State Building in Cold War Asia

Departing from conventional studies of border hostility in inter-Asian relations, Yin Qingfei explores how two revolutionary states – China and Vietnam – each pursued policies that echoed the other and collaborated in extending their authority to the borderlands from 1949 to 1975. Making use of central and local archival sources in both Chinese and Vietnamese, she reveals how the people living on the border responded to such unprecedentedly aggressive state building and especially how they appropriated the language of socialist brotherhood to negotiate with authorities. During the continuous Indochina wars, state expansion thus did not unfold on these postcolonial borderlands in a coherent or linear manner. Weaving together international, national, and transnational-local histories, this deeply researched and original study presents a new approach to the highly volatile Sino-Vietnamese relations during the Cold War, centering on the two modernising revolutionary powers' competitive and collaborative state building on the borderlands and local responses to it.

YIN QINGFEI is Assistant Professor of International History (China and the World) at the London School of Economics and Political Science.

State Building in Cold War Asia
Comrades and Competitors on the Sino-Vietnamese Border

Yin Qingfei
London School of Economics and Political Science

CAMBRIDGE
UNIVERSITY PRESS

Shaftesbury Road, Cambridge CB2 8EA, United Kingdom

One Liberty Plaza, 20th Floor, New York, NY 10006, USA

477 Williamstown Road, Port Melbourne, VIC 3207, Australia

314–321, 3rd Floor, Plot 3, Splendor Forum, Jasola District Centre,
New Delhi – 110025, India

103 Penang Road, #05–06/07, Visioncrest Commercial, Singapore 238467

Cambridge University Press is part of Cambridge University Press & Assessment, a department of the University of Cambridge.

We share the University's mission to contribute to society through the pursuit of education, learning and research at the highest international levels of excellence.

www.cambridge.org
Information on this title: www.cambridge.org/9781009426640

DOI: 10.1017/9781009426633

© Yin Qingfei 2024

This publication is in copyright. Subject to statutory exception and to the provisions of relevant collective licensing agreements, no reproduction of any part may take place without the written permission of Cambridge University Press & Assessment.

When citing this work, please include a reference to the
DOI 10.1017/9781009426633

First published 2024

A catalogue record for this publication is available from the British Library.

Library of Congress Cataloging-in-Publication Data
Names: Yin, Qingfei, 1987– author.
Title: State building in Cold War Asia : comrades and competitors on the Sino-Vietnamese border / Qingfei Yin, London School of Economics and Political Science.
Description: Cambridge, United Kingdom ; New York, NY : Cambridge University Press, 2024. | Includes bibliographical references.
Identifiers: LCCN 2024008615 (print) | LCCN 2024008616 (ebook) | ISBN 9781009426640 (hardback) | ISBN 9781009426664 (paperback) | ISBN 9781009426633 (epub)
Subjects: LCSH: Nation-building–Vietnam. | Nation-building–China. | Borderlands–Vietnam | Borderlands–China. | China–Foreign relations–Vietnam. | Vietnam–Foreign relations–China. | Vietnam–Politics and government–1945-1975. | China–Politics and government–1949-1976. | Cold War.
Classification: LCC DS556.58.C5 Y56 2024 (print) | LCC DS556.58.C5 (ebook) | DDC 909.82/5–dc23/eng/20240321
LC record available at https://lccn.loc.gov/2024008615
LC ebook record available at https://lccn.loc.gov/2024008616

ISBN 978-1-009-42664-0 Hardback

Cambridge University Press & Assessment has no responsibility for the persistence or accuracy of URLs for external or third-party internet websites referred to in this publication and does not guarantee that any content on such websites is, or will remain, accurate or appropriate.

Contents

List of Figures	*page* vi
List of Maps	vii
Acknowledgments	viii
Notes on Romanization, Names, and Pseudonymization	xi
List of Abbreviations	xii
Introduction: Internationalism, Nationalism, and Transnational Localism at the Sino-Vietnamese Border	2
1 Asymmetric State Building (1949–1954)	36
2 Joint State Building (1954–1957)	76
3 Negotiated State Building (1958–1964)	118
4 Thwarted State Building on the Sea (1954–1964)	158
5 Reversed State Building (1965–1975)	201
Conclusion: Cold War Asia: A Borderlands Perspective	248
Bibliography	259
Index	286

Figures

I.1 A French army legionnaire observes Dongxing from Móng Cái during the First Indochina War	*page* 18
I.2 Sino-Vietnamese border markers	25
1.1 Đồng Đăng during the First Indochina War	54
1.2 Nam Quan/Zhennan Guan in 1900	56
2.1 PAVN soldiers took over Cẩm Phả from the French troops in 1955	82
3.1 Beilun/Ka Long River at the end of the rain season	141
4.1 A household temple in Wanwei, Guangxi	166
4.2 Sampans in Hạ Long Bay	180
5.1 Cultural Revolution in Guangxi	206
5.2 Hoàng Văn Thụ (1906–1944)	234

Maps

I.1 Border area between the People's Republic of China and the
    Democratic Republic of Vietnam, circa 1970   *page* 1
I.2 Ethnic composition on the Guangxi–Northeast Vietnam
    borderlands based on official categorization, circa 1970   14
1.1 Border towns and crossings on the Guangxi–Northeast Vietnam
    borderlands, circa 1970   37
4.1 Northern Gulf of Tonkin, circa 1973   157

Acknowledgments

This book began as a dissertation, and I have accrued many debts to individuals and institutions during the nearly decade-long journey that has led up to the publication of this book. My interest in the Cold War in East and Southeast Asia came from studying with and reading Niu Jun and Zhang Qingmin at the School of International Studies (SIS) of Peking University. Both of them offered enthusiastic support for my aspiration to pursue research on the complicated relations between China and Indochina during the Cold War, a history that still shapes the regional order today yet has many gaps and is difficult to study. They haved remained invaluable resources for knowledge, wisdom, and support for me ever since.

This intellectual interest in contemporary international history brought me to the George Washington University (GWU) to pursue a PhD. I am extremely grateful to my PhD committee – Gregg Brazinsky, Edward McCord, and Shawn McHale – for their guidance and support. Gregg encouraged me to bring theory and history together instead of abandoning the former. Ed, with his deep knowledge of China, helped me weave disparate ideas on diplomatic history and social history together to form a coherent narrative on borderland state building. Shawn introduced me to the field of modern Southeast Asian history and taught me to think about Vietnam outside the box created by Vietnam War historiography. They jointly supervised a rigorous comprehensive exam preparation, which equipped me with the knowledge base and analytical framework that allowed me to respond to the "crisis" created by the reclassification of Chinese Foreign Ministry Archives by reorienting this project with a bottom-up approach that encompasses transnational, national, and local histories. I thank my outside examiners, Odd Arne Westad and Yafeng Xia, who offered sharp insights on what this project is about and not about.

I also benefited immensely from the intellectual atmosphere at GWU and in Washington, DC, more broadly. My knowledge and understanding of the Cold War and contemporary Asia have been enriched by conversations with fellow historians James G. Hershberg, Ronald Spector, Daqing Yang, Xiaofei Kang, and Benjamin Hopkins. I wish to thank Yan He, then librarian of the GWU

Acknowledgments ix

China Documentation Center, and her husband, Xin Fan, for their support and friendship that began at GWU and continues on this side of the pond. I am grateful to scholars who offered their valuable time to discuss my research with me during their visits to GWU or other institutions in Washington: Pierre Asselin, Christopher Goscha, Sinae Hyun, Li Ya'nan, Shi Hongfei, Đỗ Diệu Khuê, and Uliji. Members of my cohort at GWU in the history PhD program – Eric Setzekorn, John Garratt, Bob Issaacson, Katharine White, Charles Kraus, Kathryn Densford, Elham Bakhtary, Milorad Lazic, Ron Leohardt, Zhongtian Han, Benjamin Young, Naz Yucel, Maria Baranova, and Katherine Yang – created a real sense of comradery.

My research in China and Vietnam would not have been possible without the support of many kind teachers, scholars, archivists, and organizations: Bac Hoai Tran, Đinh Thị Hồng, and Nguyễn Thị Thuận, who were language instructors of the Southeast Asian Studies Summer Institute (SEASSI) at the University of Wisconsin–Madison, taught me Vietnamese. SEASSI also offered me a tuition scholarship to attend the course. The SIS of Peking University and the Institute of Chinese Studies of Vietnam Academy of Social Sciences (VASS) kindly sponsored my archival research in China and Vietnam, respectively. I thank Deng Yingwen for connecting me to VASS. The Resources Center of Contemporary Chinese History of East China Normal University kindly allowed me to consult their material. I would like to thank, in no particular order, scholars who kindly offered various help and advice during my field research: Shen Zhihua, Li Danhui, Nguyễn Xuân Cường, Li Chen, Zhou Taomo, Nguyễn Thị Phương Hoa, William Z. Y. Wang, Chen Bo, You Lan, Lu Juexuan, Feng Yiming, Jiang Huajie, and Wang Anran. A very special gratitude goes out to the archivists who offered patient support to my research and important insights in archival materials.

Over the past five years, I have been fortunate to have extremely supportive colleagues at the Virginia Military Institute (VMI) and the London School of Economics (LSE) as I have worked to transform a dissertation into a book. I am grateful to my colleagues at the VMI history department, especially my mentor Mark Wilkinson and Timothy Dowling, for helping me balance teaching and book revision. I thank Turk McCleskey for organizing the "McCleskey workshop," where I received productive critiques on my book proposal from Mark, Tim, Turk, Geoffrey Jensen, Elena Andreeva, Houston Johnson, Bradley Coleman, Eric Osborne, Jochen Arndt, Madeleine Ramsey, Liz Elizondo Schroepfer, and Christopher Blunda. The walking group Tim, Jochen, and Jochen's wife, Sherri, formed with me was essential to my mental and physical health during the pandemic. At the LSE international history department, I thank Anthony Best for his outstanding mentorship. Ronald Po, Taylor Sherman, Tanya Harmer, and Elizabeth Ingleson also offered invaluable advice on how to work with the publisher as a first-time book author.

I also thank my colleagues at the LSE Saw Swee Hock Southeast Asia Centre, especially Hyun Bang Shin, Katie Boulton, John Sidel, and Kent Deng, for their kind advice.

I presented work-in-progress from this project at conferences and talks hosted by the American Historical Association, Association for Asian Studies, Society for Military History, University of California–Berkeley, East China Normal University, Yale University, Oxford University, and the Woodrow Wilson Center for International Scholars. I thank the commentators and panelists for their constructive critiques on my work: Chen Jian, Shen Zhihua, Li Danhui, Kosal Path, Xiaofei Kang, Paul Kramer, Kevin Boylan, Henrietta Harrison, Denise Ho, Vũ Minh Hoàng, and Zhang Ning.

The research, writing, revision, and production of this book is financially supported by the GWU History Department Summer Research Grant, GWU Sigur Center for Asian Studies Summer Field Research Grant, GWU Columbian College of Arts and Sciences Dissertation Completion Fellowship, Henry Luce Foundation/American Council of Learned Societies Program in China Studies Predissertation-Summer Travel Grant, Association for Asian Studies China and Inner Asia Council Small Grant Award, VMI Jackson-Hope Fund for Professional Development, VMI Grant-in-Aid of Research, and the LSE International History Department Research Infrastructure and Investment Fund.

I received immense help during the "last mile" of producing this book. I was fortunate to have the full manuscript, or the majority of it, read by Edward McCord, Shawn McHale, and Anthony Best. The two anonymous readers strongly recommended publication of my book and offered astute comments. Christian Lentz and Philip Thai, whose scholarship I admire greatly, kindly advised on cartography. Christian introduced me to Devon Maloney, my outstanding cartographer. P. A. Crush kindly granted me permission to use a photo from his Chinese Railway Collection. Lucy Rhymer and Rosa Martin shepherded a smooth acquisition process of this manuscript.

This journey from manuscript to book would not have been possible without the unconditional support of my family. My grandparents cultivated my curiosity toward the outside world and were enthusiastic supporters of my pursuit of the highest academic degree. My parents nurtured me through this long process with their care, patience, and support. They are my greatest cheerleaders in this journey. My husband, Mark, came into my life during the revision of this manuscript. I learned a lot from him about navigational science and fisheries, which inspired me to explore the history of the fishing community in the Gulf of Tonkin with greater depth. I thank him for his wisdom, sense of humor, encouragement, and other things.

Having said that, any mistakes and shortcomings in this book are my own.

Notes on Romanization, Names, and Pseudonymization

For Chinese terms, this book uses pinyin romanization except for two names, "Sun Yat-sen" and "Chiang Kai-shek." If a commonly used romanization in Wade-Giles or other vernacular exists, it is noted in parentheses following the term in pinyin, for example, "Beihai (Pakhoi)." Vietnamese terms in this book adhere to the Vietnamese spelling (with diacritical marks) except for three place names, Vietnam (Việt Nam), Hanoi (Hà Nội), and Haiphong (Hải Phòng). Following Chinese tradition, this book puts the family name first followed by the given name when presenting Chinese names. Similarly, Vietnamese names are ordered surname, middle name, and given name as per Vietnamese convention. Due to the limited number of Vietnamese family names, the full names are cited in later references. There are two exceptions: (1) when a person with a Chinese or Vietnamese surname has a non-Chinese or non-Vietnamese given name or (2) when a person with a Chinese or Vietnamese name has presented their given name first or chosen not to use diacritical marks in their publications.

Some names of borderlanders who were labeled as lawbreakers or class enemies in unpublished archival sources are pseudonymized, although they have all died prior to the date of publication of this book. The following names are pseudonyms: Huang Deqin, Fan Shimin, Huỳnh Thị Anh, Chen Shiguang.

Abbreviations

AMFEAF	Archives of the Ministry of Foreign and European Affairs of France
BGV	Bộ Giao thông Vận tải
CIA	Central Intelligence Agency
CPC	Communist Party of China
CPSU	Communist Party of the Soviet Union
CPV	Communist Party of Vietnam
CREST	CIA Records Search Tool
CWIHP	Cold War International History Project
CZMA	Chongzuo Municipal Archives
DRV	Democratic Republic of Vietnam
ECNURC	East China Normal University Resources Center of Contemporary Chinese History
FDA	Fangcheng District Archives
FMAPRC	Foreign Ministry Archives of the People's Republic of China
GBMT	Guangzhou Bureau of Martime Transportation
GDPA	Guangdong Provincial Archives
GSBN	*Zhonghua renmin gonghe guoshi biannian*
GZAR	Guangxi Zhuang Autonomous Region
GZARA	Guangxi Zhuang Autonomous Region Archives
ICP	Indochinese Communist Party
ISC	International Supervisory Commission
JYZWX	*Jianguo yilai zhongyao wenxian xuanbian*
KTTTB	Khu tự trị Tây Bắc
KTTVB	Khu tự trị Việt Bắc
LDTL	*Lịch sử Đảng bộ tỉnh Lạng Sơn*
LDTM	*Lịch sử Đảng bộ thị xã Móng Cái*
MOPS	Ministry of Public Security
NARA	The National Archives and Records Administration
NAVC III	National Archives of Vietnam Center III
NLF	National Liberation Front of South Vietnam
NMA	Nanning Municipal Archives

NXB	Nhà xuất bản
PAVN	People's Army of Vietnam
PLA	People's Liberation Army
PRC	People's Republic of China
PTTg	Phủ Thủ tướng
RMB	Renminbi
ROC	Republic of China
SEATO	Southeast Asia Treaty Organization
SLDQ	*Những sự kiện lịch sử Đảng, tỉnh Quảng Ninh*
UBHC	Uỷ ban Hành chính
UBKCHC	Uỷ ban Kháng chiến Hành chính
UKNA	The National Archives of the United Kingdom
VKDTT	*Văn kiện Đảng toàn tập*
VNĐ	Vietnamese đồng
WPV	Workers Party of Vietnam
YBJZ	*Youyiguan bianfang jianchazhan zhanzhi*

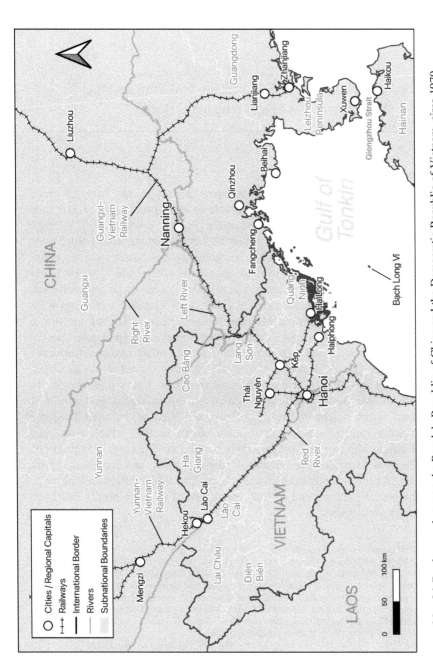

Map I.1 Border area between the People's Republic of China and the Democratic Republic of Vietnam, circa 1970
Source: Devon V. Maloney, creator. Map data from OpenStreetMap contributors and available from www.openstreetmap.org/copyright. Created using Free and Open Source QGIS, version 3.26.

Introduction
Internationalism, Nationalism, and Transnational Localism at the Sino-Vietnamese Border*

During the COVID-19 pandemic, the international boundary between China and Vietnam became legally impermeable to most people for the first time since the end of the Sino-Vietnamese border conflicts (1979–1991). On February 1, 2020, Vietnam closed the 1,300-kilometer land border to its northern neighbor and main market, becoming the first Southeast Asian country to adopt such a measure to fight against the coronavirus.[1] As the Lunar New Year holiday in late January had already delayed cargo transportation, this precipitous shutdown soon caused a backlog of Vietnamese products at the border. A week later, Prime Minister Nguyễn Xuân Phúc had to issue a remedial directive asking for "uninterrupted import and export activities via the two countries' border" while continuing the ban on international travelers.[2] Even as the growth of domestic COVID-19 cases slowed down in China, community infections increased in more countries; China thus decided to tighten its own border control. On March 31, the provincial government of Yunnan, which neighbors Myanmar, Laos, and Vietnam, required its border authority to restrict "unnecessary travel across the border."[3] Three days later, the Chinese Ministry of Foreign Affairs notified the Vietnamese Embassy of its decision to reduce the number of ports of entry and proposed a joint pandemic control mechanism chaired by provincial authorities on both sides of the border.[4] By the end of May, seven out of the nine border entries in Guangxi were closed.[5]

---

* A few paragraphs in the introduction on the historical border trade have been developed from my earlier publication "The Mountain Is High, and the Emperor Is Far Away: States and Smuggling Networks at the Sino-Vietnamese Border." Copyright © 2018 Institute for Far Eastern Studies, Kyungnam University. This article first appeared in *Asian Perspective* 42, no. 4 (October–December 2018). Published with permission by Johns Hopkins University Press.
[1] Pham and Murray, "Behind Vietnam's COVID-19 Response, Deep Distrust of China."
[2] Vietnam News Agency, "Border Gates with China Start to Reopen."
[3] Zhuang and Wang, "Zhiji Yunnan bianjian diyixian."
[4] Minh Chiến, "Trung Quốc siết nhập cảnh tại biên giới Việt-Trung do dịch Covid-19 diễn biến phức tạp."
[5] Li, "Guangxi guanbi qige lulu kou'an, yu Yuenan sisheng dingqi hutong yiqing."

Introduction 3

Under draconian measures ranging from increasing checkpoints and vigilant patrols to robust tests and government supervised quarantine hotels to curb imported cases, the daily lives of people living on the border were increasingly subject to state scrutiny. Truck drivers, who were among the very few allowed to cross the border legally, had to wait significantly longer than usual for customs clearance and to comply with quarantine requirements.[6] Five months after Hanoi suspended travel from China, the border guard leader of Quảng Ninh province acknowledged that stopping illicit entries was a complicated and sometimes thankless task. Among the more than seven hundred people detained and put in quarantine by the border authorities from February to July 2020, over six hundred were Vietnamese citizens who crossed the border just to return home, including those who swam across the border river (named Beilun River in Chinese and Ka Long River in Vietnamese) from Dongxing to Móng Cái after all the bridges were blocked.[7] After the more contagious and deadly Delta variant hit the region, several Chinese and Vietnamese border checkpoints established joint commands and dispatched squads consisting of officers from both sides to strengthen the state presence at previously less patrolled mountain trails.[8] Two Chinese provinces, Guangxi and Yunnan, also geared up to accelerate vaccinations in border counties by dispatching roving vaccination vehicles and helicopters to remote villages.[9]

During the pandemic, China sped up the construction of border fences – an ambitious and costly project that started in 2018 to combat smuggling, drug dealing, and human trafficking – to prevent border jumpers that might circumvent medical inspection and quarantine measures.[10] Smuggling at the Sino-Vietnamese border had long concerned Beijing and Hanoi because it drained customs revenues for both governments;[11] it became an even more salient security issue after COVID hit. Frozen meat smuggled from India and Brazil and entering the Chinese market via Vietnam had been one of the most profitable goods of the cross-border shadow economy as the rising Chinese middle class created a soaring demand for high-end beef. After clusters of COVID cases were widely reported in slaughterhouses overseas, this

---

[6] Minh Chiến, "Trung Quốc siết nhập cảnh tại biên giới Việt-Trung do dịch Covid-19 diễn biến phức tạp"; Zhuang and Wang, "Zhiji Yunnan bianjian diyixian."
[7] Lã Nghĩa Hiếu, "Quảng Ninh duy trì 74 chốt kiểm soát dọc biên giới Việt-Trung để phòng Covid-19."
[8] An Kiên – Trung Dũng/VOV-Tây Bắc, "Lực lượng biên phòng Việt Nam và Trung Quốc tuần tra phòng chống dịch."
[9] Liang, "Guangxi xinguan bingdu yimiao jiezhong wancheng 2000wan jici"; Han, "Yunnan bianjing diqu mubiao renqun xinguan bingdu yimiao diyiji jiezhonglü yu 97%."
[10] Thu Hằng, "Trung Quốc tính gì khi tăng tốc xây tường biên giới với Việt Nam, Miến Điện?" Also see Huang, "Chinese Authorities Take a Leaf from the Trump Playbook and 'Build the Wall' as Part of Covid-19 Curbs."
[11] See Yin, "The Mountain Is High, and the Emperor Is Far Away."

contraband was also labeled as a vexing public health threat.[12] In a global health crisis, the state buttressed the border with coercive institutions or physical barriers, not against military invasion but against an invisible virus.

While the Sino-Vietnamese confrontations over overlapping sovereign claims in the South China Sea are often thrust in the spotlight, security challenges at the border that are not disputed, such as infectious diseases, rarely attract much public attention.[13] The confrontation between the state and non-state actors (bandits, smugglers, human traffickers, dissidents, and border jumpers) reflects one of the most profound political changes China and Vietnam experienced in the second half of the twentieth century – the complete territorialization of the state.[14] To derive power from "the control of bordered political space," modernizing states extended their authority to the far corners of their territories.[15] In the ruins of the Chinese empire, European colonial empires, and the short-lived Japanese empire, the Chinese and Vietnamese communist leaders, like the ruling elites of many other postcolonial countries, strived to transform borderlands, where no single authority had previously gained supremacy, into real "borders" where stateness has to be marked, performed, and defended to reduce the ambiguities of power.[16] As Christian Lentz demonstrates in his study of Vietnamese state building at the Black River borderlands, later becoming Northwest Vietnam, during the First Indochina War, territory "is an ongoing social process, a ruling strategy, and a contingent outcome." State formation was not simply a result of war making; it largely accompanied mundane logistics work such as the mobilization of

---

[12] Ibid., 552; Cui, "Zousi dongrou, weihe changqi lüjin buzhi?"

[13] Not all border disputes are about demarcation. Emmanuel Brunet-Jailly categorizes border disputes into (1) territorial – "those that threaten the very existence of a state"; (2) positional – those about the location of the boundary line or cross-border resources; and (3) functional – those about conflicting interpretations of the function of a certain border (*Global Encyclopedia of Border Disputes*, xxi–xxii).

[14] George Gavrilis provides a theoretical discussion on how a state copes with security threats that are not disputed with another state but posed by non-state actors at the border (*The Dynamics of Interstate Boundaries*, 1–4).

[15] Maier, "Consigning the Twentieth Century to History," 808. Tongchai Winichakul argues that "Territoriality involves three basic human behaviors: a form of classification by area, a form of communication by boundary, and an attempt at enforcing" (*Siam Mapped*, 16).

[16] This development toward exclusive dominions of states is also characterized as the transition from borderlands to "*bordered*" lands, where the political autonomy of local people was narrowed. Adelman and Aron, "From Borderlands to Borders," 816 (emphasis in original). Except in a proper noun, the words "communist" and "communism" are mostly spelled with a lower case "c" in this book to refer to the policies and programs of communism pursued by the state. In specific occasions of borderlands state building, these policies and programs might emphasize different elements of the broadly defined Marxist-Leninist ideology, ranging from internationalism, anti-imperialism, collectivism, to a disciplined party. Because the weakness of party organization in the borderlands is a recurring theme in both Chinese and Vietnamese government documents, this book avoid overusing capital "C" as the words "Communist" and "Communists" imply formal party membership or affiliation.

labor and food.[17] Territorialization was often coupled with the "securitization" of the border, namely the state project of transforming spontaneous cross-border connections into matters of security in order to allow for the use of extraordinary measures to keep enemies out, potential escapees in, and cross-border activities visible.[18]

In comparison with state building in other parts of Asian borderlands in the second half of the twentieth century, the formation of new political configurations featuring the dominion of states was a particularly intense process at the Sino-Vietnamese border. The rise and fall of the Sino-Vietnamese Cold War partnership and the revolutionary social programs in the two countries created highly dynamic inter-state relations at the border. Chinese and Vietnamese authorities encountered a fundamental paradox: the borderlands where the two states interacted on a daily basis were crucial for constructing and performing their socialist brotherhood as well as for mobilizing resources to support the continuous military conflicts in Indochina. Historically, though, these borderlands were among the places under the least centralized control, the least cultural uniformity, and with the greatest regional autonomy. The relatively dense population in the region also created a complicated social fabric that was incompatible with the exclusive dominance of state power and their nationalizing policies. Nonetheless, although the unprecedentedly coercive capacity of government institutions heightened the potential for conflict during state building at the Sino-Vietnamese border, and some friction was unavoidable, the result was not always violence. Instead, the borderlanders themselves frequently maneuvered to maintain the permeability of the often arbitrarily imposed international boundary through compliance and negotiation.

The Cold War and Joint State Invasion

This is a book about how the Cold War magnified and distorted the process of state building in places where political authority had been historically flimsy. The consolidation of the Chinese and Vietnamese states at the border between Guangxi of the People's Republic of China (PRC), formally known as the Guangxi Zhuang Autonomous Region (GZAR) since 1958, and the three northeastern provinces of Cao Bằng, Lạng Sơn, and Quảng Ninh, part of the region commonly referred as Việt Bắc (Northern Vietnam), of the Democratic Republic of Vietnam (DRV) from 1949 to 1975, right before the collapse of their Cold War partnership, provides a piquant example of the development of territoriality, as well as the challenges to it, against the background of drastic

---

[17] The quote and paraphrasis are from Lentz, *Contested Territory*, 3.
[18] For the definition of "securitization," see Buzan, Wæver, and de Wilde, *Security: A New Framework for Analysis*, 23–25.

political contests in the second half of the twentieth century.[19] This geographically, economically, and ethnically diverse border region includes highlands, lowlands, and access to the Gulf of Tonkin ("the Northern Gulf," Beibu Wan in Chinese and Vịnh Bắc Bộ in Vietnamese) (Map I.1). Departing from the conventional narrative that views borders exclusively as a source of hostility in inter-Asian relations due to their arbitrary demarcation by imperial powers and postcolonial nationalists,[20] this book is not about how the two sides disputed or settled their boundaries.

Instead, I tell a story of how two revolutionary states launched movements and pursued policies that echoed each other and collaborated in extending their authority to the border to temper the transnational tendencies there – a process that I characterize as "joint state invasion." At the same time, this book also reveals how the border people responded to such unprecedentedly aggressive state building, especially how they appropriated the language of socialist brotherhood to negotiate with the authorities. I argue that the Cold War partnership between Beijing and Hanoi did indeed strengthen the presence and authority of the Chinese and Vietnamese states in the border area; yet it did not do so in a coherent or linear manner because of the concurrent trends of nationalism, internationalism, and

---

[19] These border provinces experienced administrative changes during the period examined. Present-day coastal Guangxi was historically part of Guangdong and under the administration of Guangdong from 1955 to 1965. Between 1951 and 1955, the central government put the area under the administration of Guangxi. State Council of the PRC, "Guowuyuan guanyu jiang Guangxisheng de Qinxian, Hepu, Lingshan, Fangcheng sixian he Beihaishi huagui Guangdongsheng lingdao de jueding," 370. For details, see Chapter 4.

The Việt Minh created five inter-zones (liên khu), which were "combined military and administrative unit[s]," in 1948: Inter-zone I, III, and X in northern Vietnam; and Inter-zone IV and V in central Vietnam. In 1949, Inter-zone I and X were merged into Northern Vietnam Inter-zone (Liên khu Việt Bắc), which included the region to the north of Hanoi: Cao Bằng, Bắc Kạn, Lạng Sơn, Thái Nguyên, Hà Giang, Tuyên Quang, Lào Cai, Yên Bái, Sơn La, Lai Châu, Bắc Giang, Bắc Ninh, Phúc Yên, Vĩnh Yên, Phú Thọ, Quảng Yên, Hải Ninh, Hồng Gai Special Zone, and the Mai Đà District of Hòa Bình. In 1953, Northwestern Inter-zone (Liên khu Tây Bắc) was detached from the Northern Vietnam Inter-zone to include Lai Châu, Lào Cai, Yên Bái, and Sơn La. Goscha, *Historical Dictionary of the Indochina* War, 231–33.

In July 1956, in response to the central government's decision to establish autonomous regions for ethnic minorities, the Northern Vietnam Autonomous Region (Khu tự trị Việt bắc) was established to include "Cao Bằng, Bắc Cạn, Lạng Sơn, Tuyên Quang (except for Yên Bình District), Thái Nguyên (except for Phổ Yên and Phú Bình districts), and Hữu Lũng district of Bắc Giang." Chủ tịch Nước, "Sắc lệnh số 268/SL về việc ban hành bản quy định việc thành lập Khu Tự trị Việc Bắc do Chủ tịch Nước Ban Hành."

In 1963, the DRV merged Hồng Quảng district into Hải Ninh province to form Quảng Ninh. "Đảng bộ Khu Hồng Quảng và Đảng bộ tỉnh Hải Ninh hợp nhất thành Đảng bộ tỉnh Quảng Ninh [The Party Committee of Hồng Quảng Region and the Party Committee of Hải Ninh Province merged to form the Party Committee of Quảng Ninh Province]," December 19, 1963, in Ban Nghiên cứu lịch sử Đảng tỉnh ủy Quảng Ninh, *Những sự kiện lịch sử Đảng tỉnh Quảng Ninh* (hereafter *SLDQ*), 187–88. For details, see Chapter 4.

[20] In the field of South Asian history, for example, borderlands history has intersected with partition studies. See Leake and Haines, "Lines of (In)Convenience," 963–65.

transnational localism. The state project of the "nationalization" of territory, resources, and people sometimes reinforced yet was often at odds with the party's cause of the "internationalization" of socialism. Transnational localism, namely the border people's endeavor to preserve local family, cultural, and economic connections across the state perimeter dampened and even undermined both the nationalist and internationalist agenda. In this border space, China and Vietnam were, simultaneously, comrades in pushing revolution forward, collaborators in overcoming state weakness, and competitors for limited resources.

Recent scholarship on borderlands history has a problematic tendency of throwing the state into the dustbin while focusing exclusively on identity, language, and culture; this book reemphasizes the role of the state in the study of borderlands because territorialization has largely been a state project, even though it inevitably had to navigate and adapt to the social and cultural landscape of the locality. A purely cultural approach to borderlands also tends to prioritize continuity while downplaying the enormous changes caused by the ebb and flow of political powers.[21] The scholarship on state power at the border pivots between two extremes. At one end there is James Scott's narrative of state evasion as he elaborates in *The Art of Not Being Governed*, that the people of the Asian highlands moved around and between states.[22] At the other end is Charles Tilly's model of "War made the state, and the state made war."[23] This volume offers a third perspective: "joint state invasion." When two revolutionary states collaborated at the border and launched social political campaigns that mirrored each other (land reform, collectivization, and crackdown on private commerce, among others), it became more difficult for borderlanders to elude the state in all its forms, including taxation, conscription, and political participation. The process of securing the border in this region thus challenges both the Scottian narrative of state evasion and the Tillyan model of state formation. This joint state invasion reflects the idiosyncrasies of state-society relations at the Sino-Vietnamese border as well as broader patterns of bordering practices.

Tilly's compelling argument on how war gave rise to bureaucratization, defined citizenship, intensified coercion, and accumulated capital, therefore creating and strengthening the state, gives the Tillyan thesis a seemingly "transhistorical" explanatory power.[24] Yet state building since the second half

---

[21] Adelman and Aron, "From Borderlands to Borders," 815.
[22] In his classic study of relations between highland society and lowland state, James Scott shows how state evasion and state prevention permeate the highland people's "subsistence routines, their social organization, their physical dispersal, and many elements of their culture." Scott, *The Art of Not Being Governed*, 8.
[23] Tilly, "Reflections on the History of European State Making," 42.
[24] For the applicability of the Tillyan thesis to ancient Chinese history and modern Vietnamese history, see Hui, "How Tilly's State Formation Paradigm Is Revolutionizing the Study of Chinese State-making," 272–75.

8   Introduction

of the nineteenth century entered a phase when states expanded and enhanced its presence to the peripheral space of its power in pursuit of uniformity and coherency. Borderlands state making thus had distinctive characteristics, often comprising a "shared binational experience," as Rachel St. John analyzes in her study of the Western US-Mexico border.[25] The sustainability of the development of states on the borderlands has been subject to what Enze Han describes as a "neighborhood effect" in his research into the history of borderlands state building of Burma.[26] The nature of the Cold War as "a conflict between the two versions of Western modernity that socialism and liberal capitalism seemed to offer" blurred the distinction between peace and war.[27] "Joint state invasion" thus illuminates some unique features of the everyday aspect of state building on the borderlands during the second half of the twentieth century. Political institutions established upon a clear ideational blueprint, deep binding military alliance or ideological partnership, and postcolonial countries' aspiration to catch up with the modernization projects yielded a particularly strong binational effect of borderlands state building. It invigorated both inter-state cooperation and competition and reduced the ambiguities inherent to frontier societies. From the mid-1950s to the mid-1960s, the capacity of both the Vietnamese and Chinese states increased significantly at the border as they doubled down and collaborated in turning communities inward, that is, away from the borderlands and toward the political center.

While Scott notes that his argument on "Zomia" as an anarchist refuge does not apply to the post–Second World War political landscape due to "the power of the state to deploy distance-demolishing technologies," Sarah Turner's historical and contemporary analysis of the highland trade at the Sino-Vietnamese border shows that "remote upland mountainous terrain" could still negate state power thus retain "Zomia like" space.[28] The analytical framework of "joint state invasion" demonstrates that technology and terrain were not the only factors, let alone the most decisive ones, in shaping whether and how borderlanders could out maneuver state control. The intensity and sustainability of the *joint* state-building projects were of fundamental importance. Collaborative and competitive efforts to establish the exclusivity of the respective Chinese and Vietnamese states up to the mid-1960s did not place borderlands state building on a preset trajectory. Countering the argument that communist states were especially effective in tightening social control during

---

[25] St. John, *Line in the Sand*, 64.
[26] Han, "Neighborhood Effect of Borderland State Consolidation," 305; Han, *Asymmetrical Neighbors*, 20–35.
[27] Westad, "The Cold War and the International History of the Twentieth Century," 10.
[28] Scott, *The Art of Not Being Governed*, xii; Turner, "Borderlands and Border Narratives," 265, 286.

wars, I contend that the Vietnam War reversed the process of state consolidation despite the two states' mounting investment in transportation technology and infrastructure in the region. The war generated new momentum for spontaneous cross-border flows of people and goods that the modernizing states had to accommodate while diverting state resources toward militarization and away from other functions it had to play at the border to sustain the joint projects of state invasion. These dynamics affected the highlands, lowlands, and maritime societies alike.

This book also complicates the traditional narrative of Sino-Vietnamese relations during the communist era, namely, that the inter-party relations between the Communist Party of China (CPC) and the Workers Party of Vietnam (WPV) "formed the core of the relationship" and the inter-state interactions between the PRC and the DRV simply "provided the public form."[29] Predominantly presenting the two countries as unitary actors, historians and political scientists have seen the American-Sino-Soviet strategic triangle and factional struggles among the top leadership in Beijing and Hanoi as determining the relationship between the DRV and the PRC.[30] Acknowledging the significance of the party-to-party dynamics, this book nevertheless emphasizes that state building was an under-addressed dynamic in Sino-Vietnamese relations. Building upon primary sources beyond the central-government level diplomatic record, I argue that the Sino-Vietnamese relations during the Cold War era could and should be studied primarily as the relations between two neighboring states ruled by revolutionary parties instead of one between two communist parties that acquired their respective state. Departing from the conventional understanding of the Sino-Vietnamese relations during 1949–1979 as a process of nationalism gradually replacing internationalism as the dominant driving force of the bilateral relations due to the breakdown of ideological bonds, this book demonstrates that internationalism, nationalism, and transnational localism were of equal importance and it was the tension between these three forces that shaped the Sino-Vietnamese Cold War partnership from its inception.

Bridging borderlands history and international history, this book challenges the purely diplomatic history approach to bilateral relations and shows that the Sino-Vietnamese border was significant during the Cold War not simply

---

[29] Womack, *China and Vietnam*, 162.
[30] Important earlier works include Chen, *Vietnam and China, 1938–1954*; Guo, ed., *Zhong-Yue guanxi yanbian sishinian*; and Ang, *Vietnamese Communists' Relations with China and the Second Indochina Conflict, 1956–1962*. Recent works benefit from the limited declassification of Chinese and Vietnamese diplomatic documents. See Chen, *Mao's China and the Cold War*; Zhai, *China and the Vietnam Wars, 1950–1975*; Yang, "Changes in Mao Zedong's Attitude toward the Indochina War, 1949–1973"; Roberts, ed., *Behind the Bamboo Curtain*; Khoo, *Collateral Damage*; Nguyen, *Hanoi's War*.

10   Introduction

because of the territorial disputes that later emerged. Except for a sometimes brief acknowledgment of the two countries' resolution to shelve territorial disputes in the 1950s,[31] the writing of the history of the Sino-Vietnamese border has been overshadowed by the political history of the rise and collapse of the Sino-Vietnamese alliance, which resulted in the resurfacing of territorial disputes.[32] The general writing on border issues meanwhile reflects a narrow understanding focused on demarcation and disputes, while ignoring other functions borders perform.[33] Providing substate and non-state actors greater agency, this book presents a history of state-society relations at the Sino-Vietnamese border against the broader geopolitical context. In doing so, it elucidates how ideology shaped the rationale, priorities, and strategies of revolutionary state building, a process that transformed both China and Vietnam. The obstacles the two centralizing states encountered along their shared borders also reveal that Sino-Vietnamese relations were driven, at least in part, by efforts to tackle the legacy of empires and colonialism.

By dissecting the ostensibly unitary state into its multiple "layers," this book offers a fresh look at the agency of the "local state" in shaping foreign relations, which has been a less explored subject in the writings of international history.[34] While economists have underscored how the local state – namely the provincial, municipal, county or district government, and their functionaries – lent momentum to the economic transformation of China and Vietnam in the reform era, historians have paid scant attention to how officials at the lower echelon of state bureaucracy interpreted, carried out, and sometimes obstructed the central government's foreign agenda and how the local state interacted with the outside world more broadly in the post-1945 period.[35] The grassroots

---

[31] Duiker, *China and Vietnam*, 37.
[32] Two important works that trace the dormant border disagreements during the heyday of the Sino-Vietnamese partnership and the reemergence of the issue during the 1970s are Path, "The Sino-Vietnamese Dispute over Territorial Claims"; and You, "Zhanhou Zhong-Yue ludi bianjie wenti de lishi kaocha ji zaisikao."
[33] A few notable exceptions to this trend mostly focus on cross-border trade and migration. Dinh Quang Hải, "Vấn đề di cư xuyên biên giới của cư dân khu vực biên giới Việt Nam-Trung Quốc giai đoạn 1954–1975"; Fan and Liu, *Zhong-Yue bianjing maoyi yanjiu*; Turner, "Borderlands and Border Narratives."
[34] Judd C. Kinzley studies the layered model of state formation in modern China in his writing of Qing and Russian competition in Xinjiang (*Natural Resources and the New Frontier*). He focuses on multiple layers of national interests, ranging from control over geographical knowledge to development of transport. This book uses the term "layer" to describe the not necessarily coherent bureaucratic levels of state.
[35] Jean C. Oi coins the term "local state corporatism" to characterize the local government officials' role in China's rural industry ("The Role of the Local State in China's Transitional Economy," 1132). For a long-range study of Vietnamese state and its local economic governance, see Dell et al., "The History State, Local Collective Action, and Economic Development in Vietnam." Charles Kraus points out that it was mainly the Chinese border provinces that bore the responsibility of assisting Vietnam during the First Indochina War, thus Beijing often had to

state apparatus examined in this book – county-level administrations, state-run border trade companies, armed units at the border checkpoints, among others – were all part of a hierarchical system and, whenever possible, led by party members to ensure ideological coherency. None of them attempted to invade or usurp central prerogatives, yet none of them were simply an arm of the centralized state that championed the interests of political centers either. Bestowed with little resources yet required to fulfill various functions, financial viability, instead of either internationalist or nationalist missions, often topped the street-level state representatives' agenda. In addition, at the lowest extremity of bureaucracy, the line between state and society blurred, and the state representatives eventually became part of the transnational local networks. Rather than toppling the state-building project, however, the local state sometimes moderated the most radical, impractical programs.

Zooming in on Asian borderlands, this book also highlights the uniqueness of Asian Communism and the idiosyncrasies of the Cold War in Asia. Soviet Communism was built upon the idea of "socialism in one country"; the Soviet border system, as Andrea Chandler argues, was thus an "institution for isolation" that aimed to maintain "airtight, impermeable boundaries."[36] Most Soviet satellite states in Central and Eastern Europe, while sometimes coordinating policies to encourage mobility within the bloc in the form of state sponsored and supervised tourism, still placed severe restrictions on cross-border movement of people and goods largely because they adopted from the Soviet Union "a deep, if not paranoid, suspicion of the outside world, and strong isolationist and autarkic tendencies, especially towards the capitalist West."[37] Deeply troubled by internal "socio-economic cleavages and ethnic rivalries," the "Sovietization" of the borderlands in these countries involved not only military conquest but also forced demographic changes through deportation and population exchange.[38] In Asia, by contrast, the idea of internationalism and socialist brotherhood served as a new discourse or norm on which to build a political community, replacing the Chinese, European, and Japanese empires. The Chinese and Vietnamese states made determined efforts to integrate the borderlands into their respective economic and administrative system through socioeconomic restructuring such as collectivization, which was similar to the Soviet practice. Instead of completely interrupting cross-border ties, however, the two governments imposed from above a contrived

---

"contend with the interests of" local institutions ("A Border Region 'Exuded with Militant Friendship,'" 496).

[36] Chandler, *Institutions of Isolation*, 3; also see Matthews, *The Passport Society* for the Soviet passport and immigration systems.
[37] Keck-Szajbel and Stola, "Crossing the Borders of Friendship," 92–93.
[38] Prusin, *The Lands Between*, 4, 202.

12   Introduction

Cold War comradeship over a spontaneous interdependence that had already existed for centuries along the border community.

The divergent experiences of Europe and Asia in the international power struggle during the Cold War have driven historians to question the applicability of the Cold War narrative to Asia.[39] Immanuel Wallerstein goes so far as to argue that "[i]t is probably not very useful to speak of the Cold War in Asia."[40] This book contradicts the argument that the Cold War has no place in the history of Asia. It demonstrates that the competition between capitalism and socialism accelerated and convoluted the process of territorialization. For revolutionary leaders in Asia, a manifestation of the geographical limit of power was essential to their project of constructing an all-encompassing state. Under the banner of proletarian internationalism, the establishment of communist institutions at the Sino-Vietnamese frontier and their collaborated combat there against the perceived American imperial design contributed to the gradual and eventual definition of Vietnam as a separate state and China's perception of this change, the latter of which was a part of the broader transition of China from an imperial entity to a nation-state. As Masuda Hajimu argues, instead of studying "Cold War in Asia" – how the international confrontation between the United States and the Soviet Union began in Europe and then spread to far corners of the world – it is more fruitful to contemplate "Cold War Asia" (or "*Asia* during the Cold War") by exploring the "social mechanism" underlying the term as an adjective.[41] This book relativizes the Cold War by interrogating how it intertwined with other historical forces – global, national, or local – in shaping Asia in the second half of the twentieth century.

Due to the prevailing impacts of the Cold War as a social mechanism, it is important to look beyond the "front line" between the conflicting blocs to interrogate the ramifications of geopolitics on borderlands. Recent scholarship on borderlands during the Cold War has largely focused on confrontational state building along the ideological fault line. In *Cold War Island: Quemoy on the Front Line*, Michael Szonyi studies the "militarization" and "geopoliticization" of Quemoy, the island at the front line of the military standoff between the PRC and the Republic of China (ROC), and the formation of "combat economy" on the island.[42] Choosing an even smaller analytical unit,

---

[39] Xiaobing Li argues that the "Cold War to East Asians was not only about international power struggle, but also about independence and modernization" (*The Cold War in East Asia*, 4).
[40] Wallerstein, "What Cold War in Asia? An Interpretive Essay," 24. Emphasizing China's constant involvement in hot battles and its commitment to defending the nation against American imperialist design, Covell Meyskens argues that "Cold War China only ever existed as a semantic entity outside the PRC's borders" ("There Never Was a Cold War China").
[41] Masuda, "The Cold War as Social Mechanism," 8 (emphasis in original).
[42] Szonyi, *Cold War Island*, 13, 79, 121.

Jason B. Johnson's *Divided Village: The Cold War in the German Borderlands* studies the experience of Mödlareuth, a farming village between East and West Germany and highlights the eastern villagers' strategies in dealing with a militarized Iron Curtain.[43] The securitization of borderlands during the Cold War sometimes built upon existing competitive state building and profoundly changed the relations between the borderlanders and state authorities. In *Shadow States: India, China and the Himalayas*, Bérénice Guyot-Réchard demonstrates that through "mutual observation, replication, and competition to prove themselves the better state," successive central authorities in China and India since the early twentieth century became each other's "shadow state" on the Himalayan frontier.[44] Sulmaan Wasif Khan's *Muslim, Trader, Nomad, Spy: China's Cold War and the People of the Tibetan Borderlands* argues that by addressing state weakness in the Tibetan borderlands, the PRC shifted from "empire-lite," allowing local autonomy to flourish, "to a harder, heavier imperial formation."[45] Sinae Hyun in *Indigenizing the Cold War: The Border Patrol Police and Nation-Building in Thailand* investigates the role of Thai Border Patrol police, with American support and royal patronage, in building a psychological "human border" where "the people themselves, their minds and hearts inoculated against the foreign disease of communism."[46]

In his groundbreaking book *Strong Borders, Secure Nation: Cooperation and Conflict in China's Territorial Disputes*, M. Taylor Fravel looks beyond the ideological confrontation to examine the pattern in the Chinese approach to territorial disputes with its Asian neighbors. Contending with the conventional wisdom, Fravel points out that domestic insecurity, especially ethnic rebellion on the frontier, had driven China to make frequent territorial concessions to its Asian neighbors, including those that were much weaker than China, such as Afghanistan and Burma. China was more willing to confront powerful neighbors such as Russia militarily to boost its strategic bargaining power.[47] This book places Chinese decisions to offer territorial concessions or escalate sovereignty disputes in the broader context of the political changes that China and its East and Southeast Asian neighbors experienced. Besides compromising and conflicting over territorial claims, these countries, situating on a broad ideological spectrum, transformed the symbolic meaning of the border in an effort to liquidate colonialism, perform solidarity and dissonance under ideational cause, and multiply the strength and function of the state via both competition and collaboration.

---

[43] Johnson's *Divided Village*. [44] Guyot-Réchard, *Shadow States*, 4.
[45] Khan, *Muslim, Trader, Nomad, Spy*, 2–3. [46] Hyun, *Indigenizing the Cold War*, 5.
[47] Fravel, *Strong Borders, Secure Nation*, 1–2, 4–5.

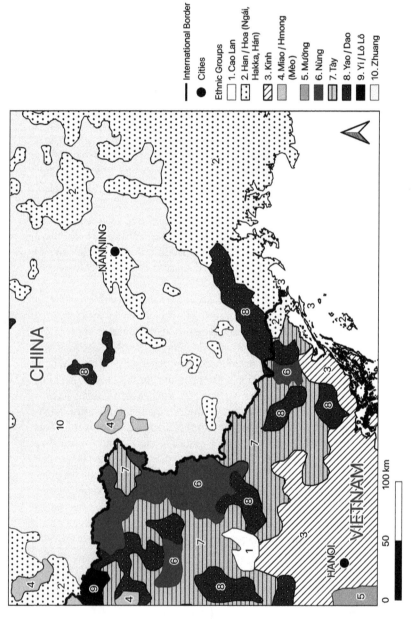

Map I.2 Ethnic composition on the Guangxi–Northeast Vietnam borderlands based on official categorization, circa 1970
Note: The ethnic composition of Quảng Ninh changed drastically during the second half of the twentieth century. The end of the First Indochina War in 1954 and the purge of ethnic Chinese in 1978 led to a mass exodus of ethnic Chinese from the region.

Map I.2 (*cont.*) This map reflects the estimated situation around 1970. The DRV had not completed the ethnic determination by the time, thus this map includes some self-identified groups (such as the Cao Lan), and the Ngái, who did not like to be referred as Ngái (See Ito, *Politics of Ethnic Classification in Vietnam*, 35), are grouped together with the Hoa.
Source: Devon V. Maloney, creator. Data on spatial distribution of ethnic groups from US Central Intelligence Agency, "Ethnolinguistic groups of Indochina 1970," https://commons.wikimedia.org/wiki/File:Ethnolinguistic_map_of_Indochina_1970.jpg; "Overview Map of GMS Ethnic Groups," Greater Mekong Subregion Atlas of the Environment (2nd ed.), 2012, http://portal.gms-eoc.org/uploads/map/archives/map/GMS-EthnicGroups_19_hi-res_11.jpg; "Carte Ethno-Linguistique du Vietnam," from Đặng Nghiêm Vạn et al., *Ethnic Minorities of Vietnam* (Hanoi: The Gioi, 1993), cited in Jean Michaud, Sarah Turner, and Yann Roche, "Mapping Ethnic Diversity in Highland Northern Vietnam," *GeoJournal* 57 (2002), 290. Created using Free and Open Source QGIS, version 3.26.

The Borderlanders

Borderlands history studies "the region on *both* sides of a state border ... as the unit of analysis" without treating people living in the unit as a homogenous group.[48] The borderlanders who accommodated, negotiated, resisted, and evaded state power at the Sino-Vietnamese border, including the northern Gulf of Tonkin, in their daily lives during the second half of the twentieth century included those who lived in, either permanently or temporarily, and traveled to the area. Reflecting the different elevations and diverse landforms within the region, the ethnic and social groups in the border area created a living from various sources and developed complicated relations with the political authorities and the state-imposed boundary (Map I.2).

The uplanders living in the Guangxi–northeastern Vietnam border region have mostly been categorized by the Chinese and Vietnamese states as "ethnic minorities."[49] As Fan Honggui points out, although the southward migration

---

[48] Baud and van Schendel, "Toward a Comparative History of Borderlands," 216 (emphasis in original).

[49] As Ito Masako argues, while both China and Vietnam adopted the Soviet policy of politics-driven top-down ethnic classification and referred to the criteria defined by Stalin – "common language," "common territory," "common economic life," and "common psychological make-up" – to determine ethnicities, the outcome of their ethnic classification differed with the Soviet one in several significant ways: Choosing federalism, the Soviet Union separated its people into "nation" and "ethnic group." Pursuing an Autonomous Region policy, Beijing and Hanoi respectively sought to unify all peoples as one nation and emphasized equality among ethnic groups with different population size. Both China and Vietnam attached greater significance to "ethnic self-consciousness" than the Soviet Union. While, by the time the PRC was founded, nine ethnic groups were recognized in China – "Mongol, Hui, Tibetan, Uyghur, Miao, Yao, Yi, Korean and Manchu" – Beijing realized through the 1953 census that nearly 400 ethnic groups demanded recognition. From 1953 to 1956, the PRC Committee of Ethnic Affairs dispatched survey teams to Yunnan, Guangdong, Guizhou, and Hunan, which identified twenty-nine new

from China over centuries formed strong ethnic ties across the Sino-Vietnamese border, the borderlanders have fallen under different ethnic groups and gained different ethnonyms in the two countries. Hmong (formally known as Mèo) is the name of a single ethnic group in Vietnam, while the Hmong people is a subgroup of Miao people in China. The population identified as Yi in China are categorized as Lô Lô and Phù Lá in Vietnam. The people identified as a single Yao ethnic group in China are recognized as three separate groups in Vietnam: Dao, Sán Dìu, and Pà Thẻn.[50] These agriculturalists, some of whom practiced swiddening, developed small societies on the rugged terrain and inhabited the eastern portion of the "continental Southeast Asian Massif" or "Zomia" – two concepts developed by Jean Michaud and Willem van Schendel, respectively, to describe the mass of Asian highland that was historically beyond the control of the valley-based government.[51] The geography, social structure, and customs had long helped these highland societies to evade or even repel the state. Meanwhile, lucrative forest products (such as rot-resistant wood, resin, herb, and spice) and the opium that some highlanders produced had attracted powerful attention from lowland societies.[52] These uplanders were oblivious to the international boundary long

---

recognized ethnic groups. The Social and Historic Survey of Ethnic Minorities that covered wider ethnic populated areas of the country and lasted from 1955 to 1964 recognized fifteen more ethnic groups. With Luoba in Tibet and Jinuo in Yunnan designated as a separate ethnic group in 1965 and 1979, respectively, the determination of fifty-six ethnic groups (the Han majority and the fifty-five state-recognized ethnic minority groups) were completed. The DRV began to investigate conditions of ethnic groups in 1955. Heavily influenced by French classification of Indochina's population, Ethnologist Nguyễn Hữu Thấu, under the auspice of the Central Committee for Ethnic Minorities, compiled the first ethnic classification list of sixty-three ethnic minority groups in 1957. The 1960 census, which allowed self-declaration of ethnicity in some areas, however, identified 125 ethnic groups in Vietnam. Despite the deteriorating Sino-Vietnamese relations since the late 1960s, the operation of ethnic determination in Vietnam resembled that of China more than the Soviet Union. The formal ethnic determination began in August 1960 and lasted more than a decade, which resulted in a list of fifty-nine ethnic groups, thirty-six in the DRV and twenty-three in the Republic of Vietnam, compiled in 1973. Following a national census after the reunification of Vietnam, the Central Committee for Ethnic Minorities completed a list of fifty-four ethnic groups at the end of 1978. Ito, *Politics of Ethnic Classification in Vietnam*, 17–39. For a study of the ethnic determination project in Yunnan, see Mullaney, *Coming to Terms with the Nation*.

[50] Fan, "Zhong-Yue liangguo de kuajing minzu gaishu," 14–15.
[51] Michaud, "Economic Transformation in a Hmong Village of Thailand," 225; van Schendel, "Geographies of Knowing, Geographies of Ignorance," 647.
[52] For the commodities of highland trade, see Turner, "Borderlands and Border Narratives." For the role of poppy cultivation, opium production, and opium trade at the Sino-Vietnamese border, see Lentz, "Cultivating Subjects"; Nguyen, "Dynamite, Opium, and a Transnational Shadow Economy at Tonkinese Coal Mines." For the history of various highlanders' relations with the state, see Culas and Michaud, "A Contribution to the Study of Hmong (Miao) Migrations and History"; Harrell and Li, "The History of the History of the Yi, Part II"; Litzinger, *Other Chinas*.

after it was spatially demarcated and challenged the boundary-making and state-building projects of the two states in their everyday life.

The international boundary also cut across the communities that live along the valleys and the lower slopes of the mountains, although lower altitude resulted in closer interactions, including military encounters, and greater proximity over the long term between them and the Kinh and Han majority in the respective countries. Nong Zhigao (in Chinese)/Nùng Trí Cao (in Vietnamese), a chieftain in Guangnan West Circuit (in today's Cao Bằng) of Song Dynasty (960–1279), sought to negotiate a space of "middle ground" and "political differentiation" by defying both the Chinese Song and the Vietnamese Lý (1009–1225) dynasties in the early eleventh century, the earliest years of Vietnam's independence from China. Nùng Trí Cao is still venerated today among the Tày, Nùng, and Zhuang people for his "rebellion" against the Chinese and Vietnamese courts, which highlights the shared regional identity and "persistent nature of transnational ethnicity" despite the boundaries created by territories and ethnic classification.[53] Beijing lumped together several distinct ethnic groups in Guangxi together to "create" the Zhuang, in the words of Katherine Palmer Kaup, "to integrate linguistically and culturally diverse peoples into a centralized state."[54] Zhuang thus became the largest ethnic minority in China and was bestowed Guangxi as their Autonomous Region in 1958, whereas their equivalent in Vietnam were five ethnic groups recognized separately – Tày (the largest ethnic minority group of Vietnam), Nùng, Pu Péo, La Chí, and Sán Chay.[55] More fertile land and well-developed irrigation methods sustained intensive cultivation of crops such as rice, maize, and sweet potato.[56] River transportation integrated these peasants and producers to distant lowland markets. The Shuikou (in Chinese)/ Bằng (in Vietnamese) River and Kỳ Cùng River confluences near Longzhou to form the Left River, which then joins the Right River to become two of the head streams of the upper West River.[57] The West River basin, by the seventeenth century, had contributed to the regional market between Guangxi and Guangdong and connected the border region economically to the Yangtzi River market and the South China Sea trade.[58] The fluctuating water level of the Left River, which could only transport small vessels, and the Shiwandashan (Hundred Thousand Mountains) between Guangxi and Guangdong nevertheless constrained the volume of trade.[59]

---

[53] Anderson, *The Rebel Den of Nùng Trí Cao*, 6, 14. [54] Kaup, *Creating the Zhuang*, 8.
[55] Fan, "Zhong-Yue liangguo de kuajing minzu gaishu," 14. The self-identified Cao Lan people were part of the Zhuang population in China and part of Sán Chay in Vietnam.
[56] Marks, *Tigers, Rice, Silk, and Silt*, 310. [57] Kaup, *Creating the Zhuang*, 31.
[58] Marks, *Tigers, Rice, Silk, and Silt*, 194, 262; Bos, *Notes on the Lung Chow T'ing, Lang Son, and Cao Bang*, 40–42.
[59] Lary, "A Zone of Nebulous Menace," 185.

Figure I.1 A French army legionnaire observes Dongxing from Móng Cái during the First Indochina War
Note: Móng Cái was the last post the French held along the Sino-Vietnamese border. Taken on October 25, 1950, the image shows Dongxing and the iron bridge that connected the city with Móng Cái. The bridge was funded by the Qing court and completed by the French in 1900.
Source: Photo by -/INTERCONTINENTALE/AFP via Getty Images. #1633625465.

Toward the east end of the Sino-Vietnamese borderlands, as the altitude further decreases, bustling trade hubs such as Dongxing and Móng Cái had emerged (Figure I.1). Located at the intersection of the Sino-Vietnamese land border and their respective coastlines, these two border towns face each other across the Beilun/Ka Long River and have been pivots to the web of commercial ties between Southern China and Vietnam. With the French colonization of Indochina and the "opening" of Longzhou and Beihai (Pakhoi) as treaty ports in the second half of the nineteenth century, border trade was increasingly woven into the global commercial network, connecting to distant markets such as British Hong Kong, Japan, and even the United States. Dongxing even won fame as "Little Hong Kong" during the Republican era.[60] The residents and

---

[60] Fan Chen [pseud.], "Dongxing: xinde Guangzhouwan [Dongxing: the new Kwangchou Wan]," *Lvxing zazhi* 18, no. 8 (1944), 65–66, in *Dacheng laojiu qikan quanwen shujuku*; Yin, "The

traveling merchants on the lowland Sino-Vietnamese frontier had actively taken advantage of the border zone, and later the borderline once it was demarcated. To dodge the Indochinese import duties, some Chinese potter masters set up large workshops in Móng Cái in 1910 and hired three hundred Chinese laborers, many of whom lived in Dongxing and walked to work every day. Producing a wide range of goods from simple utensils to high-end porcelain to the entire Indochina by the late 1930s, these pottery workshops elevated Móng Cái to the status of one of the handicraft-industry centers of the region.[61]

The coastal societies along the northern Gulf of Tonkin further demonstrate the complexity of frontier livelihood. Fishery, including the auxiliary salted fish production, was the buttress of the Gulf economy, especially for the coastal Chinese society. During the Qing era (1636–1912), China's population increased from fifty-six million to four hundred million, which drove southward migration to previously unexploited frontiers;[62] therefore, the freshwater and inshore fishery could no longer sustain the densely populated coastal societies. Intricate commercial ties that connected the interior market to the coastal economy emerged over time between the fisherfolk, merchant guilds, wholesale fish mongers, and interprovincial trans-shippers.[63] Sea fishery had historically contributed less to the food staple in northern Vietnam. According to French scholars in the 1930s and 1940s, coastal Vietnamese in the north were mostly "peasants-cum-fishers" who engaged in fishing "on a part-time basis."[64] In places such as Hải Ninh, the livelihood of the coastal population nevertheless relied heavily on the sea. The fiscal state of French Indochina derived significant revenue from the thriving salt-making industry by imposing a monopoly on salt.[65] In the piscatorial societies, the boundary between seafaring and land-living was porous.

Another community in the Gulf that was often invoked as a reason for government intervention was the *haizei/haifei* (in Chinese) or *hải phỉ* (in Vietnamese), which has generally been translated as "pirates" in Western literature. In the context of maritime Asia, this translation is highly problematic, as it ignores the different understandings of armed violence on the sea

---

Mountain Is High, and the Emperor Is Far Away," 555; also see Lary, "A Zone of Nebulous Menace," 181–97.

[61] United States Provost Marshal General's Bureau, "Civil Affairs Handbook, French Indo-China," 20–21. I thank Mark Hoskin for pointing me to this source.

[62] Deng, "Unveiling China's True Population Statistics for the Pre-Modern Era with Official Census Data," 59.

[63] For recent studies of the Chinese fishery market during the late imperial and early modern era, see Muscolino, *Fishing Wars and Environmental Change in Late Imperial and Modern China*, 13–35.

[64] The observation was made by French geographers Pierre Gourou and Charles Robequain, cited in Kleinen, "Stealing from the Gods," 250.

[65] The other two commodities under state monopoly were opium and alcohol. Jerez, "Colonial and Indigenous Institutions in the Fiscal Development of French Indochina," 117–18.

between European powers and Asian societies. The European term "pirates" in the era of rapid expansion overseas assumed the meaning "maritime raiders who operated without the authorisation of a lawful sovereign."[66] In the Gulf of Tonkin, by the first half of the twentieth century, the *haifei* or *hải phỉ*, while engaged in armed robbery on the sea, acknowledged a sovereign and were part of an organized society. They usually practiced fishing, plundering, smuggling, trade, and farming, depending on the circumstances, and these activities had been integral parts of the local economy and the means of livelihood of the coastal poor.[67] This book, therefore, translates *haifei* or *hải phỉ* into "sea thieves" or "sea robbers," who engaged in "maritime raiding," in the words of Jonathan Chappell, instead of piracy.[68] This distinction is important particularly because "piracy" was a ubiquitous term in French records to label both banditry and nationalist movements with the aim of delegitimizing the anticolonial protests.[69]

Up to the first half of the twentieth century, Vietnam had been one of the destinations for Chinese people who fled political instability in the empire, or Republic, or sought fortune abroad. The Chinese migrants who settled or lived temporarily along Vietnam's border with China added up to the ethnic mosaic, the commercial networks, and the dynamic relations with the state authorities of the frontier region. The French colonial regime's receptive policy toward the Chinese immigrants – who contributed significantly to the fishing sector, became laborers in rising industries, and acted as middlemen in the transnational commerce – lent further momentum to the southward migration from China.[70] The Chinese in the northeastern border region of Vietnam, who arrived during different waves of migration, spoke different dialects, and came from different provinces of origin, were far from homogenous. Among this diverse community were Chinese citizens – later referred to as *người Trung Quốc* during the DRV era – who carried China-issued travel documents and spent some time at the border region. The itinerant traders among them traveled between urban centers and sustained the economic connections between Southern China and Vietnam. A considerably larger group were the ethnic Chinese who spoke a dialect of Chinese, followed Chinese customs, and had lived in Vietnam, mostly in the rural area, for

---

[66] Amirell, *Pirates of Empire*, 24.
[67] Anthony, "'Righteous Yang,'" 5–8; Roszko, *Fishers, Monks, and Cadres*, 91.
[68] Chappell, "Maritime Raiding, International Law and the Suppression of Piracy on the South China Coast," 476–77. Chappell also discusses the different understandings of piracy between the British and the Qing government.
[69] Amirell, *Pirates of Empire*, 201.
[70] Amer, "French Policies towards the Chinese in Vietnam," para. 47, 58; Trần Khánh, *The Ethnic Chinese and Economic Development in Vietnam*, 57, 72.

generations. Being considered "subjects" of the Nguyễn dynasty (1802–1883; it nominally ruled the French protectorates of Annam and Tonkin after 1883 and during the Japanese occupation of 1945), the French colonial regime, and the DRV state, they had been referred to with various names such as *Hoa Kiều* or *Hán* and have been consistently categorized as *người Hoa* after 1973.[71] In addition, some Chinese in Vietnam were officially or unofficially identified as from a particular subgroup of ethnic Chinese, such as the Khách (or Hắc-Cá) and the Ngái. Both groups were Hakka in origin, yet the Khách spoke a Guangdong dialect whereas the Ngái followed a Guangxi dialect and mostly lived in Hải Ninh.[72] Another example was the Tàn Cá or Đản – the "boat people" who lived exclusively on junks, forming floating villages, and were known in China as the "Danjia" (Tanka).[73] Lastly, several groups were unofficially identified as from a particular region of China, such as *người Tiều Châu* (from Chaozhou, Guangdong) and *người Hải Nam* (from Hainan). Both the imperial Vietnamese state and the French colonial government demanded that the urban Chinese immigrants joined one of the dialect- or province-of-origin-based *bang*, or *congrégations*, which partly explains the compartmentalization of the Chinese community.[74]

The identities of the various subgroups of the Chinese community had long been fluid or overlapping, which also prevented a coherent categorization by successive political authorities. The French colonial state, for instance, lumped various ethnic groups of Chinese descent in Hải Ninh as Nùng, which meant "agriculturalist."[75] The DRV, in its early years, referred to all ethnic Chinese as *Hoa Kiều* ("overseas Chinese") at the national level, but at local levels, it distinguished different subgroups.[76] This book refers to people of Chinese origin, and their descendants, in the border provinces as "ethnic Chinese" (or "Chinese community" when describing the group as a whole) and uses the ethnonym if it is specified in sources.

The implication of this altitudinal variation of ethnic composition and geographic diversity to state building is the main reason that this book focuses on the Guangxi-Northeast Vietnam border instead of the Northwest Vietnam-Yunnan borderlands, which is made up of mostly highlands (except

---

[71] Nguyễn Văn Chính, "Ethnic Chinese in the Sino-Vietnamese Borderlands," 28–29. I thank Shawn McHale for encouraging me to unpack the problematic concept of *Hoa Kiều*.
[72] Nguyễn Văn Chính, "Memories, Migration and the Ambiguity of Ethnic Identity," 209; Luong, "A Handbook on the Background of Ethnic Chinese from North Vietnam," 6–9.
[73] Nguyễn Văn Chính, "Ethnic Chinese in the Sino-Vietnamese Borderlands," 7; He and Faure, "Introduction," 2.
[74] Amer, "French Policies towards the Chinese in Vietnam," para. 48–55.
[75] Nguyễn Văn Chính, "Ethnic Chinese in the Sino-Vietnamese Borderlands," 9–10.
[76] See further details in Chapter 1.

for the Red River Valley in Hekou-Lào Cai region) populated by both original settlers and successfully indigenized migrants of various ethnic backgrounds.[77] The historic power dynamics between the political centers and the local communities in the eastern and western sections of the Sino-Vietnamese border shared notable similarities. Armed conflicts, especially during dynastic changes in China, drove southward migration, some across the border to Vietnam, which formed a "migration corridor" and "language corridor" between the two countries.[78] Chinese and Vietnamese courts had delegated power and granted significant autonomy to tribal chieftains (*tusi* in Chinese and *thổ ty* in Vietnamese) in exchange for their flimsy loyalty and annual tributes.[79] In the second half of the twentieth century, both Yunnan and Northwest Vietnam experienced assertive nation building and state building driven by the respective Chinese and Vietnamese states, which transformed Yunnan "from a corridor of transnational trade to a remote cash crop cultivation base of the PRC political economy" and "fashioned diverse inhabitants" of the Black River Basin "into citizens of Vietnam and subjected them to nation-state power."[80]

The contradictions between internationalism, nationalism, and transnational localism were nevertheless more pronounced at the Guangxi-Northeast Vietnam border than on the western part of the two countries' border due to greater intensity of joint state building. As a culturally and socially transitional zone between East Asia and Southeast Asia, the altitudinal diversity of the eastern section of the Sino-Vietnamese border defied any state projects that pursued uniformity. Unlike Northwest Vietnam's border with Yunnan, which also neighbors Laos and Burma, state building at the Guangxi-Northeast Vietnam border had a stronger binational feature.[81] During the period of 1949–1975, the eastern part of the Sino-Vietnamese border witnessed higher volume of trade and aid in transit. It was also more vulnerable militarily to the adversarial camp due to the challenges with coastal defense, and Northeast Vietnam suffered from heavier American bombing during the Vietnam War. The significance of the Guangxi-Northeast Vietnam border to the two neighboring socialist countries heightened both the collaboration and competition between the two revolutionary governments to consolidate their authorities in the region.

---

[77] Duan, "At the Edge of Mandalas," 22.   [78] David, "The language corridor revisited," 71.
[79] Vũ Đường Luân, "Contested Sovereignty," 498, 507.
[80] First quote from Duan, "At the Edge of Mandalas," 143; second and third quotes from Lentz, *Contested Territory*, 3. For works on northwestern Vietnam during the nineteenth century, see Davis, "Black Flag Rumors and the Black River Basin"; Le Failler, *La rivière Noire*.
[81] The multilateral dimension of borderlands state building at the Yunnan-Myanmar, Laos, and Vietnam border during the Cold War needs further study.

Distracted State Building before the Cold War

Under our flag, many mountain people will enlist immediately to exterminate the remaining bandits of Liu Yongfu, who will seek refuge in the very rugged region between Cao Bằng and Lạng Sơn, after the upcoming evacuation from Lào Cai. We should not waste a minute for the new organization, but keep in mind that the Tonkinese are far from having the same character as the natives of Lower Cochinchina...
—M. A. Aumoitte, Chancelier du Consulat de France a Hanoi, 1884[82]

The three provinces of Yunnan, Guangxi, and Guangdong all bound Vietnam. Yunnan is for trade, Guangdong for coastal defense, and Guangxi for land border defense.
—Zhang Zhidong, Governor of Liangguang (Guangxi and Guangdong), 1885[83]

Aumoitte and Zhang's visions on the border around the time of the Sino-French War (1884–1885) merely hint at the variety of ways in which historical states on both sides of the Sino-Vietnamese border viewed and expressed concerns about the border and the people who lived in the borderlands. It is important to acknowledge, then, how state activities at the border in the second half of the twentieth century were initiated in the context of historical precedents of successful and, equally importantly, unsuccessful state intrusions into the borderlands and sometimes even encountered institutional remnants of these earlier efforts at exerting state authority and controls. Surveying this history, though, also reveals the shared experience of states across all periods in their need to deal with borderland realities where the movements of people took place and broad social and economic networks existed with little regard to state borders. It is the argument of this study, though, that there was a qualitative difference between state activities on the Sino-Vietnamese border that began in the Cold War period and those that came before, where "distracted states" facing continuous wars were often unable to devote full attention or resources to the task of border making. More importantly, limited coordination between the successive Chinese governments and the French colonial state left the border people significant "wiggle room" to circumvent the political authority.

In comparison with North American and some other Asian borderlands, the Sino-Vietnamese border emerged much earlier, remained relatively stable, and was characterized by intensive cross-border activities. State agents who served the Ming Dynasty (1368–1644), for instance, understood that borders between China and Annam existed and that "imperial sovereignty extended only that far

---

[82] Aumoitte, *Tong-King*, 44.
[83] "Dai Li Huyuan zhi zongshu [Telegram to the Premier's Office for Li Huyuan]," April 20, 1885, in Zhang, *Zhang Wenxianggong quanji*, 15.

and not an inch beyond."[84] Up to the late nineteenth century, the borders between China and Vietnam continued to be negotiated and defined largely as a result of a quest for autonomy by local communities and local disputes over economic resources such as fresh water, arable lands, and mines.[85] The border was nevertheless not understood, manifested, or enforced as a continuous line that divided two adjacent nations but as strongholds at several mountain passes. The local people rarely had to answer to the border authorities as the countless trails in between the guarded gates fostered close economic and cultural ties that held the border community together. Over the nineteenth century, neither the Nguyễn court and the later French colonialists in Vietnam nor the Qing court in China managed to impose their respective central state's priorities at the Sino-Vietnamese borderlands; instead, they all had to negotiate with frontier power brokers. One of the best examples of these power intermediaries was the bandit leader Liu Yongfu, whose Black Flag Army was enlisted to aid the Qing campaign against the French in the Sino-French War.[86] The war, which was followed by demarcation of the borderline, only changed state-society relations at the border to a limited extent.

At the end of the Sino-French War, France and Qing China signed the Treaty of Tianjin in 1885, which required China to recognize the French protectorate of Annam while obtaining France's guarantee that its troops would not cross the border that separated China and Indochina. The two sides also agreed to start the demarcation of clear borderlines between them.[87] The 1887 French-Qing Convention and the Additional Convention in 1895 changed the nature of the Sino-Vietnamese border, in that a border was demarcated on an agreed map, marked physically and consistently on the ground, and enforced by the French and Chinese military forces.[88] The Qing government and French colonial state also established several bordering practices that

---

[84] Brook, "What Happens When Wang Yangming Crosses the Border?," 74. For other studies on the Sino-Vietnamese border awareness, see Vũ Đường Luân, "Contested Sovereignty"; Shin, "Ming China and Its Border with Annam."
[85] See Baldanza, *Ming China and Vietnam*; Vũ Đường Luân, "Contested Sovereignty."
[86] For Liu and the Black Flag Army, see Davis, *Imperial Bandits*.
[87] The treaty was named "Traité de Paix, d'amitié et de commerce entre la Chine et la France" in French and "Zhong-Fa huiding Yuenan tiaoyue shikuan." For articles of the treaty, see Chere, *The Diplomacy of the Sino-French War (1883–1885)*, 193–99.
[88] "CONVENTION between China and France respecting the Delimitation of Frontier between China and Tonkin, signed at Peking 26th June 1887," *Hertslet's China Treaties*, 314–15; "CONVENTION between China and France complementary to the Convention for the Delimitation of Frontier between Tonkin and China of the 26th June 1887 signed at Beijing 20 June 1895," *Hertslet's China Treaties*, 321–23. According to William J. Duiker, border markers were often laid out "several kilometers apart" thus failed to demarcate the precise border (*China and Vietnam*, 37). For a summary of French and Chinese military deployments at the frontier, see *Notice sur le Kouang-Si*, 24–32, 36–39. For an analysis of the relationship between map-making and boundary-making in French Indochina, see de Rugy, *Imperial Borderlands*, 230–54.

Figure I.2 Sino-Vietnamese border markers
Note: The historical no. 53 marker on the left was erected in 1896 after the Sino-French border demarcation. It faces the Vietnamese side and shows the Chinese characters "Guangxi border of China" and the French words "Frontière Sino-Annamite." The new no. 835 marker was jointly established in 2001 after the two countries signed the Sino-Vietnamese Land Border Treaty on December 30, 1999. The side that is carved with the Chinese characters "China" faces the Chinese territory, and the side with the Vietnamese words "Vietnam" faces the Vietnamese territory. They are located near the Bản Giốc/Detian Waterfall between Cao Bằng and Guangxi.
Source: Ken Marshall (kenner116), "Sino-Vietnamese border near Ban Gioc - Detian Falls," originally posted at www.flickr.com/photos/50178625@N00/5387254060 on January 18, 2011. Wikimedia Commons, https://commons.wikimedia.org/wiki/File: Sino-Vietnamese_border.jpg. CC BY 2.0. Color to black and white.

would be inherited by the communists. The growing economic integration and expanding social ties across the border, nevertheless, gave rise to a shadowy yet vibrant market system and a cosmopolitan frontier society that proved to be the greatest hurdle to any boundary-making efforts (Figure I.2). Regime change and continuous wars further obstructed the downward extension of administrative institutions.

The Guangxi–northeastern Vietnam border revealed to Europeans who traveled to the area in this period a mixed picture of the consequences of

East-West encounters in a society at the periphery of state power. Many mountain passes, fertile valleys, and river ports, from their perspectives, seemed to be destined to develop into commercial centers and enjoy certain prosperity.[89] The Europeans, though, also saw indigenous responses to Western colonialism as threatening to the development of agriculture, industry, and commerce by destabilizing the border region. The Taiping Rebellion, an uprising beginning in Guangxi that eventually became the bloodiest civil war in the mid-nineteenth century, epidemics such as cholera and plague, and the pressing problem of "piracy" during the troubled times that followed the French war of conquest destroyed the economy and reduced the population in the region.[90]

Meanwhile, the political authorities of French Tonkin and Qing China initiated measures that resembled each other to increase the strength of their respective states at the border, which gradually integrated the area into modern political systems that centered on territoriality. Based on the Sino-French Convention in 1895, the two countries established local border authorities called "Double Military Posts" (*Postes Militaires Doubles* in French and *Duixun* in Chinese) along the borderline to patrol boundary markers, maintain local security, and communicate with the opposite side.[91] The efficacy of the cooperation between the border police forces, however, should not be overestimated due to the absence of formal agreements on the ground regarding hot pursuit or extradition.[92] Moreover, both the Chinese and French local administrations attempted to organize the border population into armed groups under village elders and to subordinate them to the nearest military post so that border troops could obtain intelligence, provisions, and assistance during military campaigns against "pirates" or bandits. An optimistic prediction was that complete security from bandits would revive the spirit of enterprise of the Cantonese traders established there and restore the once prosperous border society.[93]

Despite these efforts, French state building at the northeastern Vietnam border was slowed because the French colonialists made a more determined attempt to establish a real presence in northwestern Vietnam. Yunnan, bordering northwestern Vietnam, under weaker central Chinese control, and

---

[89] Bos, *Notes on the Lung Chow T'ing, Lang Son, and Cao Bang*, 2–4.
[90] Ibid., 3, 42–46. During the Taiping Rebellion, Wu Yuanqing (also known as Wu Lingyun), a Zhuang secret-society leader who claimed affiliation to the Taipings, established Kingdom of Tingling in Taipingfu (in today's Chongzuo, Guangxi). Laffey, "In the Wake of the Taipings," 66–67.
[91] For details of each double military posts, see Gérard, *Ma Mission en Chine*, 336–43; Wu, *Guangxi bianwu yangeshi*, 39–71; Wang and Liao, *Guangxi bianfang jiyao*, 95–152.
[92] De Rugy, *Imperial Borderlands*, 248.
[93] Bos, *Notes on the Lung Chow T'ing, Lang Son, and Cao Bang*, 3, 45.

significantly resource-richer than Guangxi, attracted more investment from France and more interest from the French agents in Asia.[94] Likewise, while the Kunming-Haiphong Railway was completed in 1910, the rail line that had been designed to connect Hanoi with Nanning, later the capital of Guangxi, stopped at the border due to inadequate funding.[95] Contemporary Catholic missionary writings on the Tonkin-China frontier also reveal great intellectual curiosity in the little known, exotic highland society in the northwest.[96] The Guangxi-Indochina border, by contrast, "was marked as much by what did not happen as by what did."[97]

Although not pursuing drastic measures, the Qing court still made dedicated and, in many ways, unprecedented efforts to beef up the Guangxi-Indochina border. The Qing state particularly sought to increase its institutional presence in the lowland, which presented less of a geographical barrier to the enforcement of the newly demarcated borderline. Facing the encroachment of Western powers on several frontiers, reform-minded Chinese elites such as Zhang Zhidong advocated strengthening land and maritime border defenses in Liangguang while opening Yunnan for trade with the West.[98] The more elaborate institutions and infrastructure established in the last two decades of the Qing empire at the Guangxi border were part of Beijing's strenuous effort to reverse the trajectory of declining state capacity on its frontiers during the chaotic nineteenth century. Late Qing state building in the border area also departed from earlier "pluralist" practices of empire and claimed "for the central state the powers that were once delegated to hybrid institutions."[99] Thus, the fortification and militarization of the border contributed to Qing success in defeating the revolutionary Zhennan Guan Uprising led by Sun Yat-sen in 1907.[100]

Early Republican China witnessed the fragmentation of state power on the Sino-Vietnamese border. Responsibility for the border defense of Guangxi shifted into the hands of provincial military strongmen – the Guangxi Clique (Guixi junfa). Distracted by civil war, the warlord authorities nevertheless

---

[94] Lary, "A Zone of Nebulous Menace," 185.
[95] Ibid., 187. The Kunming-Haiphong Railway was built in 1904–1910, destroyed during the Second World War, and reopened in 1957. For an overview of the rail line, see Rousseau, "An Imperial Railway Failure"; Del Testa, "Workers, Culture, and the Railroads in French Colonial Indochina."
[96] See Michaud, *'Incidental' Ethnographers*. The Yunnan frontier also attracted the attention of Chinese elites who were concerned with nation-building. See Guo, "'Going to the Land of Barbarians.'"
[97] Lary, "A Zone of Nebulous Menace," 187.   [98] "Dai Li Huyuan zhi zongshu," 15.
[99] Giersch, "'Grieving for Tibet,'" 4.
[100] For a firsthand account of the Zhennan Guan Uprising, see Kyōkichi Ike's *Shina kakumei jikkenki* (1907), translated as *Zhongguo geming shidi jianwenlu*. Ike was a close friend of Sun Yat-sen and participated in the uprising.

improved the staffing of and the training for border institutions. This enhanced performance of state building was part of the broader reform programs that answered to "Sun Yat-sen's deathbed call for the awakening, organizing, and training of the masses" that won Guangxi the reputation of being a model province in the 1930s.[101] In 1927, the provincial government set up the Guangxi School of Border Affairs (Guangxi bianwu xuexiao) in Longzhou with full funding for students. Priority topics in the school's curriculum were French, border geography, and law enforcement, which prepared graduates for positions at military posts along the border.[102] After visiting China's borders with Russia, French Indochina, and British Burma in the early 1930s, Ling Chunsheng, a French-trained anthropologist and a forerunner of frontier studies in China, lauded the border defense infrastructure in Guangxi as more advanced, "being able to resist neighboring countries internationally and serve as a model to other border provinces domestically."[103] Thus, in spite of the decentralization of power, political elites still strived to maintain the "geo-body" of China within the frontiers of the ruined Manchu Empire.[104] Meanwhile, the Double Military Posts barely managed to carry out their duties to maintain transportation across mountain passes and public order near their posts. These joint French and Chinese border institutions fell short of their original mission of eliminating bandits, armed opium dealers, sea robbers, and smugglers.[105]

Complicating state control over these borderlands, Chinese communists and Vietnamese revolutionaries contended with Nationalist Chinese and French Indochinese authorities, foreshadowing their eventual success in overthrowing and replacing both governments. As early as the 1920s, Wei Baqun, the son of a wealthy landlord family in northwestern Guangxi, launched a peasant revolt near his native town even before the CPC noticed him.[106] In February 1930, a communist rebellion in Longzhou, which included Deng Xiaoping among its participants, temporarily established "the Left River Soviet Region."[107] In 1941, the Indochina Communist Party (ICP) set up a front organization called the Alliance for the Independence of Vietnam (Việt Nam Độc Lập Đồng Minh Hội), better known as the Việt Minh. The Việt Minh leadership then

---

[101] Levich, *The Kwangsi Way in Kuomintang China*, 3.
[102] Wu, *Guangxi bianwu yangeshi*, 109–12.
[103] Ling Chunsheng, "Zhong-Fa Gui-Yue guojie ji biandi jiaoshe [The national borderline of Guangxi-Vietnam between China and France and frontier negotiation]," *Waijiao pinglun* 7, no. 5 (1936), 70, in *Dacheng laojiu qikan quanwen shujuku*.
[104] "Geo-body," the spatial creation of nationhood, is a concept elaborated by Tongchai Winichakul in *Siam Mapped*, 16.
[105] Davis, *Imperial Bandits*, 121–56; also see Grémont, "Pirates et contrebandiers le long de la frontière sino-vietnamienne."
[106] Han, *Chinese Discourses on the Peasant*, 121, 150; Han, *Red God*, 63–78.
[107] Quinn-Judge, *Ho Chi Minh: The Missing Years*, 159.

gathered at Pác Bó, an isolated village in Cao Bằng three kilometers from the Chinese border, where they passed a resolution in support of "all-class nationalism" that downplayed the Marxist notion of class struggle. In doing so, they sought to revive Vietnamese patriotic traditions to unify the entire population against both the French and the Japanese, who had already emerged as a new player in the politics of the border.[108]

Ironically, what eventually helped rebuild a thriving economy in the Sino-Vietnamese borderlands was not peace but war. The outbreak of the Second World War, while leaving the French and Chinese governments' endeavors to increase state strength at the frontier unfulfilled, contributed to a paradoxical wartime prosperity. After the fall of Guangzhou to Japanese troops in October 1938, the rail lines, highways, and rivers across the Sino-Vietnamese border became China's lifeline to transport supplies from the West via Indochina.[109] To cut off this cross-border supply line, the Japanese Imperial Army invaded Southern Guangxi from the Gulf of Tonkin, capturing the capital Nanning and occupying the border counties in November 1939.[110] On June 20, 1940, the colonial government of French Indochina headed by Georges Catroux complied with the Japanese demand to close its border with China. In negotiations with Japan, France granted the Japanese the right to station troops in northern Tonkin and transit through Indochina.[111] Following a brief undeclared expedition to French Indochina, most Japanese troops withdrew from southern Guangxi. But most of the urban areas of the province fell under Japanese control again during the Ichi-Go Campaign of 1944–1945.[112] Finally, on March 9, 1945, the Japanese staged a coup d'état against the French colonial forces, which essentially dismantled the French Indochina regime.[113]

This interrupted state building and suspended legal transportation across the border contributed to a lucrative shadow economy. The Sino-Vietnamese border became an adventurers' paradise for those engaged in shipping, mining, and money lending, as well as salt and opium businesses. Artificial procurement prices established by the Chinese government over strategic ores such as wolfram,

---

[108] Bradley, *Vietnam at War*, 34; Chu Văn Tấn, *Một năm trên biên giới Việt-Trung*, 5–6.

[109] Chen Derong, "Kangzhanzhong de Zhong-Yue jiaotong yunshuxian," Chen was the son of Chen Xiuhe, who was a Special Executive Officer of the Division of Military Industry of the Ministry of Military Affairs of the ROC and in charge of communicating with the French Indochinese government regarding transporting military equipment through Indochina. For an overview of the transportation project, see Liu, "Kangzhan qianqi guomin zhengfu dui Yinzhi tongdao de jingying."

[110] Hutchings, "A Province at War," 663.

[111] Marr, *Vietnam 1945*, 14–19. Catroux was replaced by Jean Decoux in July 1940. See Decoux, *A la barre de l'Indochine*, 69–72.

[112] Hutchings, "A Province at War," 667–79.

[113] Marr, *Vietnam 1945*, 13; Dommen, *The Indochinese Experience of the French and the Americans*, 78.

antimony, and tin also gave rise to a thriving black market across the border controlled by armed smugglers.[114] Opium dealers were particularly notorious for their advanced weaponry, which often outstripped the standard army.[115] Nonetheless, the "regulation" of the opium trade also yielded significant revenue for Chinese provincial governments.[116] Both Chinese and French local administrations sought to take a bite from the wartime prosperity at trading centers like Dongxing and Móng Cái. Casinos boomed in Móng Cái as many merchants accumulated significant wealth during the war, and wartime infrastructure building brought Chinese government officials. Gambling houses were conveniently set up next to the bridge that connected the town to Dongxing. Charging an annual fee of 480,000 piasters from each casino owner, the French border authorities allowed Chinese to enter Móng Cái for gambling without a visa. This worked in tandem with a similar arrangement on the Chinese side, where after a monthly payment of 1,800 piasters from these casinos, the local Chinese border authorities allowed gamblers to pass the checkpoint without travel documents.[117] In the end, it was in the interests of local Chinese and Indochinese administrations and border guards to manipulate and thus profiteer from "the permeability of borders."[118]

The end of the Second World War brought peace to neither China nor Indochina. Hồ Chí Minh declared the independence of Vietnam on September 2, 1945, taking advantage of the political vaccuum of Japan's defeat. Following an agreement made by the Allies at the Potsdam Conference in July 1945, Chinese Nationalist troops moved into northern Indochina above the sixteenth parallel on September 8 to accept the Japanese surrender. Although causing rampant inflation and exacerbating the existing food shortage in north Vietnam, the eight-month occupation nevertheless delayed the return of French colonial troops. The Chinese command, headed by Lu Han, were mostly sympathizers of the Việt Minh cause and established good rapport with Hồ Chí Minh.[119] During the Chinese Civil War and the

---

[114] Provincial government of Guangxi, "Gui-Yue bianjing kuangpin zousi [Smuggling of ores at the Guangxi-Vietnam border]," *Guangxi sheng zhengfu gongbao* 1241 (1941), 2–3, in *Dacheng laojiu qikan quanwen shujuku*.

[115] Nguyen, "Dynamite, Opium, and a Transnational Shadow Economy at Tonkinese Coal Mines," 1900–1901. Opium was smuggled to Vietnam in exchange for dynamites from the coastal coal mines.

[116] "Neizhengbu jinyan weiyuanhui zhi minzhengsi han [Correspondence from anti-opium committee of Ministry of Interior to Ministry of Civil Affairs]," March 30, 1943, in Second Historical Archives of China, *Minguo shiqi xi'nan bianjiang dang'an ziliao huibian: Yunnan Guangxi zonghejuan*, vol. 88, 115–17; "Neizhengbu jinyan weiyuanhui zhi minzhengsi han," December 28, 1943, in Second Historical Archives of China, *Minguo shiqi xi'nan bianjiang dang'an ziliao huibian: Yunnan Guangxi zonghejuan*, vol. 91, 303–4.

[117] Fan Chen [pseud.], "Dongxing: xinde Guangzhouwan," 65–66.

[118] Van Schendel & de Maaker, "Asian Borderlands," 6.

[119] See Worthing, *Occupation and Revolution*. For a firsthand account from the Chinese perspective on the occupation, see Zhu, *Yuenan shouxiang riji*.

early stage of the First Indochina War, grassroots units of Chinese communists and Vietnamese revolutionaries also forged greater ties. Defeated CPC guerrilla units retreated and regrouped in Vietnamese border provinces. While receiving financial support from Việt Minh, the CPC members helped the latter train and organize the overseas Chinese regiments. From 1948, guerilla forces from both sides launched several small-scale joint military operations in the border region.[120] The highly porous border and the resilient trade connections between Southern China and overseas Chinese in Indochina formed complex supply lines for the Việt Minh to obtain weapons, medicines, and other necessities to fight the more powerful French colonial troops.[121]

Since the late nineteenth century, the French colonial state and consecutive Chinese governments sought to turn the demarcated boundary between China and Vietnam from a line on paper to one of physical reality. Military defeats by the colonial powers and the desire to emulate Western countries propelled state building in late Qing China and increased the role of the state in the economy.[122] The establishment of border defense and inspection institutions as concrete manifestations of the modern state at the China-Vietnam border was a direct result of the Sino-French War.[123] Because the boundary between China and Vietnam had been relatively stable, the most significant changes brought by European colonialism to the Sino-Vietnamese frontier was not the borderline itself but the physical structures of the state at the border. International treaties stipulated the establishment of state institutions ranging from custom houses to passport systems to regulate cross-border mobility and homogenize people within the borderline. Cross-border activities were categorized into those that were innocuous, such as farming and marriage, or pernicious, such as gambling, smuggling, and human trafficking.[124] State-building efforts at the Sino-Vietnamese border, however, were distracted or even reversed by continuous armed conflicts, change of governments, and the inconsistency of state policies. Conflicts among warlords in China and the Japanese invasion during the Second World War reversed the growing presence of state institutions at the border, forcing the political authorities to divert resources elsewhere. The closure of the border, which was meant to deplete China's wartime supply, fell short of interrupting the cross-border economy. On the contrary, war twisted

---

[120] Gao, "Fighting Side by Side," 123–24.
[121] Goscha, "The Borders of Vietnam's Early Wartime Trade with Southern China."
[122] Lai, "Li Hung-chang and Modern Enterprise," 19–51.
[123] On the maritime frontiers, Chinese naval encounters with the French also made the Chinese elites realize the importance of coordination of its northern and southern navies. Elman (Ho, ed.), *Science in China, 1600–1900*, 204–7.
[124] See Lessard, *Human Trafficking in Colonial Vietnam*; Grémont, "Pirates et contrebandiers le long de la frontière sino-vietnamienne."

supply and demand in favor of opportunists and adventurers who managed to profiteer from the shadow economy.

The complicated and contradictory impact of war on the strength of the state at the border would recur during the communist era as mobilization during the Indochina Wars improved transportation and infrastructure yet deprived local administrations of the resources needed to sustain the border institutions. At the same time, though, in many ways the PRC and the DRV also began to revive the border-making projects of their predecessors. Thus, the Chinese and Vietnamese revolutionaries, after assuming the power of the state at the border, took on the task of the "maintenance of territoriality."[125] Nonetheless, they redefined the preexisting challenges to state building through an ideological lens and viewed the legacy of colonialism from the perspective of capitalist-communist competition. Meanwhile, although still encountering delicate central-local tensions, both revolutionary parties sought to improve the consistency and reach of the state bureaucracy in ways that mirrored previous efforts but with considerably greater success.

Sources

This book crafts its narrative mainly from the cracks in the officially constituted and selectively declassified archives. Most of the archival research for this book was conducted between 2013 and 2017 at different levels of archives in China and the National Archives of Vietnam Center III (NAVC III) in Hanoi. Documents from the Foreign Ministry Archives of the PRC (FMAPRC) were collected before 2012, when the administration reclassified about two-thirds of the materials, making them unavailable for most researchers. This book relies heavily on previously unused materials from the Guangxi Zhuang Autonomous Region Archives (GZARA) in Nanning and several county and municipal level archives in Guangxi's border counties. Because the present-day coastal counties of Guangxi were governed by Guangdong before May 1951 and between 1955 and 1965, sections dealing with state building on the maritime frontier of the Gulf of Tonkin also use documents from the Guangdong Provincial Archives (GDPA). Primary sources collected in the NAVC III are mainly from four collections: the Prime Minister's Office, the Administrative Committee of Việt Bắc Autonomous Region (Khu tự trị Việt Bắc, KTTVB), the Ministry of Foreign Trade, and the Ministry of Transportation.

In the archives of both countries, scholars have better access to materials between the 1950s and the late 1960s, the period before the bilateral relations

---

[125] Ishikawa, *Between Frontiers*, 10.

deteriorated. Government documents created between 1969 and 1971 are mostly absent in the archives of Guangxi. This was the period when Mao Zedong ordered the PLA to restore order in local Chinese societies from the anarchy of Cultural Revolution created by his support of Red Guards' relentless attacks on government institutions and factional struggles, which were particularly violent in Guangxi.[126] This meant that most official documents from this period might have ended up in military archives, which generally remain closed to researchers. In NAVC III, which I visited in 2015, my requests to read any documents that included the term "overseas Chinese" (*Hoa Kiều*), "Chinese people" (*người Hoa*) or "ethnic minorities" (*dân tộc thiểu số*) in the title were declined. Materials with their information in the content but not in the title and published sources partly help identify and fill out the missing information on these subjects.[127]

Despite being highly redacted and created in support of the master narrative of revolution, official publications by the two governments and ruling parties actually reveal the highly dynamic nature of state-society relations at the border, including the challenges the state representatives encountered. Of particular value are the *Văn kiện Đảng toàn tập* (*VKDTT*, Complete Documents of the Party) series published by the Communist Party of Vietnam (CPV), *Zhonghua renmin gonghe guoshi biannian* (*GSBN*, Chronological History of the PRC) series compiled by the Institute of Contemporary China of Chinese Academy of Social Sciences, local gazetteers and official histories created by provincial and county governments and the corresponding party committees, and newspapers of provincial authorities. In addition to published and non-published sources in Chinese and Vietnamese, materials in French and English ranging from French colonial officers' firsthand account of the border region to American intelligence reports supplement important details about the military situation on the border. For example, although not always accurate in all details, declassified Central Intelligence Agency (CIA) materials reveal the pattern of militarization in the border region during the Second Indochina War.

Structure

This book follows a chronological order to trace the history of state building at the Sino-Vietnamese border based on turning points that significantly affected

---

[126] For the increasing influence of military in the Cultural Revolution, see Nelsen, "Military Forces in the Cultural Revolution."

[127] A few unpublished documents are provided by individuals who do not wish to be acknowledged. The citation of such a source provides the document title and date. Secondary sources and some published primary sources are cited in shortened forms in footnotes with the full citation provided in bibliography. Translation of non-English sources are my own.

the agenda and capabilities of the state. Chapter 1, "Asymmetrical State Building," examines how the Chinese and Vietnamese communists' perceptions of the border, and their priorities and ability to project state power there, changed as they transformed from revolutionary insurrectionists to ruling elites during 1949–1954. State building at the border was asymmetrical during this period because for the Vietnamese revolutionaries engaged in armed struggle against the French colonial troops, a permeable border offered strategic and material gains that temporarily outweighed the concerns over transnational connections across the border. At the beginning of the 1950s, therefore, the Chinese state was more active and assertive in hardening the border than its Vietnamese counterpart.

Chapter 2 analyzes the goals of the two states' regulation of long-existing cross-border connections and their strategies to differentiate between acceptable and non-acceptable cross-border movements and to extract revenues from the acceptable ones between 1954 and 1957. Titled "Joint State Building," this chapter reveals how the two revolutionary states worked collaboratively to turn their respective border societies inward toward the political centers while imposing a Cold War partnership across the border. The different elements of the cross-border social fabric were viewed through the lens of whether they were conducive to the comradeship between the DRV and the PRC or detrimental to it.

State building nevertheless backfired against the background of aggressive collectivization movements from 1958 to 1964, before the escalation of the Second Indochina War. Chapter 3, "Negotiated State Building," investigates the coercive measures by the two states to extract resources from the border and the border people's strategy of resisting state invasion by taking advantage of the porous international boundary, at time even voting with their feet to seek better conditions across the border. Due to the widening gap beween the goals of the two centralizing governments and the capabilities of grassroots state organs, coercive state building became a highly contested process.

Shifting away from the borderlands toward the littoral societies along the northern Gulf of Tonkin, Chapter 4 focuses on coastal state-building efforts during the decade from 1954 to 1964. Titled "Thwarted State Building on the Sea," this chapter demonstrates that the tensions between internationalist, nationalist, and transnational local agendas were greater at the maritime border than on the borderlands. The defining policies of a communist revolution – the nationalization of commerce, the collectivization of production, and restrictions on movement – encountered more determined resistance from the seafaring people whose livelihood relied on an open and integrated maritime space.

Titled "Reversed State Building," Chapter 5 examines the simultaneous development of the expansion and contraction of state power at the Sino-Vietnamese border between 1965 and 1975. The escalation of the Second

Indochina War geopoliticized the Sino-Vietnamese border region by connecting a remote society to global politics. In particular, the area witnessed ambitious infrastructure construction sponsored by Beijing and Hanoi to transport aid to Vietnam and social mobilization campaigns launched by local Chinese and Vietnamese administrations to support the war effort. The militarization of the border region, along with chaos of the Cultural Revolution, however, diverted government resources away from the state-building project of turning border societies toward the political centers. The two states had to accommodate and endorse the revival of cross-border networks.

The Epilogue begins with a brief overview of the ebb and flow of state power at the Sino-Vietnamese border since the mid-1970s onward, revealing the patterns of state-society relations at the border during the decade-long conflict between the two countries and the ensuing era of rapprochement and reform, when the two states had to be "rebuilt," again collaboratively. It then discusses the broad themes this book illuminates. The interaction between the Chinese and Vietnamese states on a daily basis underlines the significance of the mundane aspect of the territorialization of state and inter-state relations. The story told in this book highlights the necessity to examine the impacts of revolutionary ideology and the global Cold War on Asia against the broader political changes that Asian societies underwent, as well as the striking continuities in the objectives and strategies of state building in the modern era.

1 Asymmetric State Building (1949–1954)*

On April 23, 1949, as the Chinese Communist troops – the People's Liberation Army (PLA) – crossed the Yangzi River and overran the national capital, Nanjing, the Việt Minh command ordered the People's Army of Vietnam (PAVN) in northeastern Vietnam to prepare for surprise attacks against the Chinese Nationalists in southern Guangxi and southwestern Guangdong. Official histories on both sides indicate that the local Chinese Communist guerrillas and the Việt Minh jointly planned the campaign to weaken the Nationalist strongholds and set the stage for the further southward advance of the PLA.[1] The attack is known in Vietnam as the Campaign of the Hundred Thousand Mountains (Chiến dịch Thập Vạn Đại Sơn), named after the mountain ranges located at the Guangxi–Guangdong border (Map 1.1). When planning the attack, Hồ Chí Minh, in a handwritten note, instructed the commander of the campaign Lê Quảng Ba, deputy commander of the First Inter-zone, with these watchwords: "Caution, secrecy, unity, friendship, victory."[2] In June, the Việt Minh troops invaded the Hundred Thousand Mountains as well as the Yunnan–Guangxi border, where the rugged terrain had, in the past, essentially denied the access of the centralized political authority. With the assistance of the local Chinese Communist guerrillas, the PAVN secured control of Chinese towns and villages adjacent to Hải Ninh by September. By the end of the month, the PAVN had pulled out of China as Chinese guerrilla units managed to establish contact with their field army that was rapidly advancing toward southwestern China.[3]

---

* A few paragraphs on smuggling in this chapter are developed from my earlier publication "The Mountain Is High, and the Emperor Is Far Away: States and Smuggling Networks at the Sino-Vietnamese Border," Institute for Far Eastern Studies, Kyungnam University, 2018. This article first appeared in *Asian Perspective* 42, no. 4 (October–December 2018): 551–73. Published with permission by Johns Hopkins University Press.

[1] CPC GZAR Committee, *Zhongguo gongchandang Guangxi lishi*, 279; Võ Nguyên Giáp, *Chiến đấu trong vòng vây*, 564–66.
[2] Nguyễn Hà, "Yuenan renmin jundui canjia shiwandashan zhanyi 60 zhounian."
[3] Ibid; Trần Minh Thái et al., *Quảng Ninh*, 105–18.

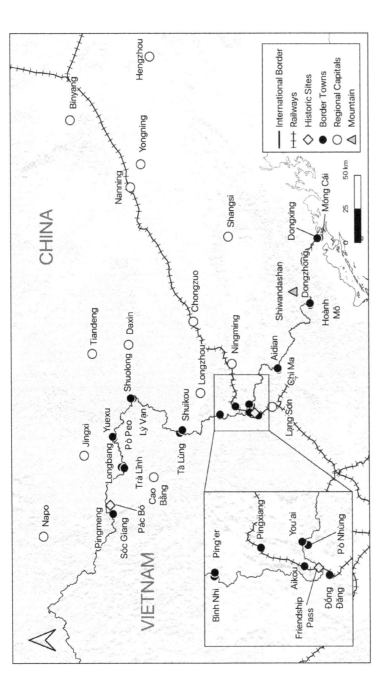

Map 1.1 Border towns and crossings on the Guangxi–Northeast Vietnam Borderlands, circa 1970

Note: Most paired border towns have also been historic markets. Border markets with significant trade volume during the period 1949–1975 are Shuikou-Tà Lùng, Ping'er-Bình Nhi, Aikou-Đồng Đăng, Aidian-Chi Ma, Dongzhong-Hoành Mô, and Dongxing-Móng Cái.

Source: Devon V. Maloney, creator. Map data from OpenStreetMap contributors and available from www.openstreetmap.org/copyright. Created using Free and Open Source QGIS, version 3.26.

Instead of a purely altruistic action fulfilling a proletarian internationalist cause, this cross-border military operation allowed the Việt Minh forces to assume tighter control over Hải Ninh, Vietnam's northeastern coastal province neighboring China. In the officially endorsed narrative, the campaign is given credit for expanding the "liberated zone," connecting it with Chinese border areas under the Communist control and opening PAVN's access to the sea.[4] Meanwhile, the Việt Minh attempted to accomplish the unannounced goal of curbing the activities of the pro-Chinese Communist Independent Regiment in Hải Ninh, especially reducing its influence among the Nùng people, who, over centuries, had migrated from Southern China.[5] The relations between the Independent Regiment and the Việt Minh leadership remained complicated, though, as the regiment also participated in the Campaign of the Hundred Thousand Mountains.[6] In the meantime, the Việt Minh also competed with the French-sponsored Nùng Autonomous Territory (1948–1954) for legitimacy in Hải Ninh. Recognizing the military strength of various ethnic minorities, mainly of Chinese descent, the French authorities brought together these armed groups under a single command to buttress the border area. As of July 1948, more than 70 percent of the residents in the autonomous region were rural ethnic Chinese – Sán Dìu, Ngái, and Hắc-Cá – who were labeled together by the French as Nùng, whereas the urban ethnic Chinese constituted about 3 percent of the total 150,000 population of the area.[7]

The coordinated cross-border military operation between the Chinese Communist forces and the Việt Minh bore out the benefits of a relatively stable yet poorly defended border, which had enabled the continuous migration from China to Vietnam, for the revolutionaries striving for political dominance in their respective countries. The Communist guerrillas in southwestern China retreated to the Vietnamese border province Hà Giang to consolidate and train their forces from June 1948 to January 1949.[8] Sporadic Việt Minh attacks on Chinese Nationalists took place in Yunnan between 1946 and mid-1949.[9] The weakness of the Chinese Nationalist and French colonial governments at the border allowed the Chinese and Vietnamese communists to create a haven where they could easily flee to or enlist assistance from their neighboring allies when enemy government crackdowns strained their resources. Once these

---

[4] Nguyễn Hà, "Yuenan renmin jundui canjia shiwandashan zhanyi 60 zhounian."
[5] Calkins, *China and the First Vietnam War*, 23–24. The Independent Regiment also coordinated with Việt Minh forces in Cẩm Phả, which had around 10,000 ethnic Chinese mine workers. Trần Minh Thái et al., *Quảng Ninh*, 132–51.
[6] Pang, "Zai Yuenan gongzuo he zhandou de suiyue," 33–38.
[7] Nguyễn Văn Chính, "Ethnic Chinese in the Sino-Vietnamese Borderlands," 4, 9–10.
[8] Guo, "Zhongguo budui zai Yuenan Heyang zhengxun de rizi," 31–33.
[9] Nguyễn Thị Mai Hoa, *Các nước xã hội chủ nghĩa ủng hộ Việt Nam kháng chiến chống Mỹ cứu nước*, 53–55.

revolutionaries ascended to power, however, they began to perceive the permeability of the border as a challenge to their authority, just as their predecessors had.

This chapter examines how the Chinese and Vietnamese Communists' perception of, and priorities at, the border, as well as their capabilities to project state power there, changed as they gradually transformed from revolutionists to ruling parties from 1949 to 1954. In late 1949, the PLA arrived at the Guangxi–Vietnam border. Although it took them another fourteen months to crush the remnant Nationalist forces and other opposition elements,[10] the party-state soon stepped up its efforts to decrease the permeability of its international boundary. On the Vietnamese side, the DRV, after a successful Border Campaign (Chiến dịch Biên giới or Battle of Route Coloniale 4) in the autumn of 1950, drove French forces out of its border with China except for the coastal trading post of Móng Cái. This victory removed major obstacles on the supply lines between Northern Vietnam and Southern China and placed PAVN in a stronger strategic position to attack French strongholds in the Red River delta.[11] As the areas under DRV's control connected with Chinese territory, the Chinese and Vietnamese Communists started to jointly enforce the international boundary, enhance the cohesion of state authorities over the margins of their power, and extract revenues by controlling cross-border flows of goods and people during the First Indochina War (Kháng chiến chống Pháp, "Anti-French Resistance War" in Vietnamese).

State building by the Chinese and Vietnamese revolutionaries at the border, however, remained asymmetric during this period, which created an "osmotic pressure between states" – in the words of Noboru Ishikawa – and left the boundary highly fluid and permeable.[12] Just like the osmosis that occurs between two solutions with different concentrations separated by a membrane, the permeability of borders has been shaped by the gap of the intensity of state building in the neighboring countries. The years from 1949 to 1954 witnessed a divergence in the Chinese and Vietnamese Communists' perceptions of the border and their priorities there due to the two parties' different status in their respective countries. Fighting the returning French colonial regime, the leaders

---

[10] Strauss, "Paternalist Terror," 83.
[11] Zhai, *China and the Vietnam Wars*, 26. This chapter uses the "DRV" (a nation-state) instead of "Việt Minh" (a movement) when referring to the Vietnamese authorities since 1950. The PRC and the Soviet Union recognized the DRV at the beginning of the year. After the Border Campaign, the Vietnamese Communists were building their state in the area neighboring China. Using "Việt Minh" also echoes unconsciously the French attempt to delegitimatize their opponent. Christopher Goscha and Shawn McHale in their latest books on the First Indochina War problematize the use of "Việt Minh" for the entire war. Goscha, *The Road to Dien Bien Phu*, ix; McHale, *The First Vietnam War*, 17.
[12] Ishikawa, "Genesis of State Space," 175. Ishikawa uses the term to characterize the impact of "the difference between two national economies" on the cross-border movement.

of the DRV, proclaimed by Hồ Chí Minh in 1945, treated the Sino-Vietnamese border as a space of opportunity to obtain Chinese aid and mobilize resources. Material gains from the porous border outweighed, at least temporarily, their concerns over the transnational connections of ethnic Chinese. Chinese leaders, however, viewed the Guangxi–Vietnam border as a space of imminent danger and potential subversion, where imperialists and domestic "counter-revolutionaries" could easily collude to challenge the authority of the newly established communist state. Hence, at the beginning of the 1950s, the PRC had to police the border unilaterally without much cooperation from the DRV.

While Beijing often attempted to micromanage the border with its Vietnamese revolutionary partners, it was the border guards, customs officials, and other grassroots state agents who were responsible for implementing the centrally devised directives. The majority of the state representatives were non-natives who came into the area with the PLA field army and therefore lacked the skill and prowess to carry out policing and administrative tasks at the border. It was, after all, very difficult for the Chinese Communists to extrapolate state-building tactics derived from densely populated peasant societies to the borderlands where the lives of traders, highlanders, and fisherfolk were not tied to a specific territory or nation. Meanwhile, the DRV's war for independence and China's involvement in the Korean War (1950–1953) further drew military resources away from enforcing the shared international boundary and distracted the two sides from concerted state building in the border region.

The consolidation of the two fledging revolutionary states at their margins over local societies thus did not unfold in a uniform manner. Borders, as "local manifestations of the claims of a state's authority," directly contribute to the realization of sovereignty. While states coerce the local people, extract revenues, and demarcate territory at the border, they do not invest in these practices to the same extent.[13] During the First Indochina War, the Sino-Vietnamese border was a site of selective coercion. The two party-states mainly targeted their political rivals, namely the French colonial expeditionary force, the Chinese Nationalist remnants, military adventurists or "bandits," and other competitors of political authorities and legitimacy. Nonetheless, given their urgent need to finance their incipient apparatus and to prime the local society for later socialist transformation, both the CPC and the Việt Minh steadily expanded the state's economic functions by extracting taxes and thrusting state-owned trade companies into the existing cross-border commercial networks.

While both sides agreed to shelve territorial disputes, the period from 1949 to 1954 witnessed the eventual definition of Vietnam, under the DRV,

---

[13] The quote and paraphrase are from Gavrilis, *The Dynamics of Interstate Boundaries*, 5–6.

as a separate state from China. Even though military advisers and supplies from China significantly improved DRV's strategic position against the French, Indochina was only one of the many foci on PRC's much broader anti-imperialist agenda in Asia.[14] Preparation for an attack on the Nationalists in Taiwan and direct involvement in the Korean War after October 1950 created major military commitments. Consolidating control in the ethnic frontiers of Tibet and Xinjiang also topped Beijing's political agenda. Under the banner of proletarian internationalism, Beijing nevertheless emphasized the importance of "self-reliance" to their Vietnamese comrades, especially in resolving the pressing issue of financial deficits.[15] Meanwhile, other than dispatching military advisers and providing material aid, the PRC avoided establishing a political presence across the border in Vietnam. Moreover, to foster a closer political and military partnership with the Vietnamese, the Chinese Communists had to accommodate and cater to the strong nationalist tendencies of the Vietnamese leadership, which drew on a long-established historical discourse of struggle against its northern neighbor.

Space of Danger or Space of Opportunity: State Perception of the Border

The Chinese and Vietnamese Communists built a revolutionary partnership during the First Indochina War through greater collaboration in high-level diplomacy as well as closer ties between their local states at the border. Simultaneously, both had to deal with various challenges to their authority at the highly permeable Sino-Vietnamese border, although not directly from each other. While the notion of the modern nation-state as a territorial entity drove all twentieth-century state building, ruling elites who ascended to power through armed struggle and encountered stiff resistance were more vigilant against the perceived treacherous infiltration from the outside world. As in Bolshevik Russia and then the Soviet Union, the philosophy of "socialism in one country" shaped border controls in newly established communist states such as the PRC and the DRV. In lieu of world revolution, the communists aimed to create a state that could confront the adversarial capitalist world and launched a class struggle at the state level. Such struggle called for sharply defined and strongly guarded state borders.[16]

---

[14] Calkins, *China and the First Vietnam War*, 60.
[15] "Liu Shaoqi jiu Yuenan kefu zhanshi caizheng kunnan wenti zhidian Yuenan Laodongdang zhongyang zhuxi Hu Zhiming [Liu Shaoqi telegrams President of WPV Central Committee Hồ Chí Minh about Vietnam overcoming wartime financial difficulty]," April 21, 1951, in *GSBN 1951*, 291.
[16] Chandler, *Institutions of Isolation*, 17.

As the Chinese and Vietnamese Communists were at different phases of their revolutionary path, however, the contested social spaces of borderlands posed greater dangers to the Chinese state while offering greater opportunities to the Vietnamese state during the First Indochina War. For the Vietnamese revolutionaries, the centuries-long transnational trade networks made its border with South China a space of opportunity with which it could mobilize resources for the armed struggle against the French. Moreover, while not ruling out the possibility that a CPC victory would press the United States to interfere directly in Indochina, the Việt Minh leadership viewed the changing strategic situation in China as a "golden opportunity."[17] In the summer of 1949, local Việt Minh cadres in the border provinces also observed that the southward movement of the PLA toward Guangxi and Yunnan had made the situation on the Sino-Vietnamese border "increasingly favorable to us."[18] For the PRC, its support of DRV's border offensive in the fall of 1950 helped to wipe out French military posts along China's border and thus improved Red China's strategic position in the south.[19] However, as armed rebellion and popular insurrection still challenged the authority of the CPC in Guangxi and the French still controlled the outpost of Móng Cái, the Chinese leaders perceived the perilous possibility of collaboration between their internal and external enemies to sabotage and subvert the communist state.

Because the PLA attacked the Nationalists southward from their power base in Northern China, Guangxi was among the last provinces where the Communists assumed control. While the PLA decimated, captured, or drove out of the territory 170,000 Nationalist troops in the first months of Guangxi's takeover, armed opponents in the province also assailed and killed over 1,400 party cadres and 700 soldiers by the summer of 1950.[20] Mao Zedong criticized Guangxi for lagging behind Yunnan in crushing "bandits" despite being liberated before the latter.[21] "Correcting" its previous "unrestrained leniency," the Guangxi provincial government executed more than 3,000 people deemed

---

[17] "TÍCH CỰC CẦM CỰ VÀ CHUẨN BỊ TỔNG PHẢN CÔNG Báo cáo của đồng chí Trường Chinh tại Hội nghị cán bộ Trung ương lần thứ sáu Từ ngày 14 đến ngày 18 tháng 1 năm 1949 [To act decisively and to prepare for a total counteroffensive: report of Comrade Trường Chinh at the Sixth Conference of Central Committee from 14 to 18 January 1949]," "CHỈ THỊ CỦA BAN THƯỜNG VỤ TRUNG ƯƠNG Về công tác tuyên truyền của ta sau những thắng lợi lớn của Quân giải phóng Trung Hoa ở Hoa Nam [INSTRUCTIONS OF THE CENTRAL COMMITTEE on our propaganda work after the great victories of the PLA in Southern China]," May 12, 1949, in *VKDTT* 10 (1949), 25–67, 216.

[18] "CHỈ THỊ CỦA BAN THƯỜNG VỤ LIÊN KHU UỶ X Về chủ trương biên giới [INSTRUCTIONS OF THE STANDING COMMITTEE OF INTER-ZONE X on border stance]," August 6, 1949, in *VKDTT* 10 (1949), 420.

[19] Duiker, *Historical Dictionary of Vietnam*, 23.   [20] Dikötter, *The Tragedy of Liberation*, 85.

[21] "Mao Zedong dui Guangxi jiaofei gongzuo tichu piping bing zuochu zhishi [Mao Zedong's criticism and instruction of bandit crushing in Guangxi]," November 16, 1950, in *GSBN 1950*, 869.

as "heads of counterrevolutionaries."[22] Against the backdrop of a "bandit suppression" campaign, which lasted until October 1951 in Guangxi,[23] the Chinese central and local government began to restore and consolidate a border check system.

In late 1949, Beijing decided to introduce a makeshift regulation at the Sino-Vietnamese border prior to fully institutionalizing its border authority. On December 29, the CPC Central Committee relayed orders to Lin Biao, commander of the Fourth Field Army of the PLA, on the necessity to regulate and inspect the people and goods that crossed the Sino-Vietnamese border: the border regulation "should make allowances for the Vietnamese Liberation Army as well as the economy and people's lives on two sides." To better fulfill the need of the Việt Minh, the two parties' central commands had established communications via radiotelegraph and the Vietnamese cadres operating in the border region would liaison with the PLA frontline command in Guangxi to work out rules on border crossing and inspection that took into consideration the Việt Minh's wartime requirement for cross-border commerce and personnel exchanges.[24] Two potentially countervailing understandings of the border space drove the CPC leadership's decision about the Sino-Vietnamese border: Whereas "proletarian internationalism" entailed cross-border support of the Việt Minh's revolutionary cause, the permeability of border with Indochina could be a subversive force to the fledging local state, which thus needed to distinguish friends, ordinary people, and enemies on the borderlands.

Obligations weighed on the coercive state institutions on the ground to transform the border from a space of neglect to a space of constraints. An important part of the state apparatus was the specialized security force devoted to selectively blocking the cross-border flows of people and goods based on the state's preferences. A report in early 1950 from the PRC Ministry of Public Security (MOPS) to Liu Shaoqi and the CPC Central Military Commission suggested that it was neccesary for the PLA to crush large groups of bandits and establish a border garrison for the immediate future in order to eradicate secret agents, reorganize stragglers and disbanded soldiers, and maintain traffic order at the Sino-Vietnamese border. Besides this, the MOPS planned to set up bureaus of border defense and public security in Hekou – a historic treaty port in Yunnan – and Longzhou, which would establish police

---

[22] "Mao Zedong jiu Gui-Yue-Xiang sansheng jiaofei ji Guangdong fangwu weiti fachu zhishi [Mao Zedong's instruction on bandit crushing in Guangxi, Guangdong, and Hunan and defense issues in Guangdong]," December 29, 1950, in *GSBN 1950*, 989.

[23] Dikötter, *The Tragedy of Liberation*, 86.

[24] The above part in this paragraph is based on "Zhonggong zhongyang jiu guiding Zhong-Yue bianjing jiancha banfa zhidian Lin Biao deng [CPC Central Committee telegrams Lin Biao on regulating Sino-Vietnamese border inspection]," December 29, 1949, in *GSBN 1949*, 829.

stations at key areas of border defense. It suggested that China should ask the Vietnamese officials to place corresponding institutions on the opposite sides of the border from the two ports. The two sides could establish telegraph communications and let party members who were familiar with the situation of their side join the bureau on the other side to strengthen liaison and intelligence sharing. While clearly endorsing proposals for the organization of border defense in cooperation with Vietnam, the CPC Central Committee more generally preferred to begin with flexible coordination and mutual assistance at the border over institutionalized collaboration there via bilateral agreements.[25] At this point, largely due to a lack of experience in border inspections or knowledge of local culture and geography at the central government level, informal cooperation initiated by state agents on the ground seemed far more effective than formal border enforcement policies that required careful premeditation by the two governments.

The focal point of border inspection was Zhennan Guan – the historic border gate connecting Guangxi and Lạng Sơn where the PRC transported military aid to Vietnam. Before the Bureau of Border Defense of the Department of Public Security of Guangxi took over responsibility for border checks in January 1951, the 151st Division of 38th Corps of the Fourth Field Army was in charge of defending this strategic mountain pass.[26] Without proper staffing or training, however, the field army was ineffective in extracting revenue or regulating a prohibitive border. In May 1950, the MOPS acknowledged in a report to the State Council that the border defense at Zhennan Guan "fell short in unified leadership, border check stations, or specialized anti-smuggling organizations." American, French, or Nationalist agents, therefore, could take advantage of the weak border defense to infiltrate into the Chinese interior, collude with "feudal forces," organize bandits to "loot the home and seize buffalo from border residents," and plant spies at important border passes.[27]

Despite the existence of border check points, both the fragmented terrain of the Sino-Vietnamese borderlands and the under-trained staff were responsible for the slow pace of institutionalization of border administration. According to the MOPS, soldiers and cadres suffered from an ambiguous understanding of the meaning of border defense and thus were less effective in enforcing any border regulations. Moreover, the troops had to devote more energy to growing or transporting grains than to undertaking the task of border defense due to

[25] "Liu Shaoqi jiu jianli Zhong-Yue jiaojie bianfang baowei gongzuo wenti zuochu pishi [Liu Shaoqi's instruction on establishing border defense at the Sino-Vietnamese border]," February 10, 1950, in *GSBN 1950*, 132.
[26] Zeng, *Youyiguan bianfang jianchazhan zhanzhi* (hereafter *YBJZ*), 44.
[27] The quote and paraphrase above are from "Zhou Enlai jiu Guangxi bianjing wenti zuochu pishi [Zhou Enlai's instruction on border issue in Guangxi]," May 23, 1950, in *GSBN 1950*, 373–74.

shortages of food and other daily necessities after the influx of cadres, officials, and soldiers into the border areas with limited arable land. The ministry's report, which was later endorsed by Prime Minister Zhou Enlai, suggested that the government should unify the command of border defense near Zhennan Guan, rectify intelligence organizations, strengthen mass work, and establish bureaus of border defense and public security along the border. In pursuing these goals, the military would still play a leading role in guarding the border, with the chief commander of the stationed troops heading the bureau and cadres with specialized skills serving as deputy heads.[28]

Beijing's concern over security in Guangxi seemed to be well-founded because state weakness at the border constantly thwarted the "bandit suppression" campaigns. In September 1950, the Central Military Commission instructed the PLA commands in Guangxi and Guangdong that it was necessary to crush remnant bandits invading from Vietnam. At the same time, it warned that the Chinese troops "should not get too close to the border; instead, they should stay a little further from the boundary line." When the bandits entered from Vietnam, the PLA field troops could "lure the enemy in depth" for about fifty to a hundred kilometers, cut off their way back, and "annihilate them from the west to the east." The PLA was instructed to avoid attacking too early thus driving the bandits back into Vietnam.[29] The CPC leadership saw that while a hot pursuit to enter Vietnam might effectively attenuate the cross-border armed oppositions to the communist state, doing so could be perceived by the West as a major escalation of the anti-French war by the socialist bloc. Moreover, an uninvited military presence in Vietnam could refresh unpleasant Vietnamese memories of past Chinese invasions.

Despite the significance of defending communism and fostering a socialist brotherhood, border issues had to compete with other items on the military agenda that assumed greater importance to Beijing. The resulting limits on resources available for the communist state to build a strong border further enhanced the danger it perceived on the margin of its power. From June 15 to 28, 1951, the MOPS held the First National Border Defense Meeting. A resolution adopted at the meeting acknowledged that because the country had just begun economic construction and needed to divert substantial resources into assisting Korea and preparing for campaigns against Taiwan, all issues related to the construction of border defense had to be solved gradually in an order of priority based on "necessity" and "possibility."

---

[28] Ibid.
[29] The above part of this paragraph is based on "Zhongyang junwei jiu Guangdong, Guangxi dengdi junshi bushu he jiaofei dengxiang gongzuo fachu zhishi [CPC Central Military Commission's instruction on military operation and bandit crushing in Guangdong, Guangxi, and other places]," September 16, 1950, in *GSBN 1950*, 681.

To allow the better-equipped standing army to fulfill more pressing military need, the meeting decided to "lay the foundations for the public security institutions to take over the task of border defense in a year and a half or two years."[30]

Meanwhile, the Việt Minh, which had operated on a fluid territorial base with hastily created structures until the early 1950s, perceived the possibility of territorializing and institutionalizing the DRV state along the area bordering its northern neighbor, with whom the Việt Minh shared a revolutionary agenda. The increasing influence of the Chinese Communists and the collapse of Nationalist rule consolidated the Việt Bắc Inter-zone – the administrative and military command unit north of Hanoi – as the DRV's base of support. As Christopher Goscha argues, the DRV was "a state born out of war," a process with a strong transnational dimension in terms of not only how Moscow and Beijing affected the trajectory of the conflict but also how the DRV drew on resources across Southeast Asia for the struggle against a much more powerful enemy.[31] The war, especially the DRV's aggressive mobilization during the campaigns to capture Điện Biên Phủ, facilitated the incorporation of the Thái-populated Black River Region into Vietnam.[32] The Việt Minh's efforts at state building and war making also intertwined in its northeastern border with China.

In January 1949, the Việt Minh started to prepare for its own "general counter-offense," as the PLA had defeated the Nationalist forces in Manchuria and were overcoming Nationalist strongholds in northern China. In an internal speech, Trường Chinh, General Secretary of the Central Committee of the ICP, which had officially dissolved into the Institute for Studying Marxism in Indochina in November 1945 but still functioned as a buttress of its front organization of Việt Minh, estimated that the nationwide victory of CPC would soon bring the revolution to the border with Indochina and that the Việt Minh should make proper preparation to take good advantage of this opportunity. At the same time, he warned against the widespread overoptimistic mentality among cadres that the Vietnamese could simply sit back and leave their Chinese comrades to force France out of Indochina. "We should remember," Trường Chinh emphasized, "if we fail to vehemently attack [the French forces], no matter how many victories the PLA achieves, France would not voluntarily exit Vietnam."[33]

---

[30] This paragraph is based on "Zhonggong zhongyang pizhuan 'diyici quanguo bianfang baowei gongzuo huiyi jueyi' [CPC Central Committee endorses 'the resolution of the first national border defense meeting']," July 15, 1951, in *GSBN 1951*, 505–6.

[31] Goscha, *Vietnam: Un état né de la guerre, 1945–1954*. [32] Lentz, *Contested Territory*, 2.

[33] "TÍCH CỰC CẦM CỰ VÀ CHUẨN BỊ TỔNG PHẢN CÔNG Báo cáo của đồng chí Trường Chinh tại Hội nghị cán bộ Trung ương lần thứ sáu Từ ngày 14 đến ngày 18 tháng 1 năm 1949," 35.

Vietnam's northeastern provinces bordering with China were of particular significance to the planned counteroffensive. The coastal Hồng Quảng region, for instance, was rich in coal resources and well-connected to the international trade system through sea lanes.[34] Although the French troops tightened its hold of the area to protect such crucial economic interests, the arrival of the PLA to South China inevitably tipped the balance of power on the ground.[35] To make the best use of the rapidly changing situation, in May 1949, as the PLA was moving close to Shanghai, the Việt Minh leadership decided to adjust its propaganda strategy. Besides using the PLA victory to woo the people already under Việt Minh control to support its revolutionary cause, the ICP Central Committee intensified propaganda toward workers, intellectuals, and businessmen, including ethnic Chinese, in the French controlled area, adopting the CPC's tactics during its swift takeover of Nanjing.[36]

Viewing the southward attack of the PLA as a favorable development, the Việt Minh nevertheless had an ambivalent attitude toward the increasing influence of the CPC in the border area, given the large ethnic Chinese population in Hải Ninh and the growing reputation of the pro-CPC Independent Regiment within the Chinese community. In the late 1940s, the Việt Minh had seemed comfortable with abdicating the responsibility for organizing the ethnic Chinese in its northeastern borderlands to overseas cadres of the CPC.[37] As the Chinese Communists approached a nationwide victory, though, the Việt Minh attitude toward leadership over the mobilization of the Chinese community underwent a subtle change. In September 1949, the party branch of the First Inter-zone issued new orders regarding preparations for the "ultimate campaign" against the French. On one hand, guerilla solders would open up a safe corridor immediately along and across the Sino-Vietnamese border for the secret movement of troops and access to the coast, the establishment of a base area, and the facilitation of foreign trade. On the other hand, the ICP would rigorously develop and consolidate the foundation of the party in the border and coastal area to effectively mobilize popular support and lead a mass movement there. In particular, the local party organs were instructed to avoid publicizing any unpleasant incidents of Chinese and Vietnamese cadres contesting for influence among the masses. The orders

---

[34] Since 1888, Société française des charbonnages du Tonkin was granted a concession in the region to exploit coal deposits. Campagne, "French Energy Imperialism in Vietnam and the Conquest of Tonkin," para. 35.

[35] "CHỈ THỊ CỦA THƯỜNG VỤ BAN CHẤP HÀNH LIÊN KHU ĐẢNG BỘ I Về những nhiệm vụ cần kíp để củng cố miền Đông Bắc Liên khu [INSTRUCTIONS OF THE STANDING COMMITTEE OF THE PARTY OF INTER-ZONE I On urgent tasks to strengthen the Northeast Inter-zone]," September 1, 1949, in *VKDTT* 10 (1949), 355.

[36] "CHỈ THỊ CỦA BAN THƯỜNG VỤ TRUNG ƯƠNG Về công tác tuyên truyền của ta sau những thắng lợi lớn của Quân giải phóng Trung Hoa ở Hoa Nam," 215–17.

[37] Ungar, "The Struggle over the Chinese Community in Vietnam," 598–99.

urged the Independent Regiment to build closer connections with the Việt Minh organizations in Hải Ninh and Hồng Quảng and avoid any conflicts, as both sides should "propagate revolutionary thoughts among the masses from a communist stance." All party members and cadres, the orders continued, "should absolutely avoid parochial nationalism, be far-sighted, and properly resolve all problems with internationalist spirit."[38]

While highlighting ideology when revolutionary solidarity worked to the advantage of the Việt Minh in its collaboration with other anti-colonial movements in Vietnam, the local cadres' attitude toward the Chinese Nationalists in the Sino-Vietnamese border was rather pragmatic, mainly aimed at obtaining weapons from the latter. In August 1949, the Tenth Interzone asked the cadres in the two provinces of Lào Cai and Hà Giang bordering with Yunnan to treat the poorly organized, less equipped Chinese Nationalists who crossed the border as bandits and confiscate their weapons. "If [they] are stronger than us," the guideline continued, "we should be flexible in negotiating with them, such as by using money, opium, and salt to buy weapons from them and split their force .... We do not need to discuss with the PLA about this modus operandi; nor do we need to share the seized weapons with them."[39] Thus, the Sino-Vietnamese border was a space of opportunity for the Việt Minh not only because the CPC was approaching nationwide victory but also because of new access to much needed weapons during the collapse of Nationalist rule in China.

After Mao Zedong declared the founding of PRC in October 1949, the Việt Minh decided to strengthen the momentum of the Vietnamese revolution. From the official dissolution of the ICP until January 1950, as Goscha argues, the DRV was almost "left out of the internationalist communist world" despite its exigent need for material assistance during its struggle for national independence. It was communist China that rebuilt the connections between Vietnam and the world communist movement.[40] Hence the period 1949–1950 was a turning point in the First Indochina War as Chinese, Soviet, and American interventions internationalized the conflict in northern and central Indochina, which not only transformed the DRV's armed struggle into a conventional war but also led to a "transnational state-making" of communist Vietnam.[41] In January 1950, as the DRV actively sought international recognition from the socialist bloc, the Việt Minh leadership renewed its publicity efforts at upholding Sino-Vietnamese revolutionary solidarity.

---

[38] The above part is based on "CHỈ THỊ CỦA THƯỜNG VỤ BAN CHẤP HÀNH LIÊN KHU ĐẢNG BỘ I Về những nhiệm vụ cần kíp để củng cố miền Đông Bắc Liên khu," 355–58.
[39] "CHỈ THỊ CỦA BAN THƯỜNG VỤ LIÊN KHU UỶ X Về chủ trương biên giới," 417–18.
[40] The quote and paraphrase are from Goscha, "Courting Diplomatic Disaster?," 60.
[41] Goscha, *Vietnam: Un état né de la guerre*, 384–95; the quoted term is from Goscha, *Vietnam: A New History*, 249.

In an order to local branches, the Việt Minh demanded an enhanced propaganda campaign on the subject of the friendship between the PRC and the Vietnamese people and revolutionary forces in order to "deter the enemy" and "invigorate our army and people" for the counteroffensive. The victory of the Chinese revolution, the orders continued, was the "most important event" since the Russian Revolution that "shook the imperialist system to its root" and declared "the complete failure of French plan to blockade the Sino-Vietnamese border. In front of us rises a powerful friend, opening a gate toward the world."[42]

With the fresh memory of Chinese occupation of northern Vietnam at the end of the Second World War and haunted by the Ming direct rule of Vietnam (1407–1427) and Qing invasion in 1788,[43] the Vietnamese leaders were alert to the possibility of PLA pursuing the Nationalist troops into Vietnam. To manage the disquiet the approaching PLA could cause across the border, the Việt Minh ordered its cadres to welcome the possible PLA's efforts to "foil the conspiracy between the French troops and the remnant Nationalists who cross the border," including their campaigns to chase the Nationalists – the "common enemy" of the Vietnamese and Chinese people – across the border. The orders further warned against "the counterrevolutionary propaganda of the enemy attempting to alienate the Chinese and Vietnamese nations," asking the cadres to educate people to distinguish the "new China" from the feudalist and Nationalist one in the past. At the end of the order, the party leadership required that all publications and speeches should stop referring to the Chinese community in Vietnam with the derogatory term "boat people" (người Tàu) and use "China's people" (người Trung Quốc or người Trung Hoa) instead.[44] Meanwhile, battles between Việt Minh guerilla forces and remnant Nationalist troops along the border lasted well into 1951.[45]

Pursuing different priorities, the Chinese and Vietnamese Communists viewed the complex social composition and volatile political situations at the border in contrasting manners. When the province was a Nationalist stronghold, the Chinese Communists in Guangxi took advantage of the fluid and porous border. However, once the CPC ascended to power, its opponents, including Nationalist army remnants and other armed rebels, exploited the

---

[42] The above part of the paragraph is based on "CHỈ THỊ CỦA BAN THƯỜNG VỤ TRUNG ƯƠNG Về việc tuyên truyền gây thiện cảm với nước Trung Hoa Dân chủ nhân dân và Quân giải phóng [INSTRUCTIONS OF THE CENTRAL COMMITTEE On propaganda in favor of the PRC and the PLA]," January 1950, in *VKDTT* 11 (1950), 3.

[43] Womack, *China and Vietnam*, 126–29, 136.

[44] The above part of this paragraph is based on "CHỈ THỊ CỦA BAN THƯỜNG VỤ TRUNG ƯƠNG Về việc tuyên truyền gây thiện cảm với nước Trung Hoa Dân chủ nhân dân và Quân giải phóng," 4–6.

[45] Trần Minh Thái et al., *Quảng Ninh*, 151–53.

same permeability of the Chinese-Vietnamese border. The fact that the French armed forces were not yet wiped out in Indochina heightened the sense of insecurity of the PRC about its southern border. The Chinese leaders thus viewed the Guangxi-Vietnam border as a space of danger, where the conflict in Indochina might spill over to China. In late 1950, the Chinese Foreign Ministry openly condemned the French for violating Chinese airspace and bombing its border towns.[46] For the Vietnamese, the poorly enforced international boundary with China provided access to trade, food, and weapons indispensable for the survival of the incipient DRV state and its increasingly battle-hardened PAVN. The cross-border revolutionary connection was one version of the long existing links between the Vietnamese anti-colonialists and various nationalist movements in China. Moreover, the presence of the PLA at China's southwestern border also tipped the strategic balance in Indochina in favor of the DRV state against the French. In light of the historically uneasy relations between the Vietnamese and ethnic Chinese migrating to Vietnam, however, the Việt Minh had to carefully manage the ramifications of the increasing strength of the PLA on the Sino-Vietnamese border despite the ideological affinity between the two revolutionary parties.

Sino-Vietnamese Revolutionary Comradeship during the First Indochina War

After the Communist victory in China, the intra-party fraternal partnership improved the political position of the Việt Minh, which began to enjoy greater political support and material assistance from the other communist countries. As military collaboration between the two sides deepened, however, divergence in their strategic interests, which would foreshadow the collapse of their partnership in the 1970s, also emerged. The interactions between the representatives of the Chinese and Vietnamese revolutionary governments on the border embodied the closer and more formal ties between the two parties but also laid bare the roots of the upcoming feud between the two nations: effective resistance of the pressure from Western powers that sought to hold fast to their colonial empires in the Far East was only one step toward the successful redefinition of China and Vietnam as modern nations.

An equally daunting task was how to properly deal with the legacy left by the Chinese empire and precolonial Vietnam, both of which had their own histories of imperial expansion. As Brantly Womack eloquently puts,

---

[46] "Waijiaobu fayanren jiu Zhong-Yue bianjing Faguo budui jinxing wuzhuang tiaoxin bing jingchang yuejing hongzha saoshe yishi fabiao shengming [Spokesperson of Chinese Foreign Ministry's statement on French troops' provocation and attacks across the Sino-Vietnamese border]," November 23, 1950, in *GSBN 1950*, 890.

"Vietnam had a more flexible notion of its southern and western boundaries, but the difference between itself and China was what defined Vietnam."[47] The Vietnamese defeat of Ming rolled back China's ambition on its southwestern frontier to "the established boundaries." Qing's involvement in Vietnamese internal factional struggles did not indicate that it sought to regain Vietnam as "a lost province."[48] Instead, as an "early-modern territorial state," characterized by Huaiyin Li, China during the high Qing era had a relatively fixed territory without "frequent interstate war."[49] Beijing's pro–status quo stance, however, did not stop Chinese miners, traders, and bandits from pursuing "local opportunities" across the border in Vietnam.[50] By increasingly adopting the Chinese revolutionary model and sponsoring institutitional connections across the border with the PRC, the Vietnamese state once again encountered the challenge of defining and defending the difference between itself and its northern neighbor. Precolonial Vietnam, by indigenizing the Confucian statecraft, had viewed Southeast Asia with a "Sinitic lens" that emphasized centricity. Although Vietnamese southward expansion against Champa and Khmer had been successful, its self-perception as the regional central power "was evangelical than natural."[51] Still, as a result of their respective imperial past, both China and Vietnam interacted with the outside world with a great sense of pride, if not a condescending perspective. The comradeship and frictions between China and Vietnam during the First Indochina War marked the beginning of the strenuous, and sometimes collaborative, efforts by the two sides to reframe one of the most intensive and fluctuating bilateral relations in Asia.

The transfer and adoption of Maoist revolutionary methods was a central theme of Sino-Vietnamese relations during the First Indochina War. Departing from the Marxist vision of an urban working-class revolution against capitalism, Maoism focused on the agrarian countryside, where the vast majority of the Chinese population lived. While sharing the Leninist emphasis on a disciplined party, Mao venerated "the spontaneous revolutionary creativity of the masses."[52] Mobilizing the predominantly rural masses allowed an archaic nation to indigenize a modern revolutionary doctrine.[53] Besides the existing connections the Vietnamese revolutionaries forged with the Chinese, it was the promise of a successful revolution of national salvation against Western imperialism by a preindustrial society that drove the Vietnamese communists to the Chinese model. Before the Border Campaign of 1950, the Việt Minh troops received training in Yunnan to prepare for the battle to

---

[47] Womack, *China and Vietnam*, 134.   [48] Ibid., 119.
[49] Li, *The Making of the Modern Chinese State*, 278.
[50] Womack, *China and Vietnam*, 133–34.   [51] Two quotes from ibid., 136.
[52] Meisner, "Leninism and Maoism," 2–3.   [53] Deutscher, *Ironies of History*, 89–90.

take Lào Cai.[54] From May 1950 to June 1954, the PRC "provided 21,517 tons of assistance to the DRV", including "machine guns, rifles, ammunition, and artillery."[55] The Chinese advisors selected from the high ranking cadres of the CPC and PLA such as Chen Geng and Luo Guibo played crucial roles in decision-making during the Việt Minh's Border Campaign and its defeat of French forces in Điện Biên Phủ in 1954, which led to "a direct transmission of strategy and tactics from China to Vietnam" and the "transformative changes" of PAVN "from a peasant rebellion force to a regular national army."[56]

Besides military expertise, land reform was another important part of the package of communist revolution that the Chinese advisors tried to transplant to Vietnam. Key land reform tactics exported to Vietnam included class categorization, peasants associations, and the "Three-Together System" (to live, eat, and work with the peasants).[57] Vietnamese land reform based on mass mobilization first began in the "liberated zones" of Cao Bằng and Lạng Sơn in 1952 and 1953.[58] Radical land reform from 1953 to 1956, although incurring miscarriages of justice and complaints from the officers and cadres from landlord families, successfully mobilized "more than 100,000 soldiers and porters" in the last year of the First Indochina War.[59] This "Sino-Soviet model for communist land reform" allowed the party to establish a "vertical control over the state" and the masses by recruiting peasants "into the bureaucracy, the army, and the security services."[60]

The border area was vital to the construction and articulation of the Sino-Vietnamese partnership for various reasons. The capacity and effectiveness of the state institutions in the border provinces of China and Vietnam were crucial to the coordination of campaigns and transportation of aid. The strength and cohesion of the Chinese and Vietnamese states were not givens; they had to be built and maintained. In particular, neither of the two states was monolithic. Beijing had to both rely on and compete with the interests of the local state along the Sino-Vietnamese border to provide material support to the DRV.[61] Moreover, both the CPC and ICP, which was refounded as the WPV in 1951,

---

[54] "Zhonggong zhongyang jiu bangzhu Yuenan budui lai Yunnan zhengxun wenti zhidian Chen Geng, Song Renqiong bing Xi'nanju [CPC Central Committee telegramming Chen Geng, Song Renqiong, and Southwestern Bureau about helping Vietnamese troops to train in Yunnan]," May 23, 1950, in *GSBN 1950*, 374.
[55] Goscha, *Vietnam: A New History*, 252.
[56] First quote from Zhai, *China and the Vietnam Wars*, 63; second and second quotes from Li, *Building Ho's Army*, 3; Also see Chen, "China and the First Indo-China War."
[57] Moïse, *Land Reform in China and North Vietnam*, 170–74.
[58] Trần Phương, *Cách mạng ruộng đất ở Việt Nam*, 139.
[59] Zhai, *China and the Vietnam Wars*, 39–42; statistics from Dommen, *The Indochinese Experience of the French and the Americans*, 207.
[60] Goscha, *Vietnam: A New History*, 254.
[61] Kraus, "A Border Region 'Exuded with Militant Friendship,'" 496.

bestowed new symbolic meanings to their shared border to signal their commitment to the revolutionary partnership. A fundamental dilemma of the Sino-Vietnamese Cold War comradeship was, however, manifested at the border. A more effective cross-border military collaboration often entailed disregard of international boundaries, which would evoke the nightmare scenario for the Vietnamese of a blurred distinction between the two countries.

The construction of the cross-border transportation systems was a characteristic example of the dual process of state building and alliance-making. In May 1950, the CPC Central Committee telegrammed its Southwestern Bureau to immediately open railway and highway lines between China and Vietnam to assist the DRV campaign in Lào Cai and to improve the delivery of military aid more generally. Emphasizing the strategic significance of this ambitious infrastructure project, the vice chairman of the Central People's Government Liu Shaoqi commented that "it was necessary to build permanent roads to Vietnam for national defense and the economic development both for now and the future."[62] On October 10, 1950, a week before intervening in the Korean War, the PRC started to extend the Hunan-Guangxi rail line, originally built during the Anti-Japanese War in 1937, to the Sino-Vietnamese border.[63] Being the first major railway project of the PRC, this decision indicated the high priority given to supporting the DRV on China's political agenda. Meanwhile, the DRV set up a liaison office in the small Chinese border town Pingxiang in Guangxi to process military aid from China, the Soviet Union, and other socialist countries.[64]

In Spring 1951, the railway construction was near completion, and the Chinese engineers needed to decide where exactly to place the finishing point of the line. On April 27, the Ministry of Railways reported to the CPC Central Financial Commission that their original plan was to build a rail line from northern Guangxi via Zhennan Guan. Because the French-constructed railroad in Vietnam had a narrow gauge, it was imperative to build a trans-loading station to connect the Chinese standard-gauge line with the Vietnamese railway. The mountainous landscape at the pass, however, precluded such a project. The first stop of the line within China was Pingxiang, which was fifteen kilometers away from the boundary and enjoyed flatter terrain and access to the highway system of South China. The ministry thus proposed that Pingxiang was an ideal location for the trans-loading station in the future. Meanwhile, the gradient of the cross-border highway passing through Zhennan Guan was too steep for effective large-scale transportation. The Ministry of

---

[62] "Liu Shaoqi dui Zhong-Yue jiaotong qingkuang zuochu pishi [Liu Shaoqi's instruction on Sino-Vietnamese transportations]," May 19, 1950, in *GSBN 1950*, 365.
[63] "Lai-Zhen duan tielu kaishi xiuzhu [Construction of Laibin-Zhennan Guan line begins]," *Guangxi ribao*, October 10, 1950, 10.
[64] Zeng, *YBJZ*, 4.

Figure 1.1 Đồng Đăng during the First Indochina War
Note: Taken in September 1950, the image shows a road sign that indicates the distances between Đồng Đăng, the border town in Lạng Sơn on the Vietnamese side of the main road to China, and Cao Bằng/Paris/Nam Quan and Beijing.
Source: Photo by AFP via Getty Images, #1628170856.

Railways, therefore, suggested that it was better to extend the rail line beyond the international boundary to Đồng Đăng, the first stop on the Vietnamese side (Figure 1.1).[65] This proposed Pingxiang-Đồng Đăng line was not new. During the Anti-Japanese War, the Chinese Nationalist Government had expanded the

---

[65] "Liu Shaoqi zuochu guanyu Zhong-Yue bianjing tielu lianjie wenti de piyu [Liu Shaoqi's instruction on connecting Chinese-Vietnamese railways at the border]," June 6, 1951, in *GSBN 1951*, 415–16.

Chinese railway line to Đồng Đăng and even established a project office in Lạng Sơn to expediate the transportation of Western aid. The construction was interrupted, however, by the Japanese invasion and occupation of Guangxi from 1939 to 1940.[66] The Ministry of Railways of the PRC suggested that since the line had been open to traffic during the war and the roadbed still existed, it would be easy to restore the project. If the DRV concurred, extending the rail line to Đồng Đăng would be a time-saving and cost-effective option to overcome the constraint of the terrain.[67]

The CPC leadership, however, had to consider factors beyond convenience and cost. On the one hand, constructing a railway across the border could be perceived by the Western powers as a major sign of escalated Chinese involvement in the First Indochina War. On the other hand, the presence of infrastructure that would allow China to gain strategic control of the modern transport system in Vietnam would strain Sino-Vietnamese relations. In June 1951, Liu Shaoqi endorsed the proposal of the Ministry of Railways to connect Pingxiang and Đồng Đăng directly by railway instead of having the line going through the narrow mountain pass of Zhennan Guan. "For now," though, the railway built by the PRC would "stop at the border first, and Chinese trains would also not go beyond it." The trains within the Vietnamese national boundary "should only be operated by the Vietnamese." If it was difficult to connect the highways of the two countries at the exact border, the construction team could connect them at Pingxiang, which was located inside the Chinese border.[68]

The Sino-Vietnamese border also became an important point of state intervention because of its symbolic meaning. Due to the importance of the Sino-Vietnamese partnership to Mao's aspirations for world revolution and the strong nationalistic sentiments among the Vietnamese leadership, Guangxi became the first place where Beijing removed the derogatory geographic terminology that had been used in Chinese history related to its borders with Asian neighbors. Zhennan Guan was a historical gateway between China and Vietnam, linking Pingxiang and the Vietnamese border town of Đồng Đăng. Vietnamese tribute missions entered China through the mountain pass during the dynastic era, whereas Việt Minh leaders including Hồ Chí Minh also used the gate many times when traveling between Northern Vietnam and Southern China. Throughout the last five hundred years, the transformation of the gate's name exemplified the changes in Chinese perception of its southern neighbor as the junior actor in an "asymmetric relationship."[69] Preparing for a military

---

[66] GZAR Gazetteers Office, *Guangxi tongzhi: tieluzhi*, 1, 12, 15; Chen Derong, "Kangzhanzhong de Zhong-Yue jiaotong yunshuxian."
[67] "Liu Shaoqi zuochu guanyu Zhong-Yue bianjing tielu lianjie wenti de piyu," 415–16.
[68] This paragraph is based on ibid., 415.
[69] Womack, *China and Vietnam*. Also see Anderson, "Distinguishing Between China and Vietnam."

A la Porte de Chine : après l'entrevue avec le maréchal Sou.
The Nam Quan (南關) frontier post 16 July 1900

Figure 1.2 Nam Quan/Zhennan Guan in 1900
Note: View from the Vietnamese side of the gate at Đồng Đăng, Lạng Sơn. The scene shows the military commander of Guangxi, Marshal Su Yuanchun and his entourage entered French Indochina via the gate on July 16, 1900, to celebrate the opening of the Hanoi-Đồng Đăng railway.
Source: Original image from September 22, 1900, edition of *L'Illustration* (copyright expired). Courtesy of the P. A. Crush Chinese Railway Collection.

campaign against Vietnam, the Ming government under the reign of the Yongle emperor named the gate Zhenyi Guan ("Barbarian Suppressing Pass") in 1407. Forced to recognize Vietnamese autonomy after a failed attempt of direct rule, in 1428, the Ming rulers changed the name to Zhennan Guan ("The Pass to Suppress the South"). In Vietnam, the site was known as "the Southern Gate" (Nam Quan or Ải Nam Quan), which is yet another symbol of Sino-centrism, as the gate was located at the northern border of Vietnam (Figure 1.2).[70] The boundary demarcated by Chinese and French officials following the Treaty of Tianjin of 1885 ran through the south of

---

[70] MacLean, "In Search of Kilometer Zero," 863.

Zhennan Guan, which made the historic border marker between China and Vietnam fall on the Chinese side of the territory.[71]

The pejorative connotation associated with the name "Zhennan Guan" became problematic when the PRC sought to forge stronger revolutionary ties with the Vietnamese to export the Maoist revolutionary model. In May 1951, Mao met Mo Wenhua, then vice commissar of Guangxi Military Region and mayor of the provincial capital Nanning, in Beijing. Mo brought up the issue of repairing Zhennan Guan, which had been severely damaged during the Japanese invasion, and invited Mao to write the inscription for the renovated gate. "Zhennan Guan is a historic gate on the Sino-Vietnamese border and thus deserves to be renovated," Mao told Mo, "with regard to its name, however, you should give it a serious thought. We now live in a different era. Would our Vietnamese comrades be happy if you continued using the term [Zhennan Guan]?" Thus, in 1953, at the height of the First Indochina War, the PRC renamed the site Munan Guan, namely, "The Gate to Establish Rapport with the South."[72] Although the Chinese government got rid of the demeaning overtone in the name of the gate, the new name was still a Sino-centric term in its geographical orientation. Twelve years later, Beijing and Hanoi gave the historical site its present name "Friendship Pass" (Youyi Guan in Chinese and Hữu Nghị quan in Vietnamese) at the onset of the American ground war in Vietnam.[73] Ironically, during the Third Indochina War, the Friendship Pass and Pingxiang were transformed into heavily guarded and mined outposts of confrontation between the two countries.[74]

At the turn of the 1950s, the DRV made a similar symbolic gesture by articulating a new policy toward the ethnic Chinese in Vietnam, signaling to Beijing that the DRV would bestow equality to the ethnic Chinese minorities without forceful assimilation. To expand allies for the cause of Vietnamese revolution, the DRV condemned the French policies toward the Chinese in Vietnam as divide-and-rule and vowed to treat ethnic Chinese on an equal footing with the Vietnamese.[75] In December 1950, after exchanging opinions with Beijing, the DRV guaranteed the political and economic rights of ethnic Chinese in Vietnam to prevent them from "following the French, damaging the resistance movement, and harming us, and to let them support and participate

---

[71] "Zhong-Fa Gui-Yue jiebeiji [Note on the border marker between China's Guangxi and French Vietnam]," 1877, no. 910000050, National Palace Museum, Taipei, cited in Chen, "Deng Chengxiu yu Zhong-Fan Gui-Yue duan bianjie jiaoshe," 21.
[72] Mo, *Mo Wenhua huiyilu*, 649.
[73] "Guanyu jiang Munan Guan gaiwei Youyi Guan dengshi [About changing the name of South-Pacifying Gate into Friendship Pass and other issues]," July 9, 1964, no. 106-D-1151-03, 4/ FMAPRC. See additional details in Chapter 5.
[74] Burstein, "Days of Danger at Friendship Pass."
[75] Trần Khánh, *The Ethnic Chinese and Economic Development in Vietnam*, 28–30.

in the resistance and construction of Vietnam."[76] Besides being eligible to elect and join local government, or administative committees (*Ủy ban hành chính*, UBHC), and own land in the countryside, the ethnic Chinese were allowed to organize their own mass organizations and activist groups as long as "close affiliation" was established with the Việt Minh. In taking this step, the Vietnamese leadership acknowledged: "Our cadres have not mastered Marxist-Leninist views on ethnic issues and, lacking in mass perspective, have been accustomed to commandism and acting in a narrow-minded and left-leaning way, which provoked discontent among the Hoa kiều."[77]

At the crucial moment of defining the postcolonial Vietnamese nation against not only the French empire but also China, the most sensitive issue about the ethnic Chinese was indeed their citizenship. While the urban Chinese businessmen carrying Chinese official documents were obviously Chinese citizens, the above policy instruction admitted that the citizenship of ethnic Chinese in the mountainous and coastal border area of Việt Bắc Inter-zone was extremely complicated. These people sometimes self-acknowledged as Hoa Kiều – Chinese nationals living in Vietnam – and at other times as Vietnamese. In light of their ambiguous nationality and fluid identity, the Vietnamese leadership decided not to bring up the citizenship issue at this moment. The cadres were required to sidestep the problem by following local customs in referring to the ethnic Chinese, instead of highlighting their nationality. For instance, the Ngái people living in Hải Ninh were to be called the "Ngái people of Hải Ninh," without specifying whether they held Chinese or Vietnamese citizenship. They, similar to the populations referred to as "Kinh, Nùng, Thổ, Mán, et cetera," were "all people of Hải Ninh", hence the equal rights they were entitled to. The local cadres were required to "unite and cooperate with" the Ngái in resisting the French forces and protecting local safety.[78] The Việt Minh went so far as to tolerate provincialism to win over the ethnic Chinese despite the urgent task of forging a national identity.

Once this order trickled down to the local institutions, however, the strategy of neutralizing the ethnic Chinese and integrating anti-colonial activists among them into the resistance movement was less fruitful than anticipated. In February 1952, as the military stalemate continued in Indochina, the DRV found it necessary to reexamine and renew its relations with the Chinese community. The WPV Central Committee noticed that several provinces in the Việt Bắc Inter-zone only countenanced Hoa Kiều's participation in

---

[76] "CHỈ THỊ CỦA BAN THƯỜNG VỤ TRUNG ƯƠNG ĐẢNG Về vấn đề Hoa kiều ở Việt Nam [INSTRUCTIONS OF THE PARTY CENTRAL COMMITTEE On the issue of overseas Chinese in Vietnam]," April 12, 1950, in *VKDTT* 11 (1950), 547.

[77] The above part of this paragraph is based on ibid., 544–50 (the quoted sentence is on 549–50).

[78] This paragraph is based on ibid., 546–47.

people's councils (*Hội đồng nhân dân*) – the local legislature – but not administrative committees. While in hindsight, the DRV endeavored to reassure the Chinese community out of a practical concern to mobilize as much popular support and resources as possible for the war against the French, the revised policy criticized that the local party branches had not fully comprehended that "the Party Central Committee sincerely let Hoa kiều participate in politics, instead of simply [using the policy as a bite] to garner their support."[79] While seeking to placate the fear among the Chinese community that they would have to give up Chinese citizenship after involvement in DRV-led politics, the WPV was determined to tap the economic resources in the hands of ethnic Chinese. While the initial policy in 1950 only stipulated that ethnic Chinese farmers were obliged to pay tax, the revised one expanded the rolls of taxpayers among the ethnic Chinese to urban merchants. At the same time, the party's stance on land ownership by ethnic Chinese changed from letting them "own land" to "use land."[80]

While the Communist victory in China opened new economic opportunities for the Việt Minh beyond the existing transnational trade networks dominated by the ethnic Chinese, the Korean War constrained Beijing's commitment to the anti-colonial war in Indochina. Economic aid and commercial connections sponsored by the PRC potentially alleviated some of the financial burden of the fledging DRV state, yet such resources were not guaranteed. According to British intelligence, at a Sino-Vietnamese conference on financial and trade issues convened in June 1950 at Longzhou, the PRC and the DRV entered into a fiduciary relations, with the former agreeing to produce banknotes for the latter backed by a Vietnamese deposit of gold to the Bank of China.[81] According to a report by the Việt Bắc Inter-zone on the general situation of the region in 1950, following the Border Campaign, the PAVN carried on the strategy of "foiling French attempts to consolidate the border line from Lào Cai to Móng Cái thus curbing communication between [the Việt Minh] and the Chinese revolutionary movement." The DRV nevertheless encountered great difficulties in mobilizing resources in Việt Bắc. The French forces still controlled several transport chokepoints, attacked Vietnamese boats, and collected and even destroyed rice from the occupied areas, all of which undermined the food supply of the DRV. The price of rice in the "liberated zone" under DRV's control increased tenfold in merely four months. Rent reductions alleviated the economic burden on the poor peasants and aided in gaining popular support,

---

[79] "THÔNG TRI Bổ khuyết Chỉ thị số 34 Về chính sách đối với Hoa kiều [NOTICE Supplementing Directive No. 34 on policy towards overseas Chinese]," n.d., in *VKDTT* 13 (1952), 34–35.
[80] Ibid., 33–34. [81] Calkins, *China and the First Vietnam War*, 50.

but rice production was still far from adequate to lend momentum to any new military campaign.[82]

Discussions of DRV requests for financial assistance showed China's reluctance to overcommit itself to the Vietnamese against the background of a military stalemate in Korea. On April 14, 1951, Luo Guibo, the CPC's liaison officer to Hồ Chí Minh, telegrammed Beijing to report on the fiscal problem of the DRV and the work of Chinese cadres who assisted the Vietnamese in that respect. He noted that the DRV had asked for the Chinese to help them by issuing new banknotes, while the Chinese advisers were against the idea of resolving the financial difficulty by increasing the currency in circulation. Luo and the Chinese advisers suggested that the DRV state should increase revenue through trade and a centralized tax system. The Vietnamese also requested Chinese aid in the form of rice. Luo, however, preferred alternative solutions to meeting their rice needs. According to Luo, the DRV's budget for the year 1951 was approximately equal to 400,000 tons of rice, and it was capable of levying 300,000–350,000 tons of agricultural tax from Việt Bắc and Interzones Three and Four. A revenue of 80,000 to 100,000 tons of rice from Việt Bắc could meet the food need of 200,000 soldiers and cadres. With other sources of tax and input from the South, they could strive to strike a balanced budget.[83] Interacting with the Vietnamese cadres on a daily basis, Luo and the Chinese advisors developed a keen awareness of the organizational problems and corruption within the PAVN and the DRV bureaucracy and thus were prone to solve Vietnamese financial problems through rectification instead of Chinese aid.

Obviously, since China was openly involved in the Korean War, the CPC leadership was concerned that financial and supply commitments to the DRV would tap too deeply into limited Chinese economic resources. In the reply to Hồ Chí Minh forwarded through Luo on April 21, Beijing agreed to provide the rice, clothes, and vehicles that the DRV requested as soon as possible. At the same time, the CPC maintained that solving wartime financial problems through self-reliance should be the basic strategy of the DRV in a protracted struggle to defeat the French colonialists. Furthermore, Beijing argued that it was essential to establish a centralized budget system and related financial

[82] "BÁO CÁO TÌNH HÌNH KHU VIỆT BẮC NĂM 1950 [Report of the situation of the base area of Việt Bắc in 1950]," n.d., in *VKDTT* 11 (1950), 675 (first quote), 681–82.

[83] "Liu Shaoqi jiu Yuenan kefu zhanshi caizheng kunnan wenti zhidian Yuenan Laodongdang zhongyang zhuxi Hu Zhiming [Liu Shaoqi telegramming President of Vietnamese Workers' Party Central Committee Hồ Chí Minh about Vietnam overcoming wartime financial difficulty]," April 21, 1951, in *GSBN 1951*, 291. A relatively centralized DRV tax system emerged in 1952. According to Vietnamese official statistics, the DRV collected 26,573 tons of agricultural tax in 1952, and the industrial and commercial tax revenues were amount to 8,232 tons of rice. Hoàng Phương, *Hậu phương chiến tranh nhân dân Việt Nam*, https://quansuvn.net/index.php/topic,30184.10.html.

institutions. The DRV, the telegram stated in a somewhat paternalistic fashion, "should relentlessly oppose people who breach financial regulations or discipline, so as to concentrate all resources and use them wisely in the anti-French struggle."[84] Beijing's message was that all issues that its Vietnamese comrades could solve without drawing on Chinese support should be resolved within Vietnam.

In May 1951, Hồ Chí Minh telegrammed Beijing to request an increase in food aid. He emphasized that crops in areas under DRV control were not ready to be harvested in the period from early June to the end of July while rice from the previous year had already been consumed. The DRV state and armed forces would run out of food if no assistance was provided. Even though they had transferred three main corps out of Việt Bắc, downsized the bureaucracy, and opted for grains other than rice, food shortage remained an obstacle to a renewed military campaign. Purchasing rice with the newly issued banknotes would cause inflation, particularly due to the lack of rice supply on the market. Hồ Chí Minh wrote that "[we] sincerely hope [China] could assist with 1,500–2,000 tons of rice so that we can get through this difficulty" and asked the Chinese government to transport the first batch of rice to Cao Bằng, Lào Cai, and Lạng Sơn before June 20 and the second batch before the end of June. Beijing soon agreed to offer a hand. However, the fragmented terrain along the China-Vietnam border rendered the Chinese aid less effective. By mid-June, China carted 1,500 tons of rice to Hekou, but the town lacked sufficient transport means or food storage. Beijing could only telegram the WPV leadership, urging them to accelerate transportation across the border.[85]

Besides direct aid, the PRC kept its domestic market open to the DRV despite a deep suspicion of commercial connections between China and the outside world that was fostered by the wariness of economic imperialism and the autarkic tendency of the Maoist development model. The Vietnamese had made effective use of existing trade networks with Southern China to obtain weapons, clothes, and medicines during the war against the French, and support from the Chinese government to sell Vietnamese goods in China could help the DRV to accumulate still more revenue. In June 1950, the PRC and the DRV signed the first intergovernmental treaty on trade, stipulating a trade plan for the next two years. The DRV would export minerals, wooden logs, and other forest and agricultural products in exchange for clothes, medicines (especially antimalarial drugs Quinacrine and Quinine and anti-infective drugs

---

[84] "Liu Shaoqi jiu Yuenan kefu zhanshi caizheng kunnan wenti zhidian Yuenan Laodongdang zhongyang zhuxi Hu Zhiming," 291.
[85] This paragraph is based on "Yuenan laodongdang zhongyang zhuxi Hu Zhiming zhidian Zhonggong zhongyang qingqiu yuanzhu Yuenan liangshi [WPV Chairman Hồ Chí Minh telegrams CPC Central Committee on assisting Vietnam with rice]," May 15, 1951, in *GSBN 1951*, 350–51.

Penicillin and Sulfamide), chemicals, machines, and manufactured goods. It was agreed that the two sides would transport the goods across the border with Guangxi at Cao Bằng and Lạng Sơn and meet in Nanning to clear the account.[86] This trade deal allowed the DRV to obtain manufactured goods at a much lower price than from the French-occupied area or other parts of Southeast Asia, while tin, lead, and antimony from Vietnam alleviated the shortage of raw minerals in China. In early 1953, upon completion of the first stage of land reform, Cao Bằng and Lạng Sơn had a surplus of 1,200–1,500 tons of paddy rice. The DRV thus instructed its local agents in these two areas to carefully plan the exchange of the grain for daily necessities in China and to transport Vietnamese goods effectively to border markets.[87]

In the summer of 1952, the DRV representatives in the German Democratic Republic told their Chinese counterparts that the French blockade since the outbreak of the First Indochina War had interrupted the sea lanes between central Vietnam and Hong Kong, which historically had been a busy route for Vietnamese exports. The DRV, therefore, proposed to break the blockade by exporting Vietnamese products without a domestic market to trade with Hainan Island of China.[88] The CPC Central Financial Commission, while agreeing that China should accept all goods exported by Vietnam, warned that transporting Vietnamese products to Hainan Island on merchant ships "could endanger national defense and leak military secrecy" and suggested that the Vietnamese cargoes be freighted to China overland.[89] Despite Beijing's reservation, the DRV still managed to establish trade relations with Hainan with the support of the local Chinese administration. The latter offered favorable tax rates and prices citing the need to support their Vietnamese comrades' guerrilla war, despite the fact that doing so made it difficult for the local Chinese state-run trade company to make a profit. Following the existing trade pattern, the DRV shipped spices, herbs, dried fish, and other agricultural products to Hainan in exchange for Western medicines and ironware. The local Chinese state even suggested that they should accept goods from the "Việt Minh

---

[86] "Hợp đồng giữa Bộ Công thương Việt Nam Dân chủ cộng hòa và đại biểu Trung Hoa Dân chủ nhân dân về việc trao đổi hàng hóa từ năm 1951 đến năm 1952 [Contract between the Ministry of Trade and Commerce of the DRV and representatives of the PRC on exchanging goods in 1951 and 1952]," June 1950, no. 2198/PTTg [1945–54]/NAVC III.

[87] Bộ Công thương [Ministry of Trade and Commerce], "Về trao đổi thóc của Cao-Lạng lấy muối của Trung quốc [About exchange rice in Cao Bằng and Lạng Sơn for salt in China]," January 29, 1953; "Bộ Công thương về trao đổi thóc lấy muối của T.Q. [Ministry of Trade and Commerce on exchanging rice for salt with China]," February 12, 1953, no. 2450, 2–13/PTTg [1945–54]/NAVC III.

[88] Commission of Finance of Bureau of South China, "Qing jiejue Yuenan tichu de wenti [Please solve issues raised by the DRV]," July 21, 1952, no. 204-1-292-169, 1–2/GDPA.

[89] CPC Central Financial Commission, "Dui Yuenan yun tutechan dao woguo zhi fushi [Reply to Vietnamese request to export local products to our country]," July 30, 1952, no. 2041-292-171, 1/GDPA.

guerrilla war zone" listed by the Chinese customs house as banned imports.[90] The economic interdependence between South China and Vietnam was strong enough to challenge the vertical control of the central government.

The commercial connections between the DRV and South China highlight the trans-local dimension of the First Indochina War. From a strategic and diplomatic perspective, the CPC victory in China certainly worked to the advantage of the Vietnamese communists. Yet the on-the-ground ramifications were complicated. Because the DRV was diplomatically isolated until early 1950, it had to "renew ancient commercial exchanges with southern China" dominated by the overseas Chinese traders "before Chinese communists arrived there in force."[91] With the assertion of organized power along the Chinese border, the DRV could no longer follow the modus operandi of trade networks between Vietnam and Southern China. Its trade with Hainan, for instance, was under the gaze of the Chinese central state, although the Vietnamese revolutionaries still enjoyed favorable treatment from their Chinese comrades. This foreshadowed more changes to come in transnational exchanges across the borderlands.

Boundary Making and Its Limits during the First Indochina War

While the CPC and the WPV perceived the Chinese-Vietnamese border differently, it was equally true that the border assumed greater importance for them than for previous governments. Socialist internationalism necessitated cross-border cooperation between the two countries, but more importantly, the First Indochina War was a transitional era for the Chinese and Vietnamese Communists. They both transformed from revolutionary to ruling parties, which required them to see themselves as centralizing states with an expanded bureaucratic scope and enhanced coercive capacity. Without effective state institutions on the ground, it was impossible for the political elites to translate their preferences and strategic goals to the local people and draw the latter into the political projects of state building and alliance-making. Without making and policing the international boundary, it was impractical for the fledging party-states to keep out their perceived enemies, let in valuable resources, and generate revenues from cross-border activities.

---

[90] Commission of Finance of Bureau of South China, "Guanyu Yuenan yunlai Haikou jinxing maoyi de jige wenti de qingshi [Asking for instruction about Vietnamese products shipped to Haikou]," March 11, 1953, no. 204-1-311-239, 1–2/GDPA.
[91] Goscha, "The Borders of Vietnam's Early Wartime Trade with Southern China," 988–89; Vu Tuong also argues that the "disregard for territorial exclusivity" contributed to the Vietnamese Communists' rise to power ("The Revolutionary Path to State Formation in Vietnam," 278).

Concretely manifesting the spatial reach of state power was not an easy task. The incipient border check institutions designed by the French and the Qing governments provided clues for the communists regarding where to police the border, such as important mountain passes and trading ports. These previous border institutions, however, never fully came into being before failing as a result of continuous civil conflicts and foreign invasions in the first half of the twentieth century. Meanwhile, the communists did not trust the staff of the previous institutions and thus sought to place their own cadres and soldiers into positions of border defense and regulation. This preference for politically reliable cadres over local elites caused major problems on the ground, especially for the Chinese. Whereas the Việt Minh had long operated in the areas close to the Chinese border, taking advantage of loopholes in French control there, Guangxi was one of the last provinces the Chinese communists seized in the Civil War. The Chinese communists brought in a large number of outsiders and filled ranks in the border institutions with recruits from their field armies, who had to deal with "unfamiliar people, unfamiliar place, and unfamiliar tasks."[92] Besides rudimentary local knowledge and language barriers among these new border personnel, border defense apparatuses were also often clumsy due to difficulties of orchestration within the bureaucracy, a persisting problem that troubled the Chinese state on its southwestern frontier.

During the first year of CPC rule of the southern border, the revolutionary state was neither strong nor complex enough to monopolize the legitimate use of force. According to an evaluation of the Bureau of Border Defense of Guangdong in early 1951, the Sino-Vietnamese border had "hundreds and thousands of gaps in control" due to the absence of regular public security forces while the field army was engaged in the "bandit suppression campaigns." The greatest challenge to the Chinese Communists came from the remnant Nationalist forces and their supporters, such as the Anti-Communist and National Salvation Army (Fangong jiuguojun). Though often not well-equipped, these units exploited the poorly guarded borders to attack communist troops and cadres. Furthermore, protection rackets established by "bandits" and "sea robbers" across the land and maritime border also competed with the communist state for authority and revenue. The local administration, for instance, denounced the sea robbers for exploiting fishermen by selling passes on the sea routes between the Vietnamese port city Haiphong and the Chinese coastal port of Beihai. Lastly, the entire border society seemed hostile to the communists. The leaders of the bureau warned that the dynamic cross-border social ties had brought strong Western influence, including Catholicism, into the area, and that too many "vagabonds" who just "idled about and did no

---

[92] Zeng, *YBJZ*, 139.

Boundary Making and Its Limits 65

decent jobs" lived in historical trading hubs such as Dongxing.[93] The revolutionaries who had built their power base in an agricultural society where peasants were tied to the land perceived the cosmopolitan and commercially vibrant border society as dangerous, chaotic, and rebellious. Such hostility toward the "corrupt, backward, and purely consumer society" led to a radical plan drafted by local cadres in May 1952 to relocate workers, smugglers, peddlers, opium addicts, suspected counterrevolutionaries and spies, landlords, and gangsters – all groups that were not directly engaged in farming in Dongxing – into the interior to "sever the city's ties with imperialists" and enforce blockades against the French occupied region in Vietnam. If implemented, the city would lose 60 percent of its slightly over 10,000 population.[94]

As the "bandit suppression campaigns" approached a reasonable degree of success in the second half of 1951, the targets of border defense shifted from armed groups that openly challenged communist authorities to "lurking" enemies that appeared to be embedded in or moving through the border society. In September 1951, Zhou Jiguang, the deputy head of the Bureau of Border Defense of the Department of Public Security of Guangxi emphasized the importance of border defense to cadres stationed along the international boundary, noting that the province was adjacent to both the areas still under French occupation and those that had recently come under the DRV's control. Because all kinds of work in the province had started before mass movements to rally popular support and establish control were launched, the border was "vulnerable to destruction by enemies." Condemning the United States for training agents around Southeast Asia and supporting sabotage by the Nationalists, Zhou demanded that enhanced border inspections should "keep spies and agents from infiltrating to the interior, prevent domestic counter-revolutionaries from escaping, and stop smugglers from destabilizing national economy."[95]

Once passed down the bureaucratic ladder, however, the state's priority to build a strong presence along the border did not always turn into a reality. Zhan Caifang, head of the Public Security Troops of the Mid-South Military Zone and attendee at the First National Border Defense Meeting held in the summer of 1951, reviewed the situation of border enforcement in Guangxi and Guangdong in a report to the military zone command at the end of the year. The national meeting had stipulated that border forces were responsible for "military defense, administrative control, and secret reconnaissance." Zhan

---

[93] The above part is based on Department of Public Security of Guangdong, "Bianfangju 1950 nian 8–12 yue gongzuo baogao [Report of the Bureau of Border Defense for August–December 1950]," March 1, 1951, no. 204-1-164-015, 17–21/GDPA.

[94] The above part is based on CPC Fangcheng County, "Dongxingshi qianyi gongzuo jihua [Relocation plan of Dongxing]," May 23, 1952, no. 1-2-6-3, 1–9/FDA.

[95] This paragraph is based on Zeng, *YBJZ*, 44.

admitted that this threefold task, especially administrative control and secret reconnaissance, was poorly implemented on the ground.[96] Although the PRC had a strong military presence at the southwestern border designed to crush bandits, state institutions had not been properly organized for border management. Zhan's observation reflected the limitation of relying on the army on the border to perform tasks that were not strictly military and echoed Beijing's decision to place the border enforcement in the hands of more specialized public security forces in the near future.

Several factors, according to Zhan, were responsible for this unsatisfactory situation. First, border institutions lacked cadres who were experienced or specialized in border management, especially regarding inspections and intelligence collection.[97] In November 1951, the Public Security Force (Gong'an jun) of the PRC replaced the Fourth Field Army in border garrisons in Guangxi and other border provinces, which indicated a first step toward creating more specialized border institutions. The PRC Public Security Force, however, was still not a police force but one branch of the Chinese military services (which was composed of the Army, Navy, Air Force, Anti-Air-Raid Force, and Public Security).[98] The vast majority of the soldiers serving in the Public Security Force were not only mostly from outside the border region but also from outside the province. To make things worse, the Communists' road to power had not equipped their state apparatus with much experience or expertise related to enforcing a national border. During the military struggle against the Nationalists and the Anti-Japanese War, the communist revolutionary bases had successfully extracted revenues from the goods traded between areas under their occupation and those under the Nationalist or Japanese control by imposing taxes.[99] Nevertheless, asserting the state's existence and authority at a national border far away from the capital city demanded a higher degree of proficiency in indigenous knowledge as well as local dialects and foreign languages.

The second constraint on the political project of border making was a lack of coordination within state institutions. The PRC had a powerful military presence at the border, including field troops, naval units, divisions of public security forces, detached battalions, coast guards, local police, and other agents, yet no unified command. In addition, it was not uncommon for local party committees or county governments to refuse to offer the assistance requested by the border garrison citing the fact that they had not received

---

[96] The above part is based on Zhan Caifang, "Diyici bianfang huiyi baogao [Report of the first border defense meeting]," 1951, no. 204-1-187-122, 1/GDPA.
[97] Ibid., 2.
[98] The Public Security Force was the predecessor of the Armed Police (Wuzhuang jingcha) of the PRC.
[99] Chinese Academy of Social Sciences, *Zhongguo geming genjudi jingji dashiji*, 12–13.

Boundary Making and Its Limits

any orders from higher authorities. Zhan warned that even the departments of public security in border provinces such as Guangxi and Guangdong failed to attach due importance to border enforcement. To conclude the report, Zhan called for stronger party leadership on border issues and greater investment in transport systems along the border. He also suggested that forces stationed at Dongxing, bordering French-controlled Móng Cái, and the counties neighboring British Hong Kong should receive better weapons and equipment not only to put up a more effective defense but also to boost the prestige of the PLA.[100]

The distribution of labor between the army and the police regarding border defense took a different direction in Vietnam in comparison to China. In early 1946, the DRV had unified all armed forces in charge of local security order and intelligence collection as the Vietnamese People's Police (Công an Nhân dân Việt Nam), which was under the direction of MOPS. The border guard was part of this public security institution.[101] It was not until March 1959, when the DRV made a firm decision to commit to military intervention in the guerrilla war in South Vietnam, that Hanoi enhanced its border guard institutions by establishing the better equipped People's Armed Police (Công an nhân dân vũ trang).[102] As the Việt Minh gradually territorialized its state during the war, it also developed increasingly uniform practices of border administration and governance, although policing the border was not necessarily a priority during the period. In August 1949, the Việt Minh branch of the Tenth Inter-zone in northwestern Vietnam suggested that patrol forces stationed on the Sino-Vietnamese border be staffed with members who could speak Chinese to "contact and host the PLA" and "negotiate with remnant Nationalists."[103] In February 1950, the PRC and the DRV decided to establish liaison regarding border defense.[104] Inspecting the cross-border movements of people then gained a more salient position on the DRV's agenda to ensure the success of the Border Campaign against the French strongholds.

In August, the border provinces in Việt Bắc received instructions from the party's Central Committee to impose more uniform control over the border society. The DRV ordered its provincial authorities along the border to

---

[100] Zhan, "Report of the First Border Defense Meeting," 3–8.
[101] Bộ trưởng Bộ Nội Vụ, "Chiếu theo Sắc lệnh số 23 ngày 21 tháng 02 năm 1946 thành lập Việt Nam Công an vụ Sau khi thỏa hiệp với Bộ trưởng Bộ Tư pháp."
[102] "NGHỊ QUYẾT CỦA BỘ CHÍNH TRỊ Số 116-NQ/TW Về việc phân công nhiệm vụ giữa Quân đội nhân dân và lực lượng Công an nhân dân vũ trang trong việc bảo vệ trị an ở miền Bắc và điều chỉnh tổ chức lực lượng Công an nhân an vũ trang [DECISION OF THE DEPARTMENT OF POLITICS no. 116-NQ/TW On the assignment of tasks between the PAVN and the Armed People's Police in protecting public security in the North and adjusting the organization of the People's Armed Police]," April 28, 1965, in *VKDTT* 26 (1965), 146; "Bộ đội Biên phòng 50 năm xây dựng, chiến đấu và trưởng thành."
[103] "CHỈ THỊ CỦA BAN THƯỜNG VỤ LIÊN KHU UỶ X Về chủ trương biên giới," 419.
[104] "Liu Shaoqi jiu jianli Zhong-Yue jiaojie bianfang baowei gongzuo wenti zuochu pishi," 132.

coordinate with Chinese local governments regarding policies toward the Vietnamese villagers who regularly attended border markets on the Chinese side or sought shelter in China during heated battles. The daily lives of border residents were more on the radar of the local state institutions on the Vietnamese side than before, as Vietnamese who traveled to China had to apply for a permit from the provincial or county administrative body – resistance war administrative committee (Ủy ban kháng chiến hành chính). The permit noted the date range as well as destination and purpose of the trip, and the document would be valid only within the border area. Furthermore, the Vietnamese communists also sought to put an end to the modus operandi of the highly decentralized, spontaneous communications with their Chinese comrades. With the exception of wartime emergencies, Vietnamese local state officials who needed to reach out to the Chinese border provinces had to receive endorsement from the DRV central government.[105] Thus the territorialization of the PRC and the DRV was coupled with the centralization of their cross-border communications. But the micro-management of the border by central political authorities, as increasing infringement and setbacks of border policies showed, often operated on problematic a priori assumptions.

Besides creating border institutions to keep aggressors out and counter-revolutionaries in, the two countries decided to collaborate in extracting the revenues created by border enforcement. Cross-border trade was the first border-making issue the two central governments chose to address due to its pertinence to various aspects of state building. Primarily, in line with the socialist ideal of building a robust, dominant public sector, the two party-states sought to have their state-run companies participate in and profit from the existing cross-border trade. Furthermore, taxing cross-border trade could contribute to the financial stability of the two states, both of which were struggling with funding their expanding bureaucracy. Third, by placing restraints on the travel of traders and cross-border flows of foreign currency, the two states sought to translate their sovereign claims into a more concrete capability to regulate the national boundary.[106]

As the DRV consolidated its control over Vietnam's land adjacent to China after the Border Campaign, the two sides decided to reopen several historical

---

[105] "THÔNG TRI CỦA BAN THƯỜNG VỤ TRUNG ƯƠNG Về việc liên lạc ở biên giới [NOTICE OF THE STANDING COMMITTEE OF PARTY CENTRAL on communication on the border]," August 1, 1950, in *VKĐTT* 11 (1950), 449–50.

[106] The influx of Indochinese piasters had concerned the ROC government. Being alert to the "economic invasion," the government of Guangdong instructed the Kwangtung Provincial Bank to open a local branch in Dongxing in 1932 to compete with Western banks and private currency exchange houses. Provincial Government of Guangdong, "Lingjin Dongxing jumin zhijie xingshi waibi [An order of banning Dongxing residents from directly using foreign currency]," *Guangdongsheng Zhengfu bongbao* 203 (1932), 68–70, in *Dacheng laojiu qikan quanwen shujuku*; Fan Chen [pseud.], "Dongxing: xinde Guangzhouwan," 61–64.

border markets for "small-scale trade" (*xiao'e maoyi* in Chinese and *mậu dịch tiểu ngạch* in Vietnamese). To "open" border markets, however, was not an accurate depiction of the situation on the ground. Spontaneous trade across the border had long existed and never ceased during the war. Such intricate trade networks, which financially benefited the local Chinese and Vietnamese administrations, were largely out of the control of the central political authorities. By "opening" the border trade, therefore, the PRC and the DRV meant to make the existing economic connections within the border region more visible, taxable, and conducive to the broader strategic objectives of the states.

Before engaging in negotiations with the PRC in March 1952, the Vietnamese Ministry of Foreign Trade pointed out in an internal report that the state-sponsored Sino-Vietnamese border trade was established upon the principle of Chinese assistance of Vietnam, which would allow the DRV to facilitate production, sell overstocked products, stablize prices and currency, and gain advantages in the economic struggle against the enemy. At the same time, the ministry warned that the border trade was meant to promote economic exchanges between the two peoples, yet it "should not be exploited by the adversarial side." Commodities from the French-occupied areas should not be transported to China via DRV-controlled territory. Similarly, goods imported from China should not flow to the enemy-occupied zone through the liberated area. Moreover, it decided to ban from the small-scale border trade the exports of two broad categories of Vietnamese goods that were largely managed by private merchants: The first were those essential to war and livelihood but still in shortage in the DRV, such as grains, gold, cotton, and buffalo. The second were those that needed to be monopolized by the state to execute the intergovernmental contracts with China, ranging from spices in high demand to raw minerals. To avoid alienating the border community, the ministry also decided to set low tax rates for the border trade and offered tax exemptions for special commodities such as salt.[107]

At the end of the negotiation in late March 1952, the DRV delegation was pleased with the political and financial benefits of the agreement for its war efforts. It observed that as a result of the trade deal, China would allow the importation of all goods the DRV sought to export, especially the forest products that were crucial sources of income for people in the border provinces. Moreover, the deal was accompanied by a currency agreement aimed at preventing the DRV-issued Vietnamese đồng (VNĐ) from devaluating. Opening up the border would also allow the border defense and public security forces of the two sides to "coordinate in exterminating all

[107] "Báo cáo của Bộ Ngoại thương: Ý kiến về Hiệp định mậu dịch Việt-Trung vào năm 1952 [Report by Ministry of Foreign Trade: Opinion on the Sino-Vietnamese trade agreement of 1952]," March 1952, no. 2198/PTTg [1945–1954]/NAVC III.

counterrevolutionaries and consolidating the people's power."[108] The two states' decision of not only participating in but also surveilling and controlling the border trade increasingly wove the commercial networks into the political project of establishing the credibility of the DRV currency and government as a whole.

In July 1952, the PRC and the DRV decided to open nine pairs of cross-border markets along the border, including Zhennan Guan-Đồng Đăng and Hekou-Lào Cai, in six months' time.[109] Besides accommodating the already long-existing commercial network across the border, opening the border markets would also allow the two governments to levy taxes from cross-border economic ties and help their state-run companies to profit from the vibrant border trade by manipulating prices. Various regulations were introduced to support these goals. Traders needed to apply for passes from the public security authority of their respective countries to attend border markets on the other side. Those who carried goods valuing more than 10,000 Renminbi (RMB) in Chinese currency (1 RMB after currency reform in 1955) to China could only trade at the border markets instead of carrying them into the interior. Cargoes exceeding the value of 10,000 RMB were also subject to customs and transaction taxes.[110] The DRV also set up similar inspection and taxation regulations. Goods worth up to 50,000 RMB (or its Vietnamese equivalent) were exempted from taxes. But the DRV required traders to use a designated route to transport commodities to border markets, thus allowing easier control and inspection by the state. The Vietnamese border trade regulations also stipulated penalties ranging from fines to confiscation for smuggling contraband, with double penalties on soldiers and government officials involved in smuggling, and rewards equaling 20 to 50 percent of the value of any contraband to those reporting infringements of the trade regulations.[111]

As the selected state-sponsored border markets were set to open, the local administrations sought to draw support from the border population for the

---

[108] "Báo cáo của đoàn đại biểu mậu dịch Việt Nam: tình hình thăm Trung Quốc năm 1952 [Trade delegation report: situation of visit to China]," March 1952, no. 2322/ PTTg [1945–1954]/ NAVC III.

[109] Military and Political Committee of Midwestern China, "Zhong-Yue bianjie diqu xiao'e maoyi [Sino-Vietnamese small-scale border trade]," July 27, 1952, no. 204-1-292-166, 1/GDPA.

[110] "UBKCHC tỉnh Lạng Sơn: Buổi họp kiểm điểm công tác chuẩn bị mở quan [Resistance Administrative Committee of Lang Son Province: Meeting to review the work of preparing for the opening of border crossings]," August 26, 1952, no. 5444, 2–11/ UBHC KTTVB 1948–1976/NAVC III.

[111] "Công văn của Bộ Ngoại Thương Số 167-TTg: Quy định tạm thời về thu thuế xuất nhập khẩu khu vực biên giới Việt-Trung [Ministry of Foreign Trade official document no. 167-TTg: Temporary regulation of import and export taxation along the Vietnamese-Chinese border]," April 30, 1952, no. 2017/PTTg [1945–1954]/NAVC III.

project. During the second half of 1952, the DRV dispatched cadres to villages in Cao Bằng and Lạng Sơn to publicize border trade policies, especially the importance of paying taxes and taking the designated routes that had been officially opened. Vietnamese border police were meanwhile assigned responsibility for maintaining the nation's economic secrets while carrying out trading with China. Furthermore, despite a shortage of staff, the Vietnamese police managed to set up more inspection stations on the border routes to crack down on the imports or exports of contraband.[112] By the end of 1952, though, the Vietnamese officials had become increasingly dissatisfied with the local population's indifference to the state-sponsored small-scale border trade. It was particularly difficult to woo the ethnic Chinese traders, who "possessed a considerable amount of capital yet took a wait-and-see attitude" toward the government endorsed cross-border trade. Vietnamese traders, who had much less capital, were also reluctant to attend border markets in China. The border residents, regardless of their ethnicity, were particularly dissatisfied with the convoluted regulations that forbade the taking of Vietnamese banknotes into China or bringing Chinese currency back to Vietnam. The administrations in Cao Bằng and Lạng Sơn, therefore, worried that the border residents would still engage in smuggling activities, not just thwarting state authority but also reducing tax revenue.[113]

The anticipated higher transaction costs explained the border population's hesitancy to be involved in the state trade project. Before the mid-twentieth century, the vibrant cross-border trade took advantage of the free flows of French Indochinese piasters and Hong Kong dollars between China and Indochina. A weak border also deprived Nationalist China and French Indochina of their ability to levy custom duties on much of the cross-border trade. An increasing state presence along the historical trade routes and mountain passes to enforce taxes and currency exchanges inevitably reduced the profits of the spontaneous commercial network. Some border traders engaged in smuggling in resistance to the DRV's project of monopolizing profitable forest products to fulfill intergovernmental trade contract with China. Instead of selling these goods to the Vietnamese state-run companies at a low price as required, these traders simply carried spices and medium-size logs directly to China where they would receive a much higher price.[114] In this state-society competition for the profits of cross-border trade, the political

---

[112] "UBKCHC tỉnh Lạng Sơn: Tổ chức công tác dân công [Resistance Administrative Committee of Lạng Sơn Province: the work of organizing civilian laborers]," December 15, 1952; "UBKCHC tỉnh Lạng Sơn: Buổi họp kiểm điểm công tác chuẩn bị mở quan," 1–11.
[113] "UBKCHC tỉnh Lạng Sơn: Buổi họp kiểm điểm công tác chuẩn bị mở quan," 4.
[114] "Báo cáo của Bộ Ngoại Thương: Một số vấn đề về việc thực hiện hợp đồng mậu dịch với Trung Quốc năm 1952 [Report of Ministry of Foreign Trade on implementing the trade contract with China in 1952]," November 12, 1952, no. 2321/PTTg [1945–1954]/NAVC III.

authorities still lacked sufficient coercive power to prevail against the private sector.

Whereas the Vietnamese cadres were concerned with the lack of interest among private traders in the state-sponsored cross-border markets, the Chinese officials, who had already begun to restrict private commerce in the domestic transformation toward socialism, worried about the dominance of private businesses and the lack of competence of state-run firms. In 1952, the CPC launched the Five-Anti Campaign, namely anti-bribery, anti-theft of state property, anti-tax evasion, anti-cheating on government contracts, and anti-stealing of state economic information. Under vague guidelines on who should be its targets, the campaign turned into a war against the entire bourgeoisie in urban China.[115] As the movement significantly alienated the commercial community, in 1953 local Chinese administrations withdrew from the most aggressive policies and encouraged people in the private economy to "actively run business" to ease the tension between the communist state and urban elites. This decision, the Division of Commerce of the Guangdong Provincial Government warned, had resulted in "a strong private economy and weak state-run sector" in cross-border trade.[116] Moreover, the state institutions at the border often pursued contradictory objectives without coherent instructions from higher-level authorities on the prioritization of different policies. The Chinese cadres in charge of foreign trade in Dongxing found themselves in an awkward situation in regard to such competing agendas. Stationed at "the front line of national defense," they were expected to respect the "historical practice" of cross-border trade and accommodate the vibrant private commerce to "win the hearts of people."[117] However, without harsh measures against smuggling, tax evasion, and the black market, state-run companies, which local administrations were supposed to buttress, had little chance to profit from the border trade.

Both the Chinese and Vietnamese authorities began to establish a stronger presence of state at their shared borderlands during the First Indochina War, which also witnessed the development of collaborative border institutions formed by the two countries to exploit resources from the border. More specifically, they sought to channel the highly profitable border trade to a space under the gaze of the state and subject to tax extraction and other state-building efforts. However, without well-trained, experienced border garrisons to enforce cross-border procedures and a monopoly of state-run companies in

---

[115] Spence, *The Search for Modern China*, 510.
[116] Division of Commerce of Guangdong Province, "Guanyu tongyi bing jiaqiang Huanan ge kou'an guoying jinchukou maoyi fang'an (cao'an) [Draft solution to strengthen state-run commerce in ports of South China]," July 24, 1953, no. X128-1-9, 23/GZARA.
[117] "Xiao'e maoyi guanli gongzuo zongjie [Summary of regulation on the small-scale trade]," 1953, no. 302-1-10-93~100, 93–95/GDPA.

the border markets, the long-existent transnational economy was able to evade the prohibitive and extractive measures of the states.

Conclusion: Continuities and Discontinuities in State Building and Boundary Making

Complicating the existing narrative of Sino-Vietnamese relations during the First Indochina War that focuses on Chinese military aid to Vietnam, this chapter emphasizes that the communist victory in China and the Việt Minh's employment of Chinese revolutionary strategy not only tilted the balance of power between the French colonial forces and the DRV toward the latter but also gradually reasserted the presence of centralized states at the Sino-Vietnamese border. Fear of capitalist intrusion in both its military and economic forms and the ambition to build socialist economies drove the two revolutionary states, especially the PRC, to secure the border against external aggressors and capture potential escapees. The Vietnamese, while being preoccupied with the armed struggle, expanded its institutional presence, including party cadres, police, and customs offices, at the border. Focusing on the often ignored international dimension of borderlands state building, this chapter illustrates how wartime strategic and logistical demands drove the communist states to extend institutions, create new functions, and attempt to mold the local society into a shape that was more conducive to state-dominated economy.

The First Indochina War was a "transnational colonial war."[118] It is evident that not only did transnational forces shape the trajectory of the war but also that the impact of the conflict went beyond the boundaries of Indochina, which transformed the Sino-Vietnamese borderlands from a space of state negligence to one of state interventions. Both the PRC and the DRV made gestures at the border to signal, forge, and confirm their emerging socialist partnership. Mao and other CPC leaders believed that the triumph of the Việt Minh could boost China's status in the communist world by underlining the "international relevance" of the Maoist revolutionary model and nudging other peoples fighting for national liberation in the same direction.[119] The CPC perceived the Vietnamese revolution as "an Asian revolution following the Chinese model," thus heavily invested in it to validate the Maoist doctrine.[120] Beijing, however, needed to meticulously manage the often bitter legacy of asymmetric relations between imperial China and Vietnam. The Sino-Vietnamese borderlands were not simply "places where states, empires, and

---

[118] Goscha, *Vietnam: Un état né de la guerre*, 282.
[119] Zhai, *China and the Vietnam* Wars, 21.
[120] Chen, "China and the First Indo-China War," 89.

other sources of governing institutional authority, demarcate, expand, and protect territories under their control."[121] They served much broader international strategic purposes.

Moreover, the First Indochina War intertwined with the expansion of the revolutionary parties and their corresponding states into previously uncontrolled lands, including the institutionalization of inter-state relations that had taken place at the border on an ad hoc basis. This process was not entirely imposed from above; it was also shaped at the local level by different segments of the party-states with a wide range of motives and interests in the border society. Nevertheless, the main form of state building during the period was military conquest and consolidation. The bandit-extermination campaign of the PLA established a state monopoly of legitimate violence in southwestern China.[122] Cao Bằng and Lạng Sơn became the power base of the Việt Minh after the Border Campaign of 1950 and thus territorialized the DRV state. Even so, violence was not the only tool of state formation at the Sino-Vietnamese border. While Beijing restored and extended the Hunan-Guangxi railway to freight its aid to the DRV, the presence of a modern transport infrastructure helped the state to wield other forms of power. The two states' expanding presence in the border trade combined coercive policies against powerful private merchants and collaborative measures to meet the daily economic needs of the borderlanders.

This initial stage of communist border making marked both continuities and discontinuities in the extension of state authorities since the late nineteenth century. The Chinese and Vietnamese decision to pair authorities at important border passes was a reenactment of the Double Military Posts established by the French colonial state and the late Qing government. The two revolutionary parties inherited the modernizing agenda to strengthen the state presence by setting up institutions, exerting coercive power, and deriving revenues in locations where cross-border flows of people and goods were more frequent. A significant discontinuity can be seen, however, in varying state perceptions of the border and their goals there. The two states' domestic political agenda carried greater weight on border making during the communist era, when "the liberation of the border peoples" formed an integral part of the broader mission "to end class oppression within their societies."[123] The socialist border making therefore went beyond defending a static line and necessitated the transformation of the border society in alignment with the revolutionary objectives. Second, driven by the need to foster a socialist partnership along the border,

---

[121] Readman et al., eds. *Borderlands in World History*, 2.
[122] For Max Weber's thesis on the modern state's monopoly on the legal use of violence, see Waters and Waters, eds., *Weber's Rationalism and Modern Society*, 11.
[123] Wade, "The Southern Chinese Borders in History," 33.

the two states politicized the quotidian cross-border connections that were hallmarks of a cosmopolitan border space. The regulation of cross-border trade expanded the role of the state in the economy at the periphery of its rule. The shifting emphasis in DRV's treatment of ethnic Chinese and their cross-border networks reflected Hanoi's strategy of striving for the maximum extent of popular support and implied to Beijing its temporary tolerance of the ambiguous loyalty of the Chinese community despite the Vietnamese anxiety for a strong national identity after living the colonial rule.

The DRV's costly armed struggle against the French and China's preoccupation with its confrontation with the United States in the Korean Peninsula, however, placed significant constraints on the resources allocated to borderlands state building. It was not until the end of the First Indochina War and the more thorough revolutionary transformation of Chinese and Vietnamese societies in the mid-1950s that the communist states gradually constrained the leeway the border people had long enjoyed in cross-border social and economic interactions.

2 Joint State Building (1954–1957)*

Huang Deqin, a landlord's daughter living in the border county Longjin in Guangxi, married a man from across the international boundary and moved to her husband's household in a Vietnamese village in 1952, following the patrilocal residence pattern of the region.[1] Land reform had begun during the winter of 1951–1952 in China's southwestern provinces of Guangxi, Yunnan, Sichuan, and Guizhou.[2] When the violent movement stormed Huang's hometown, the work team, which had been sent down by the state to agitate in favor of peasants' grievances against the rural elites, classified Huang's family as landlords. Fearing persecution, Huang's widowed mother and younger sister fled to Vietnam to take refuge in Huang's home. The Chinese land reform work team pursued and captured Huang and her mother, took them back to Guangxi, and handed them over to the "masses" for control and supervision for their "stubborn resentment against the government and the people."[3] Less drastic than execution and imprisonment, the punishment of "control and supervision by the masses" (*qunzhong guanzhi*) placed restrictions on the political rights, movements, social contacts, and speech of the landlords and their families.[4]

---

* A portion of this chapter, in its earlier form, has been published as an article "From a Line on Paper to a Line in Physical Reality: Joint State-Building at the Chinese-Vietnamese Border, 1954–1957." This article first appeared in *Modern Asian Studies* 54, no. 6 (November 2020), 1905–1948. Reprinted with permission by Cambridge University Press. A few paragraphs on smuggling in this chapter are developed from my earlier publication "The Mountain Is High, and the Emperor Is Far Away: States and Smuggling Networks at the Sino-Vietnamese Border." Copyright © 2018 Institute for Far Eastern Studies, Kyungnam University. This article first appeared in *Asian Perspective* 42, no. 4 (October–December 2018). Published with permission by Johns Hopkins University Press.

[1] Border work committee of Buju, Longzhou County, "Dizhu jiating chushen zhi funü chujia Yuenan kefou zhunxu chujing bao qingshi zun [Seeks instruction on whether to allow a landlord class woman who is married to a Vietnamese to exit the border]," October 6, 1955, no. X1–12–263, 26/GZARA.

[2] Kaup, *Creating the Zhuang*, 84; Qiao, "Guangxisheng tudi gaige jiben zongjie."

[3] Border work committee of Buju, Longzhou County, "Dizhu jiating chushen zhi funü chujia Yuenan kefou zhunxu chujing bao qingshi zun," 26.

[4] Benton and Ye, "Translators' Introduction," in Yang, *Eight Outcasts*, 7.

In October 1955, after being forcibly separated from his wife for almost three years, Huang's husband demanded her release and return through the local Vietnamese police, who maintained regular contacts with the authorities of Chinese border counties. Noting the party line that landlords being monitored were not allowed to go abroad, the border authorities of Longjin decided to relay the request to the Office of Foreign Affairs of Guangxi. They suggested that, because Huang was already married to a Vietnamese citizen, she should be permitted to migrate to Vietnam "as long as she did not conspire with any spies or bandits."[5] The provincial authorities, however, overruled this moderate proposal and banned her emigration until the period of control and supervision ended, citing her background as a "diehard landlord" who refused to rehabilitate.[6] The fate of Huang and her family is a vivid example of how spontaneous cross-border movement became a target for increasing state control in the 1950s. The provincial government of Guangxi, in this case, was determined to divide a cross-border household when the marriage ran counter to its revolutionary agenda. Border residents, such as Huang's family, however, were not passive spectators of border making and state building. By complying, evading, and negotiating with state institutions, the borderlanders actively shaped the priorities and strategies of the two states in exercising control at the fringe of their authority.

Investigating how the two communist governments regulated long-existing transnational connections and how they differentiated between acceptable and non-acceptable cross-border movements – and extracted revenues from the acceptable ones – presents a revealing story. The Chinese and Vietnamese communists pursued two interrelated goals at the territorial limits of their countries. First, they wanted to build an inward-oriented economy and society at their respective borders by consolidating the national administration of territory. Second, they sought to impose a contrived Cold War "comradeship" between the PRC and the DRV over and in place of the organic interdependence of peoples within the borderlands that had already existed for centuries. The Sino-Vietnamese border, therefore, encountered "joint state building" by the two communist governments, which made the cross-border movement of people and goods more visible, malleable, and, more importantly, taxable to the state. The two modernizing states nonetheless confronted a twofold challenge in their borderlands. First, the states did not extend their reach in a

---

[5] Border Work Committee of Buju, Longzhou County, "Dizhu chengfen funü yinyu Yuenan jumin jiehun yaoqiu qu Yue [A woman with landlord background married with a Vietnamese resident asks to move to Vietnam]," October 11, 1955, no. X1–12-263, 25/GZARA.

[6] Foreign Affairs Office of Guangxi, "Fu guanyu dizhu jiating chushen funü chujia Yuenan kefou zhunxu chujing wenti zhi chuli [Reply on whether to permit the woman from landlord family married to a Vietnamese to migrate to Vietnam]," October 14, 1955, no. X1–12-263, 23–24/GZARA.

uniform fashion but through their discrete parts, which made coordination within the bureaucracy, particularly between the center and local administrations, difficult. The pursuit of both national and international communist goals by central governments often left the local state apparatus, which bore the burden of implementing these policies, confused and bogged down by conflicting priorities. Second, the more culturally diverse and fluid on-the-ground realities of the borderlands did not fit easily into the nationalist or internationalist agenda of the two states.

Following the end of the First Indochina War, both the PRC and the DRV not only implemented what were certainly expected policies derived from the Soviet practice of communism, including the nationalization of trade and the collectivization of agriculture, but also imposed measures based more on their common goal of consolidating political control such as restrictions on migration. Border residents thus found it increasingly difficult to circumvent the state by exploiting different political situations on the two sides of the boundary as they had done in the past. Local states in China and Vietnam meanwhile cooperated in their efforts as they sought to mobilize resources from the frontier and saw advantages in reducing people's motives and abilities to cross the border. The ambition of Chinese and Vietnamese leaders to construct socialist societies and to foster a "comradeship plus brotherhood" translated into efforts to manage the permeability of the border.[7]

Imposing restrictions on the spontaneous movements of goods and people across the border therefore emerged as a top item on the agenda of the two communist countries. In the mid-1950s, the international relations of East Asia and the domestic politics of the PRC and the DRV underwent a period of relative stability. With the end of the Korean War in July 1953, the CPC shifted away from a radically revolutionary perception of international affairs to adopt a more modest approach to foreign policy. To create a favorable international environment for domestic consolidation and counter American pressure, Zhou Enlai, the premier and foreign minister of the PRC, exploited the differences between the United States, France, and Britain at the Geneva Conference of 1954, jointly introduced the Five Principles of Peaceful Coexistence with India and Burma, and called for cooperation between Asian and African countries at the 1955 Bandung Conference.[8] Meanwhile, China's First Five-Year Plan (1953–1957) set ambitious economic objectives, including promoting socialist industrialization through Soviet-assisted projects, developing agricultural cooperatives, and establishing state capitalism

---

[7] The term "comrade plus brother" was characterized and popularized by Hồ Chí Minh at the height of PRC-DRV solidarity.

[8] Chen, "China and the Bandung Conference," 132–34; Wang, "Neutralizing Indochina," 3.

in commerce.⁹ The DRV, emerging victorious from the First Indochina War, likewise faced the pressing issue of regime consolidation and thus took a pragmatic "North-first" policy to preclude American intervention and to heal the wounds of war.[10] In late 1954 and early 1955, the DRV leaders formulated their Three-Year Plan for Economic Recovery (Kế hoạch khôi phục kinh tế trong ba năm 1955–1957). Centering on land reform and moderate collectivization, the project was designed to return production to the 1939 level.[11] The shared priorities on economic growth, political centralization, and regional stability geared both Beijing and Hanoi toward more concerted efforts to increase their institutional presence at the border.

Similar to border formation in other parts of the world, the actions of the Chinese and Vietnamese governments to draw and sustain the borderline were also inherently connected to other functions of the state. Borders incorporate three elements: "the legal borderline," "the physical structures of the state," and "frontiers."[12] State building, border making, and diplomacy were thus closely interwoven. During the First Indochina War, the goals of the Chinese and Vietnamese states at the border were rather one-dimensional and military oriented. After the end of the First Indochina War, however, the border became relevant to broader social and economic reforms for the two Communist leaderships. It was then, as the two states began trying with greater effect, to generate revenues from the frontier and to intervene into the daily lives of the borderlanders during their respective socialist movements, that they realized the poor delineation of boundaries. The seemingly unbridgeable gap "between abstract lines drawn on a map and the on-the-ground realities of borderlands" underlined the limits of state power at the border.[13] At this point, diplomatic and ideological concerns came into play. The needs to forge socialist solidarity and to support the socialist reforms of the comrade country shaped the two states' approach to the often-ambiguous membership of the Chinese, Vietnamese, and those categorized as "ethnic minorities" in nations and states.

The Long 1954: The End of the First Indochina War and the Sino-Vietnamese Border

In the wake of the French defeat at Điện Biên Phủ, the Soviet Union, the United States, France, Britain, the PRC, the DRV, the State of Vietnam, and

---

[9] "Zhonghua renmin gongheguo fazhan guomin jingji de diyige wunian jihua, 1953–1957 [The first five-year plan to develop national economy of the PRC, 1953–1957]," in CPC Central Literature Research Center, *Jianguo yilai zhongyao wenxian xuanbian* (hereafter *JYZWXB*) 6, 410.
[10] Asselin, *Hanoi's Road to the Vietnam War*, 13–14.
[11] Lê Văn Yên, *Đảng Cộng sản Việt Nam*, 640–43.
[12] Wilson and Donnan, "Nation, State and Identity at International Borders," 9.
[13] Schoenberger and Turner, "Negotiating Remote Borderland Access," 668.

representatives from Cambodia and Laos negotiated over the fate of French Indochina in the summer of 1954 at the Geneva Conference. The Geneva Agreements, which theoretically put an end to the war between French Union forces and PAVN, stipulated a partition of Vietnam at the 17th parallel into two states, one controlled by the DRV in the North and a French-backed State of Vietnam in the South. The implementation of this agreement immediately brought about marked effects on the economy, flows of people, and state institutions on the border.

The resumption of long-distance trade at end of the war obstructed the state's project of heightening control over cross-border commerce. Following the ceasefire, Vietnamese products stockpiled in northern Vietnam due to wartime interruption of transportation flooded into Chinese border towns, including those officially opened for small-scale border trade under the bilateral agreements during the war. The state-run West Guangxi Trade Company and later an investigation team dispatched by the PRC Ministry of Commerce, for example, reported that merchants (especially ethnic Chinese traders) from Hanoi and other major cities were eager to expand their sales northward to the borderlands to sell off overstocked goods. Peddlers and store owners from other parts of China, such as Guangdong, Tianjin, Hankou, Xi'an, and Shanghai, also traveled for days and weeks to the border to purchase Vietnamese herbs, spices, and dried fish, which revived long-distance commercial networks yet ran counter to the state's vision of the goods on the small-scale trade markets as "self-produced, self-sold, self-purchased, self-used" and only flowing within the border region.[14] The rising number of private merchants at the border markets drove up the price of Vietnamese goods and impeded the Chinese state-run firms' purchase of Vietnamese products at a fixed low price – a standard practice of the socialist economy to accumulate surplus from the agricultural sector to fund the nascent heavy industry. Meanwhile, sales of Chinese light industrial products and salt plummeted after July 1954, which reduced the profits of the Chinese state-owned trade companies and impaired the public sector in the border economy.[15] The volatile border market prompted the two states to interfere in cross-border commerce in the following years.

---

[14] West Guangxi Trade Company, "1954 nian Zhong-Yue bianjing xiao'e maoyi gongzuo zongjie [Summary of Sino-Vietnamese small-scale border trade in 1954]," March 10, 1955, no. X1–8-364, 6/GZARA; Investigation team of ethnic trade in Guangxi dispatched by Ministry of Commerce, "Guangxisheng Longjinxian Shuikou kou'an xiao'e maoyi diaocha qingkuang baogao [Investigation report of border small-scale trade in Shuikou, Longjin County, Guangxi]," May 25, 1955, no. X41–1-232, 109/GZARA.

[15] West Guangxi Trade Company, "1954 nian bianjing xiao'e maoyi qingkuang [Situation of small-scale border trade in 1954]," December 10, 1954, no. X1–8-364, 82–83/GZARA.

Promising reunification through a nationwide election in July 1956, the Geneva Accords allowed a 300-day period within which forces of either party and civilians could freely cross the provisional military demarcation line and relocate to the other Vietnam.[16] This arrangement produced complicated social effects on the ground, including in the Sino-Vietnamese border area. The grace period resulted in the emigration of around 310,000 French Union soldiers and civilians, including around 45,000 ethnic Chinese, from the DRV to the South, with the assistance of the American Navy. Among the fleeing ethnic Chinese were about half of the population of the Nùng Autonomous Territory. The Eisenhower administration and the South Vietnamese government showcased the relocation as Vietnamese people's voting with their feet against communism.[17] Facing a serious drain of its tax base, the DRV officials in Hải Ninh accused Western powers of provoking ethnic divisions and "enticing the Hoa and Dao" to follow the withdrawing French colonial forces. To curb the emigration, the grassroots cadres resorted to measures ranging from organizing anti-American propaganda to sending out letters in the name of northern priests to persuade the evacuated parishioners to return.[18]

People nevertheless did not only vote with their feet across the boundary of the ideological blocs. Disturbed about the ailing economy and uncertain of the DRV's ethnic policy, many ethnic Chinese in Northern Vietnam decided to relocate to China, at least until the dust settled in Indochina. Among them were mining workers in Haiphong and Cẩm Phả (two industrial centers in North Vietnam still controlled by the French), merchants residing in main cities in the north and the south, and fisherfolk (Figure 2.1).[19] The Chinese government set up service stations at several border towns to record the migration and to help with resettlement. The coastal counties of Dongxing and Beihai made contingency plans to receive fishing families from Vietnam who did not possess any

---

[16] "Agreement on the Cessation of the Hostilities in Viet-Nam, July 20, 1954," in US Congress, *Background Information Relating to Southeast Asia and Vietnam*, 32.
[17] Prados, "The Numbers Game"; Nguyễn Văn Chính, "Ethnic Chinese in the Sino-Vietnamese Borderlands," 15. For the resettlement of Nùng after evacuation to South Vietnam, see Trần Đức Lai, *The Nung Ethnic and Autonomous Territory of Hai Ninh-Vietnam*, 124–204.
[18] The quote and paraphrase are from "Khu Hồng Quảng và tỉnh Hải Ninh chống địch dụ dỗ, cưỡng ép dân đi cư vào Nam [Hồng Quảng area and Hải Ninh province resisted the enemy's seduction and coercion to migrate people to the South]," April 1955, in *SLDQ*, 24–25.
[19] PRC Ministry of Foreign Affairs, "Lü Yue huaqiao yaoqiu fanYue shi [Issues about Chinese residents in Vietnam who migrated back to China and asked to return to Vietnam]," May 13, 1955, no. X1-12-256, 4–5/GZARA. Before the French, the local Annamites and Chinese immigrants had extracted minerals from surface deposits for centuries, and the Chinese remained an important source of mining labor during the French colonial era. Miller, "Mineral Resources of Indo-China," 268; also see Nguyen, "Dynamite, Opium, and a Transnational Shadow Economy at Tonkinese Coal Mines."

Figure 2.1 PAVN soldiers took over Cẩm Phả from the French troops in 1955
Source: Photo by Keystone-France\Gamma-Rapho via Getty Images. #558675417.

identity cards or legal travel documents.[20] The protective function of the Chinese state at the border thus unfolded against the backdrop of increasing cross-border flows of people.

When the 300-day period ended in May 1955, however, the Chinese government encountered new problems. As social order was restored in Vietnam, some of the sojourning Chinese asked for permission to return to Vietnam. Ideological competition imbued the Chinese government's reactions to these requests with political overtones. Citing the necessity to consolidate the DRV and undermine the West-backed State of Vietnam, the Chinese Ministry of Foreign Affairs instructed the Office of Foreign Affairs of Guangxi that Chinese citizens from areas under DRV control should be allowed to return but those from South Vietnam needed "to be persuaded to stay." Beijing also alerted the Guangxi provincial government that, given the food shortage in Haiphong and Cẩm Phả, the influx of Chinese workers to

---

[20] PRC Central Committee for Overseas Chinese, "Qingzuo shourong jiuji you Bowan taolai Dongxing, Beihai yumin de zhunbei [Please prepare for receiving and relieving fisherfolk from Bowan to Dongxing and Beihai]," February 15, 1955, no. X1–12-256, 6/GZARA.

these mining centers would encumber the Vietnamese government if industrial production could not restart promptly. Returning workers from these two port cities, therefore, should stay in China until the local Vietnamese administration stabilized the economy.[21]

The food shortage indeed posed a significant challenge to the DRV leadership after the war ended. WPV Central Committee member Nguyễn Duy Trinh had warned in early 1955 that after the DRV took over the mines in Haiphong and Hòn Gai and withdrew all troops from the South in the near future, "the demand for rice will grow and the food situation will further deteriorate."[22] The relocation of factories and business to the South left many urbanites unemployed and struggling to make ends meet.[23] Whether the Chinese government's decision to require these industrial workers to stay in China was a genuine move to buttress the DRV against the South or a competition with the Vietnamese comrades for skilled labor for the sake of economic recovery, the spontaneous economic connections between Southern China and Southeast Asia represented by the notion of *xia Nanyang* (going to Southeast Asia for economic opportunities) were now under increasing state scrutiny.

Besides the ethnic Chinese who sought to return to work in Vietnam, among the people who asked to leave China for Vietnam after the war were overseas Vietnamese (*Việt Kiều*) who had moved into the border area during the conflict. Many overseas Vietnamese had been assigned land during the land reform or owned homes in China, and they sought to monetize their properties before returning to Vietnam. To support the DRV's economic reconstruction but probably also to reduce the ethnic diversity of its border society, the CPC Guangxi Provincial Committee decided to allow them to sell off their houses. The committee insisted, however, that because most of them had acquired land during the land reform or by reclaiming wasteland, they "should be persuaded" to submit the land to the local Chinese government and be compensated at a price slightly lower than the land value before the land reform.[24]

---

[21] PRC Ministry of Foreign Affairs, "Lü Yue huaqiao yaoqiu fanYue shi," 4–5
[22] "THÔNG TRI CỦA BAN BÍ THƯ SỐ 07-TT/TW Về việc phát động phong trào thi đua sản xuất và tiết kiệm vụ xuân, đẩy mạnh việc phòng đói, chống đói [ANNOUNCEMENT OF THE SECRETARIAT 07-TT/TW On the launching of the spring crop production and saving emulation movement to promote hunger prevention and fight against hunger]," January 29, 1955, in *VKDTT* 16 (1955), 29. The food crisis in Hải Ninh was particularly severe as a storm hit the coastal province in Septermber 1955. "Khu Hồng Quảng tập trung lực lượng khôi phục hậu quả nạn bão lụt [Hồng Quảng area gathers strength to recover from storms and floods]," September–October 1955, in *SLDQ*, 37.
[23] "Khu Hồng Quảng giải quyết nạn đói, nạn thất nghiệp sau tiếp quản [Hồng Quảng area solves hunger and unemployment after taking over]," May 1955, in *SLDQ*, 26.
[24] "Zhonggong zhongyang pifu Guangxi shengwei he Guangdong waishichu 'guanyu guiguo yueqiao de fangwu chuli wenti de baogao' [CPC Central Committee's instruction on 'report on the settlement of house and land owned by migrated *Việt kiều*']," January 10, 1955, in *GSBN 1955*, 29.

The end of the First Indochina War also accelerated the institutionalization of border authority by bringing in a third-country presence. The Final Declaration of the Geneva Conference on the Problem of Restoring Peace in Indochina stipulated the formation of an International Supervisory Commission (ISC) constituted by Canada, India, and Poland to oversee the cessation of hostilities.[25] The arrival of ISC members at the Vietnamese border constrained the cross-border activities of the cadres working for border authorities in many ways. According to Zeng Fusheng, a soldier in the Chinese border garrison at Friendship Pass (then named Munan Guan), in the early days "China and Vietnam were simply two abutting villages" in the view of the border staff. It was not uncommon for them to go shopping in Đồng Đăng, to help Vietnamese police with interrogating suspects (or the other way around), or to collect intelligence on fleeing Nationalist troops without formal, cross-border procedures. Facing a shortage of facilities, the Việt Minh cadres who entered China to coordinate military aid sometimes asked the Chinese border authority to print their entry and exit permit, which should have been issued by a Vietnamese authority.[26] After the arrival of ISC representatives, however, Chinese garrison soldiers' presence in Vietnam could be reported as a Chinese violation of the Geneva Accords. When the situation at this remote corner of the country became pertinent to the international image of China, which had publicly pledged peace and coexistence in Southeast Asia, interactions with international authorities such as the ISC shook the "village mentality" and forged the national identity of the border garrison soldiers. Their changing conceptualization of the international boundary accentuates the problematic divide between state and society when studying state building at the border. Without the intervention from higher authorities to strengthen border-crossing procedures, the common soldiers themselves benefited from a fluid, porous border and did not necessarily have a stronger national consciousness than the local populations.

Whereas the Geneva Accords brought new norms to the border bureaucracies, the ISC also operated under the gaze of the Chinese and Vietnamese authorities. In 1954, the ISC members in Vietnam reportedly trespassed the border twice.[27] On December 1, 1954, the Guangxi provincial government set up a foreign affairs liaison office in Pingxiang, in charge of communicating with local Vietnamese officials and receiving ISC members and foreign delegations.[28] Sulmaan Khan argues that defining lines that separated countries

---

[25] "Indochina-Final Declaration of the Geneva Conference on the Problem of Restoring Peace in Indochina, July 21, 1954," *The Avalon Project*, http://avalon.law.yale.edu/20th_century/inch005.asp.
[26] Zeng, *YBJZ*, 191. [27] Ibid., 48.
[28] GZAR Gazetteers Office, *Guangxi tongzhi: washizhi*, 16.

often took place simultaneously with drawing lines dividing the countries' citizens.[29] At the Sino-Vietnamese border, other lines were drawn in relation to international visitors. In 1954, people from ten countries besides China and Vietnam traveled through Friendship Pass.[30] An order issued by the Chinese Central Command of Public Security Force in 1955 required border authorities to conduct stringent inspections of the documents and personal belongings of visitors from Western countries and to be more flexible toward those from the communist bloc.[31]

The end of the First Indochina War generated mixed outcomes at the Sino-Vietnamese border, especially for the Chinese state. For Beijing, the French retreat meant that the Vietnamese border no longer posed a major, open threat to China's national security. The CPC provincial committee of Guangxi optimistically reckoned in March 1955 that "after the ceasefire in Indochina, the situation of struggle against the enemy at the border of our province changed fundamentally, which is favorable to us."[32] The end of conflicts in Indochina, however, created unexpected cross-border mobilities that often caught the local Chinese state and border authorities off guard and demonstrated the exigency of increasing institutional strength at the frontier and taming the border society.

Watch Out for the Enemy Inside: The Development of Border Police

After the restoration of peace in Indochina, the two communist states adopted the Stalinist model of treating border controls as integral parts of the institutions that reinforced domestic political stability. Borders epitomized the all-encompassing communist party-state by performing "both economic and internal-security functions." Highly restrictive regulations on cross-border movements safeguarded the Soviet national defense, internal surveillance, and planned economy.[33] The ideal relations that the two states sought to foster with their border societies, however, did not mimic that of the Soviet Union. Xiao Hua, then deputy head of the PLA Department of Political Affairs, found the Soviet practice of letting border forces live in barracks isolated from nearby villages, banning recruits of local ethnic minorities from the border authorities, and forcefully relocating border communities to the interior highly problematic

---

[29] Khan, *Muslim, Trader, Nomad, Spy*, 3.   [30] Zeng, *YBJZ*, 154–55.   [31] Ibid., 132.
[32] "Zhonggong Guangxi shengwei guanyu jiaqiang bianfang duidi douzheng de zhishi [Instruction of the CPC Guangxi Provincial Committee on strengthening border defenses and struggling against the enemy]," March 30, 1955.
[33] The quote and paraphrase are from Chandler, *Institutions of Isolation*, 3.

and risking "the alienation of the mass."[34] A similar stress on mobilizing people's support for the border police's duty and being sensitive to ethnic and religious policies was also pronounced in Hanoi's orders to its border forces, which indicated caution against overuse of coercion.[35]

The institutionalization of the Chinese and Vietnamese border police mirrored the public security campaigns of the mid-1950s to consolidate border defenses in the two adjacent countries more broadly. The PRC and DRV leaders held a disturbing vision of frontiers as part of an international environment that was hostile and subject to exploitation by domestic counterrevolutionaries. Although the two communist countries were then Cold War partners that did not pose a direct political or military threat toward each other, they needed to address the historical legacy of state weakness at the borderlands. Borders are not simply "lines of separation between states" but "institutions that directly contribute to state formation and state authority."[36] The Chinese and Vietnamese attempts to buttress national borders through police deployment were as much about preventing internal counterrevolutionaries from escaping the country as they were about keeping external enemies out of their territories.

The end of the First Indochina War coincided with the nationwide effort by the PRC to formalize its border police system. At the Sixth National Meeting of Public Security held in Beijing in May–June 1954, Minister of Public Security Luo Ruiqing cautioned that the "border defense issue is long overdue" and confirmed the guidelines stipulated at the First National Border Defense Meeting in 1951 that the border police should undertake the missions of armed patrols, administrative management, and covert surveillance. Reminding the attendees of the "rampant armed provocation" and the lack of presence of troops in some border areas, Luo required the border defense institutions to combine military and political defense; coordinate open and secret struggle; strengthen unified leadership of party, state, military, and police; and "rely on the mass" in the border region.[37] This broad conceptualization of frontier defense, as Taylor Fravel argues, reflected China's ethnic geography as an "empire state" and its concerns over unrest at the frontiers. Border defenses thus necessitated both preserving "the internal political

---

[34] "Muqian Yunnan bianfang douzheng zhong de jige wenti [Several issues in the border defense struggle in Yunnan]," June 1, 1956, in Editorial Group, *Xiaohua wenji*, 199.

[35] "CHỈ THỊ CỦA BAN BÍ THƯ Số 34/CT-TW Về việc tăng cường công tác an biên phòng (gồm biên giới, bờ bể và giới tuyến) [Directive of the Secretariat No. 34/CT-TW On strengthening border security work, including land and maritime borders]," July 7, 1956, in *VKDTT* 17 (1956), 278–84.

[36] Gavrilis, *The Dynamics of Interstate Boundaries*, 5.

[37] The quote and paraphrase above are based on Luo Ruiqing, "Luo Ruiqing zai diliuci quanguo gongan huiyishang de zongjie."

stability of China's frontier regions (*bianjiang*)" and protecting "the borders (*bianjing*)" from outside intrusion.³⁸ The southern border assumed strategic importance to the political center due to both perceived hostility from the outside world and unceasing political challenges from the newly pacified border provinces.

Because the French retreat from northern Vietnam largely eliminated any immediate external threat from Indochina, the Chinese border inspection in the region was gradually reoriented from its wartime mode. During the First Indochina War, in April 1952, the Guangxi provincial border defense authorities set forth three broad tasks for the border inspection stations: the border police should inspect people who entered or departed the country, detect and arrest "counterrevolutionaries, bandits, agents, spies, fugitives, capitalists and merchants identified with illegal activities during the 'Three-Anti' and 'Five-Anti' Campaigns, and other criminals," and work with the customs to curb smuggling. After the Geneva Accords entered into force, while the border police's responsibilities remained undiminished, the border-crossing procedure became less convoluted and prohibitive. The border police at Friendship Pass, for instance, were allowed to "simplify procedures" to shorten the clearance time. The officially open period of the border gate changed from night to daytime following the drop of the air defense alert level. In July 1955, at the end of the 300-day grace period of the Geneva Accords, the Friendship Pass inspection station dissolved the branch that had been in charge of wartime military surveillance.³⁹

Despite the subsiding direct danger posed by the neighboring country, potential threats from the United States and the Washington-backed ROC on Taiwan remained an abiding concern of Beijing at the southern border. Citing the establishment of the Southeast Asia Treaty Organization (SEATO) and the coming into force of the Mutual Defense Treaty between the United States and the ROC as signs of an American encirclement, a Guangxi provincial directive in March 1955 required the border counties to guard against American-supported "conspiracies against our border area" and "counterrevolutionaries who fled from the inland to the frontier." It urged all border counties to establish border work committees – consisting of personnel from the military, the border police and inspection stations, the public security authorities, banks, and transportation, customs, and trade offices – at the earliest possible date.⁴⁰ This call responded to the lingering problems of cadres and officials from different branches of the government and the military receiving orders

---

[38] Fravel, "Securing Borders," 709–10.
[39] This paragraph is based on Zeng, *YBJZ*, 130–31, 166.
[40] The quote and paraphrase are based on "Zhonggong Guangxi shengwei guanyu jiaqiang bianfang duidi douzheng de zhishi."

from their respective higher authority without much consultation with each other. The priorities of the border authorities also shifted from detecting immediate military threats from Indochina to crushing conspiracies between their internal and external enemies. The revolutionary state was determined to transform its southwestern border from a historical asylum for politically ostracized individuals into a socialist stronghold against challenges in all forms.

The WPV took similar steps in institutionalizing its border police. Following a military campaign in August 1955 to consolidate its control of the mountainous regions of Hải Ninh, where the Nùng Autonomous Territory had been located, the Vietnamese state managed to subdue open armed resistance in northeastern borders and ensure the presence of cadres in village (xã) level administrative units. Perceiving the area as a "corridor" for bandits and pirates, "kingdoms" of landlords and feudalists, and "bases" of reactionaries and "reactionaries under the guise of religion," the Vietnamese state launched a series of military and political campaigns to arrest those labeled as bandits, to force armed bandit leaders to surrender, and to confiscate private weaponry in the region, which lasted into 1956.[41] In October 1955, the MOPS of the DRV convened a national border security meeting in Hanoi, where it admitted that the weak organization of the Vietnamese border garrison and the loose control of the local party committees over border defense left many loopholes for enemies. The DRV government stipulated that the mission of the border police was "to incorporate the three aspects of administrative management, secret surveillance, and armed patrols under the leadership of the Party Central, with reliance on the people, and in close collaboration with other departments."[42] The wording of this statement showed the clear impact of the Chinese military doctrine of border defense that treated the inspection of cross-border activities and the transformation of border societies as inseparable.

With the Sino-Vietnamese partnership in place, the DRV was more lenient regarding spontaneous cross-border connections with China than with other neighboring countries, which mirrored the relaxation of defensive measures on the Chinese side. In July 1956, Hanoi demanded that the Vietnamese border police investigate the geography, population, and society of the borderlands and the coast, "striking hard on the conspiracy between the imperialists and the bandits at sea." On the land border, the DRV government decreed, in the same

---

[41] The quotes are from "Mở đợ củng cố các xã vùng rừng núi Đông Bắc [To establish and consolidate communes in the Northeast mountainous region]," August 1955, in *SLDQ*, 30; the information on campaigns is from "Khu Hồng Quảng và tỉnh Hải Ninh tiểu phỉ vùng Đông Bắc để củng cố chính quyền nhân dân [Hồng Quảng area and Hải Ninh province cracks down on bandits in the Northeast to strengthen the people's government]," 1956, in *SLDQ*, 49–51.
[42] "CHỈ THỊ CỦA BAN BÍ THƯ Số 34/CT-TW Về việc tăng cường công tác an biên phòng," 278–79.

order, that the administration of the border police be extended twenty kilometers from the border with China and that the border defense zone with Laos, in the absence of diplomatic relations between the DRV and the Royal Lao Government, be expanded to fifty kilometers. At the Vietnam-China border, the focal point of regulation was regular inspections at border ports such as Móng Cái, Đồng Đăng, Tà Lùng, and Lào Cai. In the communities bordering Laos, however, the border police were to monitor the activities of residents who sought to enter Laos to visit family or trade. The local officials were to conduct a thorough investigation at the border villages, make lists and create profiles of people engaged in cross-border activities, and only permit those who were politically trustworthy to travel to Laos.[43]

The Sino-Vietnamese Railway and Geopolitization of the Border

The Chinese-Vietnamese border acquired even greater importance to Beijing and Hanoi after the railway systems of the two countries connected in 1955. Linking the Vietnamese transport system with China was vital to the economic revival of the DRV, as the country was located on the periphery of the socialist camp and was geographically separated from the Soviet Union.[44] In December 1954, the DRV decided to repair the railroad between Hanoi and Đồng Đăng and to connect the line with the main Chinese rail network near Friendship Pass. Under the "Agreement of the PRC Assisting the DRV in Repairing Railways," the Chinese Ministry of Railway provided locomotives, vehicles, and other equipment to the DRV and sent technicians and construction teams to restore 166.9 kilometers of the Hanoi-Friendship Pass railroad.[45] The Vietnamese railroads in this area, originally constructed by the French, used a 1,000 mm (3 ft, 3 3/8 in) narrow gauge due to the mountainous terrain along, whereas the Chinese railroad used the standard gauge of 1,435 mm (4 ft, 8 1/2 in). To solve the problem of incompatible gauge, the two countries agreed to have the Vietnamese narrow-gauge rail extend into Pingxiang, the first station within China, where the Chinese would construct a reloading yard. The Vietnamese railway authority would also operate the trains between Pingxiang and Đồng Đăng.[46] Due to concerns about security and secrecy, the PRC put the PLA General Logistics Department in charge of reloading and transporting materials in Pingxiang, while the representatives of the Vietnamese Ministry of Transportation set up a liaison office in the town.[47]

---

[43] This paragraph is based on ibid., 279–80.
[44] PTTg, "ý kiến về đường sắt lm. VA 1435 [Opinions on railway lm. VA 1435]," circa 1956, no. 7607, 8/PTTg/NAVC III.
[45] Editorial Board of the Contemporary China Series, *Dangdai Zhongguo de tiedao shiye*, 355–56.
[46] Ministry of Railway of the PRC, *Zhong-Yue guojing tielu xieding*, 1.
[47] Fan, "Lengzhan shiqi Zhong-Yue tielu guoji lianyun guankui," 100.

This arrangement of extending the Vietnamese managed rail into China instead of the other way around might indicate Beijing's accommodation of Vietnamese sensitivity to the presence of Chinese infrastructure on its soil. The project was completed in February 1955, and the line was officially opened on August 1, 1955. This turned the Guangxi-Vietnam frontier into a bustling land transport hub between the two communist countries.

The railway also connected the DRV with the socialist camp – "unite us more closely with the 900 million people from friendly countries" in the words of Hồ Chí Minh – when twelve European and Asian socialist countries decided to establish the Organization for Cooperation of Railways in May 1956, improving the DRV's trade with Eastern Europe.[48] Furthermore, these agreements enhanced the importance of the railway vis-à-vis the historically prominent riverways and sea lanes. Acknowledging that railways would not dominate the Vietnamese transport system as it did in the Soviet Union and China, where the landmass supported an extensive rail network, the DRV was determined to capitalize on its modernizing infrastructure. In particular, it sought to distinguish the transportation system operated by the DRV, which followed the "advanced and scientific" regulatory methods of the socialist countries, from that created under French control, which DRV leaders criticized as under-equipped, poorly managed, and "a tool for exploitation."[49] On the other side of the border, Guangxi assumed a pivotal role in China's transportation system and military defense. Because high mountains surrounded Guangxi from the west to the north and only break at its southeastern border with Guangdong, Guangxi's connection with the outside world relied on the West River flowing into Guangdong and concentrated on its southeastern part, which was also the political center of the province.[50] The railroad section in Guangxi extended from the northeast to the southwest, thus significantly improving the transportation in the western part of the province, providing the province with better access to other parts of China while enhancing its strategic importance.

The massive construction of modern transport infrastructure was not always welcomed in the border society, even if these projects brought jobs. The new rail station in Pingxiang built in November 1955, for instance, took up a large amount of the arable land in the town, where peasants already operated in

---

[48] "NHÂN DỊP KHÁNH THÀNH ĐƯỜNG XE LỬA HÀ NỘI – MỤC NAM QUAN [On the occasion of the opening of Hanoi-Munan Guan railway]," February 28, 1955, *Hồ Chí Minh Toàn tập – Tập 9*, 348. The participatory countries were Albania, Bulgaria, Hungary, Vietnam, East Germany, China, North Korea, Mongolia, Poland, Romania, the USSR, and Czechoslovakia.
[49] PTTg, "ý kiến về đường sắt lm. VA 1435," 8–9.
[50] Kaup, *Creating the Zhuang*, 29–30; Lary, "A Zone of Nebulous Menace," 187; Fan, "Lengzhan shiqi Zhong-Yue tielu guoji lianyun guankui," 101.

a demanding environment over the mostly mountainous terrain. While the households dislocated by the project were "generously compensated," as reported by the authority of West Guangxi Zhuang Autonomous Region, those who lived near the site and lost their land, orchards, or aqueducts did not receive any payments and thus harbored resentment against the officials who oversaw the project. The project hired 3,200 laborers locally and from nearby counties without offering adequate housing or food, which demoralized these construction workers, many of whom ended up deserting their work. While promising to improve the "political work" and solve "thought problems" among the workers, the local government asked for approval for more funds to compensate for the economic losses of the households affected by the project and to increase food supplies at grocery stores.[51]

The moderate position of the cadres in their bargaining with the laborers and local community highlighted the delicate state-society relations at the border. Guangxi's border with Vietnam was one of the last areas reached by the PLA on mainland China. It took the military and party cadres almost another year to eliminate banditry and remnant Nationalist forces. Pingxiang and many other border towns were cosmopolitan, remote, and migration-based societies, lacking in nationalist sentiments, traditional clans, conspicuous class cleavages, or strong communist influence. Mobilization methods like "criticism and self-criticism," "thought reform," and "rectification," which had brought stunning victories to the CPC elsewhere proved less fruitful on the frontier, even though the party was generally adaptable to geographic variations during its revolution.[52] The communist state had to resort to economic incentives to draw the borderlanders into state projects.

The militarization and geopoliticization of the Guangxi border laid a considerable bureaucratic and fiscal burden on local state institutions. From 1955 to 1956, the population of Pingxiang rose from 14,860 to 24,000 (with 13,461 registered as peasants) following the influx of government employees and laborers.[53] In a telegram to the State Council on March 9, 1956, the Guangxi provincial government requested to upgrade Pingxiang from a township to a municipality, citing the scarce resources of the town in comparison to its growing significance after the opening of the Sino-Vietnamese Railway.

---

[51] This paragraph is based on "Zhongguo gongchandang Guixi Zhuangzu zizhiqu weiyuanhui baogao [Report by CPC West Guangxi Zhuang Autonomous Zone]," January 19, 1956, no. 1-6-27-13, 104–11/CZMA.

[52] Perry, "Moving the Masses," 112.

[53] Investigation team on ethnic trade in Guangxi of the Ministry of Commerce, "Guangxisheng Ningmingxian Pingxiang shichang kou'an xiao'e maoyi diaocha baogao [Investigation report of small-scale border trade in Pingxiang, Ningming County, Guangxi]," May 21, 1955, no. X41–1-232, 102/GZARA; the statistics for 1956 come from Nong, *Zhongguo gongchandang Pingxiang lishi*, 315.

The small town hosted 589 civil officers from 13 different national and provincial level state institutions who "scattered around the town and all had their own superiors." A lack of coordination and contradictory opinions "often undermined the important task the town undertook in foreign relations."[54] Receiving so many branches of the state in Pingxiang left local cadres with little bargaining power against senior officials. Most of the newly arrived state representatives were of higher rank in the bureaucratic hierarchy than the town officers, not to mention the military personnel who also had a strong voice in resource allocation.

The various international and domestic tasks that the local cadres were expected to perform were beyond the fiscal capability of Pingxiang. In the Chinese fiscal system of the 1950s, a town-level government like Pingxiang did not have its own budget and thus struggled financially in hosting the high volume of international visitors, including Vietnamese and overseas Chinese. Furthermore, the Guangxi provincial government admitted to Beijing that even though it had tried to transfer better-educated cadres and those more experienced in foreign affairs to work in Pingxiang, the meager income they received in a remote town offered few incentives. Meanwhile, some 145,517 people entered or left Pingxiang through Friendship Pass in 1955, and the number was expected to increase. Uplifting Pingxiang to the municipal level, the provincial government recommended, would grant officials there adequate funds and enhanced status to receive foreign delegations. In November 1956, the State Council acceded to the local request and elevated Pingxiang into a municipality, a rare status for a small border town.[55]

Along with the growing military and economic significance of border towns such as Pingxiang and Đồng Đăng, the two revolutionary states also tightened social controls along the railway. Because socialism was a modernization project, the communists actively employed advanced transportation technologies to make domestic mobility "an instrument of social change" yet maintained an ambivalent attitude toward the opportunities unendorsed by the state these technologies afforded the citizens in terms of transboundary mobility.[56] After the opening of the Sino-Vietnamese Railway, the border authority at Friendship Pass took charge of the customs inspections at the Pingxiang station. It investigated the social conditions around the locality and created detailed records on "suspected enemies." Among those arrested were ordinary people who confessed their plans to flee to Saigon by hopping on a passing train and alleged spies who purportedly collected intelligence while disguised as rail workers.[57] The Chinese state's close surveillance of the communities

---

[54] The above part is based on Nong, *Zhongguo gongchandang Pingxiang lishi*, 315.
[55] Ibid., 315–16.   [56] Keck-Szajbel and Stola, "Crossing the Borders of Friendship," 92.
[57] The quote and paraphrase are from Zeng, *YBJZ*, 52, 140, 166.

along the railroad echoed similar trends on the other side of the boundary. In June 1955, the WPV decided that the land reform in minority regions would not commence as early as in the lowland provinces populated by the Kinh people. Areas along the Sino-Vietnamese Railway, however, were an exception to this lenient policy because some of the ethnic groups there had collaborated with the French during the First Indochina War.[58] Clearly, it was decided that the agrarian reform process would help the Vietnamese state detect and crack down on potential defiers of its political authorities along the strategic supply lines of the country. Border garrisons and a closely monitored railway line, among other border-making institutions, helped the two states to turn, with force if necessary, the long-existent transnational economic and social ties to their own advantage.

A Farewell to Business: The Marginalization of Spontaneous Cross-border Trade

When deciding to open markets for small-scale border trade during the First Indochina War, the two governments had already sought to make state-owned trade companies the most powerful buyers and sellers there. Transformation to "socialist" cross-border trade accelerated after the war, spurred in part by the flood of Vietnamese goods sold by private merchants in Chinese border markets that reduced the profits of state-run firms on both sides. Marginalizing private merchants in the border markets hewed to the two countries' broader revolutionary project of establishing a predominantly socialist trade system. China's socialist transformation (*shehui zhuyi gaizao*) of handicraft industry and private commerce, which started in the second half of 1954, took the form of "public-private joint management" and practically abolished the private sector.[59] In the DRV, the socialist transformation (*cải tạo xã hội chủ nghĩa*) did not become national policy until 1958. The food crisis in 1954–1955 following the ceasefire drove the Vietnamese leaders to pursue a socialist trade system, especially in the supplies of staples, but without a state monopoly, which created "a *modus vivendi* between the state grain sector and the private economic actors."[60] Committed to nationalizing private commerce to differing extents, the Chinese and Vietnamese nevertheless shared an interest in increasing the influence of state-run companies in the border markets.

---

[58] Szalontai, "Political and Economic Crisis in North Vietnam," 397–98.
[59] Chen, "Socialist Transformation and the Demise of Private Entrepreneurs," 240.
[60] Yvon, "The Construction of Socialism in North Vietnam," 43.

Deeply concerned about any returning bourgeois elements that might threaten its autarkic agenda, the Chinese state decided to place restrictions on itinerant traders from outside the border area. In late 1954, it tried to quarantine the border markets from the rest of the country by not issuing trade licenses to people who lived more than twenty kilometers – the radius of the designated border defense zone – from the border.[61] By defining the border in this way, the state restructured the relations between the borderlands and the inland. Under the broader nationalization of commerce, the share of private commerce compared to the public sector (including state-run companies and village selling and buying cooperatives) at the border markets significantly dropped from 1953 to 1955. The suppression of private business not only expanded the market share of local state-owned firms but also disrupted the transnational trade pattern between Southern China and Indochina.

As the state-run companies strived to secure a monopoly at the Chinese border markets as a by-product of the socialist war on commerce, the tension between local administrations and border dwellers heightened. Once Beijing's decision to exclude outside merchants trickled down the bureaucratic hierarchy, the policy translated into "a widespread hostility among the cadres against all private shopkeepers."[62] The Guangxi provincial administration, for instance, decided to push the socialist transformation of private commerce earlier at the border area than inland.[63] Most merchants of the border towns fell into poverty after late 1954, as they were deprived of the right to trade at the border markets and yet "not arranged properly" to secure an alternative livelihood.[64] Local peasants had no choice but to sell their goods to the state-run companies at lower prices. Residents grumbled that these firms forced down prices more aggressively than the entrepreneurs had done during the Nationalist era. A report from the Ministry of Commerce confirmed this, acknowledging that the procurement price arbitrarily determined by the state-owned companies "had incurred a negative impact among the masses."[65] Restrictions on private merchants in China, however, did not guarantee profits for state-run companies due to the volatile demand from Vietnam. In April 1955, Chinese state trade agents at Dongxing complained about the unpredictable cross-border market that was supposed to be already under their

---

[61] West Guangxi Trade Company, "1954 nian Zhong-Yue bianjing xiao'e maoyi gongzuo zongjie," 5.
[62] Investigation team on ethnic trade in Guangxi of the Ministry of Commerce, "Guangxisheng Ningmingxian Pingxiang shichang kou'an xiao'e maoyi diaocha baogao," 103.
[63] Investigation team of ethnic trade in Guangxi dispatched by Ministry of Commerce, "Guangxisheng Longjinxian Shuikou kou'an xiao'e maoyi diaocha qingkuang baogao," 110.
[64] Investigation team on ethnic trade in Guangxi of the Ministry of Commerce, "Guangxisheng Ningmingxian Pingxiang shichang kou'an xiao'e maoyi diaocha baogao," 103.
[65] Ibid., Investigation team of ethnic trade in Guangxi dispatched by Ministry of Commerce, "Guangxisheng Longjinxian Shuikou kou'an xiao'e maoyi diaocha qingkuang baogao," 110.

supervision. With Vietnam still a "free market," they reported, "our trade is poorly planned. We can hardly draft realistic plans because it is difficult to obtain reliable information on what exactly the Vietnamese side needs."[66]

This awkward situation was a striking example of the resilience of cross-border commercial networks against state manipulation of trade when the social economic conditions in the two neighboring countries differed significantly. The CPC had consolidated its authority and credibility through a series of political campaigns, especially a nationwide suppression of "reactionaries" during the Korean War.[67] By contrast, the primary concern of WPV leaders in the mid-1950s was to avoid alienating the masses who had supported the Việt Minh's war efforts for national independence. In an attempt to stabilize the urban economy after the ceasefire, Hanoi decided to leave trade and handicraft business in private hands.[68] It was not until the DRV also carried out more drastic measures to exclude private traders from the border markets in 1957 that the state-run companies of the two communist countries could seriously undermine the centuries-long transnational trade network.

Besides competition with itinerant traders, the Chinese trade companies faced the dilemma of simultaneously shouldering the responsibilities of accumulating wealth for the state, supporting local livelihoods, and strengthening the DRV economy. When the PRC and the DRV opened small-scale trade during the First Indochina War, Beijing required its state-run companies to buy the vast majority of the goods brought by the Vietnamese to the border markets in order to boost sales of Vietnamese products in China to fund the DRV's military struggle, regardless of whether there was a Chinese demand for them or whether the items were of satisfactory quality. The influx of Vietnamese goods after the end of the war left the Chinese trade companies severely overstocked with firewood, cane, and bamboo, which were without a ready market in China.[69] In addition, the postwar famine in the DRV made border crossings crucial for Vietnamese supplies of rice, oil, and daily necessities. This reversed Guangxi's historical role as an importer of rice from Indochina to an exporter. To help relieve the food shortage in Vietnam, the Chinese state-run companies adopted different policies toward Chinese and Vietnamese buyers at the border markets. Whereas Chinese citizens were limited to a strict monthly ration on rice and cooking oil and had to use ration coupons to obtain

---

[66] Dongxing port of Fangcheng, "Guangxisheng Fangchengxian Dongxing kou'an gongzuo weiyuanhui baogao [Report of Dongxing Border Work Committee, Fangcheng County, Guangxi Province]," March 9, 1955, no. X1–12-267, 7/GZARA.
[67] Chen, *Mao's China and the Cold War*, 88.
[68] Duiker, *Vietnam: Revolution in Transition*, 135; Szalontai, "Political and Economic Crisis in North Vietnam," 400.
[69] Dongxing port of Fangcheng, "Yiyuefen gongzuo zonghe baogao [Comprehensive report for work in January]," February 18, 1955, no. X1–12-267, 2/GZARA.

cotton clothes, the Vietnamese could buy 15 kilograms of rice and 250 grams of oil per person and any quantity of cotton clothes they wished each time they attended the market. When local Chinese officials realized that a sizeable number of buyers from Vietnam were itinerant merchants who resold the rice on Vietnamese markets, where food prices had been driven high by the famine, they applied a five-kilogram limit on the amount of rice each person from Vietnam could purchase. The Ministry of Commerce, however, overruled this decision as "inappropriate." Worried that failure to help the DRV feed its starving populations would compromise the socialist partnership, the ministry suggested that the provincial government should bolster the border markets by increasing grain supply.[70] This highlighted the obstacles to implementing a centrally coined international strategy of a large country in a local context. The perceived importance of foreign policies sometimes lessened further down the bureaucratic hierarchy, especially when they diverted the already meager resources from other tasks that were locally deemed just – if not more – important, including ensuring the fiscal survival of local state institutions.

In July 1955, Beijing and Hanoi revised the protocol on small-scale border trade and signed a new treaty to establish direct trade relations between local state-owned trade companies. The two agreements marked a coordinated attempt to marginalize small-scale border trade, to overcome "the frailty of Vietnamese state-run commerce at the border," and to nationalize the border economy.[71] Three forms of state-sponsored or endorsed cross-border trade took place at the border henceforth – the intergovernmental trade conducted between the two central states, the local trade operated by provincial or regional state-owned trade firms, and the small-scale border trade among the borderlanders. Earlier that year, Hanoi had decided to monopolize the purchase of major cash crops, such as coffee beans and tea, following the Chinese model, which helped narrow the price gap between the two countries.[72] With local Chinese and Vietnamese companies directly trading based on seasonal plans, the historic border markets for small-scale trade would decline in importance based on the two states' schemes. The object of the revised protocol, according to the PRC State Council, was "to respond to the DRV's transition into a period of peaceful construction and the market change in the

---

[70] Investigation team of ethnic trade in Guangxi dispatched by Ministry of Commerce, "Guangxisheng Longjinxian Shuikou kou'an xiao'e maoyi diaocha qingkuang baogao," 111–12.

[71] PRC Ministry of Foreign Trade, "Guanyu tong Chaoxian, Yuenan bianjing difang maoyi wenti de qingshi baogao [Report on issues of local border trade with North Korea and Vietnam]," August 21, 1962, no. X50-3-81, 136/GZARA. I thank ECNURC for sharing this document with me.

[72] Investigation team of ethnic trade in Guangxi dispatched by Ministry of Commerce, "Guangxisheng Longjinxian Shuikou kou'an xiao'e maoyi diaocha qingkuang baogao," 109.

small-scale border trade after the ceasefire in Indochina, to prevent private businessmen from engaging in speculation and profiteering at the border markets, and to supply the means of production and subsistence to the border dwellers on the two sides."[73] The protocol explicitly stated that only residents within the twenty-kilometer radius could attend the border markets, with a daily limit of commodities valued at ten yuan RMB or equivalent VNĐ.[74] To discourage the private cross-border economy, the DRV abolished an existing tax exemption policy for people who brought commodities under a value of five yuan RMB or equivalent VNĐ.[75]

Both the variety of goods and the number of participants at the border markets subsequently plummeted. The socialist campaign against private business, however, was not an easy victory; even local state representatives had reservations about repelling private traders from the border markets. They admitted that private merchants had competed with state-run companies to purchase Vietnamese products by offering higher prices or by placing orders in advance, and some of them might have even undertaken subversive political activities. Excluding them did more harm than good, however, as the public trade firms had focused on monopolizing the trade in major commodities and thus fell short of meeting the daily demands of the border residents, especially regarding medicines, herbs, and buffalo.[76]

The two Communist leaderships already had the final nationalization of all cross-border trade in mind. Viewing both small-scale border trade and local state-run trade as makeshift, transitional arrangements, the two parties determined to gradually incorporate all cross-border transactions under "formal, intergovernmental trade."[77] In the spring of 1956, Beijing and Hanoi decided to close all border markets by the end of June 1957, while making allowance for local dwellers to cross the border carrying small numbers of gifts or

---

[73] State Council of the PRC, "Guanyu zhixing 1955 nian Zhong-Yue bianjing xiao'e maoyi yidingshu de zhishi [Instruction on implementing the protocol of Chinese-Vietnamese small-scale border trade in 1955]," August 17, 1955, no. X1–12-294, 1/GZARA.

[74] "Zhonghua renmin gongheguo zhengfu yu Yuenan minzhu gongheguo zhengfu guanyu liangguo bianjing xiao'e maoyi de yidingshu [Protocol of small-scale border trade between the PRC and the DRV]," July 7, 1955, no. X1–12-294, 7–8/GZARA.

[75] State Council of the PRC, "Guanyu zhixing 1955 nian Zhong-Yue bianjing xiao'e maoyi yidingshu de zhishi," 2.

[76] CPC Pingxiang Township Committee, "Guanyu Zhong-Yue bianjing xiao'e maoyi qingkuang baogao [Report of Chinese-Vietnamese small-scale border trade]," September 20, 1955, no. X1–12-293, 17/GZARA.

[77] PRC Ministry of Commerce, Ministry of Foreign Trade, and Ministry of Finance, "Wei zhixing 'Zhong-Yue guanyu liangguo bianjing difang guoying maoyi gongsi jinxing huowu jiaohuan de yidingshu' de zhishi [Instructions on implementing 'the agreement on exchanges of commodities between local state-run companies at the border']," September 5, 1955, no. X1–12-294, 25/GZARA.

personal items.[78] Even though the plan was not carried out, the two countries' ambition to fix frontier people on either side of the borderline by monopolizing the supply of goods was manifest. In May 1957, the Forestry Department of Hồng Quảng was founded to manage timber – one of the most profitable exports of the region besides coal. Vowing to distinguish itself from the French colonial practice of "indiscriminately exploiting" precious woods "without a plan," the department was bestowed the responsibility of "combining forest exploitation with protection."[79] Under this seemingly ideological agenda of controlling the cross-border trade, a nationalist overtone of reversing the chronic fragmentation and decline of the authorities of the Chinese and Vietnamese state in the political economy was pronounced. Over the century before the mid-1950s, treaty ports and sphere of influence of Western powers, as well as warlord finances, had largely squeezed the Chinese state out of the economic life of China's frontier. In response, successive Chinese governments since the late Qing waged, with varied success, a "war on smuggling."[80] Along Vietnam's northern border, a booming colonial economy in mining and forestry controlled by French companies was a financial bonanza for the colonial mother country. Local inhabitants' use of forests for their own livelihood, however, came under tight restrictions.[81]

Although the two states' joint scrutiny and regulation increasingly targeted the cross-border commercial networks, itinerant merchants proved resilient, especially in the DRV. Unlike in China, where businessmen had lost management rights through state-imposed public–private joint ownership, the DRV did not hastily push for a state monopoly of commerce for fear of alienating the urban population. It was thus more challenging for the Vietnamese officials to block itinerant retailers from border markets. In April 1957, the Vietnamese Prime Minister's Office ordered local governments along its border to take tougher measures to exclude "greedy merchants" who "exploit the shortage of commodities in the domestic markets." Hanoi blamed stores opened by these traders in the border area for creating "disorderly and complicated" supply and demand. More importantly, these non-native shopkeepers had managed to dominate the Vietnamese border markets and to smuggle contraband by bribing businessmen, ordinary people, and cadres. The DRV government

---

[78] PRC Ministry of Foreign Trade, "Zhengxun Zhong-Yue bianjing tingzhi xiao'e maoyi wenti [Consultation about stopping Chinese-Vietnamese small-scale border trade]," April 13, 1956, 235-1-394-051~052, 51/GDPA.
[79] "Thành lập Ty Lâm nghiệp khu Hồng Quảng [Establishment of Forestry Department of Hồng Quảng area]," May 1957, in *SLDQ*, 58–59.
[80] Thai, *China's War on Smuggling*. I thank one of my anonymous reviewers for suggesting I contextualize Chinese pursuit for the centralization of trade with its experience of unequal treaties and warlordism.
[81] Namba, "Colonization and Forestry in French Indochina," 24.

therefore required that by August 1957 retailers taking commodities to the border from Hanoi, Haiphong, and other interior areas had to sell their goods to local Vietnamese state-run companies instead of trading directly with the Chinese. Moreover, only agricultural products from the border provinces could be exported to China via small-scale border trade, and Chinese imports were not to be sold to merchants outside the border area.[82] These orchestrated state efforts to interfere with and profit from the border trade shrank the border markets greatly, with fewer people applying for trade licenses and more crossing the border illegally through the less-patrolled trails. Chinese border authorities at Aikou, an official border market near Pingxiang, noted that while they used to welcome approximately five hundred traders from Vietnam per day, almost no foreign visitors appeared in August 1957.[83]

Given the pivotal role of overseas Chinese traders in the commercial networks between Southern China and Southeast Asia and their strong regional connections, across land and maritime borders, their experience during the marginalization of private border trade merits special attention. Even during the period of close socialist comradeship between Beijing and Hanoi, the overseas Chinese merchants enjoyed favorable treatment at the Chinese border markets because of their ethnic affinity and language skills. In June 1955, Vietnamese officials complained to the Chinese authorities about the unfair treatment toward the Vietnamese vis-à-vis ethnic Chinese merchants at the Chinese border markets. The Chinese state-owned companies reportedly refused to purchase the dyeing yam brought by the Vietnamese because of their low quality, while accepting the exact same batch sold by the Chinese traders the next day. "It has become a common experience among the Vietnamese," the Vietnamese officials added, "that it is better to ask the Chinese merchants to sell products on behalf of the Vietnamese" at the Chinese border markets. An inspection group dispatched by the Guangxi provincial government confirmed that many Vietnamese peddlers believed that they were discriminated against by the Chinese trade firms and thus chose to hide their nationality and pretend to be ethnic Chinese during transactions.[84]

The different treatment of ethnic Chinese and Vietnamese traders at the border markets incurred serious political consequences, which, as noted by the inspection group, "was a far cry from the principle of fostering the solidarity

---

[82] The above part is based on PTTg, "Sô 5294 TN v/v biện pháp quản lý buôn bán qua biên giới và chống lậu ở biên giới Việt-Trung [No. 5294 TN on regulations of cross-border trade and anti-smuggling at the Vietnam-China border]," August 7, 1957, no. 7642, 29–30/PTTg/NAVC III.
[83] Editorial Committee of Gazetteer of Pingxiang City, *Pingxiang shizhi*, 377.
[84] This paragraph is based on Foreign Affairs Committee of Guangxi, "Munan Guan kou'an maoyi gouxiao jinkou yinqi Yuenan shangfan buman you [Import policy of trade company at Munan Guan causing discontent among Vietnamese peddlers]," June 16, 1955, no. X1–12–293, 41–42/GZARA.

between the two peoples at the border – an internationalist spirit that drove us to open the small-scale border trade at the very beginning."[85] Alerted that the Sino-Vietnamese "lips and teeth" relationship promoted by the political centers did not translate to a persuasive sense of unity with the Vietnamese among the grassroots Chinese cadres, the Guangxi provincial government emphasized the strategic significance of the small-scale border trade, urging Chinese officials at the border to "cast off the remnants of great-nation chauvinism or narrow nationalism, and uplift internationalism." Favoring Chinese merchants from Vietnam while discriminating against the Vietnamese people, it warned, would result in a serious political loss.[86] This disparity along ethnic lines suggested a striking continuity in the cross-border economic exchanges, in which personal and ethnic ties gave rise to favoritism, despite an engineered friendship between the two political centers that required impartiality.

The marginalization of small-scale border trade after the First Indochina War was the result of both the domestic campaigns for socialist transformation in China and Vietnam, which sought to construct a centrally planned, command economy, and cooperation between the two communist states at the border markets to take hold of economic exchanges. The decisive advantage of the modern state apparatus was as much in paperwork as in arms. Effective tax extraction was the end product of "cadastral surveys," "settlement reports," censuses, "identity cards," and "a growing body of regulations and procedures."[87] The communist state, which had long mobilized from the bottom-up with a finely woven network of officials, was exceptionally efficient in capturing and recording the status of each inhabitant, each piece of land, and each activity of the state's concern. The logic behind the two countries' regulation of border trade was to make it legible and taxable to the state by prescribing the locations of economic exchanges. They then excluded private merchants and established a monopoly of state-run companies in the hope that the inhabitants would turn their back on the border and commit to a nationalized economy supervised by the political centers. Ordinary people could, however, turn their back on the state apparatus by exploring alternative spaces for cross-border exchanges. The authorities could not construct an all-encompassing state structure without alienating some of the people in the borderlands.

---

[85] Ibid., 42.
[86] Nanning Customs, "Zhuanfa 'guanyu Munan Guan Aikou kou'an maoyi gouxiaozu shougou jinkou shulang yinqi Yuenan shangfan buman de tongbao' ji zuzhi xuexi you [Forwards and studies 'the notice about trade company at Aikou, Munan Guan, importing dyeing yam and leading to discontent among the Vietnamese peddlers']," July 1, 1955, no. X1–12-296, 9/ GZARA.
[87] Scott, *The Moral Economy of the Peasant*, 94.

Turning Border Society Inward: Severing Cross-Boundary Social Ties

The hunt for potential subversive individuals and the struggle against private cross-border trade were not sufficient to create a socialist border. The two revolutionary states collaborated in making the border a point of contrast by turning the respective frontier societies inward. This joint state building and border making required government intervention in people's daily lives and greater control over local economies beyond the restructuring of commerce. For example, by reducing cross-border farming, the socialist states could more efficiently tax the borderlanders and integrate the border societies into the planned economy. The state would also reach into more intimate aspects of the interactions between the border people, such as marriage.

If the two communist countries' policies to nationalize cross-border trade made border crossings "points of differences," their decision to eliminate cross-border farming highlighted a more ambitious goal in enforcing a linear border. Cross-border farming initially emerged as a tax problem. After the end of the First Indochina War, the Vietnamese local government asked Chinese farmers who owned or harvested land in Vietnam to pay "overdue agricultural taxes" for the period 1951 to 1954, when the DRV only had a fluid territorial base.[88] From surveys of cross-border croplands, the two governments quickly realized the financial implications of an ambiguous border, where the attempt to extract agricultural surplus by one modernizing state could encounter claims made by the neighboring country engaged in similar state building projects.

Continuous wars and social upheavals in the China-Vietnam border region since the second half of the nineteenth century had undermined the strength of the central states in the area and given the local population significant leeway against political authorities. Before 1948, people from Guangxi and west Guangdong who had land in Vietnam paid an agricultural tax in the form of rice to the French colonial state. As the population increased in Southern China, landlords purchased land in Vietnam, and agriculturalists expanded their fields across the border through swiddening.[89] After the outbreak of the First Indochina War, some of them moved back to Guangxi while keeping

---

[88] "Guanyu Zhong-Yue bianjing guojing gengdi nongyeshui qingli yu jinhou fudan banfa de chubu yijian [Preliminary solution on clearing agricultural tax of cross-border farming at the Sino-Vietnamese border and future tax policy]," n.d., no. X1–12-290, 25/GZARA.

[89] Bureau of Finance of Guangxi Province, "Guanyu Zhong-Yue liangguo guojing tudi ji nongyeshui fudan wenti de qingkuang he yijian [Situation and suggestions about agricultural tax of the cross-border land between China and Vietnam]," January 17, 1955, no. X1–12-290, 11/GZARA.

their land in Vietnam.[90] Rent or transfer of land as dowry or betrothal gifts also created cross-border farming and land ownership.[91] In 1949 and 1950, neither the colonial state nor the Việt Minh was able to levy much on its northern border, and the fledging DRV only started to collect tax in the area after 1951.[92] Hence most of the landowners from China were able to escape Vietnamese agricultural taxes during the war.

The different pace of state building in China and Vietnam also allowed perceptive borderland residents to exploit the disparity. They defended themselves before local Chinese officials by asserting that Chinese customs had blocked their attempts to carry rice to Vietnam to pay tax due to a lack of legal documents to export crops or the Vietnamese officials had declined the payment due to uncertainty about tax rates. While a few peasants admitted that they took a gamble in assuming that the Vietnamese government was too weak, others pleaded innocence, explaining that the DRV usually collected tax in February and March, when they had almost consumed the harvest from the previous year. With the Sino-Vietnamese socialist partnership in mind, the local Chinese officials labeled and condemned these state-evasion strategies as "great-nation chauvinism."[93] The Guangxi provincial government estimated that Chinese residents from ninety-four border towns owed the Vietnamese government between 750,000 and 1,000,000 kilograms of rice for the period from 1951 to 1954. In contrast, most Vietnamese citizens who farmed in China had paid agricultural tax to the Chinese government.[94]

The tax implications of the consolidation of the Vietnamese communist state, however, soon reached the Sino-Vietnamese border. As instructed by Hanoi, the Vietnamese provincial administrations started communicating with Chinese border counties in late 1954 about their "overdue" agricultural taxes. They required that Chinese border residents who had land in Vietnam pay back taxes from 1951 to 1953, based on the DRV tax regulations of the time. As for the taxes from 1954 on, they proposed adding up the individual harvests in China and Vietnam, calculating the per capita output of rice in the household,

---

[90] CPC Fangcheng County Committee, "Guanyu Zhongguo jumin zai Yuenan gengzhong tudi zhi nongyeshui zhengshou wenti [About Chinese residents paying agricultural tax for their land in Vietnam]," March 14, 1954, no. X1–12-290, 30/GZARA.
[91] Zheng and Wang, *Xinan diqu haiwai yiminshi yanjiu*, 161.
[92] CPC Fangcheng County Committee, "Guanyu Zhongguo jumin zai Yuenan gengzhong tudi zhi nongyeshui zhengshou wenti," 30.
[93] The above part is based on CPC Jingxi County Committee, "Youguan woguo zai Yuenan tudi jiaona gongliang ji Zhong zai Yue tudi jiaohuan wenti [About agricultural tax of Chinese land in Vietnam and land exchange with Vietnam]," December 8, 1955, no. X1–12-290, 39–41/GZARA.
[94] Bureau of Finance of Guangxi Province, "Guanyu Zhong-Yue bianjing guojing tudi nongyeshui linian jiqian qingli yijian de qingshi baogao [Report seeking instruction about clearing overdue agricultural tax of cross-border land at the Sino-Vietnamese border]," March 28, 1955, no. X1–12-290, 65–66/GZARA.

and then levying taxes according to the Chinese tax rate. People from Vietnam who had land in China would pay agricultural taxes in the same way.[95]

Although the Vietnamese government's request was an overt response to the postwar food shortages, it was also linked to other, subtle issues. For instance, the Vietnamese clearly desired to present the image of a functioning, legitimate, socialist state to its northern neighbor. The agricultural tax issue certainly made the Chinese government more aware of the problem of contested sovereignty as well. Due to discrepancies between cartographic records, some of the land claimed by the Vietnamese government fell under the administration of China according to one map, while belonging to Vietnam on another. The Foreign Affairs Office of Guangxi noted that the issue was thus pertinent to national territorial sovereignty and should be reported to the central party authorities.[96] At the same time, Chinese local governments considered various international and domestic factors when seeking a solution with the Vietnamese. As Hanoi's most important ally, China felt obliged to uphold Vietnam's right to extract resources from Vietnamese territory. Hence Fangcheng County ignored its grassroots authorities' suggestion to ask the Vietnamese to reduce taxes for impecunious peasants and ethnic minorities.[97]

Nationalist sentiments in favor of delineating and defending sovereignty nevertheless shaped the Sino-Vietnamese relations even during the heyday of their "socialist brotherhood." None of the Chinese provincial institutions involved in the internal discussion agreed with the Vietnamese proposal of calculating total rice output from both sides of the border as the basis for taxation. Instead, provincial financial and foreign affairs offices came up with a program aimed at both keeping China's agricultural statistics confidential and reducing cross-border land ownership. They proposed that each government should levy taxes from lower-income people according to the local tax rate and the average output of the town where the land was located. Since the majority of people engaged in cross-border farming were classified as "poor peasants" whose harvest fell below average, this tax scheme would discourage them from farming across the international boundary. The Chinese government, moreover, would treat each foreign holder of land on its territory as one household and impose progressive taxation, which would increase their tax

---

[95] Bureau of Finance of Guangxi Province, "Guanyu Zhong-Yue liangguo guojing tudi ji nongyeshui fudan wenti de qingkuang he yijian," 11.

[96] Foreign Affairs Office of Guangxi, "Zhong-Yue shuangfang jumin guojing gengdi de nongyeshui zhengshou banfa [Methods to levy tax from cross-border farmland owned by Chinese and Vietnamese residents]," August 10, 1955, no. X1–12-290, 4–5/GZARA.

[97] Border Work Committee of Dongzhong Port, "Guanyu Zhongguo jumin zai Yuenan gengzhong tudi zhi nongyeshui zhengshou wenti [About agricultural tax of land in Vietnam farmed by Chinese residents]," March 10, 1955, no. X1–12-290, 29–31/GZARA.

burden.[98] The Chinese local government also dwelled on the possibility that charging the poor peasants for all taxes deemed "overdue" to Vietnam in full at one time would spark social protests. The Guangxi provincial officials thus proposed to Beijing that the Chinese government pay the taxes from 1951 to 1954 to the DRV on behalf of the poor. It further suggested that Beijing make payments for those categorized as rich peasants, landlords, and businessmen but that these amounts should be deducted from their salaries.[99] This proposal shows that the local state agents were protective of the border community, where the population identified as "ethnic minorities" often overlapped with economically disadvantaged groups.

The tax lever aimed at reducing cross-border land ownership soon took effect. In late 1955, Jingxi County reported to the Guangxi provincial government that some border people had tried to solve the "new problem" of cross-border farming by swapping land. In December, the provincial administration not only gave the green light to land swaps on "a voluntary and mutually beneficial basis" but also decided to simplify the legal procedures to encourage future exchanges.[100] In January 1956, the International Department of the CPC Central Committee instructed the local officials to "actively create favorable conditions to gradually reduce and eventually eliminate cross-border farmland" and forests.[101] The local state accordingly put forward plans that combined economic compensation and political campaigns. Following a preliminary survey of plots owned by Chinese citizens in Vietnam and land farmed by Vietnamese households under their administrations, some Chinese counties decided to offer monetary compensation equal to the total agricultural output of one to three years to people who had to give up their harvests in Vietnam. Party cadres also sought to inculcate a national awareness among the borderlanders through the settlement of cross-border farming despite the fact that, whenever possible, the farmers would exchange land with or hand it over to their close relatives across the border to make sure that the wealth circulated within the extended family. Through rallies and posters, party cadres attempted to persuade the local people to "lift the internationalist spirit, respect the territorial integrity of the DRV ... and to make use of the abundant sources

---

[98] Foreign Affairs Office of Guangxi, "Fu 'guanyu Zhong-Yue bianjing guojing tudi nongyeshui fudan wenti de yijian' [Reply to 'opinions on agricultural tax on cross-border land on Sino-Vietnamese border']," January 17, 1955, no. X1-12-290, 14/GZARA.

[99] Bureau of Finance of Guangxi Province, "Guanyu Zhong-Yue bianjing guojing tudi nongyeshui linian jiqian qingli yijian de qingshi baogao," 66.

[100] Liaison Department of CPC Committee of Guangxi, "Fu Jingxixian bianjing gongzuobu Jing Bian (55) zi di 27 hao baogao [Reply on Report no. 55-27 by the Department of Border Affairs of Jingxi County]," December 16, 1955, no. X1-12-290, 36/GZARA.

[101] CPC Fangcheng County Committee, "Guojing gengdi, shanlin de chuli fang'an (cao'an) [Draft solution of cross-border land and forest]," October 11, 1956.

of our homeland to develop socialism and improve living standards instead of relying on foreign countries."[102]

Because the two communist states were assertive in claiming resources from their territory and turning border society inward, the traditional strategies employed by borderlanders to maintain autonomy, such as moving between and around states, became less promising.[103] Stateless space disappeared not only on the map but also in terms of administrative oversight. Starting in early 1956, the Vietnamese state pushed the inchoate cooperatives movement in the form of mutual-help groups (tổ đổi công, where individual peasants came together to help each with farming) to its northeastern borderlands and launched land reform in Hải Ninh in May.[104] Similar institutions designed to channel agricultural revenues more effectively to the state and enforce grass-root governance emerged on both sides of the border. The effects of the policy to discourage cross-border farming, however, should not be overestimated. It was not until a comprehensive land survey along the border was completed by the spring of 1957 that the central governments realized the number of households involved in cross-border farming and forestry.

Besides economic connections, cross-border marriage and family ties formed a solid cultural foundation of borderlands society that even aggressive boundary making could not shake. The integration of cross-border marriage into the realm of the state illustrates the ramifications of state building on the fringe of political power, which historically had been a space of juridical exception. Marriage became a practice of concern to the Chinese and Vietnamese states because extended families, arranged marriages, child marriages, and polygamy were among the traditional social institutions that came under attack for thwarting the two nations' aspirations for modernity. The Civil Code of the Republic of China, implemented in 1931, marked a significant break from the state's role in regulating matrimonial practices in the past and legitimized the state's intervention into people's intimate relations in the name of fostering citizens' loyalty to the modern nation. Nevertheless, the reach of the state was too limited to shake gender inequity and patriarchal structures, especially in rural area.[105] While the New Marriage Law of 1950 was among the first legislative acts promulgated by the PRC, it was not until the mid-1950s that the provisions of the law, such as the establishment of civil

---

[102] The above part is based on ibid. For an overview of the farmland swap, see You, "Zhanhou Zhong-Yue ludi bianjie wenti de lishi kaocha ji zaisikao," 67–68.
[103] Scott, *Seeing Like a State*, 1; Scott, *The Art of Not Being Governed*, 24.
[104] "Tỉnh Hải Ninh đẩy mạnh phong trào tổ đổi công sản xuất trong nông nghiệp [Hải Ninh province fully launches movement of mutual-help groups in agriculture]," 1956; "Ba huyện: Đông Triều, Thủy Nguyên và Yên Hưng tiến hành cải cách ruộng đất [Three districts: Đông Triều, Thủy Nguyên and Yên Hưng carry out land reform]," May 1956, in *SLDQ*, 44–47.
[105] Li and Friedman, "Wedding Marriage to the Nation-State in Modern China," 148–51.

registries, were widely publicized and enforced.[106] In the DRV, the codification of marriage law did not take place until 1959. Strongly influenced by the Chinese New Marriage Law of 1950 and Soviet marriage laws in its vocabulary, the Marriage and Family Law of the DRV vowed to protect monogamy, gender equality, and the rights of women and children.[107]

To resolve potential conflicts between the New Marriage Law and Vietnamese marriage traditions in the absence of a DRV marriage law, as well as between the rather progressive written law and the customary marriages that followed diverse local practices, Beijing issued an administrative guideline in June 1954 on marriage between Chinese and Vietnamese citizens in the border area. Cross-border marriage requests "should be permitted as long as it is not against the Marriage Law of our country or laws of the Vietnamese state."[108] Based on this central decree, the Guangxi provincial government established administrative procedures for cross-border marriage, divorce, and marriage-based migration in June 1955.[109] All cross-border marriages, including those among ethnic minorities such as the Hmong/Miao, required approval by and registration with the local authorities, although such regulation was difficult to enforce.[110]

What concerned local officials most was not whether to endorse individual cross-border marriage requests but how to contain the ripple effects of cross-border conjugal disputes, which required not only considerable time but also local knowledge beyond their understanding. The Guangxi provincial government initially advised that when a Chinese citizen requested to divorce a Vietnamese citizen who did not live in China, the Chinese local administration should consult the opinions of the Vietnamese person and the Vietnamese authorities through the Vietnamese consulate in Nanning.[111] The local state agents nevertheless found this instruction "too general" and "difficult to

[106] Wong, "Family Reform through Divorce Law in the PRC," 275–76.
[107] Kim, "The Marriage and Family Law of North Vietnam," 441–42.
[108] "Zhengwuyuan jiu Guangxisheng Zhong-Yue bianjie diqu Zhong-Yue liangguo renmin yaoqiu tonghun yishi pifu zhongnan xingzheng weiyuanhui [State Council's reply to the Mid-West Administrative Committee about cross-border marriage request at the China-Vietnam border area]," June 12, 1954, in *GSBN 1954*, 409.
[109] Foreign Affairs Office of Guangxi, "Guanyu wosheng Zhong-Yue bianjing jiehun, lihun yinci er chansheng de chuguo shouxu wenti de jidian chubu yijian [Preliminary opinions on cross-border marriage and divorce and the ensuing issue of people going abroad in our province]," June 16, 1955, no. X1-12-263, 4–5/GZARA.
[110] Department of United Front of CPC Guangxi Provincial Committee, "Guanyu Miaozu nan qingnian yu Yuejing nü qingnian jiehun wenti de qingshi [Seeking instructions over marriage between Hmong young men and women in Vietnam]," July 26, 1955, no. X1–12-263, 21/GZARA.
[111] Foreign Affairs Office of Guangxi, "Guanyu wosheng Zhong-Yue bianjing jiehun, lihun yinci er chansheng de chuguo shouxu wenti de jidian chubu yijian," 4–5.

implement," and they often confronted a dilemma between interfering in and stepping back from resolving family disputes, especially those involving settlements of property and children.[112] The borderlanders often did not bother to register their marriage, yet were ready to resort to the state authorities of their home country when they believed this would help them bargain for a better deal when a marriage broke down.

A typical cross-border marriage dispute involved bigamy among women from Vietnam. It was not uncommon in the rural area for a married woman to escape her household and remarry. As marriage in the area almost always involved betrothal gifts from the groom to the bride's family, and a commissioning fee to the matchmaker if he hired one, marital disputes often emerged simultaneously with financial tangles. When the disagreement emerged between families on two sides of the border, an intricate "international problem" arose. Resolving cross-border marital conflicts became burdensome for local officials. In one such case, Fan Shimin, a peasant living in Ningming County, Guangxi, married Huỳnh Thị Anh, Vietnamese woman, via a Vietnamese matchmaker. It soon turned out that Huỳnh Thị Anh already had a husband in Vietnam, and she left Fan for her Vietnamese hometown after the wedding. Fan rushed to Vietnam without any travel documents and asked the matchmaker to return the commission and Huỳnh Thị Anh's family to return the betrothal gifts. After being rejected bluntly, Fan angrily took the matchmaker's buffalo and wrangled with his wife's family. The Vietnamese border authorities then notified the county authorities of Ningming, where the Chinese cadres reprimanded Fan for being "chauvinist" and "disregarding border regulations ... even if it was the woman's fault for not divorcing first before remarrying." In the end, the Chinese and Vietnamese local administrators managed to persuade Fan to return the buffalo and the bride to return the betrothal gifts.[113]

Given the deep-rooted transboundary ethnic connections and the considerable number of unresolved marriage disputes brought before it, the provincial court of Guangxi issued a guide that encouraged local border authorities to mediate between the two litigants through "work"(*gongzuo*) that observed the local customs or to let the couple and their families directly resolve the

---

[112] Ibid., 7.
[113] This paragraph is based on Provincial Court of Guangxi, "Guanyu Ningmingxian <name pseudonymized> yu Yuefang funü <name pseudonymized> hunyin jiufen wenti de cailiao [Material on marriage disputes between <name anonymized> of Ningming County and Vietnamese woman <name anonymized>]," April 11, 1955, no. X1-12-263, 30/GZARA; another file also records the incident: Foreign Affairs Office of Guangxi, "Guanyu Zhong-Yue bianjing liangjumin de hunyin jiufen wenti [About the marriage disputes between a Chinese and a Vietnamese citizen in the border area]," August 4, 1955, no. X1-12-263, 31-32/GZARA.

disputes by consultation.[114] This position contradicted the provincial government's initial policy that prescribed a solution via diplomatic channels. Nonetheless, as early as during the Yan'an period of the early 1940s, the Chinese Communist cadres had used persuasion or conciliation to resolve family disputes, considering these techniques more valuable than legal procedure.[115] In the end, the provincial authorities steered clear of a diplomatic or legislative settlement of cross-border matrimonial disputes based on practical concerns. The court's instruction admitted that formal legal proceduress often dragged on "because it not only involved diplomatic relations between the two countries, but also the applicability of different laws."[116]

Thus, the reality at the border rolled back the legalist approach toward settling cross-border marital disputes and problematized the tendency of treating all transnational connections as international issues. While the enshrined sovereignty provided the nation-state with a justification to interfere with intimate aspects of frontier life, it also imposed significant administrative burdens on local state agents. Largely because of the non-interventionist attitude of the local administration, problems inherent in transnational marriage, such as citizenship, legal residence, and conflicts over marriage laws, remained shelved until a meeting between the border provinces in November 1956.

Tensions between Borderline Administration and Borderland Realities

From November 6 to 9, 1956, representatives from China's Guangxi and Guangdong provinces and Vietnam's Cao Bằng, Lạng Sơn, and Hải Ninh provinces met in Nanning to attend the first inter-provincial border conference, which underlined that state building and border making at the China-Vietnam borderland was an internationally coordinated project. The creation of all-encompassing states by two communist parties necessitated joint efforts by Beijing and Hanoi to make a soft and poorly delineated and defended frontier space into a hard, clearly defined border, the crossing of which came with higher political risks and economic costs. The fact that the meeting was between provincial governments from the eastern part of the China-Vietnam border indicates that the two countries were eager to work out a solution for border issues in the lowlands, where the states enjoyed stronger institutional

---

[114] Provincial Court of Guangxi, "Dui Jingxixian Nalin kou'an gongzuo weiyuanhui qingshi baogao de yijian [Opinion on the reports of Nalin Border Work Committee]," August 1, 1955, no. X1–12-263, 37/GZARA.
[115] Wong, "Family Reform through Divorce Law in the PRC," 266, 275.
[116] Provincial Court of Guangxi, "Dui Jingxixian Nalin kou'an gongzuo weiyuanhui qingshi baogao de yijian," 37.

strength and identified more issues of concern, via a mechanism separate from the highland provinces. The Chinese and Vietnamese delegates admitted that, for the immediate future, they needed to respect centuries-long customs and cross-border connections for the sake of social stability and production. Nonetheless, they also envisioned turning the borderland population away from the borderline in the long run.

Except for the rather sensitive issue of border demarcation, the provincial governments were granted the authority to negotiate over measures for monitoring and reducing the mobility of people and goods across the border, such as land and forest ownership, buffalo trade, debts between border residents, conflicting nationalities, marriages, and the management of border defense zones, which allowed Beijing and Hanoi to extricate themselves from administrative issues that required local knowledge. This division of responsibility between the central and provincial governments manifested itself in the meeting agenda. The delegates shelved the resolution of physical border disputes but still agreed that "some of the boundary markers have been moved, which could incur disputes if the two parties do not resolve the problem." With the blessing of the CPC and the WPV central authorities, the party committees of the border provinces would scrutinize the issue, discuss a settlement, and report to party leaders.[117]

The resolution of the meeting endorsed the established practices for reducing the residents' motives to cross the borderline and for managing transnational social networks. The states' attitudes toward cross-border farming and forestry best signaled their determination to intrude into everyday life in the borderlands: "To strengthen border management and avoid disputes, the two sides will actively, firmly, and gradually decrease and withdraw altogether from land farmed across the border." Besides encouraging voluntary swaps between holders of land and forests, the provincial authorities scheduled a land investigation, to be followed by a formal exchange of farmland and forests starting in the spring of 1957. Whereas cross-border farming on existing crop fields was temporarily permitted for peasants "facing genuine economic difficulties," further swiddening or transactions of land across the border were prohibited. For cross-border ties less likely to create contested territorial claims, the authorities decided to respect "historical customs." They agreed,

---

[117] This paragraph is based on UBHC KTTVB, "Trích Biên Bản Ghi Những Vấn Đề Biên Giới Được Trao Đổi Trong Cuộc Toạ Đàm Giữa Đại Biểu Các Tỉnh Cao Bằng, Lạng Sơn, Hải Ninh-Việt Nam Và Quảng Tây, Quảng Đông-Trung Quốc Họp Từ Ngày 6 Đến 9 Tháng 11 Năm 1956 [Memorandum on the border issues discussed at the round table meeting between representatives of Cao Bằng, Lạng Sơn, and Hải Ninh of Vietnam and Guangxi and Guangdong of China, 6–9 November 1956]," no. 5523, 1/UBHC KTTVB 1948–1976/ NAVC III.

for instance, not to restrict fishing or the passage of boats from either country on the boundary river. They granted county authorities the power to mediate debt disputes based on the laws of the creditor's home country and made arrangements for repaying government bonds and debts incurred by guerrillas and local troops to people on the other side of the border during the Chinese Civil War and the First Indochina War.[118]

Policies regarding cross-border marriage and nationalities, however, reflected the two communist countries' uneasiness with the transnational fraternity fostered by ethnic ties. In 1955, the PRC, which did not recognize dual citizenship, agreed in talks with the DRV that "all subjects of Chinese origin living in the DRV should be encouraged to assimilate on a voluntary and gradual basis into Vietnamese society."[119] This decision toed the line of China's overall approach, which took shape during 1953–1955, to the overseas Chinese problem. Vowing to coexist peacefully with its non-communist Southeast Asian neighbors, Beijing encouraged overseas Chinese to become nationals of the countries where they lived to dispel the image that they could serve as agents of communist infiltration or of Chinese influence on local politics more broadly.[120]

This approach to nudge the Chinese in Vietnam to take on Vietnamese citizenship soon created anxiety among the Chinese community in the border area and sparked stiff resistance. In August 1956, in preparation for the border provinces meeting, Hải Ninh dispatched work teams to investigate the opinion of ethnic Chinese on the issue of nationality. Being vigilant against the heralded DRV move to impose Vietnamese citizenship, mass protests broke out and "illegal" meetings were convened in Chinese populated areas such as Đại Lại village and the coastal town of Hà Cối between August and October. They refused to discuss the citizenship issue with Vietnamese government officials and demanded that they select their own representatives to talk to the Chinese Consulate. The open resistance culminated in a mass demonstration in Hà Cối between October 20 and 24 that attracted more than 500 Chinese, among whom 320 decided to move to China.[121] In March 1957, demonstrations took place again following the mysterious destruction of a Chinese temple in Móng Cái. Ethnic Chinese workers from the pottery workshops and agriculturalists of Chinese descent in nearby villages gathered in the

---

[118] This paragraph is based on ibid., 1–5   [119] Duiker, *China and Vietnam*, 40.
[120] FitzGerald, *China and the Overseas Chinese*, 104–5.
[121] "Tỉnh Hải Ninh đập tan âm mưu gây rối loạn của bọn phản động người Hoa ở Hà Cối [Hải Ninh province smashed the plot to cause disorder of the Chinese reactionaries in Hà Cối]," August 20–October 24, 1956, in *SLDQ*, 48–49. This official history is obscure on how the Vietnamese authorities responded to the resistance. It uses expressions such as "increasing the number of cadres in the town" and "mobilize the mass to detect and isolate the leaders."

border trading hub, denouncing the incident as a Vietnamese government–instigated attack on the Chinese community.[122]

Regarding the Vietnamese living in China, Beijing mostly adopted a non-assimilationist approach. At the 1956 border provinces meeting, the Chinese delegates conveyed Beijing's opinion to their Vietnamese counterparts: the ethnically Vietnamese people who migrated to China after the PRC was founded were considered Việt Kiều – Vietnamese citizens living overseas. Those who had moved to China before October 1949, had a legitimate occupation, and settled down in China would also be "persuaded to keep their Vietnamese citizenship." Only those insisting on obtaining Chinese nationality and Vietnamese women who married Chinese men might be allowed to change their citizenship.[123] Beijing's non-assimilationist stance indicates its concerns over the ethnic mosaic at the edge of its territory and the possibility of Vietnamese demanding favorable treatment if they became an ethnic minority with a significant population.

For cross-border marriages, the two countries agreed to adopt a "not banning but not encouraging" policy as long as the marriage was not illegal in the country where it was registered. More flexible regulations, however, were employed in the highlands. The two sides admitted that it was difficult to determine the citizenship of those considered "ethnic minorities" who constantly moved back and forth across the borderline; therefore, their nationality would be determined by residence at the time of registration. The provincial authorities instructed grassroots cadres to "respect the long-established social, cultural, and family connections between the Mèo, Mán, and Lô Lô people" dispersed along the border and to refrain from interfering in their marriage traditions, such as dowry and betrothal gifts.[124] The decision to differentiate border policy implementation with ethnic minorities and to selectively reduce the ambiguities in citizenship indicated a rather realist approach to state building at the border.

---

[122] "Nhanh chóng đập tan âm mưu gây rối của bọn phản động người Hoa ở Móng Cái [Quick smash of the disruptive plot of the Chinese reactionaries in Móng Cái]," March 1–7, 1957, in *SLDQ*, 55–56.

[123] The above section is based on UBHC KTTVB, "Trích Biên Bản Ghi Những Vấn Đề Biên Giới Được Trao Đổi Trong Cuộc Toạ Đàm Giữa Đại Biểu Các Tỉnh Cao Bằng, Lạng Sơn, Hải Ninh-Việt Nam Và Quảng Tây, Quảng Đông-Trung Quốc Họp Từ Ngày 6 Đến 9 Tháng 11 Năm 1956," 6. The historic survey team dispatched to the ethnic Việt populated islands in southern Guangxi emphasized the difference between "Vietnamese overseas" (*Yueqiao*) and "ethnic Việt" (*Yuezu*), citing the fact that the latter had lived in the region for 400 years. Zhang, "Zhong-Yue bianjie kuajing jiaowang yu Guangxi Jingzu kuaguo shenfen rentong," 108.

[124] The above section is based on UBHC KTTVB, "Trích Biên Bản Ghi Những Vấn Đề Biên Giới Được Trao Đổi Trong Cuộc Toạ Đàm Giữa Đại Biểu Các Tỉnh Cao Bằng, Lạng Sơn, Hải Ninh-Việt Nam Và Quảng Tây, Quảng Đông-Trung Quốc Họp Từ Ngày 6 Đến 9 Tháng 11 Năm 1956," 7.

Finally, the border provinces drafted a special legal procedure for border crossing by borderlanders who lived within a twenty-kilometer radius of the boundary. Heeding to the local population's subsistence, social, and schooling needs across the border, the two countries decided to "open" – which in reality meant to endorse the existing practice – more unpatrolled trails managed by civil cadres of the border towns instead of by border garrisons. Border residents who sought to cross the border for "legitimate reasons," such as paying homage to tombs, reuniting with relatives, or seeing a doctor, could apply for a temporary travel permit valid for three to six months. In principle, they were supposed to use official border crossings, but exceptions could be granted to people in remote towns.[125] In 1957, the police authorities of Guangxi decided to impose stricter restrictions on the migration of border residents, requiring that any requests to move into or out of the country be reviewed by county-level public security institutions and endorsed by the Vietnamese side. To reinforce the political hierarchy created by the revolution, however, "key members of reactionary secret societies, bandits, bullies, spies, former Nationalists still committed to counterrevolutionary positions, and criminals should not be permitted to migrate."[126] Through this selective blocking of cross-border flows, the two parties aimed to translate their nationwide revolutionary victories into increased authority at the border. It was, nonetheless, in the interests of the two governments to keep borders as passable "political membranes,"[127] given that neither of them was able to secure the basic livelihood of the borderlanders on their own.

Among all the measures to implement the agreement reached at the 1956 border provinces meeting, land swaps or transfers to eliminate cross-border farming received the most meticulous state attention, although enforcing a clear-cut line in the borderlands economy was easier said than done. During the scheduled land survey conducted by Guangxi and Guangdong in the frontier counties, provincial officials finally realized the scale of cross-border farming. According to a report from Guangxi to the Chinese Foreign Ministry, more than eight hundred households in the province, including a considerable number of Zhuang, Yao, Miao, Lo Lo, and Kinh ethnic minorities, farmed on the other side of the borderline. More importantly, except in a few commercially oriented towns such as Dongxing, people involved in cross-border agriculture depended on a good harvest in Vietnam for their survival.[128]

---

[125] The above section is based on ibid., 9.
[126] GZAR Gazetteers Office, *Guangxi tongzhi: gong'an zhi*, 693.
[127] Wilson and Donnan, "Nation, State and Identity at International Borders," 9.
[128] The above section is based on "Zhonggong Guangxi shengwei guanyu Guangxi Zhong-Yue bianjing shewai wenti ji chuli yijian [CPC Guangxi Provincial Committee on coping with foreign affairs at the Chinese-Vietnamese border]," circa 1956, no. 105-00440-02 (1), 36–37/ FMAPRC, cited in Zheng and Wang, *Xinan diqu haiwai yiminshi yanjiu*, 160.

In late 1956, Hanoi rescinded its original demand for overdue taxes from cross-border farming largely due to the bureaucratic hassle of figuring out the exact amount. The two sides agreed to levy agricultural taxes on cross-border farming starting in 1957 based on the rule of the country where the land was located.[129] In March 1957, Beijing decided not to press the borderlanders further on the issue of cross-border agriculture and instructed Guangdong to maintain the status quo of cross-border farming (except for plots that had already been swapped or returned). To take into account the border residents' livelihood needs, the border authorities of Guangdong could be more flexible in regulating mountain trails and activities such as grazing cattle and obtaining firewood across the border "so long as doing so [did] not jeopardize the interests of the Vietnamese people." Meanwhile, border counties were granted more discretion to solve cross-border issues through consultation with the local Vietnamese officials.[130] By the fall of 1959, Guangxi, which had more cross-border land ownership in Vietnam than vice versa, had handed over 5,019 *mu* of farmland to Vietnam, which, in return, transferred 922 *mu*. The two governments declared that the issue of cross-border farming had been mostly settled and confirmed the non-recognition policy toward the "wasteland" reclaimed by citizens across the border onwards.[131]

The changing attitudes of Beijing and Hanoi toward cross-border agriculture indicated the gap between policymaking and implementation at the political periphery. While local administrations became more capable of discovering and recording the cross-border movements of people and goods than before, be they considered legal or illegal, the state did not always end up containing these activities because severing the close-knit ties across the border was costly, both fiscally and politically. To compensate and secure alternative livelihoods for the borderlanders who quit cross-border farming could hurt the financial viability of the bureaucracy, while failure to do so would sap the

---

[129] "Guangdongsheng dui Guangdong he Haining liangsheng bianjing diqu yixie juti wenti de chuli yijian [CPC Committee of Guangdong's suggestion on how to solve the concrete problems between Guangdong and Hải Ninh]," circa 1959.

[130] "Guowuyuan jiu Guangdongsheng yu Yuenan guojing tudi wenti pishi Guangdongsheng renmin weiyuanhui [Instruction from State Council to Guangdong on cross-border farming between Guangdong and Vietnam]," March 28, 1957, in *GSBN 1957*, 199.

[131] GZAR Border Work Committee, "Bianjing gongzuo huitan jiben neirong de baogao [Report on the basic content of border work talks]," March 22, 1962, no. X50-3-81, 115/GZARA, cited in You, "Zhanhou Zhong-Yue ludi bianjie wenti de lishi kaocha ji zaisikao," 68. 1 *mu* = 1/15 hectare or about 666.67 m². "Zhonghua renmin gongheguo Guangxi Zhuangzu zizhiqu Jingxixian, Yuenan minzhu gongheguo Yuebeizizhiqu Gaopingsheng Chongqing, Heguang, Chalingxian: yijiao guojing tudi shanlin zhengshu [Jingxi County of PRC's GZAR and Trùng Khánh, Hà Quảng, and Trà Lĩnh Counties of DRV's Cao Bằng Province: certificate of transferring land across the border]," April 3, 1959, no. 5523, 13–17/UBHC KTTVB 1948–1976/NAVC III. This certificate contains the detailed records of the location, category (paddy field, dry land, forest, or orchard), size, and annual yield of the transferred plots.

political support of the state. Spontaneous border-crossing for livelihood and survival continued defying the ideational design of an airtight boundary. After Hanoi placed additional restrictions on people from outside the border region of Vietnam to attend markets in China in August 1957, the Chinese border police patrolling the Friendship Pass area detected approximately one hundred undocumented Vietnamese citizens each day who entered China through small mountain trails and traded without any permits. The number was only around ten before August.[132] As the Anti-Rightist Movement in 1957 purged alleged political opponents across China and the Great Leap Forward began in 1958, the reported cases of Chinese sneaking into Vietnam near Friendship Pass doubled from 132 in 1957 to 291 in the subsequent year (not including fugitives). Most border jumpers who were considered innocuous ordinary folk (*qunzhong*) were required to attend an education session on the government policy and then released, which was a rather weak deterrence against future attempts.[133]

The revolutionary states carefully designed an internationally coordinated project to extend their reach into the borderlands yet were pushed back by the realities on the ground. This illustrates the gap between the demanding tasks placed on border administrations and their limited ability to fulfill them. In the border region, the state had to pursue multiple objectives, including but not limited to foreign policy goals. It produced coercive institutions but had to promise prosperity – goals that could be at cross purposes in some cases. Guidelines for border inspection drafted by the Guangxi Military Region Command in October 1956 stipulated that the border garrison and police should

> enforce the border check rules and regulations while taking into consideration the long-existing customs between inhabitants of the two sides, the political awareness of the people, and the real situation in Vietnam. They needed to crush the enemy efficiently and to win the sincere support of the people at the same time. And overall, they had to strengthen the Sino-Vietnamese comradeship and consolidate border defense by striking a balance and making steady progress.[134]

Similarly, the resolution passed by the provincial meeting on border issues convened by Hải Ninh in November 1957 required the state apparatus and military units on the border to "educate" the border residents to raise "patriotism" and the "spirit of proletarian internationalism," to respect the laws of the two countries, to stay vigilant for border defense, and to promote solidarity with the people in the Chinese border region. Meanwhile, to address the historical state weakness at the border and late integration of northeastern

---

[132] Editing Committee of Gazetteer of Pingxiang City, *Pingxiang shizhi*, 377.
[133] Zeng, *YBJZ*, 141, 161.   [134] Ibid., 132.

borderlands into the postcolonial Vietnamese state, the provincial authorities emphasized the exigency of "building a solid mass base" for the government, military, militia, and police to implement policies, detect and suppress insurgents, and fight against smuggling and illegal border crossings.[135] Being part of the street-level bureaucracy dispatched to a remote, unfamiliar society that had historically resisted intrusion by the central state, border institutions were asked to be everything for everyone.

Conclusion: Cold War Comradeship and Joint State Building

In traditional narratives of Chinese-Vietnamese relations, the years immediately after the end of the Geneva Conference of 1954 witnessed the consolidation of the "lips and teeth relationship" between the two countries. Converging strategic interests eased the disatisfaction between the Chinese and Vietnamese leaders created by their disagreement in Geneva over ceasefire terms. Perceiving a threat from the American-sponsored SEATO, Beijing "viewed the DRV as the keystone of their national security perimeter in Southeast Asia."[136] Meanwhile, diplomatic support and economic assistance from China buttressed the DRV's reconstruction, although the backfiring of Vietnamese land reform led the WPV leaders to question the Maoist revolutionary model.[137] The border issues that eventually became the pretext for China's punitive invasion of the Vietnamese border provinces during the Third Indochina War appeared in this initial period to be a matter of relatively little significance.

Borderlands state building in the mid-1950s, however, epitomized a profound transformation in the nature of the Sino-Vietnamese frontier and in the characteristics of Chinese-Vietnamese relations. The border region underwent a "long" 1954 that underscored the interconnectedness between Indochina and Southern China. These spontaneous connections became increasingly intolerable to the two centralizing states, which were determined to launch socialist revolutions to obliterate whatever was deemed to be feudal, market-driven, and outward-oriented – the causes of the two societies' impuissance against imperialism and colonialism. With the end of the First Indochina War, the border transformed from a place where the two states could experiment with ways to monitor cross-border activities to a strict national border. The two states discouraged mobility on the part of the borderlanders in order to build an

---

[135] "Hội nghị cán bộ của Tỉnh ủy Hải Ninh bàn công tác vùng biên giới [Cadres meeting of Hải Ninh Provincial Party Committee to discuss border works]," November 23–24, 1957, in *SLDQ*, 66–67.
[136] Duiker, *China and Vietnam*, 36.
[137] Zhai, *China and the Vietnam Wars*, 69–91; Womack, *China and Vietnam*, 164–71.

inward-oriented, socialist society on their respective sides while preventing permitted cross-border movements from hindering their carefully forged communist partnership.

Under the veneer of inter-party bonds between the CPC and the WPV, the two socialist countries began to interact as modern states in making boundaries and strengthening border institutions. The period from 1954 to 1957 witnessed their mutual endeavors to adjust their revolutionary strategies to the everyday statecraft by, in the words of James Scott, "seeing like a state" in the border region.[138] The transnational commercial and social ties that had accelerated the two revolutionary parties' path to power became obstructive to the clear definition and effective enforcement of state authorities. The two states launched large-scale authoritarian plans that did violence to the complex interdependencies on the frontier that were not and could not be fully comprehended by state institutions that pursued uniformity. In the end, sources reveal a border that served to bind states together rather than set them at odds.

That the PRC and the DRV had a similar political system and trajectory of social revolution apparently worked to the advantage of the two centralizing states at the border. On the one hand, the Cold War geopoliticized the border region and led the two communist countries to cooperate in guarding against any potential subversion. On the other hand, addressing the ambiguity at the border was essential to a socialist country that strived to be more "centralized, bureaucratic and mass-incorporating" with "enhanced great-power potential in the international arena."[139] Located between two newly established communist governments, the Sino-Vietnamese border was subject to parallel state schemes to increase institutional presence, strength, and coherency, which often took the shape of bilaterally coordinated efforts to remold the murky "soft" boundary into a clearly defined "hard" one. While border making also occurred in other border provinces of the two countries, and in all postcolonial states more broadly, what distinguished the China-Vietnam border was a distinct international dimension of state building in the form of the localization of Cold War partnership. This joint state-building project made it increasingly difficult for the local residents to escape or evade the state, due to collaborative measures introduced by the two communist states to make the borderlanders' daily lives more visible, trackable, and exploitable.

This, however, does not indicate a linear process toward a stronger state at the border. Instead, the state had to strike a balance between the construction of socialism and political pragmatism. This dilemma was often complicated by cultural nationalism, the presence of disputed areas, the prevalence of local hierarchies, and the inconsistency of central authority. Moreover, limits to the

---

[138] Scott, *Seeing Like a State*.   [139] Skocpol, *States and Social Revolutions*, 41.

Conclusion: Cold War Comradeship and Joint State Building 117

reach of the state at the border were in no small part due to both different priorities and gaps of available resources between the political center and the local state. This problem was especially severe in China, where the southwestern border was a distant corner of the country. The structural and geographical location of the local state at the border meant that it sometimes was more prone to the challenge of being "asked to be all things to all people" than with inland officials.[140] It had to deal with international affairs on a daily basis yet did not always have the organizational complexity, cultural expertise, or fiscal capability to carry out a coherent foreign policy. It was not an uncommon belief among local officials that pursuing foreign policy objectives diverted resources from programs that contributed more directly to socialist transformation. Furthermore, the conflation of the Communist Party with the administrative state led to the "essential indivisibility of ideology, civil administration and national defence" and to conflicts among the goals of the three spheres.[141]

---

[140] Remick, *Building Local States*, 6.
[141] Whitson and Huang, *The Chinese High Command*, 519.

3 Negotiated State Building (1958–1964)*

Chen Shiguang and his wife (who left no name on the government record) raised four children in Daxin County of Guangxi, bordering Cao Bằng. At the beginning of the 1960s, woes hit this poor peasant family as Chen fell into chronic illness and his wife was injured. With their compromised physical capabilities, the couple failed to earn enough "working credits" – therefore enough food – by farming their unit of the people's commune. Facing starvation, the couple sent a ten-year-old daughter away for "adoption" in a neighboring county.[1] Not an uncommon practice in rural areas, the "adopted daughter" typically became a child bride for the family that adopted her; hence the Marriage Law of the PRC promulgated in 1950 banned this age-old custom for its violation of women's rights.[2] The couple then separated, with the three remaining children living with the wife. To support the children by herself, she had to spend more time foraging for food in the forests than in collective farming. The commune cadres cited this as evidence of her "laziness" and refused to allocate her emergency food. Still unable to make ends meet, she had to send another four-year-old daughter to a Vietnamese family across the border for "adoption" in April 1961.[3]

This "adoption," although it robbed girls of their agency, was but one aspect of long existing cross-border mutual assistance networks, which enabled borderlanders to survive economic adversity. Such practices became an issue of great concern for the Chinese government when emigration was involved, not only because it diminished the labor force but also because it exposed the

---

* A few paragraphs on smuggling in this chapter have been developed from my earlier publication "The Mountain Is High, and the Emperor Is Far Away: States and Smuggling Networks at the Sino-Vietnamese Border." Copyright © 2018 Institute for Far Eastern Studies, Kyungnam University. This article first appeared in *Asian Perspective* 42, no. 4 (October–December 2018). Published with permission by Johns Hopkins University Press.

[1] CPC Daxin County Committee, "Guanyu jiejue bianmin liu-Yue gongzuo qingkuang baogao [Report on resolving the issue of border residents fleeing to Vietnam]," June 13, 1961, no. 1-36-13-6, 19/CZMA.

[2] Kang, "Editors Introduction," in *Women, Family and the Chinese Socialist State*, 10.

[3] CPC Daxin County Committee, "Guanyu jiejue bianmin liu-Yue gongzuo qingkuang baogao," 19.

fallacies of the Maoist model of radical agricultural collectivization to their Vietnamese comrades, who also began to push for collectivization to boost agricultural growth.[4] The Chinese borderlanders' defiance of the international boundary amid the struggle for survival, which was matched in turn by the state's efforts to curb emigration, points to the externalities of political radicalization during the years leading up to the Cultural Revolution and the escalation of the Vietnam War. Against the background of the aggressive collectivization movement, state building by the two revolutionary states at the border, like elsewhere in the two countries, became increasingly coercive. The border people nevertheless sought to take advantage of the porous international boundary to resist state incursion by voting with their feet, making the extension of state authority and its functions a highly contested process. This phenomenon of "negotiated state building" is the focus of this chapter.

Examining the macro-level and micro-level dynamics of cross-border interactions, I argue that the years from 1958 to the escalation of the Vietnam War in 1964 witnessed a widening gap between what the two centralizing governments sought to achieve at their shared border and the capabilities of the state organs stationed on the ground to pursue the diplomatic and state-building tasks assigned to them by the political centers. At stake was the eagerness of Beijing and Hanoi to translate their meticulously forged Cold War comradeship, as well an ambitious socialist agenda, into concrete cooperation projects at the border such as trade between state-run enterprises, Chinese aid to Vietnam, and cross-border transportation networks. Furthermore, the two leaderships hoped to find and accurately interpret any signs of each other's position in the unfolding Sino-Soviet split through the daily interactions between local officials across the border.

The disastrous Great Leap Forward (1958–1962), however, led China into an era of self-imposed trouble. It hindered the process of increasing strength and cohesion of the Chinese communist state in border areas and generated unpleasant political and economic spillover effects on Vietnam. Thus, the economic disasters and starvation caused by the Great Leap Forward, which promoted production at the expense of livelihood supports, drove an increasing number of unauthorized border crossings. This severely tested the ability of the Chinese and Vietnamese local officials to enforce their recently established border control institutions, making this a prominent issue between the two countries. More importantly, even as the radicalization of domestic politics in China since the late 1950s made Beijing's international strategy more aggressive, it actually hindered in turn the capability of the Chinese state to

---

[4] "BÁO CÁO Về nhiệm vụ kế hoạch ba năm (1958–1960) phát triển và cải tạo kinh tế quốc dân [Report of the Three-Year Plan (1958–1960) to develop and reform national economy]," n.d., in VKDTT 19 (1958), 466.

implement its assertive policies in the borderlands. The Vietnamese leaders, who initiated their own cooperative movement in 1958, perceived the emerging chaos in China as detrimental to the consolidation of the DRV state at the border. Indeed, encountering aggressive collectivization campaigns on the two sides of the border, the Chinese and Vietnamese border citizens, including the "ethnic minorities," joined hands in passively resisting the political authorities. Ironically, when the communist states attempted to extract resources from a fragmented society at the edge of their power, they risked creating social chaos and losing "face" in front of their revolutionary comrades.[5] This provided the borderlanders seeking alternative means of livelihoods through the maintenance of a soft boundary with considerable bargaining power against the political authorities.

The year 1958 was pivotal for the CPC and the WPV, as both aimed to rapidly transform their respective countries from an agrarian economy into a socialist society through industrialization and collectivization. With the recovery of the national economy under the First Five Year Plan and the silencing of political opponents during the Anti-Rightist Movement, Mao and the CPC leadership considered the conditions ripe for a Great Leap Forward in early 1958.[6] Mandatory agricultural collectivization to enhance grain production took the form of people's communes (*renmin gongshe*), which practically eliminated private ownership and constituted a major "leap" from earlier forms of collectivization such as mutual aid teams and producers' cooperatives.[7] Simultaneously productive and administrative units, the communes also extended governmental functions into rural China.[8] At the same time, Mao's vision of surpassing the United Kingdom and the United States in a short time in terms of steel production drove an industrial battle featuring "backyard steel furnaces."[9] As an "attempt at making a shortcut to communism and industrialism," this simultaneous revolution and development agenda, however, soon threw the Chinese economy into disarray and eventually caused the Great Famine (1959–1961).[10]

---

[5] David Yau-Fai Ho defines the sociological concept deriving from the East Asian cultural context as "the respectability and/or deference which a person can claim for him from others, by virtue of the relative position he occupies in his social network and the degree to which he is judged to have functioned adequately in that position as well as acceptably in his general conduct" ("On the Concept of Face," 883).

[6] For different interpretations of the origins of the Great Leap Forward, see Domenach, *The Origins of the Great Leap Forward*, 111–19; Bachman, *Bureaucracy, Economy, and Leadership in China*, 189–90; Chan, *Mao's Crusade*, 17–34.

[7] Ahn, "The Political Economy of the People's Commune in China," 632.

[8] O'Leary and Watson, "The Role of People's Commune in Rural Development in China," 593.

[9] Zhang, "Rural Industrialization in China," 64–66.

[10] Ahn, "The Political Economy of the People's Commune in China," 632.

In the meantime, the WPV leadership decided to take more concrete steps to construct a centrally planned socialist economy via the Three-Year Plan for Socialist Transformation and Development of Economy and Culture (Kế hoạch ba năm cải tạo xã hội chủ nghĩa và phát triển kinh tế - văn hoá 1958–1960), which was approved by the National Assembly in February 1958.[11] Despite debate over the pace of collectivization, the WPV Central Executive Committee resolved in November 1958 to abandon the gradualist approach of forming voluntary and intermittent labor-exchange groups and to complete low-level cooperatization in the form of "agricultural cooperatives" (hợp tác xã nông nghiệp) by the end of 1960.[12] Besides the desire to boost industrialization through agricultural collectivization, the party leadership was also worried about the reconcentration of land in the hands of the rich if rural living standards further crumbled. The reported high yields of Chinese agricultural collectivization and the ambitious targets of Soviet Union's Seven-Year Plan made the WPV leaders more optimistic about the faster implementation of socialism.[13]

The shifting directions of the domestic politics of China and Vietnam were intertwined with the reorientation of their foreign policies, both of which moved toward a more confrontational stance against the great powers. To halt "the chronic decline of the revolutionary vigor" and to mobilize the Chinese people's support of the Great Leap Forward, Mao decided to shell Jinmen (Quemoy) and harden the PRC's policy toward Taiwan.[14] The leap, on the other hand, also deepened the divergence between the Soviet Union and China. Khrushchev's criticism of the people's communes not only indicated Sino-Soviet disagreements over the correct path for socialist development but also increased Mao's resolve to challenge Moscow publicly both in domestic policies and foreign strategies.[15] For the WPV leadership, the domestic socialist transformation served the paramount goal of a forceful unification of Vietnam. Saigon's suppression of the opposition since 1954 threatened the survival of the communist movement in the South, but the popular discontent against Ngô Đình Diệm also created an auspicious revolutionary condition.[16] Morevover, passive peasant resistance to the rapidly unleashed collectivization

---

[11] "BÁO CÁO Về nhiệm vụ kế hoạch ba năm (1958–1960) phát triển và cải tạo kinh tế quốc dân," 451–524.
[12] Nguyen, Hanoi's War, 40.
[13] The above portion is based on Kerkvliet, The Power of Everyday Politics, 67–69; alse see Wiegersma, Vietnam: Peasant Land, Peasant Revolution, 147.
[14] Chen, Mao's China and the Cold War, 174.
[15] Shen and Xia, "The Great Leap Forward, the People's Commune and the Sino-Soviet Split," 878–79. Lorenz Lüthi argues that the transformation of Mao's preference from "Bureaucratic Stalinism" to "Revolutionary Stalinism" in domestic programs led to an anti-Soviet stance in other policy areas (The Sino-Soviet Split, 80).
[16] Duiker, The Communist Road to Power in Vietnam, 200.

intensified the factional struggles between the "North-firsters," who wanted to concentrate resources on state building in the DRV, and the "South-firsters," who urged for "reunification through war." Because the "North-firsters" such as Phạm Văn Đồng and Võ Nguyên Giáp attempted, yet failed, to bring about a successful socialist revolution in the North, Lê Duẩn and Lê Đức Thọ managed to usurp power and gear the country toward war preparation in 1959, believing that launching a war against the South "could provide the rallying cry that the Party needed to reinvigorate the masses and bolster its position within the DRV."[17]

The Sino-Soviet split and Hanoi's preparation for a war of reunification had complicated implications for the Sino-Vietnamese relations. Mao's post-1958 aspiration to be the leader of the world national liberation movements did not bring about Beijing's support of the DRV's position on armed struggle in the South at least until 1960.[18] Meanwhile, Hanoi, which could not afford to alienate either Moscow or Beijing, strived to avoid being trapped in the schism between them. Indeed, driven by its reliance on the unity of the Soviet-led socialist bloc for attaining international support and assuaging factional conflicts between the "moderates" and the "militants" within the WPV leaders, Hanoi attempted to mend the breach between Beijing and Moscow. Not until Khrushchev took a clearer stance on peaceful coexistence with the United States at the Geneva Conference on Laos and after the Cuban Missile Crisis in 1962 did the WPV distance itself from Moscow's foreign policy line.[19] Converging Sino-Vietnamese interests in foreign strategies led to Beijing's "general security commitments" to Hanoi in late 1962 and early 1963. By playing up the external threats, Mao also sought to strengthen the dynamics of continuous revolution and to regain the upper hand over other party leaders he deemed as "revisionists" after the recession caused by the Great Leap Forward undermined his authority.[20] Despite frequent consultations between Hanoi and Beijing regarding domestic and foreign policies, however, the two countries chose not to form a "military alliance to the exclusion of the Soviet Union."[21]

The closer political and military collaboration between the PRC and DRV made their shared border an even more important area of state intervention than before. State building at the borderlands as a result became increasingly convoluted, however, due to the intertwined effects of high-level strategic calculations and local dynamics. The Chinese and Vietnamese states sought

---

[17] Nguyen, *Hanoi's War*, 42–43. [18] Zhai, *China and the Vietnam Wars*, 82–83.
[19] Ibid., 86–91; the information on the "moderates" and the "militants" is based on Asselin, *Hanoi's Road to the Vietnam War*, 77–86.
[20] The sentences above are based on Chen, *Mao's China and the Cold War*, 207, 210–11.
[21] Ang, *Vietnamese Communists' Relations with China and the Second Indochina Conflicts*, 213.

to extend their reach to the outlying society through infrastructure building and to tame the cross-border shadow economy against the backdrop of radical collectivization. The borderlanders in turn managed to bargain with the political authorities during the period of economic difficulties by taking advantage of the delicate socialist partnership between Beijing and Hanoi.

Performing the Socialist Partnership: Expanding International Cooperation at the Border

Thanks to the period of joint state building by Chinese and Vietnamese communists after the end of the First Indochina War, the two states extended their reach and expanded both the size and complexity of state institutions at their shared boundary by the late 1950s, which allowed them to perform new tasks. With the Guangxi-Vietnam railway open to traffic in 1955 and the French-built Yunnan-Vietnam rail line restored in 1957, the border was integrated into a modern transportation system that was beyond the experience of many frontiers elsewhere in Asia, even if the volume of the border economy by itself did not necessitate these rail linkages. Moreover, the state-run enterprises of the two countries established their presence at the official border crossings to manage international trade. George Gavrilis divides the function of the state at the border into "positional and administrative tasks," which include "the actual delimitation and demarcation of the boundary on the ground," on one hand, and the regulation of legal border crossing, crackdown of smuggling, and extraction of customs duties, on the other.[22] In the case of the Sino-Vietnamese border, the two central authorities pursued goals beyond undertaking such tasks when they created these institutional foundations. Specifically, Beijing and Hanoi sought to reap the benefits of a friendly border to promote their respective ambitious socioeconomic plans that were designed to transform agrarian society toward an industrialized one.

For centuries, the forbidding topography of southwestern China (especially the Yunnan-Guizhou Plateau) had rendered opening domestic roads that directly connected the area with the coastal provinces a costly option. Traders, therefore, developed efficient networks that moved goods and people between these geographically separated places by way of Indochina. The central governments recognized the importance of these routes. In 1930, the French and ROC governments signed the Pact on the Relations between Vietnam and Border Provinces of China, which entered into force in 1935 and stipulated that ordinary merchandise going through Vietnam enjoyed a favorable tariff rate of 1 percent and strategic goods shipped by the Chinese government such

---

[22] Gavrilis, *The Dynamics of Interstate Boundaries*, 3.

as weapons and ore were exempted from customs duties.[23] Whereas the Sino-French conflicts in the late nineteenth century, the Second World War, and the First Indochina War had bound infrastructure building at the borderlands to military needs, by the late 1950s the modern transport system across the Sino-Vietnamese border began to serve more economic purposes as a result of the increasing intra-bloc trade among socialist countries and the accelerated domestic economic integration in China and Vietnam.

The connections between the Chinese and Vietnamese transportation systems were grafted onto the organic centuries-long trade routes over land and the sea but business itself became increasingly nationalized to serve the centrally planned economy. In January 1958, the PRC and DRV signed an agreement covering the transport of Chinese domestic goods to and from Yunnan by way of Vietnam. Agricultural products from Yunnan such as rice, brown sugar, and tobacco would enter Vietnam through the Yunnan-Vietnam Railway and then either return to China overland on the Guangxi-Vietnam Railway at Pingxiang or arrive at the port of Haiphong to be shipped back to Guangzhou or other Chinese coastal cities. Industrial products from other parts of China could be transported to Yunnan by taking the opposite direction of these routes.[24] Although charged a Vietnamese domestic shipping fee, China was able to facilitate the movement of goods between its landlocked southwestern frontier and the wealthier coastal provinces at a lower cost and faster speed than conveying the materials by its own domestic transport system.[25] Until the opening of Yunnan-Guizhou Railway in 1966, the Yunnan-Vietnam Line was the only railroad that connected the mountainous province with the outside world.[26]

The long-existent cross-border transportation networks were revived yet nationalized by the two communist governments to strengthen "control of both society and the domestic economy."[27] Typically, the diminishment of state power at the outlying territories enabled "the development of trans-boundary regions, many of which may reflect a form of spatial or social transition from one core area to another."[28] As a consequence, integration within these transition zones, such as road networks, was often stronger than

---

[23] "Zhong-Fa guiding Yuenan ji Zhongguo biansheng guanxi zhuantiao," 109–10.

[24] "Guanyu Zhonghua renmin gongheguo wuzi zai Yuenan minzhu gongheguo guojing yunshu de yidingshu shishi xize [Rules of implementation of the agreement between PRC and DRV on transporting Chinese materials through Vietnam]," January 1958, no. 290-1-105-43~51, 48–50/ GDPA. The transit transportation went through Pingxiang (in Guangxi), Đồng Đăng (in Lạng Sơn), Hanoi, Lào Cai (in Lào Cai), and Hekou (in Yunnan) from east to west. The cross-border transportation for this purpose mostly stopped after 1964 following the escalation of the Vietnam War.

[25] GZAR Gazetteers Office, *Guangxi tongzhi: haiguan zhi*, 187. [26] Mei, "Tiedaobing lishi."

[27] Chandler, *Institutions of Isolation*, 3. [28] Newman, "On Borders and Power," 18.

the connections between the border provinces and other parts of their home country. In a period of relatively amicable bilateral relations, the central governments did not necessarily perceive integration across the border as dangerously centrifugal but actively derived benefits from it, especially when the cross-border links such as the railway were in the full control of the state.

Closer connections between the transportation systems helped translate the political will for a stronger socialist fraternity between Beijing and Hanoi into frequent and institutionalized communications between state apparatuses on the ground, although the local officials often cared more about getting material things done than promoting the Sino-Vietnamese partnership. From 1957 on, the Vietnamese Ministry of Transportation, the Railway Bureau of Liuzhou (Guangxi), and the Railway Bureau of Kunming (Yunnan) formed a joint committee to meet annually in China and Vietnam alternately, where members exchanged annual cargo plans, set import and export goals, and settled charges and payments. Interestingly, the two countries had to devote significant time to improving liaison between the Chinese and Vietnamese border stations at Pingxiang-Đồng Đăng and Hekou-Lào Cai, which were often criticized by the higher authorities for not completing relevant paperwork or lacking in cross-border coordination.[29]

Besides transportation overland, the shipping lines between Southern China and Vietnam, which had been a significant part of the maritime economy of the South China Sea, were restored under the socialist partnership. In mid-1958, the port authorities of Guangzhou and Haiphong met to improve communication, streamline loading processes, increase ship journeys, and complete sea route maps.[30] Showing deference to China has always been an expedient path for Vietnam to appease the northern power while maintaining autonomy.[31] This could explain why the Vietnamese promised to grant preferential treatment to Chinese ships vis-à-vis other Soviet bloc vessels in the port – though the Vietnamese were no doubt equally driven by the desire to increase exports

---

[29] Bộ Giao thông vận tải hợp tác quốc tế [Department of International Cooperation of Ministry of Transportation of DRV], "Báo cáo về hôi nghị ủy ban liên hợp đường sắt biên giới Việt-Trung lần thư 7 họp tại Hà Nội từ ngày 2/3 đến 9/3/1964 [Report of the 7th meeting of the Vietnamese-Chinese joint border railway commitee in Hanoi from 2–9 March 1964]," March 1964, no. 1084, 2/BGV/NAVC III; Bộ Giao thông vận tải tổng cục đường sắt [Directorate of Railway of Ministry of Transportation], "Nghị định thư, báo cáo về hội nghị ủy ban liên hợp đường sắt biên giới Việt-Trung lần thứ 6 họp tại Côn-Minh [Agreement and report on the 6th meeting of the Vietnamese-Chinese joint border railway committee in Kunming]," March 13, 1963, no. 7965, 1–8/PTTg/NAVC III.

[30] Bộ Giao thông vận tải hợp tác quốc tế, "Hội đồng xếp hàng hóa giữa cục quản lý hải vân khu Quảng châu Trung Quốc và cảng Hải Phòng năm 1958 [Confirmation of the meeting between the management office of the Guangzhou harbor and the Haiphong port in 1958]," July 1, 1958, no. 1025, 1–8/BGV/NAVC III.

[31] Elliott, *Changing Worlds*, 258; Womack, *China and Vietnam*, 84.

via coastal trade.³² At least in the years immediately after the meeting, this promise was not hollow. Moreover, the Vietnamese Ministry of Transportation and the Guangdong Provincial Department of Shipping met every half a year to improve the efficiency of transit transportation, primarily seeking to reduce the loss of Chinese goods during transit and to deal with overstocked cargos in Haiphong.³³

To "perform" the Chinese-Vietnamese socialist comradeship before ordinary border dwellers, the two countries decided to build a new bridge on the Beilun/Ka Long River to connect the Chinese border town of Dongxing with Vietnam's Móng Cái in place of the poorly maintained iron bridge originally funded by the Qing court and completed by the French in 1900. To indigenize the intimate political relations between Beijing and Hanoi, a committee composed of Chinese and Vietnamese local officials and engineers hired workers from both countries to construct the project, even though language barriers hindered the timely completion of the work. To mobilize the Chinese and Vietnamese workers, the joint committee turned to "socialist competition," a widely practiced method employed in the socialist bloc among state enterprises or individuals to encourage the rapid accomplishment of economic tasks.³⁴ When the bridge opened to traffic and pedestrians in May 1958, the two sides replaced a legacy of colonialism with a symbol of socialist internationalism. Furthermore, by building border inspection stations at the two bridgeheads, the two states drew a more distinct line between legal and illegal border-crossings. Only people and goods with valid documents and endorsements were able to cross the bridge, whereas those engaged in border jumping, smuggling, and trading contraband took unpatrolled mountains passes or crossed the river at night.

The goals of such measures, then, were not only to create more effective collaborations between the state-run firms of the two countries but to shore up the desired socialist monopoly over cross-border trade. As discussed in Chapter 2, soon after the First Indochina War ended, Beijing and Hanoi waged a socialist war on private cross-border commerce by gradually closing small-scale border markets and replacing them with international trade operated by either the central governments or provincial trade companies. This effort continued into the late 1950s. In February 1958, a Vietnamese trade delegation

---

[32] Bộ Giao thông vận tải hợp tác quốc tế, "Hội đồng xếp hàng hóa giữa cục quản lý hải vân khu Quảng châu Trung Quốc và cảng Hải Phòng năm 1958," 4.

[33] Guangdong Provincial Department of Shipping, "Guanyu Zhong-Yue shuangfang disanci zhongzhuan lihui de baogao [Report of the third meeting between China and Vietnam on transit transportation]," August 16, 1960, no. 220-226-054~057, 1–4/GDPA.

[34] PRC Ministry of Foreign Trade, "Dongxing-Mangjie Beilunhe daqiao jianqiao weiyuanhui zongjie baogao [Summary report of the construction committee of Dongxing-Móng Cái Beilun River bridge]," June 4, 1958, no. 221-1-12-171~182, 3–4/GDPA.

visited Beijing, where the two governments agreed to "take efforts to ban merchants on the respective side from pariticipating in the border trade." To save its reserves of Chinese currency, the Vietnamese delegation proposed to reduce the allowance for currency exchange at the small-scale border trade markets from ten yuan RMB or the Vietnamese equivalent to only one yuan.[35]

To implement the two governments' decision to limit the volume of small-scale border trade, representatives of the Chinese and Vietnamese border provinces met in June to make necessary revisions to the protocol on small-scale border trade signed in 1955. The two sides decided to remove goods that fell under state purchase and marketing monopoly from the list of items allowed for small-scale border trade and shut down two pairs of border markets between Guangxi and Lạng Sơn. More importantly, the border provinces agreed to set up state-run local products stores at major border crossings to purchase goods from residents and sell basic daily necessities to "restrict the number of people having to enter and exit the border [for trade]" so that "the bad elements would not take advantage of the opportunities to sabotage public security and the people would have a peace of mind to participate in laboring instead of wasting time in trade."[36]

At the same time, state-run companies between the Chinese and Vietnamese border provinces entered into formal trade deals, which, nevertheless, not only fell short of meeting the constantly changing local demand but also raised the cost of transactions. The yearly or quarterly contracts and settlements through governmental bank accounts left little flexibility. The end result was to encourage, rather than eliminate, smugglers who could profit by offering better trade terms. The Vietnamese, therefore, proposed that the local state-run companies barter at border crossings such as the Dongxing-Móng Cái area to secure supplies for the mountainous areas in Vietnam.[37] By endorsing the proposal,

---

[35] The above information on the visit is based on "Báo cáo của KTTTB về biên bản cuộc hội đàm về buôn bán biên giới giữa đại biểu nước Việt-nam dân-chủ Cộng-hòa với đại biểu nước Cộng-hòa nhân-dân Trung-hoa [Report by the Northwestern Autonomous Region: Meeting between the DRV and the PRC delegates on border trade]," February 25, 1958, no. 5335/UBHC KTTTB/NAVC III.

[36] "Báo cáo của Bộ ngoại thương tóm tắt cuộc đàm phán về mậu dịch tiểu ngạch trong khu vực biên giới Việt-Trung [Report of the Ministry of Foreign Trade: Summary of the negotiation on Sino-Vietnamese small-scale border trade]," June 28, 1958, no. 5368/UBHC KTTTB/NAVC III.

[37] Foreign Trade Bureau of Guangdong, "Zhong-Yue difang maoyi zhixing qingkuang ji 1959 nian kongzhishu yijian [Implementation of local Sino-Vietnamese trade and opinion on the quota for 1959]," October 10, 1958, no. 302-1-273-154~155, 2/GDPA; Chinese Delegation of Sino-Vietnamese Trade Negotiation, "Guanyu wubanian Zhong-Yue difang bianjing xiao'e maoyi tanpan gongzuo jieshu baogao [Report on the completion of negotiation over Chinese-Vietnamese local and small-scale border trade of 1958]," June 2, 1958, no. 296-1-100-85, 2/GDPA.

the two sides hoped that a more flexible barter system would help the state-run companies to outstrip the organized smugglers.

The Vietnamese government was highly active in shaping the negotiation agenda on state-sponsored cross-border trade. As Brantly Womack points out, big nation–small country relations do not always work to the disadvantage of the latter largely because the smaller power has "a more acute sense of the risks and opportunities offered by the relationship."[38] For the Vietnamese, the border trade with China generated a significant amount of state revenue and helped stabilize a planned economy in the border region. In December 1958, the Vietnamese National Bank, citing very promising statistics that indicated the revenue of Vietnamese companies from the border trade with China had risen by a factor of six from 1956 to 1957, decided to increase loans to national and local state-firms to stimulate their investment in cross-border trade.[39] To coordinate exports to China, Hanoi decided to establish a Department of Foreign Trade in KTTVB in September 1959. Besides working out trade deals with Guangxi, the most important tasks of the department were to concoct procurement plans, boost the production of goods for export, and sign purchase contracts with local farms and companies.[40]

From the late 1950s to the escalation of the Vietnam War in 1964, then, Beijing and Hanoi consistently expanded their cooperation at the border on issues such as defense, trade, transportation, and resource extraction, motivated by a shared cause of anti-imperialism and a common goal of strengthening their socialist economies. At the same time, the two central authorities took considerable effort to "perform" a subtle friendship at the border to overcome the problematic legacy of the Chinese empire claiming suzerain authority over the adjacent states, which, by the mid-twentieth century, had been delegitimized by the Westphalian notion of sovereign equality and the decolonization movement.

Comradeship Strained: Radicalization of Chinese Politics and Its Implications

With the dramatic inauguration of the Great Leap Forward and Mao's increasing dissatisfaction with the Soviet development model, Beijing invested more heavily in its relations with the socialist countries. Its state apparatus at the border with Vietnam, which interacted with their comrades on a daily basis,

---

[38] Womack, *China and Vietnam*, 1.
[39] Ngân hàng Quốc gia Việt Nam, "Thông tư 195-VP/PC năm 1958 về biện pháp cho vay Mậu dịch xuất nhập khẩu biên giới Việt-Trung."
[40] Bộ Ngoại thương, "Nghị định 257-BNT/TCCB năm 1959 về việc thành lập Sở Ngoại thương Khu tự trị Việt Bắc."

nevertheless lacked sufficient institutional complexity and financial prowess to embrace the central government's agenda. In October 1958, the CPC Central Committee decided to strengthen economic and technical assistance to "the underdeveloped brotherly countries within the socialist bloc and peaceful neutral countries that have gained national independence or are striving for it in Asia and Africa."[41] Behind the stated goals of promoting intra-bloc solidarity, building ties with postcolonial countries, and furthering the anti-imperialist cause, an undercurrent of competing with the Soviet Union for leadership of the Third World was palpable. Uncomfortable with the lack of attentiveness within the bureaucracy to "internationalist obligations" amid intense domestic mass mobilization, the central government demanded that all institutions and provinces responsible for foreign aid "should display the spirit of the Great Leap Forward and complete their foreign aid tasks meticulously, punctually, instead of setting the work aside or procrastinating with excuses of the exigency of domestic projects, because tiny slips in foreign aid projects might lead to damaging political consequences."[42] As such instructions trickled down the bureaucratic ladder, however, it became obvious that grassroots institutions were often neither willing nor capable of placing the fulfillment of internationalist duties at the top of their political agenda.

For the Chinese local import-export companies, for instance, the fact that international trade was primarily meant to serve strategic needs turned out to be burdensome, especially during the Great Famine. Ideally, the deals between the Chinese and Vietnamese state-run companies should have struck a trade balance and consolidated the autarkic socialist economy in both countries. In reality, the Chinese central government, in the hope of helping the Vietnamese stablize socialism, instructed its local companies to accept piled-up goods from Vietnam without quality control. The Foreign Trade Bureau of Guangdong complained in 1959 that their local affiliated trade firms were capable of neither selling these Vietnamese products in China due to poor quality or lack of demand nor purchasing enough domestic goods to trade with Vietnam. Besides slipping into deficit, the Chinese enterprises encountered other awkward situations such as being asked by their Vietnamese counterparts to trade commodities that were only exportable under contract between the central governments, such as rice, rubber, and coconut oil.[43]

---

[41] "Zhongyang pizhuan Chen Yi tongzhi he Li Fuchun tongzhi 'guanyu jiaqiang duiwai jingji, jishu yuanzhu gongzuo lingdao de qingshi baogao' [CPC Central Committee endorses and circulates comrades Chen Yi and Li Fuchun's 'report on strengthening leadership on foreign economic and technical assistance']," October 29, 1958, no. 1-34-17-13, 2/CZMA.

[42] The above portion is based on ibid., 1–2.

[43] Foreign Trade Bureau of Guangdong, "Jinnian lai Zhong-Yue difang guoying maoyi qingkuang [Situation of Sino-Vietnamese local trade in the recent years]," March 1959, no. 302-1-101-96~107, 99–104/GDPA.

Promoting the Sino-Vietnamese partnership, therefore, was expensive for the local state apparatus of China, which, unlike higher state organs, had to operate on a tighter budget. In August 1962, as Mao had retreated to the "second line" and pragmatists such as Liu Shaoqi and Deng Xiaoping took charge of the day-by-day direction of the state, the Ministry of Foreign Trade of the PRC admitted that while China should accommodate the demands of the DRV and North Korea in intergovernmental trade deals, trade at the border between local state-run companies needed to adhere to the principle of "mutual benefit and reciprocity." To avoid stretching thin national finances, the authorities of border provinces were called upon to tap resources within own provinces should they prefer to do their Korean or Vietnamese comrades a favor.[44]

The nationwide campaign to boost agricultural and industrial output in the Great Leap Forward also put an unprecedentedly heavy load on the cross-border railway, which was crucial for both the transit transportation between Yunnan and southeastern China through Vietnam and the delivery of Chinese aid to Vietnam. This was particularly the case for the Pingxiang Railway Station, which was responsible for unloading and reloading cargo between the Chinese standard-gauge rail and the Vietnamese narrow-gauge one. Both the volume of transit transportation and total freight numbers rocketed in 1958, doubling the figures for 1957. A backlog of untrans-loaded cargo began to pile up at Pingxiang station and continued into 1960 as the amount of transit transportation going through the port tripled from 1958 to 1960.[45]

Taking the rapid expansion of industry and the growth of agriculture as their paramount tasks, the cadres at the station devoted most of their labor to transloading materials shipped from Yunnan through the Vietnamese railway while delaying uploading cargoes of Chinese aid to Vietnamese trains. The Chinese Export Company of Complete Equipment Sets once complained that its aid packages to Vietnam were continuously held at the Pingxiang station where cargoes that had arrived in August 1959 were not shipped to Vietnam until early 1960. Although a cross-departmental committee was in place to accelerate the transportation of aid to Vietnam that had piled up at the station in the hope of minimizing negative political ramifications, the situation only improved after transit transportation dropped in late 1960 when Beijing put a halt to its inflexible government procurement policy in order to pull China out of the Great Famine.[46] Before the Great Leap faltered, the high volume of transit transportation for China caused similar stockpiling in Haiphong, which

---

[44] The above portion is based on PRC Ministry of Foreign Trade, "Guanyu tong Chaoxian, Yuenan bianjing difang maoyi wenti de qingshi baogao," 136.
[45] GZAR Gazetteers Office, *Guangxi tongzhi: haiguan zhi*, 180.   [46] Ibid., 180–81.

was responsible for trans-loading cargos between trains and vessels.[47] As in the case of deficits accumulated by local state-run trade companies, grassroots transport authorities also lacked the resources and infrastructure to prioritize the internationalist agenda in their daily operation, especially when the entire society was under immense pressure to boost production statistics.

As Beijing and Hanoi carefully fostered their Cold War partnership, the elephant in the room was the Sino-Soviet split. From late 1962 to mid-1963, Sino-Soviet relations quickly deteriorated due to Mao's decisive "ideological resurgence" after a brief post-Leap decline in power and the "Soviet-American nuclear rapprochement" that led to the Limited Nuclear Test Ban Treaty.[48] While initially worrying about the negative effects of the squabbles between Beijing and Moscow on the prospects for a Vietnamese unification war, the WPV leaders soon realized that they could appeal to China's support of their armed struggle against the South while maintaining Vietnamese autonomy by playing the Chinese and the Soviets off against each other.[49] In the delicate triangular relationship that emerged, Beijing was eager to understand Hanoi's position in ideological disputes, whereas Hanoi kept a close watch on the possibility of a truce between Moscow and Beijing and sought to exploit any opportunities offered by changes in Sino-Soviet relations. Due to ambiguities sometimes intentionally preserved by the leadership, the two sides had to sound out any slight signs of changes in the other side's position during their interactions.

The border passes and ports, where the Chinese and Vietnamese cadres met and interacted on a daily basis, became convenient sites of such grassroots-level intelligence collection. Right before Tết, the Vietnamese New Year, in 1963, Hanoi instructed cadres of the border regions to organize holiday parties to be attended by local Chinese officials and people, citing the necessity of "promoting solidarity between the peoples of the two nations."[50] As reported by the Chinese state-run freight shipping companies to their superior authorities, since early 1963 Chinese sailors and cadres who spent time in Haiphong, Hòn Gai, and Cẩm Phả – the destinations of Chinese cargo ships – encountered increasing inquiries from their Vietnamese counterparts on the status of Sino-Soviet relations. In these ports, Vietnamese and Chinese from a variety of social strata, ranging from Chinese sailors and Vietnamese dockworkers to ethnic Chinese pilots sent by the Vietnamese port authorities to Chinese vessels, intermingled. Vietnamese officials and captains of Chinese ships,

---

[47] Bộ Giao thông vận tải tổng cục đường sắt, "Nghị định thư, báo cáo về hội nghị ủy ban liên hợp đường sắt biên giới Việt-Trung lần thứ 6 họp tại Côn-Minh," 5.
[48] Lüthi, *The Sino-Soviet Split*, 246–47. [49] Nguyen, *Hanoi's War*, 48.
[50] PTTg, "Công văn của PTT v/v tổ chức vui chơi ở biên giới Việt-Trung nhân dịp Tết năm 1963 [Official dispatch on organizing celebration activities at the Sino-Vietnamese border for the New Year of 1963], January 10, 1963, no. 5672, 1/UBHC KTTVB 1948–1976/NAVC III.

who were typically party cadres, were able to meet and communicate on different occasions, such as during registrations, inspections, cargo work, and parties organized by the Vietnamese authorities. In April 1963, for instance, two Vietnamese policemen who were in charge of registering and inspecting a Chinese cargo ship in Haiphong asked for brochures on counter-revisionism that were published in Vietnamese.[51]

While Chinese cadres were rather outspoken about their anti-Soviet stance, the Vietnamese officials were more reticent about their views toward the ideological rifts between Beijing and Moscow.[52] In April 1963, the Foreign Office of Guangdong instructed crew members on the state-owned vessels outbound for Vietnam to embrace a more assertive propaganda line abroad. The office asked them to "take a proactive attitude towards the Vietnamese comrades by articulating our anti-modern revisionist stance based on published articles or presenting brochures as gifts instead of waiting for them to ask first" but to "avoid being regarded as imposing our opinion on them."[53] The sailors, who spent days and months on their ships, some of whom never received any formal education, obviously lacked the savvy to be part of the propaganda machine. In the same month, therefore, the Chinese Ministry of Transportation asked the Guangzhou Bureau of Maritime Transportation (GBMT) to hold "anti-revisionist study programs," in the hope of promoting political discipline among the sailors.[54] To the disappointment of local Chinese officials, the Chinese sailors often failed to sound out the views of their Vietnamese counterparts. Most Vietnamese they met and interacted with, especially those from official backgrounds, were far more active in obtaining Chinese publications on its foreign stance than voicing their own opinions on the Sino-Soviet split.[55] Their caution was a by-product of Hanoi's strategy of not openly taking sides in the ideological conflict between the two senior powers, thus leaving itself enough room for maneuver.

As the Vietnamese cadres were prone to dodge any inquiries, the Chinese tried to probe the Vietnamese stance in more subtle ways. The ethnic Chinese

---

[51] GBMT, "Guanyu hangxing Zhong-Yue xian chuanbo zai Yuenan gangkou qingkuang de fanying [Report on situations the vessels on the Sino-Vietnamese lane encountered in Vietnamese ports]," May 22, 1963, no. 290-1-136-52, 1/GDPA.
[52] For the Vietnamese media outlets' reaction to the Sino-Soviet split, see Chen, "Zhong-Su fenlie yu Yuenan Laodongdang dui guoji gongyun de renzhi he biaoda."
[53] Foreign Office of Guangdong, "Fu guanyu hangxing Zhong-Yue xian chuanbo zai Yuenan gangkou suo yudao yixie qingkuang baogao de yijian [Reply of the situation the vessels on Sino-Vietnamese lanes encountered in Vietnamese harbors]," April 8, 1963, 290-1-136-45, 1/GDPA.
[54] PRC Ministry of Transportation, "Guanyu hangxing Zhong-Yue xian chuanbo zai Yuenan gangkou yudao de yixie qingkuang [Report on the situation the vessels on Sino-Vietnamese lanes encountered in Vietnamese ports]," April 17, 1963, 290-1-136-44, 1/GDPA.
[55] Foreign Office of Guangdong, "Fu guanyu hangxing Zhong-Yue xian chuanbo zai Yuenan gangkou suo yudao yixie qingkuang baogao de yijian," 2.

in Vietnam turned out to be an important source of intelligence. In early 1963, for instance, an ethnic Chinese cadre in a Vietnamese state-owned freight forwarding company in Cẩm Phả told the captain of a Chinese ship that ordinary Vietnamese cadres were confused by the WPV leadership's decision of not expressing any opinions on anti-revisionism and that the WPV was organizing cadres with more than five years of party membership to study articles published by China and the Soviet Union.[56] In addition, Chinese cadres paid close attention to Vietnamese treatment of Soviet and Chinese vessels at the ports, trying to detect any signs of Soviet-Vietnamese fraternity. In late 1962, the Chinese cadres still believed that they "were well-attended and given preferential treatment," such as enjoying faster resupply and unloading or uploading of cargos.[57] During the first half of 1963, however, the Chinese vessels allegedly experienced longer time waiting for pilots outside the ports, were resupplied with low quality coal, and were declined support for ship repairs. Unable to confirm whether these unpleasant encounters were a result of mismanagement or deliberate arrangement by the Vietnamese authorities, the local Chinese state officials interpreted them as tacit Vietnamese distancing from the Chinese.[58] In the years leading up to the breakup of Sino-Soviet relations, the daily interactions between the Chinese and the Vietnamese at the border thus operated in a milieu of mutual observation and suspicion, which gave rise to overinterpretation of each other's actions.

Efforts by Vietnamese local officials to strike a balance between their treatment of Chinese and Soviet vessels mirrored Hanoi's intentionally ambiguous position in the Sino-Soviet debate over the correct line of the socialist movement. At the end of PRC President Liu Shaoqi's visit to Hanoi in May 1963, Hồ Chí Minh and Liu issued a joint communique that pledged the two parties' support of revolutionary struggles in the Third World and identified "revisionism, or rightist opportunism" as a dire threat to the revolutionary cause – without blaming the Soviets for posing such danger, singling out Yugoslavia instead. More importantly, Hồ Chí Minh emphasized in the communique that the unity between the Communist Party of the Soviet Union (CPSU) and the CPC, the two largest parties that bore the greatest

---

[56] GBMT, "Guanyu wo hangxing Zhong-Yue xian chuanbo zai Yuenan gangkou suo yudao de yixie qingkuang de baogao: diyiqi [On the situation our vessels on Sino-Vietnamese lanes encountered in Vietnamese ports, no. 1]," March 15, 1963, no. 290-1-136-67, 2/GDPA.

[57] China Ocean Shipping Co. Canton Branch, "Dui Yuenan xiangkuoda yuwo hangyun hezuo qingkuang de fanying [Reports on Vietnam wants to expand cooperation with us on maritime transportation]," November 8, 1962, no. 291-1-34-5~5, 1/GDPA.

[58] GBMT, "Guanyu hangxing Zhong-Yue xian chuanbo zai Yuenan gangkou qingkuang de fanying," 2–3.

responsibility in the world communist movement, was the pillar of the solidarity of the socialist bloc.[59]

In Summer 1963, it became evident that the divergence between Moscow and Beijing went beyond abstract ideological disagreements over the character of Marxism and had developed into a struggle for leadership of the world socialist revolution, with Mao coveting the "mantle of the chief Marxist-Leninist."[60] In June 1963, the CPC Central Committee published "The CPC's Proposal Concerning the General Line of the International Communist Movement," which sought to legitimize a more militant policy to promote world revolution and repudiate the possibility of "peaceful coexistence."[61] In July, a CPC delegation headed by Deng Xiaoping went to Moscow with the intention of "removing discord and strengthening unity." Yet the Chinese delegation leveled strident criticism at the Soviet positions on "peaceful transition," which Beijing deemed as "against Marxism-Leninism" and "the full, groundless denunciation of Stalin under the pretext of the so called 'struggle with the cult of personality.'"[62] The CPSU responded to the CPC with its "Open Letter of the Central Committee of the CPSU to All Party Organizations and to All Communists of the Soviet Union," which condemned the CPC's inimical actions and polemics in exacerbating tensions and declared the significance of "peaceful coexistence" between communist and capitalist countries "for averting a world thermonuclear catastrophe."[63] The hostility in China's position and the Soviet open letter made public the ideological rift that had thus far been kept mostly in private form.

The Vietnamese were eager to gauge the implications of the Moscow meeting to the palpable tensions between the CPSU and the CPC. When invited to take a tour on a Chinese ship staying in Haiphong in August 1963, a group of students from the Vietnamese University of Transportation asked the Chinese sailors to brief them on the result of the Moscow meeting, admitting that Vietnamese radio and newspapers covered little about it. They also told the Chinese that they had visited a Soviet ship and made the same

---

[59] State Council of the PRC, "Liu Shaoqi Zhuxi he Hu Zhiming Zhuxi lianhe shengming," 171–72.
[60] Radchenko, *Two Suns in the Heavens*, 25.
[61] "Guanyu gongchanzhuyi yundong zongluxian de jianyi [The CPC's proposal concerning the general line of the international communist movement]," *Renmin ribao*, June 14, 1963, 1.
[62] "Meeting of the Delegations of the Communist Party of the Soviet Union and the Chinese Communist Party, Moscow, 5–20 July 1963," July 8, 1963, History and Public Policy Program Digital Archive, SAPMO Barch JIV 2/207 698, 187–330, obtained by Vladislav Zubok and translated by Benjamin Aldrich-Moodie, http://digitalarchive.wilsoncenter.org/document/111237.
[63] "Open Letter of the Central Committee of the Communist Party of the Soviet Union to All Party Organizations and to All Communists of the Soviet Union," July 13, 1963, in CIA, *Daily Report, Foreign Radio Broadcasts*, Issue 135, BB-11.

request, yet the Soviet captain declined to comment. Tactfully blaming the Soviet Union for not letting Vietnam publish any articles or express opinions regarding the rift between Beijing and Moscow, the Vietnamese students told the Chinese crew members that they had to resort to radio programs in Vietnamese made by China or, for those who read Chinese, the *People's Daily*, to figure out the situation. Pandering to the Chinese, they reassured them that even though the WPV media outlets did not reprint Chinese publications that criticized the Soviet Union, the country nevertheless stood with China.[64]

As China's domestic socialist program grew increasingly utopian and its polemics with the Soviet Union escalated, both Chinese and Vietnamese local states at the border had to fulfill new functions. The border became a unique contact zone between grassroots cadres of the two states eager to receive and interpret signals of the changes in each political center's foreign strategy. The extent to which such intelligence reached the upper echelon of the state apparatus remains unknown. Nonetheless, the prominence of the Sino-Soviet split in the conversations between the local officials – as well as among those only remotely associated with the state, such as crew members – was a vivid example of how the Cold War politicized the mundane aspects of interactions between states at the border. The language and deportment of individuals, who could be largely uninformed about either Beijing or Hanoi's political stance, came under interpretation and overinterpretation by their counterparts. In addition, pressed by the national zeal to boost production during the Great Leap Forward, the local Chinese officials tended to prioritize not falling behind the "leap" over advancing internationalist obligations. Borderland state building was a negotiated process even viewed from within the bureaucracy. Without seeming to obstruct the tasks stipulated by the political center, the local state had to decide where to allocate their limited financial resources, personnel, and attention. In particular, at the turn of the 1960s, both the local Chinese and Vietnamese authorities were besieged by resurging cross-border ties caused by the devastating catastrophe of the Great Leap Forward.

The Socialist Borderlands during the Collectivization Campaigns

For Chinese and Vietnamese officials stationed in the border area, the paramount task in the late 1950s, as for cadres elsewhere in the two countries, was to make sure that the collectivization campaigns reached down into the far corners of their respective territories. The first round of the agricultural

---

[64] GBMT, "Wo hangxing Zhong-Yuexian chuanbo huibao zai Yuenan gangkou suoliaojiedao de qingkuang [Report by vessels on the Sino-Vietnamese lane on situations they find out in Vietnamese ports]," September 22, 1963, no. 290-1-136-60, 2–3/GDPA.

cooperatization movement in China in the mid-1950s had accomplished little in the border areas aside from deeply straining the relations between Han and the ethnic minorities. Facing grievances, disturbances, and even armed rebellion, Chinese leaders had been forced to adopt more moderate methods to extract grain due to concerns over the centrifugal tendencies of these places and the limited strength of the state there.[65] At the onset of the Great Leap Forward, the Chinese state made a more determined effort to enforce cooperatization, which further alienated the ethnic minorities and eventually caused an exodus of villagers into Vietnam. The border county authorities in Guangxi and Guangdong dispatched work teams in the spring of 1958 to organize villages, many of which were populated by ethnic minorities, into cooperatives, priming them for the Great Leap.[66] In August, Vietnam's agricultural cooperatization movement (*phong trào hợp tác hóa nông nghiệp*) reached the coastal Hải Ninh province, although Hanoi did not decide to push cooperatization into the northern mountainous region until November 1959.[67]

In March 1958, the Dongxing County People's Commune Committee dispatched several ethnic work groups to the hill villages neighboring Vietnam in the hope of recruiting the Yao people into the "advanced cooperatives" (*gaojishe*).[68] The "socialist" advanced cooperatives, in which private land ownership was essentially eliminated, developed from the lower-level "semi-socialist" agricultural producer cooperatives where land had been collectively farmed but each family retained ownership of land and farming tools.[69] Given the fact that the movement to create lower-level cooperatives in the mid-1950s either never reached some of the remote areas or soon disintegrated after initial organization efforts, any attempt to impose advanced cooperatives directly was doomed to encounter stiff resistance because it canceled the dividend payments for land and other materials brought into the collective, as was allowed under the lower-level cooperatives, and distributed income solely based on labor contributions.[70] At the same time, the work groups deplored the "backward" slash-and-burn agriculture they saw. This kind of "illegible agriculture" had been an essential element of the highland

---

[65] Wang, "Radical Agricultural Collectivization and Ethnic Rebellion," 281–82.
[66] Ethnic Work Group of Dongxing Autonomous County of Multiple Ethnicities, "Jianli Xikengshe zongjie [Summary of establishing communes in Xikeng village]," July 14, 1958, no. 1-2-84-17, 87/FDA.
[67] "Mở đầu phong trào hợp tác hoá trong ngành nông nghiệp ở tỉnh Hải Ninh và khu Hồng Quảng [Initiating the movement of cooperation in the core industry in Hải Ninh province and Hồng Quảng area]," August 1958, in *SLDQ*, 85–86; Hội đồng Chính phủ, "Nghị quyết về việc tiến hành hợp tác hóa nông nghiệp kết hợp hoàn thành cải cách dân chủ miền núi."
[68] Ethnic Work Group of Dongxing Autonomous County of Multiple Ethnicities, "Jianli Xikengshe zongjie," 86–91.
[69] Meisner, *Mao's China and After*, 143.
[70] Chinn, "Cooperative Farming in North China," 279.

way of life and the centuries-long tactics of the highlanders to evade the levy of the lowland state.[71] Villagers identified by the Chinese state as Yao lived in geographically scattered hillsides and often spoke diverse dialects. The international boundary, which played little to no role in the Yao people's lives, sometimes cut across the villages or the mountain trails that connected two neighboring settlements. The majority of the Yao villagers, as the ethnic work groups observed, made a living by reaping mountain products and selling them in Vietnam in exchange for grain while cultivating wet rice on small-sized mountain terraces.[72] The cooperative system that aimed to secure state extraction of grains based on excessively inflated production figures, therefore, would fundamentally alter their traditional livelihood.

Upon entering the villages, the work groups encountered an unfamiliar population highly adroit at escaping the state. Their original plan was to transplant a series of mobilization tactics to the highlands that had proven effective in typical Chinese villages, such as establishing a good rapport between cadres and the people by the "three togethers" – dining together, living together, and cultivating together with the peasants.[73] Harboring lingering suspicion toward the highland people, however, some cadres avoided living or dining with the villagers out of fear of being poisoned or plotted against.[74] The Yao villagers meanwhile resorted to their centuries-long strategies of circumventing state authorities. During the day, adult males who were typically heads of the households hid in the mountains to avoid meeting with the cadres while leaving at home only young kids and elderly women, who could equally evade the state by not understanding Hakka or Cantonese (two languages widely used in eastern Guangxi) or pretending ignorance of any ongoing socioeconomic campaigns.[75]

The cadres then tried to employ another mobilization strategy that had been tested as useful elsewhere – discovering sympathizers to the communist cause among the poor and converting them into the "backbone" (*gugan*), or pro-party political activists, of the political movement. Ideally, these activists would become the nucleus of the collectivization movement by voluntarily signing up to join the advanced cooperatives and other villagers would follow their lead. In reality, however, individuals deemed as politically credible by the

---

[71] Scott, *The Art of Not Being Governed*, 77–79.
[72] Ethnic Work Group of CPC Shiwanshan County Committee, "Minzu gongzuo zongjie [Summary of ethnic work]," April 12, 1958.
[73] Ibid.
[74] CPC Dongxing County Committee, "Xian jiang Banba Xikeng yaozu qunzhong taopao qingkuang baogao [Report of the situation of fleeing Yao people from Xikeng Village, Banba Town], August 24, 1958.
[75] Ethnic Work Group of Dongxing Autonomous County of Multiple Ethnicities, "Jianli Xikengshe zongjie," 88–91.

party cadres were usually the same people who got promoted to the status of "backbone" during the campaign to set up lower cooperatives in 1956. With already strained personal relations with the villagers due to their role in this earlier effort, these former "backbones" resisted appointment as the activists for the intensified cooperatization and expressed their grave concern of being "scolded by the masses again."[76]

The highlanders defiantly objected to the cooperatives and outspokenly expressed their distrust of political authorities, especially its local apparatus. A Yao villager told the ethnic work group that "we Yao people, unlike other ethnic groups, are not obliged to join the cooperatives .... We will only follow the policy if the ethnic Yao cadres dispatched by the central government visit our village. You came to the job half-prepared, so we do not trust you."[77] The highland villagers on the Sino-Vietnamese border were especially resentful of the cadres' demand to collectivize buffalo, which was prized as family property in the mountainous areas due to extensive use of animal power in wet rice plowing and thus also the most valuable commodity of Sino-Vietnamese cross-border trade.[78] What was beyond the knowledge of contemporary party cadres was the fact that buffalo were not merely means of production for the local population but served broader social functions, such as key goods in dowries and betrothal prices, and even as a safety net against financial disaster. A senior widow who lived on her own, yet was no longer physically capable of farming by herself, would spend a fortune on a buffalo and then rent it out to secure a stable annual income.[79]

In an aggressive collectivization campaign, the villagers' endeavors to maintain private ownership by hiding buffalo, not attending study meetings, or even threatening suicide achieved little under the resolute will of the cadres. With the collaboration of activists, the ethnic work groups targeted "diehard opponents of collectivization" who "needed to be trained, educated, and warned individually." The cadres coerced these antagonists to comply, threatening them with dire political consequences given the fact that they had committed "historical crimes" by voicing opposition against the party-state in previous political movements. After numerous meetings that combined persuasion and coercion, the work teams imposed cooperatives, and later communes, on the Yao communities in the border area and forced the villagers to accept inflated production goals simply to keep pace with other communes.[80] The people continued resisting

---

[76] Ibid., 89.   [77] Ibid., 90.
[78] For the role of buffalo in the border economy, see Turner, "Borderlands and Border Narratives."
[79] CPC Shiwanshan County Committee, "Tansanxiang Kenghuaicun yaozu de jiben qingkuang huibao [Report of the Yao people in Kenghuai village, Tansan Township]," March 16, 1958, no. 1-2-84-17, 82–85/FDA.
[80] The portion above is based on Ethnic Work Group of Dongxing Autonomous County of Multiple Ethnicities, "Jianli Xikengshe zongjie," 89–91.

the "last enclosure" of the valley state in a more passive way by procrastinating over any change toward intensive cultivation.[81] Thus, in the border town of Tansan, the party cadres reported the slow speed of production and the low morale of the population, with most villagers devoting little effort to plowing or fertilizing the land. One villager outrightly complained about the unrealistic production goal arbitrarily set for such a barren land.[82]

In lieu of openly defying the political authorities – especially the aggressive state procurement of grain – many villagers took advantage of the different pace of agricultural collectivization in the two countries and voted with their feet by fleeing to Vietnam, where living standards were higher and political pressure lighter – at least temporarily. A political and legal affairs work team dispatched in August 1958 to a Yao village with a population of 244 people in 44 households found that 14 families had moved to Vietnam right after the mobilization for collectivization started in May, and 5 more did so after being recruited into the cooperative. To the cadres' disappointment, the escaping villagers included not only former prisoners, rich peasants, and other "class enemies" but also the ostensible allies of the revolution such as poor peasants, heads of work brigades, members of security and defense committees, and militiamen. Many of those who fled to Vietnam also took their buffalo with them. The local officials lamented that, "even those we used to trust as active and credible are now running away." Rumors that the government was offering a bounty for capturing the organizer of the flight prompted his relatives to flee to Vietnam as well. Blaming the instigation of "class enemies," officials warned that the mass outflow of villagers would "not only have negative international influence but also hamper the consolidation of agricultural cooperatives and production activities and especially pose a danger to public order on the border."[83] Similarly, the police in Mubian County, which had a large Miao population, reported in September 1958 that after being notified of the forthcoming shift to communal dining, a Miao village of thirty-seven people moved to Vietnam overnight, building new homes across the border facing their previous hamlet in China. Determined to start a new life in Vietnam, they took with them all their buffalo and pigs as well as farming tools and hunting guns.[84]

---

[81] For an analysis of the "last enclosure," see Scott, *The Art of Not Being Governed*, 4–9.
[82] CPC Shiwanshan County Committee, "Tansanxiang Kenghuaicun yaozu de jiben qingkuang huibao."
[83] The above part is based on CPC Dongxing County Committee, "Xian jiang Banba Xikeng yaozu qunzhong taopao qingkuang baogao."
[84] Foreign Office of Guangxi, "Wochu yu Yuenan zhu Nannning lingshiguan jiaotan wenti jilubiao [Record of conversation between our office and DRV Consular in Nanning]," September 15, 1958, no. X50-2-266, 17/GZARA. I thank ECNURC for sharing this document with me.

These resettlements were aided by the survival of robust trans-boundary mutual help networks based on resilient kinship and cultural ties that had long enabled the border villagers to evade the monitoring of officials and to leverage policy differences in the neighboring countries. Upon entering Vietnam, for instance, they lived outside existing settlements to escape surveillance. When the Vietnamese police were about to patrol the area, the local villagers often divulged the information beforehand to the runaways from China – with whom the villagers often shared family ties – so the latter could temporarily take refuge in forests.[85] Meanwhile, whereas rural private markets in China were prohibited during the Great Leap Forward, private commerce in the northern mountainous area of Vietnam still came under less state scrutiny prior to the launch of the agricultural cooperatization movement there at the end of 1959. Borderlanders from Chinese communes near the international boundary thus could still exchange light industrial products for food in Vietnam. State authorities had little means of breaking up these mutual help networks beyond brushing them all into the same category as illicit smuggling.

Indigenous knowledge and trust-based relationships within the cross-border community also contributed to a resilient shadow economy. Intermediaries brokered deals between buyers from China and sellers in Vietnam and helped the two parties seal transactions using code words or secret signals that were hard to detect by the state apparatus. Chinese buyers could even temporarily store the purchased goods in Vietnamese border villages to avoid police patrols during the day and wait until the night to transport them back to China through only locally known mountains trails or along the Beilun/Ka Long River (Figure 3.1).[86] Thus, instead of subsiding under continuous government crack-downs, organized smuggling rings revived in a time of widening gaps in living standards and political pressures on the two sides of the border.

After the nationwide famine hit the border region in the winter of 1960, the outflow of refugees from China to Vietnam changed from an isolated phenomenon restricted to the ethnic minority–populated mountainous areas into a widespread one along the border. Government procurement based on exaggerated harvest statistics dramatically reduced the food quotas in the people's communes and resulted in a violent breakdown of the relationship between grassroots cadres and villagers. Daxin County, for instance, reported that some heads of work brigades forcefully extorted grains from the villagers, embezzled food that should have been distributed to brigade members, and

---

[85] CPC Shiwanshan County Committee, "Yuenan minzhu gongheguo Haining shengwei bangongting fuzhuren Wang Tingzhen tongzhi dao woxian jiaohuan woguo hezuohua qingkuang [Deputy head of the Administrative Office of Hải Ninh Province of DRV Comrade Vương Đình Trấn come to our county to communicate the situation of cooperative movement]," September 29, 1958.

[86] Ibid.; Yin, "The Mountain Is High, and the Emperor Is Far Away," 561.

Figure 3.1 Beilun/Ka Long River at the end of the rain season
Note: Taken from Dongxing (right side of the picture). Móng Cái is on the left side of the photo.
Source: Author, September 2015.

relentlessly beat up those who committed misdemeanors for survival such as pilferage.[87]

Famine and persecution fueled a widespread feeling of despair and rumors of an imminent political collapse. A landlord in Tiandeng, a county in Southwest Guangxi located about twenty kilometers away from the border, was labeled a "bad element" for convincing some villagers and previously purged cadres that the CPC was about to lose power and inciting them to "go to Vietnam to carry out revolution and return next year when the communist regime collapses."[88] While the Chinese and Vietnamese governments had hitherto attempted to restrict outsiders' access to the border zone – places

---

[87] CPC Daxin County Committee, "Guanyu jiejue bianmin liu-Yue gongzuo qingkuang baogao," 19–20.

[88] CPC Tiandeng County Committee, "Guanyu bianmin yuejing, wailiu de baogao [Report on border residents crossing the border and migrating to Vietnam]," June 26, 1961, no. 1-36-13-5, 13–14/CZMA. For the political label of "bad elements," see Benton and Ye, "Translators' Introduction," in Yang, *Eight Outcasts*, 6–7.

within twenty kilometers from the boundary line – many citizens who lived outside now realized that they could travel miles and cross the boundary line without any documents, taking advantage of the unguarded, unpatrolled paths. Those who managed to return revealed the limited coercive strength of the state at the frontier, encouraging others to do the same. According to the statistics collected by the border check station at Friendship Pass, border guards stopped 442 Chinese citizens (not including "criminals") for illegal boundary crossing to Vietnam in 1959, and the number reached 1,057 in 1961, with the vast majority being "educated and released."[89] Unlike the highland Yao or Miao people who fled the country in 1958, many people from interior communes had no plan to resettle in Vietnam, except for those married to or adopted by Vietnamese citizens. Instead, they sought grain from their relatives in Vietnam; exchanged light industrial products; "sold" young children for rice, oil, and meat; or worked as casual laborers or housemaids in Vietnam. The Tiandeng county officials bemoaned the unsettling phenomenon of "speculation and profiteering across the border," as many Chinese citizens obtained food from Vietnam not only for consumption but for resale in the interior.[90]

The catastrophic leap into a communist society was only one reason behind the borderlanders' attempts to challenge the state's bordering practices. A myriad of other factors pitted the local society against the two states in a sustained hostility. Many political outcasts who had fallen victim to unremitting political campaigns to identify the "enemies of the people" decided to flee China as a hedge for survival, especially after pressure on them built up during the Anti-Rightist Movement. In 1958, the Chinese border guards at Friendship Pass arrested 142 "criminals" who were attempting to flee the country, including 116 who were caught by the Vietnamese police and repatriated to China. The number in the following year was 101, including 71 who were returned to China by the Vietnamese authorities. Among those arrested were suspected spies, rightists, fugitives from the prison camps, and smugglers. Cadres at the border pass proudly reported in 1959 that, "after the nationwide rectification and anti-rightist campaigns," the enemies "have nowhere to hide in our country thus have to run away."[91]

Meanwhile, Beijing and Hanoi demilitarized the border enforcement system at the Sino-Vietnamese border in the late 1950s, which the borderlanders perceived as a sign of downgraded state control. In August 1958, Chinese border troops that served under the authority of the Central Military Commission were replaced with salaried People's Armed Police Corps

---

[89] Zeng, *YBJZ*, 161.
[90] CPC Tiandeng County Committee, "Guanyu bianmin yuejing, wailiu de baogao," 14.
[91] Zeng, *YBJZ*, 167–68.

accountable to the provincial public security authorities. In December 1961, the border police were put under the dual control of public security and the military, with the latter mainly in charge of ideological education, equipment, and logistics.[92] Mirroring this change, in March 1959 Hanoi established its own People's Armed Police composed of border guards and internal protection forces under the leadership of the MOPS.[93] Once placed within the state bureaucracy, the border check points were often understaffed during political movements as the local cadres were not exempt from meetings, study sessions, or persecution.

Disturbed by the spontaneous movements across the border that confronted their joint campaigns to tie the border citizens to their respective land, the two countries decided to reduce the legal permeability of the border – a hasty decision that turned many previously legitimate cross-border activities into crimes. When the local Chinese and Vietnamese state-run trade companies started to barter at the Dongxing-Móng Cái border crossing in July 1958, citizens were no longer allowed to attend the border market on the other side for small-scale border trade so that the state monopolized all legal cross-border trade at the locality.[94] Encouraged by the reduction of cross-border farming, the Hải Ninh and Guangdong provincial authorities decided at a meeting over border issues in August 1959 to close down some mountain pathways that had been opened in the early 1950s to allow citizens who needed to cross the boundary on a daily basis for farming or schooling to travel to the other side as long as they carried identification cards.[95] In a time of economic downturn, the space for legitimate cross-border contacts shrank.

Equally important, as Hanoi began its own campaign of socialist agricultural cooperatization, the two central governments' interests overlapped in not only enforcing an international boundary but also collectivizing the border economy. In November 1958, a resolution emanated from the WPV Central Executive Committee set the ambitious goal of forming collective cooperatives throughout the north by the end of 1960.[96] The dread of food shortage accompanying the collectivization reignited the tension between the ethnic Chinese community and the local Vietnamese state in Hải Ninh. At the end of 1958, following a widely circulated rumor that the state-sponsored supply and

---

[92] Ibid., 86.
[93] Thủ tướng Chính phủ, "Nghị định 100-TTg năm 1959 về việc thống nhất các đơn vị bộ đội quốc phòng, công an biên phòng, cảnh sát vũ trang thành Công an nhân dân vũ trang."
[94] CPC Dongxing County Committee, "Guanyu Zhong-Yue bianyuanqu xiao'e maoyi wenti de baogao [Report on small-scale trade in the Sino-Vietnamese border area]," January 24, 1960, no. 1-2-101-3, 47–48/FDA.
[95] "Yuenan minzhu gongheguo Hainingsheng he Zhonghua renmin gongheguo Guangdongsheng guanyu shuangfang bianjing diqu yixie wenti de huitan jilu [Record of meeting between Hải Ninh Province of DRV and Guangdong Province of PRC]," August 10, 1959.
[96] Kerkevliet, *The Power of Everyday Politics*, 58–59.

sale stores would no longer sell rice anymore to individuals, ethnic Chinese in Móng Cái and Tiên Yên, including some soldiers serving in the local army units, besieged the stores in these towns and attacked the cadre managers.[97]

In November 1959, the WPV spread the cooperatization campaign into the ethnic minority–populated mountainous areas, including its northern border with China, in the hope of enhancing the production of food, cash crops, and livestock and gradually building industrial centers for mining, electricity, and food processing. Acknowledging that the border societies had "undifferentiated class divisions" and that gangs and spies were still active in some areas, the Vietnamese government decided to "implement agricultural cooperation in combination with completing democratic reform," explicitly targeting disruptive challengers to state authorities. To avoid alienating highlanders, Hanoi required that the collectivization of buffalo should be limited to families that owned large numbers of the draft animals and that those who complied would be compensated with a bonus for three to five years.[98]

Because of geographical proximity and ideological affinity, Vietnamese cadres were eager to draw on the experiences of collectivization from its northern neighbor while avoiding the mistakes that had been made there. In April 1959, the WPV Central Committee instructed provincial authorities along the border to "promote collaborative relations and enlist the help of local party committees of China to improve work at the border."[99] Showcasing the Great Leap Forward and convincing their Vietnamese comrades that the Maoist development model wrapped around the idea of the impregnable human spirit was superior to that of the Soviet Union became the primary objective for local Chinese officials tasked with receiving the Vietnamese. During the first quarter of 1959, the government of Hải Ninh sent 30 delegations totalling 2,500 people to visit factories, collective farms, and communes in Chinese counties near the border.[100] Inspired by the "backyard furnaces" of China, Hải Ninh province established a primordial steel furnace in Móng Cái to facilitate steel manufacturing.[101]

---

[97] "Đối phó với âm mưu đen tối của bọn phản động người Hoa [Coping with the dark conspiracy of the reactionary Chinese]," 1958, in *SLDQ*, 88–89.

[98] Hội đồng Chính phủ, "Nghị quyết về việc tiến hành hợp tác hóa nông nghiệp kết hợp hoàn thành cải cách dân chủ miền núi."

[99] KTTVB, "Nghị quyết cửa Ban Thường vụ khu ủy đối với viện trợ cửa bạn và một số công tác biên giới năm 1961 [Resolutions of the regional party standing committee on aid from China and some border affairs in 1961]," May 5, 1961, no. 5638, 1/UBHC KTTVB 1948–1976/ NAVC III.

[100] CPC Dongxing County Committee, "Yijiuwujiu nian diyijidu Zhong-Yue bianjing – Dongxing Haining youhao laiwang de qingkuang zonghe baogao [Friendly communication between Dongxing and Hải Ninh during the first quarter of 1959]," April 25, 1959, no. 1-2-92-4, 60–61/FDA.

[101] CPC Dongxing County Committee, "Yijiuwujiu nian wu yuefen waishi gongzuo qingkuang baogao [Report of foreign affairs in May 1959]," June 9, 1959, no. 1-2-92-4, 95/FDA.

The Socialist Borderlands 145

To impress the Vietnamese cadres who frequently visited Dongxing, local Chinese cadres mobilized the residents in the border town to flaunt the accomplishment of the Great Leap.[102] The Vietnamese officials were particularly interested in how to mobilize the masses into a series of socialist movements launched simultaneously in the countryside. Hoàng Chính, Party Secretary of Hải Ninh, visited Dongxing in June 1959 and asked the local Chinese administration to introduce their experience of undertaking "democratic reform," establishing cooperative leadership, organizing people's communes, and promoting the Great Leap Forward among ethnic minorities, because the mobilization of ethnic groups was the most urgent task in his province.[103] In September, the Autonomous Region of Thái-Mèo – renamed the Northwest Autonomous Region (Khu tự trị Tây Bắc,KTTTB) in 1962 – and Hải Ninh Province sent a delegation to Dongxing to learn about the Chinese experience of introducing the socialist reform of capitalist industries and commerce. The Vietnamese cadres told the Chinese that they had great difficulties relocating the "surplus population in business" from urban areas to the Autonomous Region of Thái-Mèo. In response, the local Chinese cadres showcased the example of a prosperous nationalized retail business in Dongxing, all the while carefully hiding the fact that the majority of shopkeepers and peddlers in this historical trade hub had long resented collectivization and complained about their declining living standard.[104]

Against the background of the nationwide drive for agricultural collectivization and the campaign to reshuffle the socioeconomic structure in the northern moutainous region, the central and local authorities of the DRV exercised vigilance toward the outflow of refugees, goods, and currency from China for their potentially disruptive effects. The outpouring of Chinese currency into Vietnamese border regions was in particular a salient problem for Hanoi. Since the state-sponsored reopening of markets for small-scale border trade in 1952, both governments pursued the unattainable goal of keeping their currency within their national boundaries, asking the borderlanders who attended the

---

[102] CPC Dongxing County Committee, "Yijiuwujiu nian di 3 jidu waishi gongzuo qingkuang baogao [Report of foreign affairs in the third quarter of 1959]," November 1, 1959, no. 1-2-92-4, 100/FDA.

[103] CPC Dongxing County Committee, "Yijiuwujiu nian wu yuefen waishi gongzuo qingkuang baogao," 95. From 1911 to 1960, the Kinh/Vietnamese population in Hải Ninh increased from 35.66 percent to 64.01 percent, while the Hoa (including Ngái, Hakka, and Hán) decreased from 38.34 percent to 24.57 percent. The Tày (4.0 percent) and the Dao (3.76 percent) were the second and third largest ethnic minorities in the province. Nguyễn Văn Chính, "Ethnic Chinese in the Sino-Vietnamese Borderlands," 11.

[104] The above section is based on CPC of Dongxing County Committee, "Dongxingzhen xiaoshang xiaofan zongluxian jiaoyu yundong zongjie [Summary of the education of overall line of socialist construction to shopkeepers and peddlers in Dongxing]," December 26, 1959, no. 222-2-278-118~137, 1/GDPA.

market to exchange any surplus amount of foreign currency after trading, which should not exceed one yuan or its Vietnamese equivalent.[105] Currency flew across the border, however, largely under the state's radar. During the Great Leap Forward, the influx of food commodities into China led to an outflow of RMB to Cao Bằng and Lạng Sơn, where every household ended up possessing some Chinese currency. As RMB depreciated quickly and exchange rates on the black market increasingly deviated from the official one, the National Bank of Vietnam began to lose control over finances in the border provinces.[106] This phenomenon may have reminded the Vietnamese of its bitter experience during the ROC troops' occupation of Vietnam north of the 16th parallel at the end of the Second World War. The large volume of Chinese currency brought in by the Chinese soldiers had thrown the Vietnamese economy into chaos.[107] Fifteen years later, the Vietnamese authorities were eager to avoid a similar nightmare.

Vietnamese officials had legitimate concerns over the cross-border mobility of people and goods, particularly because they were already barely able to meet the demands of their own citizens in the border provinces. These concerns were complicated by the fact that many outlying Vietnamese villages already heavily relied on economic connections with China due to difficulties in transportation between the mountainous area and the Red River Delta. Because most Vietnamese border provinces were short of surplus food, exporting a large amount of goods to China could be an onerous task. KTTVB thus instructed the local governments that they needed to make efforts to help the Chinese comrades solve their immediate food shortage difficulties but "only to a reasonable extent."[108]

The increasingly lucrative transboundary private trade in a time of economic slump and food shortage in China, however, attracted even more people in Vietnam into this business, which Hanoi believed would derail its project of tying labor to agricultural cooperatives, buttressing collective ownership, and pushing for food self-sufficiency of the border provinces. According to a report from KTTVB to Hanoi, a substantial number of Chinese citizens had illegally traveled across the border to Cao Bằng since August 1960 – sometimes several hundred people a day – which drove up food prices. While initially bartering for food in small amounts, more and more Chinese citizens began purchasing

---

[105] Thủ tướng Chính phủ, "Nghị định 486-TTg năm 1958 về bản điều lệ quản lý mậu dịch tiểu ngạch nhân dân trong khu vực biên giới Việt-Trung."
[106] PTTg, "Về một số vấn đề trong quan hệ mậu dịch tiểu ngạch biên giới giữa hai tỉnh Cao-bằng, Lạng-sơn với tỉnh Quảng-tây [On some issues in border trade between two provinces of Cao Bằng, Lạng Sơn with Guangxi]," September 7, 1961, no. 7839, 79/PTTg/NAVC III.
[107] Worthing, *Occupation and Revolution*, 94.
[108] PTTg, "Về một số vấn đề trong quan hệ mậu dịch tiểu ngạch biên giới giữa hai tỉnh Cao-bằng, Lạng-sơn với tỉnh Quảng-tây," 80.

larger quantities of grain and non-staple food regardless of cost, being willing to pay with whatever they had – which suggested some of these purchases were destined for resale in China. This situation obviously encouraged many Vietnamese citizens to engage in the illegal trade across the border, which official documents warned had allowed Vietnamese border people to "gain undue advantage" and impelled them to "give up [agricultural] work and venture into the market."[109] What bothered the Vietnamese cadres more was the revival of smuggling rings – some remotely controlled by merchants in Hanoi – connecting cities with the border region. On one hand, light industrial products were smuggled inland as far as Hanoi; on the other hand, merchants outside the border region stealthily brought grain to Lạng Sơn for sale to the Chinese. As cross-border movements not under the state's gaze increased, profiteers could "take advantage of that opportunity to blend in with the people."[110]

With the alarming growth of illicit trade, the two states renewed their collaborative campaign to snatch the borderland economy out of private hands. In August 1960, Guangxi and the two Vietnamese border provinces of Cao Bằng and Lạng Sơn agreed to close six out of ten border markets to "restrain border residents from participating in small-scale border trade."[111] At the request of the Vietnamese Ministry of Foreign Trade, the two countries also reduced the quota of small-scale border trade at the officially opened crossings from ten yuan RMB or Vietnamese equivalent to five yuan per person each day in order to reduce private commerce and consolidate collective ownership in Vietnamese border communes.[112] In December 1960, the Vietnamese Minister of Foreign Trade proudly stated in his report to the central government that fewer and fewer Vietnamese people in Hải Ninh attended markets in China because domestic trade had already begun to meet the demand of border residents for manufactured goods.[113]

The reality, however, was that the Vietnamese citizens at the border were as much in need of the shadow economy as their Chinese counterparts. Beginning in early 1961, the Vietnamese state moved to exert tighter control over the lives of agricultural labor in response to a nationwide campaign for food self-sufficiency and surplus. Vowing not to "rely on thousands of tons of food from

---

[109] The above part is based on ibid., 79–81.   [110] Ibid., 79.
[111] "Guowuyuan pifu Guangxi zhuangzu zizhiqu renmin weiyuanhui, tongyi Guangxi yu Yuefang xieshang de yijian [The State Council endorsing the opinion of consultation between GZAR and Vietnam]," August 20, 1960, in *GSBN 1960*, 541.
[112] UBHC tỉnh Hải Ninh [Administrative Committee of Hải Ninh], "Về việc đề nghị đóng cửa khẩu Pohen [About the proposed closure of Pò Hèn gate]," October 21, 1960, no. 7839, 1/ PTTg/NAVC III.
[113] Bộ trưởng bộ ngoại thương [Minister of foreign trade], "Việc đóng cửa khẩu Pohen [About the closure of Pò Hèn]," December 27, 1960, no. 7839, 2/ PTTg/NAVC III.

central government," Hải Ninh began to resettle the Dao people from the mountainous region to permanent villages, where they would grow rice, develop terraced cultivation to maximize arable land, and raise buffalo for ploughing, all of which made agriculture more labor intensive for the highland population.[114] In a draft speech in October 1961 prepared for a meeting with the trade office of Guangxi, the trade delegation of KTTVB noted that with agricultural cooperatives established along the Vietnamese border, local officials had decided to restrain "unnecessary daily commuting" to the Chinese side "for labor management in production." However, the speech also admitted that after the de facto closure of the border, Vietnamese officials had failed to procure local products from the Vietnamese border community in a timely fashion or to provide in return the light industrial products desired there. No longer allowed to sell their mountain products – such as herbal medicines – in exchange for manufactured daily necessities by attending border markets in China, these Vietnamese citizens instead turned to black markets or illegally crossed the border to China in search of these commodities.[115] Thus, the micro-management of the border by higher authorities eventually led to legal sanctions against the innocent, who did not mean to openly deny the regulation of the state yet were simply forced to resort to what the state deemed as illegitimate to support their own livelihood.

Besides squeezing out space for legitimate cross-border contacts between individual citizens in the two countries, the hasty occlusion of the border significantly harmed the capabilities of grassroots cadres on the two sides to settle cross-border issues. Local solutions were typically more effective than communications overhead through layers of bureaucracies in dealing with the crisis of starvation that arose in many Chinese communes during the Great Leap Forward. Thus, when the CPC leadership met in Lushan, a historic resort in Jiangxi, in July 1959, to discuss how to contain "leftist tendencies" during the leap, local Chinese cadres were searching for ways, on their own, to pull society back from starvation. The Bureau of Commerce of Hainan Island and the Dongzhong Commune of Dongxing County, for instance, bartered with Vietnamese border communes without endorsement from the higher authorities.[116] At the center of the power

---

[114] "Phong trào sản xuất tự túc của nhân dân tỉnh Hải Ninh [Self-sufficient production movement of the people of Hải Ninh province]," 1961, in *SLDR*, 153; "Hội nghị chuyên đề về phát triển hợp tác xã và sản xuất nông nghiệp vùng cao tỉnh Hải Ninh [Meeting on the cooperative movement and highland agricultural production in Hải Ninh province]," November 14, 1962, in *SLDR*, 174.

[115] "Phát biểu của đoàn đàm phán khu tự trị Việt Bắc v/v Tổ chức phục hồi lại một số cửa khẩu mậu dịch [Speech of the delegation of the KTTVB on restoring some trading ports]," October 13, 1961, no. 7839, 37/PTTg/NAVC III.

[116] Ministry of Foreign Trade, "Fu guanyu Dongxing Dongzhong renmin gongshe zhijie tong Yuefang jinxing maoyi wenti [Reply on the problem of direct trade between Dongzhong People's Commune and Vietnam]," August 1, 1959, no. 302-1-101-139~139, 1/GDPA.

structure, though, the Lushan Conference not only failed to shift the country away from political radicalization but also re-radicalized the leap after Peng Dehuai, the Minister of National Defense, was purged for criticizing the inflated production figures of the people's communes.[117] Reflecting this harsh line against moderate economic policy, the Ministry of Foreign Trade excoriated the local officials in Hainan and Dongxing for "violating the policy of national control of foreign trade and the principle of unified action toward the outside world" and banned any similar deals in the future.[118] From the other side, in 1961, the Vietnamese Foreign Ministry prohibited Vietnamese border cooperatives from initiating any contacts with the Chinese authorities without the direction of the county or provincial government, except for issues related to marriage or divorce.[119]

These state interventions into the spontaneous collaborations initiated by local cadres constituted a vivid example of how ideological affinity, ironically, drove the two countries apart. Basking in the glow of socialist brotherhood, local Chinese and Vietnamese officials had indeed institutionalized liaison with each other, yet the initiative for such communication was only supposed to occur at the behest of the superior level of the bureaucracy. From the perspective of the political centers, local resolutions of crises, problems, or disputes were seen as a dangerous tendency of decentralization. An internal policy guideline on "remedying China-Vietnam border issues" ratified by the CPC Central Committee in 1959 warned against "proceed[ing] solely from the interests of the frontier" and "imperial power mindset" in dealing with the Vietnamese over border issues. Keenly aware of the fact that "there are quite a few regions that state power had difficulty reaching or almost never reached" and that "inhabitants of the borderlands are increasingly forming a discrete ethnicity," Beijing perceived the management of border as "not just a question of international issues between states" but also "a question of struggling for and uniting national minorities with the interior."[120]

---

[117] Bernstein, "Mao Zedong and the Famine of 1959–1960," 429–34.
[118] Ministry of Foreign Trade, "Fu guanyu Dongxing Dongzhong renmin gongshe zhijie tong Yuefang jinxing maoyi wenti," 1.
[119] "Bản dự thảo về quy định lề lôí quan hệ cửa các tỉnh biên giới bên ta vơí các tỉnh cửa Trung Quốc cửa Lãnh sự Bộ Ngoại giao năm 1961 [A copy of the regulation on the relations between our border provinces and the border provinces of China by Consul Department of Foreign Ministry]," October 13, 1961, no. 5636, 2/UBHC KTTVB 1948–1976/NAVC III.
[120] The quote and paraphrase are based on "Policy Documents for Expatriate Affairs related to the CCP Central Committee, Expatriate Committee, and District Committees (1956, 1957, 1959)," January 4, 1959, History and Public Policy Program Digital Archive, GZARA, X42-1-72, obtained for CWIHP by Hongwei Fan and translated by Max Maller, 3–4, http://digitalarchive.wilsoncenter.org/document/118258.

Negotiating the Permeabililty of the Border

Living along the Sino-Vietnamese border both provided opportunities and posed dangers to citizens who searched for alternative methods of supporting their livelihood when suffering under intolerable conditions. Border residents enjoyed stronger bargaining power against the state than people living in the interior thanks to the porous boundary, which empowered the borderlanders to vote with their feet as a hedge for their survival. The famine created by the Great Leap Forward institutionalized "a state-designed rural-urban divide" that gave urbanites better access to food than farm households in a time of extreme economic difficulty.[121] The survival of citizens in rural areas who attempted to escape this highly exploitative system were jeopardized not only by the possibility of political persecution but also by the scarcity of food supply for them outside the commune. Those living close to the border, by contrast, could resort to the cross-boundary mutual-help networks.

However, the fact that the borderlanders lived between two neighboring socialist states that were actively pursuing a collectivization agenda reduced their leeway for migration in comparison with those living close to a Cold War front line, as in the case at the Guangdong-Hong Kong border. The years of Great Famine witnessed the first wave of Cantonese fleeing to Hong Kong since 1949, which resulted in tougher measures by the British colonial government against illegal immigration. In practice, the exclusionary policy turned out to be highly ineffective even in identifying the illegal immigrants.[122] On the Sino-Vietnamese border, however, cross-boundary mobility and migration were subjected to concerted interventions by both Chinese and Vietnamese governments, even though the approaches they adopted were not always coercive. Meanwhile, the fate of the émigrés fleeing China to Vietnam was also in sharp contrast to those to North Korea – mainly ethnic Korean in Northeast China – during the Great Famine. In competition with the Soviets for North Korean support, Beijing deferred to Pyongyang's choice of selectively accepting able-bodied laborers, skilled workers, and ethnic Korean families among the illegal immigrants, which flew in the face of the border agreements reached between the two governments in the 1950s.[123]

In a time of surging cross-border movements unendorsed by and potentially subversive to the state, "bandit suppression" (*jiaofei* in Chinese and *tiểu trừ nạn phi* in Vietnamese) regained salience on the agenda of local administrations. In Autumn 1958, the Vietnamese police informed the Chinese border

---

[121] Thaxton, Jr., *Force and Contention in Contemporary China*, 27–28.
[122] Ku, "Immigration Policies, Discourses, and the Politics of Local Belonging in Hong Kong," 336.
[123] Shen and Xia, *A Misunderstood Friendship*, 154–58.

authorities about a series of armed robberies of granaries and shops by people from China. For the first time after the PLA eliminated the remnant Nationalist forces from its border provinces in the early 1950s, the Chinese officials used the term bandits to refer to people wandering across the boundary, not only highlighting the violent nature of the latter's activities but also treating them as political opponents. The Vietnamese police showed their determination to strike hard against these armed challengers, telling their Chinese counterparts that they planned to plant agents among the refugees and ambush the bandits. The Vietnamese and Chinese police vowed to share intelligence and "effectively mobilize the people" so that they would not "join, hide, or assist the bandits."[124] In May 1959, the WPV established the Border Work Committee, which urged Beijing to restore order at the border by reinforcing the local party and state institutions.[125]

Hanoi had long viewed northern Hải Ninh as a "reactionary corridor," citing the history of the French-sponsored Nùng Autonomous Territory and the continuous penetration by spies supported by the United States and South Vietnam.[126] In August 1958, a bandit leader, Trình Coóng Phí, established his base in the forest region of Hà Cối, with about eighty followers. Later that year, his force amalgamated with that of the commandos Lương Mù, who broke into the North across the 17th parallel, and with the "bandits" who fled from China, which made the group the prime target of Vietnamese bandit-suppressing efforts. Condemned as an "American-South Vietnamese spy," Trình Coóng Phí and his followers were also charged with killing cooperative leaders and robbing food from the people. In May 1960, the police of Hải Ninh arrested him alive, and the banditry started to subside.[127] In January 1961, the provincial authority cracked down on a group of forty-seven people in Hoành Bồ area for their armed resistance against the cooperative movement, which included killing the commune leader's wife and children at the instigation of a "reactionary Chinese" fleeing from China.[128] In February, following another raid against "bandits," Hải Ninh arrested and deported to China twenty-nine

---

[124] Bureau of Public Security of Dongxing County, "Zhong-Yue bianjing jiaofei gongzuo baogao zhisan [Report on crushing the bandits in the Sino-Vietnamese border, no. 3]," October 15, 1958.
[125] International Department of CPC, "Zai Yue-Zhong bianjing gongzuo fangmian yaoqiu youfang dangbu bangzhu de juti neirong [Details on the request of help from the friendly party committee on work at the Sino-Vietnamese border]," April 14, 1959, no. X50–3-37, 10–12/ GZARA, cited in You, "Zhanhou Zhong-Yue ludi bianjie wenti de lishi kaocha ji zaisikao," 68, 79.
[126] Thanh Nga (Trung tâm TT&VH), "Vàng không mua nổi lòng người Dao theo Đảng."
[127] "Tiểu trừ nạn phỉ, bảo vệ các huyện miền Đông tỉnh Hải Ninh [Eliminate bandits and protect the security of eastern Hải Ninh]," May 1960, in *SLDQ*, 124–25.
[128] "Đập tan một tổ chức phản động của địch ở khu Hồng Quảng [Smash an enemy's reactionary organization in Hồng Quảng area]," January 1961, in *SLDQ*, 142–43.

people labeled as loyalists to Chiang Kai-shek.[129] These militant measures only went so far against those who violently flouted state authorities or openly questioned its legitimacy; the two countries' reactions to the refugees and the resilient smuggling networks indicated that the ordinary borderlanders could still manipulate the Sino-Vietnamese alliance to their benefit.

Curbing the exodus of refugees to Vietnam turned out to be a tricky task for the local Chinese administration because forced repatriation would further alienate border residents and belie the carefully created positive image of Chinese socialism. Besides these issues, upwardly accountable cadres who needed to keep pace with other communes in production were especially concerned with the decline of grain output due to a shortage of labor. Large-scale coercion could dampen the morale of the border villagers precisely at the time that high spirit was needed to boost productivity. Thus, the local Chinese government had to resort to persuasion, propaganda, and most importantly, economic incentives. Cadres who were dispatched to Yao villages to investigate the situation, for instance, believed that the government should "absolutely avoid arresting or detaining villagers who organized the exodus because the masses are not yet mobilized thus the enemy is not yet isolated." They recommended that the higher authorities "liaison properly with the Vietnamese" and persuade the refugees to return home and warned against policies that "blindly copy the experience of collectivization in Han-populated area."[130] In 1959 and 1962, the Chinese and Vietnamese border provinces held several border work meetings, where they agreed to assist each other in persuading "the working people" among the refugees to return home, allowing those who had established a stable livelihood and wished to stay in Vietnam to resettle in the new home permanently following Vietnamese laws, while forcibly repatriating those identified as "landlords, rich, counterrevolutionaries, and criminals."[131]

Meanwhile, local Chinese governments launched a propaganda campaign on patriotism and internationalism along the border targeting not only ordinary villagers but also grassroots cadres. County-level public security authorities dispatched circuit work teams to each border village to investigate the situation

---

[129] "Tỉnh Hải Ninh tiễu phỉ, chống vượt biên trái phép [Hải Ninh province suppresses bandits and fights against illegal border crossing]," February 2, 1961, in *SLDQ*, 145–46.

[130] CPC Dongxing County Committee, "Xian jiang Banba Xikeng yaozu qunzhong taopao qingkuang baogao."

[131] Public Security Department of GZARA, "Guanyu woqu he Yuenan Yuebeizizhiqu bianjing gongzuo huitan qingkuang [About our region's border work meeting with KTTVB of Vietnam]," June 14, 1962, no. X53-3-81, 98–99/GZARA, cited in You, "Zhanhou Zhong-Yue ludi bianjie wenti de lishi kaocha ji zaisikao," 68, 79. Quotes are from "Yuenan minzhu gongheguo Hainingsheng he Zhonghua renmin gongheguo Guangdongsheng guanyu shuangfang bianjing diqu yixie wenti de dierci huitan jilu [Record of the second meeting between Hải Ninh Province of DRV and Guangdong Province of PRC]," September 23, 1962.

and explain government policies of boundary control to the citizens. Party committees of border communes were ordered to attach greater importance to border management instead of letting the exodus go unchecked. The Tiandeng County administration conveniently summarized the theme of the education as "three checks (to check unauthorized border crossing, illegal emigration, and illicit trade)" and "two calculates (to calculate the loss in production and the negative international political impact)."[132] The fact that the propaganda campaign aimed to mobilize both ordinary villagers and commune heads revealed the incoherency of the state below the county level. Grassroots leaders with locally invested interests and social networks sometimes had neither the will nor the capability to uphold the political agenda of the higher authorities.

In the end, though, neither persuasion nor propaganda could solve the refugee problem without concrete steps to narrow the gap between food supplies in China and Vietnam. Rising food quotas became the key to keeping the border villagers on the Chinese side. In early 1961, the administration of Daxin County, for instance, enhanced the per capita food ration to fourteen kilograms per month and allowed the peasants to keep the spring harvest for themselves so that the actual grain each person possessed reached fifteen to twenty kilos. It also set a higher quota, of fifteen kilograms per capita per month, for refugees who agreed to return to China.[133] Similarly, Tiandeng County raised food and salt allowances and supplied borderlanders with more kitchenware, much of which had been forcibly seized earlier for steel production.[134] By spring 1961, just less than half of the villagers from Daxin County had allegedly returned home to China under the combined measures of persuasion, education, and moderated procurement.[135] In December 1961, Beijing admitted in an internal document that food shortage in China had allowed the Vietnamese border residents to "sell agricultural and other products at a high price at the border markets in China." Having little to purchase there, though, these Vietnamese citizens often took Chinese currency back to Vietnam, exacerbating the exiting problem of unendorsed cross-border flow of bank notes. Thus, it was decided that the border provinces should relax the food and clothes rations and prioritize the supply of salt, farm tools, and other necessities to border residents and furnish more goods to the border markets for the Vietnamese to curb the outflow of Chinese currency.[136] Given a highly

---

[132] CPC Tiandeng County Committee, "Guanyu bianmin yuejing, wailiu de baogao," 15.
[133] CPC Daxin County Committee, "Guanyu jiejue bianmin liu-Yue gongzuo qingkuang baogao," 20.
[134] CPC Tiandeng County Committee, "Guanyu bianmin yuejing, wailiu de baogao," 17.
[135] CPC Daxin County Committee, "Guanyu jiejue bianmin liu-Yue gongzuo qingkuang baogao," 20.
[136] The above portion is based on "Guowuyuan zhuanfa Waimaobu 'guanyu jiejue Zhong-Yue xiao'e maoyi cunzai wenti de jidian yijian' [State Council forwards 'opinion on problems in

permeable border, the Chinese state in the end had to resort to market rules to enforce the international boundary instead of relying solely on coercion.

Whereas the disastrous impact of the Great Leap Forward shook Beijing's self-perceived status as a socialist model for Hanoi, the revival of unexpectedly resilient cross-border networks in a time of a widening gap between living standards on the two sides of the border posed a significant challenge to the emerging planned economy in Vietnam. After the shutdown of several historic border markets during the cooperatization movement, the central Vietnamese state had failed to provide the alternative sources of income it had promised. The border villagers, therefore, resorted to the black market, which not only sustained their livelihood but also helped them dodge the monitoring of and tax-collection by the state. Furthermore, while state-run trade companies held firm control on the price of commodities at the officially established border markets, the government had little leverage in the shadow economy. Heightened smuggling and a thriving black market brought back speculative merchants, especially among the ethnic Chinese traders, whom central and local Vietnamese administrations had tried so hard to exclude from border markets. In the hope of reasserting the state in the border economy, in September 1961 the Vietnamese government suggested to its Chinese counterpart the restoration of the six historic border crossings and markets between Guangxi and the two provinces of Cao Bằng and Lạng Sơn that had been shut down by 1960 under a series of bilteral agreements. Once these border towns reopened for cross-border trade among ordinary people, the Vietnamese government also instructed its border check stations, tax divisions, and bank branches to collaborate more closely in stabilizing prices, regulating the transactions, and collecting taxes.[137] Hanoi made a radical departure from its original policy of pushing for the closure of border and nationalization of cross-border trade. It was evident to the Vietnamese administrations that coercion did not necessarily lead to more effective extraction of revenues from the border economy.

Smuggling nevertheless did not subside despite the two states' synergetic efforts against it. Realizing that many grassroots cadres such as militia and communal police either had directly engaged in illegal trade or lacked the political motivation to crack down on the smuggling rings, the Vietnamese government decided to resort to monetary incentives to buy support from local cadres.[138] In December 1962, the Vietnamese Ministry of Finance stipulated

---

the Sino-Vietnamese small-scale border trade' by Ministry of Foreign Trade]," December 25, 1961, in *GSBN* 1961, 794.

[137] PTTg, "Về một số vấn đề trong quan hệ mậu dịch tiểu ngạch biên giới giữa hai tỉnh Cao-bằng, Lạng-sơn với tỉnh Quảng-tây," 79–81.

[138] An earlier version of this paragraph appears in Yin, "The Mountain Is High, and the Emperor Is Far Away," 562.

the payment of compensation to the militiamen, rangers, and commune police involved in smuggling control "to mobilize various forces in the society to participate in the implementation of tariff policy."[139] In the spring of 1964, a grain shortage in the Vietnamese border provinces drove thousands of Vietnamese citizens to travel without documents to the border markets in Guangxi to buy food from the Chinese state-run stores.[140] Alerted by the unauthorized cross-border flows of daily necessities, the Vietnamese government expanded the remuneration from military and police units to "people who help the financial agency to execute tax policy and detect smuggling cases" in June 1964.[141] Hanoi's anti-smuggling measures highlighted the delicate relationship between the central and street-level bureaucracies. The distance between Hanoi and the border provinces was much shorter than that between Beijing and its southwestern frontier. However, the distance between the central state and its on-the-ground apparatus was as hierarchical as it was physical. Grassroots administrations and cadres could manipulate or dodge the broad strategies decided upon by the central government and only selectively carry out particular policies. Hanoi, therefore, had to offer material incentives to keep its bureaucracy disciplined.

Conclusion: Revolutionary States at the Border on the Eve of the Escalated Vietnam War

What was the implication of the revolutionary agenda pursued by two neighboring communist countries to the strength of their states and lives of people along their shared border? This chapter provides a complicated answer. Beijing and Hanoi preferred socialist partnership fostered from above to fraternity built from below. The two centralized governments, therefore, often hastily intervened against cross-border collaborations initiated by grassroots officials and rescinded the autonomy previously granted to the local border authorities. A vigorous socialist partnership and similar trajectory of state building provided an "arena for communications" between Chinese and Vietnamese administrations at both central and local levels and enhanced the "monitoring capacity" of the border authorities to tackle security challenges at the border.[142] The imposition of communes and cooperatives – a symbol of

---

[139] Bộ Tài chính, "Thông tư 140-TC-TQD-T năm 1964 bổ sung Thông tư 802-TC-TQD năm 1962 về việc trả thù lao cho những người tham gia bắt lậu."

[140] "Yuenan bianmin jixu guojing mailiang qingkuang [Situation of Vietnamese border residents continuing buying grain across the border]," June 13, 1964, no. X50-3-136, 147–48/GZARA. I thank ECNURC for sharing this document with me.

[141] Bộ Tài chính, "Thông tư 140-TC-TQD-T năm 1964 bổ sung Thông tư 802-TC-TQD năm 1962 về việc trả thù lao cho những người tham gia bắt lậu."

[142] Gavrilis, The Dynamics of Interstate Boundaries, 32–33.

socialist state building – however, resulted in setbacks to the two revolutionary states' strength and authority on their shared border and compromised the organic interdependence among the borderlanders. At the beginning of the Great Leap Forward and the Vietnamese cooperatization movement in 1958, the two countries, which undervalued the significance of cross-border ties for the people while overestimating the capabilities of the local administrations to deal with the economic consequences of shutting down the border, pushed forward an ambitious plan to nationalize border trade. The hasty closure of borders on land and, as shown in Chapter 4, at sea brought about abrupt changes to the livelihood of border residents, which heightened the tension between the centralizing states and border societies.

The countervailing tendencies at the border revealed several fundamental challenges the communist countries encountered at the frontier during the Cold War. First, the socialist partnership sometimes worked to the advantage of the border citizens in their bargaining with political authorities. Chinese administrations, which had long possessed a sense of superiority in front of the Vietnamese, risked losing their assumed status as a mentor of socialism when a mass of border villagers migrated to Vietnam during the Great Leap Forward. Coercive measures useful elsewhere did not suffice to alleviate the situation at the frontier. Thus, the state had to be responsive to the economic needs of the border society instead of simply relying on force to tackle the refugee issue. Second, the socialist, centrally planned economy aimed at self-reliance often conflicted with the way in which border society operated. The elaborate, resilient cross-border networks restrained by the two neighboring communist countries could easily be restored whenever the monitoring or coercive capacity of the political authorities slumped. The borderlanders had been socialized by the community's age-old interactions with the expanding states with a shrewd acumen of perceiving the changes in state strength and the opportunities ensued. Third, interactions between two countries near their shared boundaries were neither purely international nor local. The tensions between macro-level and micro-level dynamics were especially severe at the Chinese-Vietnamese frontier. The two central governments reaped the benefits of a rather secure border and tailored an ambitious agenda for the border provinces to perform and bolster their ideological and strategic partnership. The border authorities on the ground, however, were not necessarily capable or politically driven to implement the grand strategies of the centralized state. A particularly serious problem was that upwardly accountable local administrations often exaggerated the achievement of top-down state building in their reports to higher authorities. Driven by a misperception of the situation, the central government pushed for measures to further reduce the ambiguities at the frontier, which enlarged the gap between policy goals and state capability.

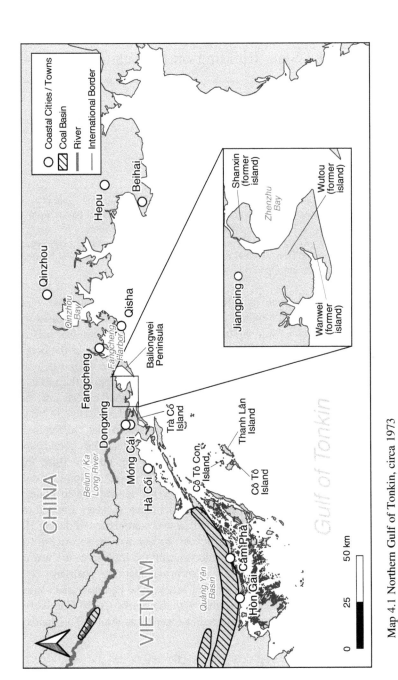

Map 4.1 Northern Gulf of Tonkin, circa 1973

Note: Wanwei, Wutou, and Shanxin were formerly three islands along Guangxi's coast near the Sino-Vietnamese border. They were connected to the mainland during land reclamation 1964–1972 (see Chapter 5).

4 Thwarted State Building on the Sea (1954–1964)

Map 4.1 (*cont.*)
Source: Devon V. Maloney, creator. Map data from OpenStreetMap contributors and available from www.openstreetmap.org/copyright. Location of coal basins from "Principal Coal Basins of Tonkin," E. Willard Miller, "Mineral Resources of Indo-China," *Economic Geography* 22, no. 4 (October 1946), 270, cited in Nguyen, "Dynamite, Opium, and a Transnational Shadow Economy at Tonkinese Coal Mines," 1884. Created using Free and Open Source QGIS, version 3.26.

On May 9, 1961, the year the DRV launched its first Five-Year Plan (1961–1965), Hồ Chí Minh flew to Cô Tô, an island fifty kilometers eastward from the shoreline of Hải Ninh. Addressing the audience as "compatriots" in his speech to the islanders, Hồ Chí Minh praised their progress in the cooperatization movement, encouraged the fisherfolk to increase their catch by applying technology, and urged the island population to support the military stationed there in defense of "the beloved island of the Fatherland" against the "sabotage of imperialists and all kinds of reactionaries."[1] Later, Hồ Chí Minh spoke to the soldiers and police on the island, telling them that "[defending] strategic locations does not only rely on heavy guns; it necessitates good heart: be loyal to the party and be devoted to the people."[2] In January 1962, the provincial authorities of Hải Ninh sought Hồ Chí Minh's permission to install a statue of him at the place where his helicopter had landed and to build a memorial house on the site where he met the assembled islanders. Erected on May 19, 1968, the statue was the only one that was commissioned during Hồ Chí Minh's lifetime.[3] The Vietnamese officials' anxiety over the security of Cô Tô Island and the allegiance of the islanders during the lead-up to the war to reunify with the South reveals the DRV's precarious maritime position.

Populated by Cantonese-speaking ethnic Chinese who had migrated southward over centuries, Cô Tô Island, together with the nearby Cô Tô Con Island and Thanh Lân Island (commonly referred to together as the Cô Tô Islands),

---

[1] "Hồ Chủ tịch về thăm quân và dân đảo Cô Tô [President Hồ visits the army and people of Cô Tô Island]," May 9, 1961, in *SLDQ*, 148.
[2] Ibid, 149. [3] Đảng Cộng sản Việt Nam, "Tượng đài Bác Hồ trên đảo Cô Tô."

were granted to Tonkin by the Convention between China and France respecting the Delimitation of the Frontier between China and Tonkin, signed in Beijing on June 26, 1887 (hereafter the "1887 Convention") because they lie to the west of the meridian 105°43' east longitude.[4] Economically self-sufficient through fishery and farming, the islanders rarely interacted with the Vietnamese mainland except for occasional trips to Móng Cái or Đầm Hà, where they could purchase manufactured goods from ethnic Chinese merchants. Living their lives without having to speak Vietnamese, they identified themselves as "Chinese immigrants," "overseas Chinese," or "Vietnamese Chinese."[5] A part of the Nùng Autonomous Territory and French stronghold during the First Indochina War, the island was brought into the perimeter of the DRV state in 1954, when Vietnamese administrators were dispatched to the island.[6] Responsible for conducting censuses, levying taxes, and later issuing food ration cards and calculating credits based on the fish catch during the cooperatization movement, the officials stationed there inserted the Vietnamese state into the everyday life of the islanders. More importantly, treating the islanders as "Hán rải" – descendants of Han, instead of Hoa Kiều, the Vietnamese state demanded that they take on Vietnamese names and citizenship, which made all the men on the islands eligible for conscription. After this, draft dodging continued in the form of escaping from service or even bribing officials for exclusion from the conscript list.[7]

The highly dynamic relations between the grassroots state apparatus and local inhabitants best illustrate why the geographic setting, economic structure, and social norms of the seafaring people often thwarted state building at the maritime frontier despite the sometimes assiduous attention the central government paid to the outlying territories. In comparison with the Sino-Vietnamese borderlands, state building by the Chinese and Vietnamese revolutionaries at the maritime border generated even more irresolvable tensions among internationalism, nationalism, and transnational localism. Social engineering projects that were essential to the communist revolution, such as the state monopoly of trade and agricultural collectivization in the countryside, as well as administrative tactics descending from ancient statecraft such as household registration, confronted tough challenges from those whom Homi Bhabha characterizes as the "wandering peoples,"[8] who refused to be tied to a

---

[4] "CONVENTION between China and France respecting the Delimitation of Frontier between China and Tonkin, signed at Peking 26th June 1887," 315.
[5] Luong, "A Handbook on the Background of Ethnic Chinese from North Vietnam," 33.
[6] Hoàng Thị Kim Thanh, *Lịch sử Đảng bộ Thị Xã Móng Cái* (hereafter *LDTM*), 75.
[7] The above section is based on Luong, "A Handbook on the Background of Ethnic Chinese from North Vietnam," 33–35.
[8] Bhabha, "DissemiNation," 316.

piece of land or contained within a national culture, let alone mobilized for ideational goals.

Shifting focus from the Sino-Vietnamese borderlands to the northern Gulf of Tonkin (Map 4.1) during the decade from the end of the First Indochina War to the escalation of the Second Indochina War, this chapter views the history of state building from the seashore. Echoing land reforms and agricultural collectivitization in the borderlands, fishery reforms and collectivization toppled the existing economic and social structure and tightened the state's control over fishery labor and catches. The "joint state invasion" culminated in the bilateral fishing agreement in 1957 and an ensuing collaborative survey of natural resources in the Gulf of Tonkin. The fact that the centralization of resource control and flows took place almost simultaneously along the Chinese and Vietnamese coasts left the fisherfolk with little leeway to avoid encountering the state. The characteristics of the reform programs and the geographic, technical, and social realities of the locality nevertheless obstructed the political centers' endeavors to establish primacy along the coastal frontier.

Beijing and Hanoi devised their political strategy toward the fishing communities following the land-oriented rationale that drew upon their past revolutionary experience of mobilizing peasant support through land redistribution and attracting intellectuals with the banner of "national regeneration."[9] The local cadres who were responsible for implementing these policies quickly realized the incompatibility between the centrally crafted revolutionary agenda and the realities of the fishing communities. While determined to claim resources, the grassroots state representatives cushioned the destructive impacts of some of the most excruciating programs of the revolution by accumulating and transmitting knowledge of the local societies back into the bureaucracy. Located between the central state and the indigenous society, the grassroots state apparatus at the coast was simultaneously predatory and protective, acting as an intermediary power between the expanding state and the marginalized population.[10]

The fisherfolk, in comparison with their counterparts living in the borderlands, were both more vulnerable and more empowered. Susceptible to unpredictable hazards, disasters, and emergencies, fishing ranked among the most

---

[9] Fairbank, "The Problem of Revolutionary Asia," 104–106. For important works on the Chinese and Vietnamese communists' strategies of mobilizing both peasants and non-peasants, see Huỳnh Kim Khánh, *Vietnamese Communism*; Luong, *Revolution in the Village*; Johnson, *Peasant Nationalism and Communist Power*; Seldon, *The Yenan Way in Revolutionary China*; Shum, *The Chinese Communists' Road to Power*; Hung, *War and Popular Culture*; Perry, "Moving the Masses"; Woodside, *Community and Revolution in Modern Vietnam*.

[10] This finding echoes Elizabeth Remick's argument in her study of the Chinese local state during the Republican and post-Mao eras (*Building Local States*, 5–6).

treacherous occupations during peace time. The centuries-old transnational cultural and social connections in the Gulf of Tonkin led to customary arrangements among the coastal seafaring communities, ranging from rescuing sinking vessels to offering shelter during storms. By facilitating the enclosures of natural resources, the state restricted the mobility of the fisherfolk and deprived them of this safety net. Despite offering protections against the "sea robbers," state building could pose a greater danger to the lives and livelihood in the maritime space than those in the borderlands, especially when the surrounding national governments coordinated the enclosure. At the same time, asserting the primacy of the state on the sea was always easier said than done. In particular, while the "agreement line" that demarcated fishing resources required engine-powered vessels to implement, the prevalence of wind-powered junks was the technical reality in the Gulf. The inherent openness and fluidity of the fishing economy and the deeply ingrained transnational network among the coastal inhabitants became the seafaring communities' bargaining chips against the state, which often lacked credible punitive power over the highly mobile fisherfolk. Thus, the fluid border between China and Vietnam in the Gulf presented enormous challenges to the nationalization of maritime resources and government control over its outlying citizens.

Current maritime disputes between China and Vietnam over the South China Sea have encouraged scholars and observers to extend this animosity backward into history. Findings in this chapter complicate the conventional narrative about Sino-Vietnamese interactions over their maritime frontier that focuses on the weaponization of fishers and fishing fleets by the Chinese and Vietnamese governments to exert their territorial claims.[11] Even in this conflict-centered narrative, Sino-Vietnamese interactions in the Gulf of Tonkin stand out as an exception. In 1947, the ROC published an eleven-dash territorial line on maps of the South China Sea after its internal circulation, and historians are still divided over whether the line indicates the geographical scope of China's authority over the South China Sea or an "islands attribution" boundary that only claimed "the islands, features, and any adjacent waters."[12] In 1953, two dashes laying in the Gulf of Tonkin were removed from atlases produced by the PRC, reflecting Beijing's warm attitude to its emerging revolutionary ally.[13] In July 1955, the PLA took over Bạch Long Vĩ (known as Fushuizhou in Chinese), an island in the middle of the Gulf, from remnant Nationalists. In January 1957, the PRC transferred the island, together

---

[11] For the weaponization of fishery, see Zhou, "Why Fishing Boats Are on the Territorial Front Lines of the South China Sea"; Roszko, "Fishers and Territorial Anxieties in China and Vietnam."
[12] Chung, "Drawing the U-Shaped Line," 38.
[13] Gao and Jia, "The Nine-Dash Line in the South China Sea," 103.

with its more than two hundred inhabitants, to the DRV, which made the island a village level administrative unit under the city of Haiphong.[14] In December 1973, the DRV, seeing the Gulf as a target for oil exploration, proposed to launch formal negotiations between the two countries to demarcate the maritime boundary there. These negotiations were soon aborted due to the deterioration of Sino-Vietnamese relations after the mid-1970s.[15] A boundary agreement between Beijing and Hanoi to demarcate Chinese and Vietnamese waters in the Gulf in 2000 became a "forgotten maritime compromise," as their territorial disputes in the South China Sea have persisted.[16]

The diplomatic history of boundary settlements between China and Vietnam provides a background to the discussion of state building at the maritime frontier in this chapter. An investigation into the politics of state claims of resources as well as the bottom-up protests against such claims from 1954 to 1964 underlines how even during the recent past, the disputed territories were only one, and not aways the most severe, among many contests taking place in the shared maritime space between China and Vietnam. The most bitter contention during the decade took place between the Chinese and Vietnamese states that spatially and institutionally expanded into the coastal and island societies along the Gulf of Tonkin, on one side, and the seafaring communities that openly or passively resisted such intensive state-making and nation-building activities in the maritime space, on the other. Two countervailing forces, therefore, shaped the history of the Gulf – a state project that territorialized and fragmented the maritime space and an established local but transnational practice that sought to keep the shared body of water open and integrated.

The Historical and Geographic Context of State Building in Northern Gulf of Tonkin

Similar to the land border, the international maritime boundary between Guangdong (later Guangxi) and Hải Ninh (later Quảng Ninh) barely reflected

---

[14] Zou, "Maritime Boundary Delimitation in the Gulf of Tonkin," 245–46; Ji, "The South China Sea Island China Gave Away"; Dan County of Hainan Province Gazetteers Office, "Juan yi: dilizhi"; Ủy Ban Nhân Dân Thành Phố Hải Phòng, "Đề nghị xây dựng Nghị quyết của Hội đồng nhân dân thành phố về cơ chế, chính sách đối với cán bộ, công chức, viên chức công tác tại huyện đảo Bạch Long Vỹ"; Trần Đức Thạnh, *Thiên nhiên và môi trường vùng biển đảo Bạch Long Vĩ*, 153–78.

[15] Zou, "Maritime Boundary Delimitation in the Gulf of Tonkin," 236.

[16] Quote from Kardon, "The Other Gulf of Tonkin Incident"; also see Amer, "The Sino-Vietnamese Approach to Managing Boundary Disputes," 31–33; De Tréglodé, "Maritime Boundary Delimitation and Sino-Vietnamese Cooperation in the Gulf of Tonkin"; Nguyen Hong Thao and Amer, "Managing Vietnam's Maritime Boundary Disputes."

the complicated ethnic, cultural, and economic landscape of the Gulf. The 1887 Convention, which drew a north-south line along the Paris meridian 105°43' east longitude, granted sovereignty over the coastal islands to the east and west of the line to the respective side of China and French Tonkin.[17] This aribitrarily drawn boundary potentially severed the social, cultural, and economic links among various seafaring communities in the northern Gulf of Tonkin and caused potential conflicts of interest that cut across national ties. The development of transnational communities along the coast of the Gulf were largely geographically determined and technologically prescribed. A shallow marginal sea located in northwestern South China Sea, the Gulf is within the East Asian monsoon region. The surface currents of the Gulf, however, are not driven purely by the monsoon wind, which would have created cyclonic circulation (counterclockwise in the Northern Hemisphere) from September through April and anticyclonic circulation in the summer. On the contrary, the Gulf features a cyclonic circulation in summertime as well due to the combined effects of the "tidal-rectified inflow from Qiongzhou Strait" from the east of the Gulf and "stratified wind-driven circulation."[18] The runoff flow of the Red River, which enters the Gulf from the west, generally flows southward along the coast. Only when heavy rain causes large discharges in the summer can the river plume turn northward driven by the southwest monsoon.[19] Over the centuries predating the invention of engine driven vessels, winds and ocean currents largely determined the fisheries in the Gulf. A Gulf-wide cyclonic circulation therefore facilitated the fishing, migration, and sojourn of fisherfolk from South China to coastal northeastern Vietnam.

This geographic feature of the Gulf created a littoral community that not only shared the fishing grounds but also maintained substantial ethnic and cultural ties, which posed challenges to any centralizing state that sought to impose uniformity to its territory. The coastal Ngái people, for example, were a Hakka-speaking ethnic group originally from Southern Guangxi and classified separately from the Hoa by the DRV.[20] An instruction from the WPV Central Committee to the party branches of Hồng Quảng and Haiphong nevertheless acknowledged the discrepancies between the official ethnonym and the cultural identity. These Ngái fisherfolk "not only refer to themselves but also are known to local people" as Hoa Kiều, or overseas Chinese who sought to

---

[17] "CONVENTION between China and France respecting the Delimitation of Frontier between China and Tonkin, signed at Peking 26th June 1887," 315.
[18] Ding et al., "Observational and Model Studies of the Circulation in the Gulf of Tonkin," 6495. For earlier research, see Wyrtki, "Physical Oceanography of the Southeast Asian Waters."
[19] Ding et al., "Observational and Model Studies of the Circulation in the Gulf of Tonkin," 6509.
[20] Ito, "The Ngái in Vietnam," 176.

maintain Chinese citizenship.[21] Similarly, the microclimate of the Gulf and the geographic location made the Cô Tô Islands a navigational pivot for fisherfolk. Due to the existence of fresh water, conditions suitable for agriculture, and ethnic connections, fishers sailing southward from coastal China had made the Cô Tô Islands a staging post for the resupply of food and water during the fishing season. Among the seven thousand people on the islands by the mid-1950s, three thousand were fisherfolk.[22] Following the extension of the Vietnamese state's authority to the islands, the fact that Chinese and Vietnamese citizens, who shared close social-cultural ties, fished alongside each other became a constant political concern for the DRV.[23]

The much less frequent clockwise currents were powerful enough to allow northward migration of Vietnamese fisherfolk along the coast during a certain period, albeit at a much smaller scale in comparison with the flow of people in the opposite direction. The boundary line demarcated in the 1887 Convention passes through the eastern point of Trà Cổ Island (also known as Wanzhu Island), which is only twenty kilometers away from Wanwei, Wutou, and Shanxin, three islands populated by a Kinh (Vietnamese) fishing community yet granted to China.[24] These three islands are off the coast of Dongxing, about eight kilometers east of the boundary with Vietnam. The Kinh in China, known as the Jing people in Mandarin, had a relatively small population of 2,690 in 1952, increasing to 4,000 by the early 1960s.[25] They traced their origin to Đồ Sơn near Haiphong and their earliest history of northward migration to 1511 CE.[26]

---

[21] "CHỈ THỊ CỦA BAN BÍ THƯ Số 41/CT-TW Về chính sách tiến hành cải cách ở miền biển Hồng Quảng [INSTRUCTION OF THE SECRETARIAT no. 41/CT-TW on reform policies in the Hồng Quảng coastal region]," July 26, 1956, in *VKDTT* 17 (1956), 312.

[22] Luong, "A Handbook on the Background of Ethnic Chinese from North Vietnam," 34.

[23] Department of Rural Affairs of CPC Guangdong Provincial Committee, "Zhuanfa Dongxing xianwei renwei guanyu Yuenan Hainingsheng fangmian tichu de jige wenti de baogao [Forwarded report by the CPC Dongxing Committee on several issues raised by Hải Ninh Province of Vietnam]," January 14, 1959, no. 215-1-52-134~138, 2–3/GDPA.

[24] "CONVENTION between China and France respecting the Delimitation of Frontier between China and Tonkin, signed at Peking 26th June 1887," 315.

[25] CPC Fangcheng County Committee, "Fangchengxian disiqu zhaokai Yuenan xiongdi minzu daibiao huiyi zongjie [Summary of the meeting with representatives of the brotherly Việt ethnic minority held by the fourth zone of Fangcheng County]," October 10, 1952, no. 1-2-5-2, 45/FDA; Ethnic Affairs Commission of Guangdong Province, "Pizhuan sheng minwei guanyu Dongxing gezu zizhixian Jiangping gongshe Jingzu diqu yaoqiu fazhan yuye de baogao [Forwarded report from provincial committee on ethnic minorities on the Kinh ethnic minority from Jiangping Commune of Dongxing Autonomous County of Multiple Ethnic Minorities asking for developing fishery]," January 5, 1961, no. 246-1-68-70~71, 2/GDPA. An identical document exists with file no. 235-1-255-205.

[26] Editorial board, *Jingzu jianzhi*, 6. For literature in English on the ethnic Kinh, see Shih, *Autonomy, Ethnicity, and Poverty in Southwestern China*, 75–94; Legerton and Rawson, *Invisible China*, 79–98; Cheung, "Regional Development and Cross-Border Cultural Linkage," 277–311.

The local folklore about the mythical formation of these four coastal islands embodies the long-existing ethnic connections across the more recently constructed international boundary. According to this myth, a centipede spirit lived inside a deep cave in Mt. White Dragon located in the northwestern coast of the Gulf. It demanded human sacrifice from passing ships and capsized those refusing to obey with huge waves. The patron sea god of the fishing community eventually killed the centipede spirit, which fell into four pieces: the head becoming Wutou Island (*tou* means head), the mouth with two big teeth turning into Wanzhu Island (*zhu* means teeth), the trunk with its heart evolving into Shanxin Island (*xin* means heart), and the tail transforming into Wanwei Island (*wei* means tail).[27] Notably, despite this holistic regional cultural context, the four islands nevertheless fell on different sides of the international boundary decided by the political centers, with three islands assigned as Chinese territory, and Wanzhu (Trà Cổ) Island becoming Vietnamese. These transnational cultural connections were nevertheless not exclusive. The creation myth of the islands bears resemblance to the local Chinese legend developed in late fourteenth century about a sea god slashing a White Dragon, which gave the Bailongwei ("White Dragon Tail") Peninsula (also known as "White Dragon Peninsula") – the area to the east of Wanwei across the Zhenzhu Bay – its name. Until today, the annual Ha Festival that worships the sea god and influential ancestors of the local Kinh community begins with the Kinh cultural leaders traveling to the Bailingwei Peninsula to receive the patron god.[28]

Besides cultural ties, the economy of the three Kinh-populated islands resembled that of the coastal communities in northern Vietnam. Unlike the nearby Chinese fisherfolk who sailed offshore on junks to catch fish, inshore fishing generated most of the income for the Kinh community. Over centuries, the Kinh fisherfolk had developed techniques such as walking on stilts through soft sand and catching fish by hand-held net on the shoal. Another nimble fishing craft was "fish ponds" – inshore waters enclosed by wooden fences and nets where small fish and shrimp entered during the rising tide to be trapped in the pond when the tide receded. Small, family-owned workshops produced fish sauce from the catch of the fishing ponds for sale in Guangdong, Guangxi, and Vietnam.[29] Similar to other rural Asian societies, a strong communal tradition developed in the Kinh community. Groups of families self-organized into mutual-help units that collectively purchased or

---

[27] Cheung, "Regional Development and Cross-Border Cultural Linkage," 281–83.
[28] Zhang, "Zhong-Yue bianjie kuajing jiaowang yu Guangxi Jingzu kuaguo shenfen rentong," 125.
[29] Ethnic Affairs Commission of Guangdong Province, "Pizhuan sheng minwei guanyu Dongxing gezu zizhixian Jiangping gongshe Jingzu diqu yaoqiu fazhan yuye de baogao," 3.

Figure 4.1 A household temple in Wanwei, Guangxi
Note: The temple was established in 1970 and renovated several times since then by three clans in Wanwei that had long worshipped together.
It commemorates a young man from one of the clans who died from shipwreck in 1968 on his way to obtain construction material to help another clan build a new home, as well as a few other enshrined ancestors of these clans.
Source: Author, September 2015

rented nets, boats, and other fishing gear as well as worshipped together (Figure 4.1).[30]

Since the founding of the PRC, the Kinh community living in the southwest corner of China attracted close attention from Beijing that was disproportionate to its population size due to the sensitivity of Sino-Vietnamese relations. During the initial years of communist rule, the Chinese government sought to bring the "brotherly Việt ethnic group" into the state's perimeter and forge their identity with the Chinese nation by promoting pro-party activists to township leadership, organizing touring delegations to Beijing, recruiting students to the South Central College for Nationalities located in Wuhan,

---

[30] Guangxi Zhuang Autonomous Region Gazetteers Office, *Guangxi tongzhi: minzuzhi*, 473.

training nurses and midwives, and granting loans on favorable terms.[31] Excessive arrests and persecution during "bandit repression," caused by the suspicion about the community's links to the ROC forces operating out at sea, and land reform nevertheless triggered an exodus of Kinh to Vietnam.[32] Embargoes on trade with French-held Móng Cái – the main market for the fish sauce produced on the three islands – during the First Indochina War was a harbinger of continued strife between the sea-reliant populace and land-oriented state over livelihood.[33] To ameliorate the Kinh community's fear over expulsion, the Guangxi provincial authorities granted Wanwei, Wutou, and Shanxin the status of Ethnic Autonomous Township.[34] In May 1958, Beijing changed the official name of these ethnic Vietnamese people from "Yue" (Việt) to "Jing" (Kinh),[35] probably in an attempt to sever their ties with the Vietnamese nation, at least nominally, and to solidify their allegiance to China. The three islands were merged into the Dongxing Autonomous County of Multiple Ethnicities, which was also home to the Zhuang and the Yao, in the same year.[36] This move officially recognized Kinh as one of the ethnic minorities in the multiethnic nation-state and incorporated it into the Regional Ethnic Autonomy System that largely formed autonomous regions based on population size.[37]

Interactions with the Ngái people of Hồng Quảng, the Cantonese of Cô Tô Islands, and the Kinh community of coastal Guangdong all underscored the challenges that the two revolutionary states could encounter when trying to establish themselves along their maritime border. Nationalist anxiety and threats from competing states in the capitalist bloc, namely South Vietnam and the ROC, necessitated the securitization of the coastal societies, which were considered more porous and vulnerable than land borders. The interconnected coastal inhabitants, however, were often culturally and economically alien to the inland society and state. Meanwhile, both the Chinese and Vietnamese communists sought to exert the supreme authority of the state over the coastal society by denying and destroying the status of old social elites. In communities that thrived on fishing, those deemed by the political

---

[31] CPC Fangcheng County Committee, "Fangchengxian disiqu zhaokai Yuenan xiongdi minzu daibiao huiyi zongjie," 45–46; Editorial board, *Jingzu jianshi*, 44.
[32] Zhang, "Zhong-Yue bianjie kuajing jiaowang yu Guangxi Jingzu kuaguo shenfen rentong," 107.
[33] CPC Fangcheng County Committee, "Fangchengxian disiqu zhaokai Yuenan xiongdi minzu daibiao huiyi zongjie," 46.
[34] Zhang, "Zhong-Yue bianjie kuajing jiaowang yu Guangxi Jingzu kuaguo shenfen rentong," 107.
[35] Editorial board, *Jingzu jianshi*, 44.
[36] Provincial People's Committee, "Guanyu tongyi wosheng jiang Shiwanshan Zhuangzu Yaozu Zizhixian gaimingwei Dongxing Gezu Zhizhixian de tongzhi [Circular on endorsement to change the name of Shiwanshan Autonomous County of Zhuang and Yao into Dongxing Autonomous County of Multiple Ethnicities]," May 8, 1958, no. 235-1-219-155~156, 1/GDPA.
[37] Zhang, "Zhong-Yue bianjie kuajing jiaowang yu Guangxi Jingzu kuaguo shenfen rentong," 108.

authorities as "class enemies" or "bad elements," such as wealthy boat owners, who could afford larger, safer fishing junks, and esteemed liturgical leaders, who claimed to be capable of communicating with the sea gods, were seen by fisherfolk as essential to their lives and livelihood. The state apparatus, imposed from above and coming from outside the local community, tended to fail as competitive substitutes for such protective roles. Any radical class struggle or collectivization that disturbed or overthrew grounded social structures would encounter substantial resistance.

The coastal societies of the northern Gulf of Tonkin also experienced major changes in administrative divisions, which reflected the shifting priorities of the two central governments. China's coast along the Gulf of Tonkin had been administered by Guangdong Province since the Ming Dynasty. In May 1951, however, the central government put the area under the administration of Guangxi to more effectively launch military and political campaigns against remnant Nationalist "bandits," before returning it to Guangdong in May 1955 "to achieve unified leadership on national defense and fishery in the South China Sea."[38] During the decade from 1955 to 1965, though, Sino-Vietnamese maritime border issues never topped the agenda of the Guangdong provincial government. Areas adjacent to Hong Kong and Macau, where people could flee from the waves of political movements by jumping the porous boundary with the capitalist world, were of greater security concern to the political authorities.[39] Thus, in 1965, Beijing again decided to have Guangxi govern the coastal counties to coordinate border defense after the escalation of the Second Indochina War.[40]

After the end of the First Indochina War, the coastal area of northeast Vietnam fell under the administration of Hải Ninh Province and Hồng Quảng Special Zone, respectively.[41] The Quảng Yên basin, where Hồng Quảng was located, had been the center of French investment of natural resources in Tonkin. The basin's reserve of anthracite coal "of exceptional quality," conveniently located on the coast, made Indochina the second largest coal exporter in the Far East during the first half of the twentieth century, only behind Manchuria.[42] The mining industries made Hồng Quảng "the cradle of

---

[38] State Council of the PRC, "Guowuyuan guanyu jiang Guangxisheng de Qinxian, Hepu, Lingshan, Fangcheng sixian he Beihaishi huagui Guangdong sheng lingdao de jueding," 370.

[39] Commission of Politics and Laws of Guangdong Province, "Guanyu dangqian yanhai bianfang zhi'an guanli he jingji zhengce zhixing qingkuang he yijian de baogao [Report on public security and implementation of economic policy in coastal border defense]," May 16, 1963, no. 217-1-13-23, 30–31/GDPA.

[40] Liang, *Guangxi jingji nianjian 1985*, 98. The geographic area covered in this chapter also includes Leizhou Peninusla and Hainan as they were both integrated parts of the economic and social network in the northern Gulf of Tonkin.

[41] Ban nghiên cứu lịch sử Đảng tỉnh ủy Quảng Ninh, *SLDQ*, 13.

[42] Brocheux and Hémery, *Indochina*, 124.

the [Vietnamese] working class" in the revolutionary narrative sponsored by the DRV.[43] In August 1954, French colonial forces withdrew from Hải Ninh but continued occupying Hồng Quảng during the 300-day transitional period stipulated by the Geneva Accords.[44] On April 24, 1955, the last French colonial soldier left the coastal mining town Hòn Gai, which marked the end of "seventy-two years of persistent and brave struggle" of the "mineworkers and peoples of various ethnicities" of northeastern Vietnam that followed the French conquest of the mineral rich area in 1883.[45] In October 1963, Hanoi decided to merge Hải Ninh and Hồng Quảng into Quảng Ninh Province to combine the former's strength in agriculture and fishing and the latter's resources in mining "to create favorable conditions of boosting massive socialist production," and to fortify the defense of northeast Vietnam.[46] Such administrative changes meant that the Chinese and Vietnamese states' policies toward their fishing population in the region often lacked consistency and stability.

Establishing the Socialist State: The Fishery Reform and Early Phase Collectivization

By the end of the 1950s, the Chinese and Vietnamese revolutionary states had established a presence in their respective coastal societies through fishery reform and become deeply involved in the fishery of the Gulf after the initial stage of collectivization. Traditional elites of the fishing communities, such as owners of large boats or enclosed fish fences, were overthrown from their dominant status, whereas fishers gradually lost control over their livelihood to the local cadres serving as agents of the centralizing state. Because, in the beginning of their political consolidation, the two governments had prioritized destroying the "feudal" land-ownership in the agricultural societies of the vast interior over reforming fishery, they pressed for reforms in the coastal societies later than the rest of their countries and in a hasty manner.[47] Transferring the tactics of land reforms to the seafaring communities often turned out to be impractical. Farmland was dividable and redistributable; junks and fishing nets were not. Moreover, the vibrant sea trade networks in the Gulf of Tonkin

---

[43] "Đảng bộ khu Hồng Quảng và Đảng bộ tỉnh Hải Ninh hợp nhất thành Đảng bộ tỉnh Quảng Ninh," in *SLDQ*, 188.
[44] Ban nghiên cứu lịch sử Đảng tỉnh ủy Quảng Ninh, *SLDQ*, 17.   [45] Ibid., 9.
[46] "Đảng bộ khu Hồng Quảng và Đảng bộ tỉnh Hải Ninh hợp nhất thành Đảng bộ tỉnh Quảng Ninh," 187–88.
[47] Commission of Coastal Defense of the South China Bureau of the CPC Central Committee, "Huanan yanhai yuye minzhu gaige zongjie baogao [Report on the democratic reform of fishery in the coastal area of South China], November 1953, no. 236-1-8-43, 3/GDPA; "CHỈ THỊ CỦA BAN BÍ THƯ Số 41/CT-TW Về chính sách tiến hành cải cách ở miền biển Hồng Quảng," 312–13.

created "international economic alliances" among the local communities,[48] with a transnational market of aquatic products that defied the governments' intensified efforts to leverage marine resources in service of state-controlled economic development.

The PRC first extended its institutional presence to the coastal society along the northern Gulf of Tonkin during the "bandit crushing campaign" in South China from 1950 to 1951. During the Second World War and the Chinese Civil War, the water-dwellers of South China had been woven into the intelligence and arms supply network with Hong Kong and Macau sponsored by the allied forces of the United States and the ROC. The continuous connections between the fisherfolk and foreign military were thus a cause for grave security concern to Beijing as the United States and the ROC placed a joint naval blockade against coastal China after the outbreak of the Korean War.[49] To strengthen maritime defenses against hostile navies, the South China Bureau of the CPC Central Committee decided to "go all out to mobilize the fishers and organize them to prevent infiltration and sneak attacks" from the enemy.[50] While military campaigns gradually wiped out open challenges to state power, integrating the piscatorial community into the state project required a delicate balance between coercive and conciliatory measures. In April 1951, the Border Defense Bureau of Guangdong reported on the "fisherfolk work" to the provincial authorities and highlighted that it was incumbent on them to promote the state's image as a protector of fisherfolk's interests and resolve the livelihood difficulties of the vulnerable to bring stability and security to the coastal border.[51]

In tandem with political consolidation, the party-state sought to assert greater control over the production methods used in the fisheries, pitching the state against existing local elites. In early 1951, local cadres in Guangdong set out to register fisherfolk, license their vessels, and organize fisherfolk into the state sponsored "fishers associations" led by pro-party "activists" identified among the community. This echoed the party's strategy of rebelling against the rural elites by organizing "peasants associations" in the 1920s. Building upon these two measures, fishing junks were formed into small brigades (of eight to ten vessels), medium brigades (of thirty vessels), and large brigades (of one hundred vessels), each led by a captain and a vice captain, who were typically the "activist" leaders in the fishers' association. Besides facilitating taxation,

---

[48] Morieux, *The Channel*, 212.   [49] Du, "Embodied Borders," 103.
[50] Hou, "Xin Zhongguo chuqi Guangdong yanhai yuye minzhu gaige yu jiaqiang haifang de douzheng," 248.
[51] Bureau of Border Defense of Guangdong Province, "Guanyu bianfang yanhai yumin gongzuo yiban qingkuang zonghe [Summary of the general situation of works among fisherfolk in the coastal border]," April 14, 1951, no. 238-1-18-1, 3/GDPA.

fishing brigades addressed the state's security concerns by giving the local authorities a pervasive influence on the movement of fishing junks, as each small brigade was supposed to set out and return together.[52] Without much prior contact with the fishing community, local cadres often meshed the state-making project with local customs to cultivate ties with the highly mobile population. Some fisherfolk encountered the state of the newly established People's Republic for the first time when attending service at church, where the local cadres announced registration policies and conducted "educational sessions" about the fishery associations.[53] Making the population and vessels visible to the state prepared the way for political authorities to control the coastal economy and generate revenues from it later on.

Most fisherfolk's attitudes toward the state-building project, however, was lukewarm at best. As the PLA had expropriated fishing junks in its attack on Hainan Island from March to May 1950, the fishing community became deeply suspicious that the fisherfolk organization would prime the population for conscription, while boat registration set the stage for the campaign against Taiwan. The Guangdong Bureau of Border Defense blamed the "political backwardness" of the seafaring people caused by "imperialist suppression and the reactionary rule of feudalists" for the slow progress of vessel registration. In addition, they warned against the "complicated social composition" of the coastal border, which had allowed "landlords, evil bullies, thugs, gangsters, and sea thieves" to maintain dominant positions.[54] The greatest cause of the strained relationship between the expanding state and the fishing population, however, was the disruptive effects of unrealistic yet stringent policies against established fishery practices. Some coastal police stations, for instance, demanded vessels setting out for fishing to return within twenty-four or seventy-two hours to enhance port security outside the time of regular patrolling. This was virtually impossible except for the "three-people dinghies," commonly known as sampans, which were employed for inshore shallow water fishing. Thus, many fisherfolk had to give up sailing out on the sea altogether.[55] Meanwhile, during the nationwide campaign to crack down on counterrevolutionaries, many fishing boats were confiscated from their owners, who were forced to abandon their businesses under political pressure. Consequently, the fishery in the region receded abruptly.[56] This initial stage of state building in the coastal society not only fell short of reshuffling the social structure in service to the unchallenged authority of the party but also

---

[52] Ibid., 3–4.   [53] Ibid., 5.   [54] The quote and paraphrases are from ibid., 5.
[55] Bureau of Islands of Guangdong, "Youguan yanhai bianfang gongzuo de yixie wenti [Issues about defense of coastal border]," July 17, 1951, no. 238-1-18-12, 2/GDPA.
[56] Commission of Coastal Defense of the South China Bureau of the CPC Central Committee, "Huanan yanhai yuye minzhu gaige zongjie baogao," 3–4.

shook the economic foundation from which the state derived taxes and revenues.

The land reform launched in June 1950 unintentionally exacerbated the existing social inequalities in the coastal counties and turned some fisherfolk into pariahs. The inhabitants of the piscatorial society were far from homogenous. Farmers and part-time fishers (those who fished and processed salted fish seasonally and farmed for the rest of the year) had long looked down upon the fisherfolk without landed property, especially the Danjia who lived entirely on junks. Lacking a presence on the land had deprived the boat people of power in the land-based political structure while rendering them relatively less fettered by state scrutiny. As the party branch of Beihai – the largest fishing port in Guangxi – admitted in early 1953, the local cadres had largely ignored the fishing population since taking power in towns where both fishers and non-fishers lived. Likewise, the fisherfolk, who were mostly away fishing at sea while mobilization meetings or other revolutionary state building were taking place, seldom heeded the political authorities seated in towns and districts.[57] Thus, the land reform, which strongly favored the agrarian population from the start, largely overlooked and jeopardized the interests of the fishing and semi-fishing community, which numbered around 160,000 in the coastal counties of Beihai, Qinzhou, and Fangcheng.[58]

The situation was such that even Beijing authorities, concerned about gaining acquiescence from the coastal population for the sake of national defense, warned against the dangerous alienation of the seafaring people during the state-led redistribution of rural wealth. The local government had simply taxed the fisherfolk while ignored the latter's difficulties with repairing junks, mending nets, and selling their catch. While not being distributed with land, vegetable plots, or homesteads during the land reform, some fisherfolk's foreshore seabed (*haidi*) and fixed netting operation (*wangdi*) on the oceanfront were reassigned to peasants, which left those who relied on shallow water fisheries with no place to fish.[59] Rather than a deliberate policy of seizing resources from fishers to benefit the farmers, the mistaken redistribution of the seabed was more probably caused by the long-existing Chinese land registration practices, which did not distinguish land and seabed.[60] As the ownership of land lot or seabed was recorded on land deeds in the same manner, cadres would not be able to tell them apart without visiting the physical sites. The fisherfolk were also vulnerable to the state-monopolized salt supply system.

---

[57] CPC Municipal Committee of Beihai, "Yumin wenti cailiao baogao [Report on fisherfolk issues]," August 1, 1953, no. 204-5-20-105~110, 2–4/GDPA.

[58] CPC Regional Committee of Qinzhou and Municipal Committee of Beihai, "Guanyu yumin gongzuo huiyi de baogao [Report on the meeting regarding fisherfolk issues]," March 4, 1953, no. 204-5-20-001~007, 2/GDPA.

[59] Ibid., 2.   [60] Hoskin, "Communication through Cartography – China 1946–1947."

Without being issued salt purchase licenses, many fishers were denied access to salt in large quantity, which was the crucial ingredient to produce salted fish or even cooking salt. Frustrated with the predatory state, some fisherfolk told the cadres that "it would be better if we and the government could just leave each other alone."[61]

Ultimately, the revolutionary state designed the fishery reform programs to achieve the ambitious goals of shaking up the social structure in coastal China to generate legitimacy among the fishing population and boosting fish catches. While the party-state promulgated its agrarian reform law in June 1950, to be applied across the nation, fishery reform along the South China coast did not begin until February 1953 but was still declared completed after a mere eight months.[62] In comparison with the large number of peasants, coastal fishers only accounted for a small fraction of the total population in South China, which clearly rendered fishery reform a less-prioritized task on the state's agenda despite the ability of the industry to bring in large government revenues. Carried out in a hasty fashion without thorough appreciation of local conditions, fishery reform met with even more stiff resistance from the fisherfolk and crew members than during vessel registration.

Inconsistency within the party cadres and bureaucracy also foreshadowed the rocky extension of the reach of the state into a society that relied on the sea for its livelihood. Implementing the tactics of agrarian reform, the government decided to dispatch "work teams" to the fishing communities and required cadres to live, eat, and work together with the fisherfolk. A veteran who had been transferred from the military to the local government of west Guangdong expressed his concern at a preparatory meeting on fishery reform that "dying in a battle is not scary; being drowned after the boat capsizes is."[63] His hesitancy was not uncommon among the "southwardly dispatched cadres" (*nanxia ganbu*) – military and civilian personnel transferred from northern China where the party had consolidated its control to fill the political vacuum left by the defeated Nationalists toward the end of the Chinese Civil War.[64] Besides language barriers, climatic differences, and culinary changes, being expected to venture out onto the sea further dampened revolutionary enthusiasm. In addition, many members of the fishery-reform work teams were

---

[61] CPC Regional Committee of Qinzhou and Municipal Committee of Beihai, "Guanyu yumin gongzuo huiyi de baogao," 3.
[62] Ibid., 3; Commission of Coastal Defense of the South China Bureau of the CPC Central Committee, "Huanan yanhai yuye minzhu gaige zongjie baogao," 1.
[63] Border Committee of CPC Western Guanggdong Branch, "Yuzheng ganbu xunlianban zongjie baogao [Summary of training sessions of cadres of fishing affairs]," April 16, 1953, 204-5-75-089~092, 2/GDPA.
[64] In October 1948, the CPC Central Committee decided to transfer 53,000 cadres from the north to the "newly liberated" south. He, "Qianli da 'shuxue,'" 34–35.

reassigned from land-reform teams and interpreted their new position as a demotion or a sign of the higher authority's dissatisfaction with their performance, as most of their former colleagues had assumed urban jobs after completing the land reform.[65] Hastily launched into a marginal society and led by half-hearted cadres, fishery reform faced gigantic challenges in its attempt to reverse the alienation of the fishing population; to forge new, class-based allegiances channeled toward the party-state in the coastal society; and to mitigate the perceived security threats along the maritime frontier.

Learning from the lessons of land reform and recognizing the abysmal lack of a protective function of the state in comparison with its extractive capacity, the CPC Central Committee urged local authorities to support the fisherfolk's livelihood and alleviate their economic hardship during fishery reform to reverse their resentment against the revolution.[66] Toeing the party line, in March 1953, the government of Qinzhou and Beihai set out a guideline of "relying on hired fishery workers and poor independent workers and uniting the general fishers (including the fishery capitalists)" while "accurately striking the very few," namely the "bandit heads, evil bullies, feudal labor contractors, gangster bosses, fled landlords, and counterrevolutionaries."[67] To amend the unequal treatment of peasants and fishers during land reform, the local state returned the redistributed inshore seabed to the fishing communities. Vegetable and housing slots were assigned to the fishing population in the hope of "reinforcing their national identity" by forging more ties between their livelihood and the land. Taxation on fish sauce was abolished, as the ingredients of the product – fish and salt – had already been taxed.[68]

Deciding on the class status of the fishing community, which did not comprise coherent classes, formed the core of the party-state's struggle to generate legitimacy in the coastal society. Many villages in South China had no distinct hierarchies of power, nor class sentiments.[69] The social composition of the piscatorial community deviated even further from the rural class structure of landlords dominating over an underclass of tenants. Many junk owners and their family members went fishing together with the crew they employed to man the ship. With more navigational knowledge and richer fishing experience, the owners were often the most skilled workers among

---

[65] Border Committee of CCP Western Guanggdong Branch, "Yuzheng ganbu xunlianban zongjie baogao," 2.
[66] Commission of Coastal Defense of the South China Bureau of the CPC Central Committee, "Huanan yanhai yuye minzhu gaige zongjie baogao," 4.
[67] CPC Regional Committee of Qinzhou and Municipal Committee of Beihai, "Guanyu yumin gongzuo huiyi de baogao," 4, 9.
[68] Ibid., 5.
[69] Siu, *Agents and Victims in South China*, 128, 141. Also see Unger, "The Class System in Rural China."

the crew. County officials observed that even large-vessel owners, who could afford not to join the hazardous fishing voyage, "invest in junks and nets and thus differ from rural landlords who simply lease their land without investment." The reform program thus categorized the ship owners as "fishery capitalists" (*yuye zibenjia*) who deserved to be "united" in the revolution instead of "landlords" who would be ousted from politically and economically powerful positions.[70]

Following the same categorizing principles, the vast majority of the coastal population were identified as an underclass that should be granted with political capital to lend the reform momentum. These included "hired fishing workers" (*yugong*) who owned few to no fishing tools and thus had to work for ship owners, "poor independent laborers" (*pinku laodongzhe*) who fished and sometimes lived on sampans without hiring anyone, and ordinary fishers (*yiban yumin*) who could afford small junks and hire a few people.[71] All of them were seen as being exploited by various groups of power intermediaries in the coastal society, notably the seafood brokers (known as *yulan*) who were the agents between the fisherfolk and wholesale fishmongers and usually formed regional monopolies via guilds.[72] Besides earning a commission on the total business done, *yulan* advanced loans to fisherfolk in financial trouble yet charged with an exceedingly high interest rate.[73] The greatest peril to the reform agenda came from those who threatened the government's monopoly of violence and potentially obstructed the extension of the state to grassroots societies, including spies and agents of the Nationalists who engaged in subversive activities, military adventurers such as bandit heads and gang leaders, and "feudalist butlers" (*fengjian batou*) who controlled the labor market in the ports by acting as the agent of privileged elites and bullying the local residents with violent gangsters.[74]

While classifying the owners of large fishing junks as capitalists spared them the violent eradication and brutal torture imposed on landlords, the reform program empowered the deck laborers to check the wealth the junk owners could accumulate. In September 1953, the local authority of Qisha in Qin County – the second largest fishery port in Guangxi – hosted a negotiation between the crew member representatives and the junk owners. While

---

[70] CPC Regional Committee of Qinzhou and Municipal Committee of Beihai, "Guanyu yumin gongzuo huiyi de baogao," 11
[71] Ibid., 10–11.
[72] Committee of Coastal Defense of the South China Bureau of the CPC Central Committee, "Huanan yanhai yuye minzhu gaige zongjie baogao," 2.
[73] Bureau of Foreign Trade of Ministry of Industry, *China Industrial Handbooks: Chekiang*, 369. I thank Mark Hoskin for pointing me to this source.
[74] CPC Regional Committee of Qinzhou and Municipal Committee of Beihai, "Guanyu yumin gongzuo huiyi de baogao," 11.

blocking the radical agenda proposed by the state-sponsored crew union to share vessel ownership, the local state buttressed the hired fishing workers' demand to split the revenue following a "thirty-two and sixty-eight rule." Namely, the owner would receive 32 percent of the after-tax revenue of the junk and the remaining 68 percent would be the crew's salary. In addition, the union, which assumed the sole power of deciding the salary bands backed by the revolutionary state, deliberately put the salaries for skilled workers such as deck bosses or helmsmen, who were often close relatives of the junk owners, into a lower bracket.[75]

The local officials then found themselves trapped in difficult labor negotiations where neither side was satisfied with the state. Not being able to break even, let alone to make profits, as a result of their reduced income from ownership and labor, many junk owners stopped investing in the basic maintenance of their vessels. An owner of two medium junks in Qisha even decided to sell them in exchange for a small family sampan so that he would not have to hire any crew and could save the rest of his funds in a bank to produce interest instead of "investing in the junks and then getting bullied [by the crew members]."[76] In light of the sapping morale of the fisherfolk and the mounting pressure of a declining fishery catch, local officials called a labor representatives' meeting to suspend the "thirty-two and sixty-eight rule" on October 27. Rumors soon spread among the poorer fisherfolk that the state was about to yield to the junk owners' demand for a forty–sixty distribution of income. Accusing the state of "relapsing to a capitalist line," some crew workers staged a strike four days later, citing inclement weather that day to stave off a head-on confrontation with officials. After a lengthy negotiation that lasted for another two months, a "thirty-six and sixty-four" income distribution deal was concluded, with the junk owners agreeing to contribute to a "labor insurance" pot to cover the medical expenditure of work-related injuries of all crew members including themselves.[77]

The result of the negotiations at Qisha indicated that while the state planned to transplant the so far successful model of land reform to the coastal area, the fishery reforms eventually adopted the party's strategy in cities, where the first task was to avoid violent class conflicts and to keep industries open and workers at their jobs.[78] Hastily launched toward the end of the nationwide campaign to oust rural elites in places where the social stratification was far removed from revolutionary theory, the reforms barely struck the delicate

---

[75] The above section is based on Department of Marine Products of Qinzhou Prefectural Commission, "Fanchengxian Qishagang tiaozheng guyong guanxi de zongjie [Summary of the adjustment of labor relations in Qisha port]," December 31, 1953, no. 204-5-20-054~062, 2–3/GDPA.
[76] Ibid., 3.   [77] The above section is based on ibid., 4–7.
[78] Spence, *The Search for Modern China*, 492.

balance between increasing the state's coercive capability and building up its protective strength. Often lacking in local knowledge, the state typically intervened in fishery issues by introducing drastic changes and then fell back to a more collaborative stance for fear of wrecking its power base or economic foundation. This pattern of unwavering yet frequently thwarted state building continued through the mid-1950s as the government made audacious departures from previous authorities' practices of controlling the fishery industry and the fishing population, even as its understaffed local institutions often fell short of projecting state power along the coast in a consistent manner.

In late 1953 and early 1954, the local Chinese state pushed on to the cooperatization movement right after declaring the fishery reform a success. At Qisha, the cadres persuaded the poor fisherfolk to join cooperatives by promising enhanced safety on large junks or motorized boats purchased with government loans in comparison to sampans or rafts that were much more vulnerable to inclement weather; meanwhile, they sought to assuage the fears among the well-off ship owners by promising dividends based on investments in junks and nets.[79] By the end of 1954, the local Chinese authorities moved more than 40 percent of the fisherfolk along the Gulf of Tonkin into fishing cooperative units or mutual aid groups and advanced loans to the cooperatives to purchase larger junks and nets.[80]

While the cadres hoped that the intensification of production would boost catches and thus "outfish" the yields under the Nationalist rule, some programs of this state-led modernization project backfired. Having operated small junks, sampans, and rafts for generations, some fisherfolk lacked the prowess demanded when handling large ships or any interest in switching to a different fishing ground farther out at sea. Setting up the woven bamboo fence (*yuhu*), a kind of trap to catch migratory fish, much earlier in the year than before, some cooperatives reported that the percentage of small fish among the catches significantly increased, reaching 70 to 80 percent in the spring. The Beihai local authorities admitted that the aggressive, single-minded pursuit of that scale and intensity would jeopardize the sustainability of fishery.[81] Financially, the state's plan to replace small vessels with larger ones left the fisherfolk heavily in debt. The villagers who fished and farmed seasonally in particular begrudged the social engineering project as they had to answer to both agricultural and fishery cooperatization policies, yet neither of these programs

---

[79] Work team of establishing Laodong Cooperative, "Fangchengxian dierqu Qishagang laodong yuye shengchan hezuoshe gongzuo zongjie [Summary of establishing Laodong Cooperative at Qisha port, of the second district of Fangcheng County]," May 1955, no. 1-2-40-13, 22–30/ FDA.

[80] "Beihai yuye gongzuo gaikuang [Brief summary of fishery in Beihai]," 1955, no. 204-5-107-040~050, 2/GDPA.

[81] Ibid.

took into consideration the particular rhythm of the part-time fisherfolk's economic life. Despite successfully wiping out the influential private agents, state-run fishery companies accumulated a large backlog because seafood imported from Vietnam and freshwater fish from Hubei and Zhejiang sometimes offered much more competitive prices.[82] As a bold move to align capture fishery with the national economic agenda, the fishery cooperatives nonetheless encapsulated the communist state's determination to modernize an economy of which it had little knowledge. In many ways, these efforts were simply a continuation of the increasing legal and institutional protection of fisheries instituted during the Republican era in response to environmental decay and escalated fishery disputes with Japan, which not only harbored territorial ambitions against China but also deployed much more effective motorized drag-net vessels on an industrial scale.[83] Departing from earlier regulatory practice, however, the communist state intervened more deeply into the technology and organization of fishing activities.

In tandem with direct state involvement into capture fishery, the seafaring communities encountered enhanced securitization of their daily lives. The Qinzhou authorities, which governed China's coastal counties along the Gulf of Tonkin, decided to incorporate the fisherfolk, including the boat people, into the household registration system, standardize the registration cards of vessels across all ports, and require different ranks of ships to berth at respectively designated areas to guard the coastal society against spies and agents. To meet the people who appeared to live adrift and standardize their information on state records, the Qinzhou authorities instructed local cadres to better understand the fisherfolk's itineraries to increase the chance of registering them when and where they moored. To overcome language barriers and illiteracy, the registration work teams were required to recruit local students, teachers, and other intellectuals who could serve as communication channels between fishing communities and the expanding state.[84]

Neither the attempts to register fishing households nor the regulations on ship registration were new to Chinese history. After the Ming Dynasty failed to apply the peasantry-based household registration system to the fishing population, the Qing government treated their boats as tax units, thus control-

---

[82] Ibid., 3, 7.
[83] Muscolino, *Fishing Wars and Environmental Changes in Late Imperial and Modern China*, 96–126. For a review of Chinese fishery laws, see Huang, *Haiyang fa yu yuye fagui*; Huang and He, "Management of China's Capture Fisheries," 176–77.
[84] This paragraph is based on CPC Qinzhou Regional Committee, "Qinzhou quyu yuchuanmin hukou jianli yu zhengdun gongzuo jihua de pishi [Instructions on the plan to establish household registration of fisherfolk and boat people in Qinzhou]," October 3, 1955, no. 1-2-32-5, 26–31/FDA.

ling the fisherfolk indirectly.[85] The Nationalist government promulgated rules to register ship masters and chief engineers and carried out fishery surveys in 1932 and 1935 – a determined state expansion interrupted by the Second World War.[86] To aid postwar reconstruction efforts, the Ministry of Agriculture and Forestry of the ROC compiled statistics on fishing households, fisherfolk, and vessels in 1946.[87] Consecutive Chinese states had sought to turn the selective, complex realities of the coastal China into numbers in official records; the responsibility of maintaining order in the port was nevertheless left in the hands of port headmen, who would inspect ships for contraband and prevent theft.[88] The renewed efforts during the communist era to register households and conduct a census of fisherfolk indicated the state's determination to assert its presence along the shoreline driven by the acute threat from ROC incursions into coastal waters. Requiring identification cards at port entry allowed the state to tie the seafaring people to "home" locations, thereby increasing its monitoring capacity over the latter's movement.

Along the DRV's northern coast, the expansion and consolidation of the state unfolded in a similar manner, beginning with the registration of vessels and followed by a fishery reform that enabled the government to seize key resources from the "exploitative class" and reallocate them to appeal to the lower class. By the time Hanoi launched its fishery reform program in July 1956, two years had passed since the DRV claimed victory in North Vietnam. Yet neither the social structure nor the geographic condition of the coastal region lent much momentum to the revolutionary agenda. Whereas many fisherfolk lived on their junks and sampans, and thus had no sustained connections to the land, the population who lived on land followed diverse occupations ranging from liturgical workers to fish sauce producers,[89] which did not present the revolutionary party with a homogenous underclass that could be mobilized to generate popular legitimacy through social engineering programs. In addition, many fisherfolk lived on islands that were impossible to reach during inclement weather and thus were extremely difficult for the political authorities on land to regulate during the rainy season from April to September (Figure 4.2).[90]

---

[85] Yang, "Government Registration in the Fishing Industry in South China during the Ming and the Qing," 33–41.
[86] Huang and He, "Management of China's Capture Fisheries," 174.
[87] Wang, *Zhonghua minguo tongjishi*, 48.
[88] Yang, "Government Registration in the Fishing Industry in South China during the Ming and the Qing," 39.
[89] "CHỈ THỊ CỦA BAN BÍ THƯ Số 41/CT-TW Về chính sách tiến hành cải cách ở miền biển Hồng Quảng," 311.
[90] Ibid.

Figure 4.2 Sampans in Hạ Long Bay
Note: Possibly taken in 1947, when the photographer was reporting in Vietnam and Cambodia.
Source: Photo by Michel HUET/Gamma-Rapho via Getty Images # 945913086.

On July 7, 1956, the WPV decided to mount greater surveillance over the coastal community as part of a general move to strengthen its border defense. The maritime border zone was defined as "coastal villages and islands where the people still went fishing in the sea." The general guideline on strengthening the border police issued that month demanded that coastal households declare and register their boats with local authorities. Vessels not in state records were therefore considered foreign and came under stricter restrictions on their mobility and access to resources on land. Foreign vessels that entered Vietnamese ports to take shelter from storms, repair machinery, or resupply food were required to berth at designated places, and their crews were banned from traveling to or communicating with the inland. Border guards and police were required to "both protect and monitor" foreign ships and report their existence to higher authorities.[91]

In the same month, Hanoi launched policy reforms in the coastal area of Hồng Quảng, where fisherfolk and salt makers accounted for 64 percent of the total population and historically had developed communities outside of agriculture-based villages and thus largely outside of the Vietnamese state authority.[92] In the propagated reform agenda, the party-state vowed to eradicate "evil bullies" (cường hào gian ác) who "usurped the river, sea, and bays to exploit and oppress the fishermen" and the leaders of sabotage activities that did not subside after the WPV's legitimacy was recognized at the Geneva Conference. By toppling traditional political elites and military strongmen, the revolutionary state sought to remove the "feudal" private possession of the sea and rivers, boost fishery catch, and increase manpower for coastal defense.[93] Similar to the fishery reform enacted in China, registering households and wooing the seafaring population into cooperatives were to follow these initial steps of eliminating the power intermediaries that had existed during the French colonial rule.[94]

Encountering a socially diverse coastal community and haunted by the prevailing hostility against land reform, however, Hanoi executed a narrower scope of class struggle in comparison with its Chinese counterparts. Among the five groups identified as large private property owners in the coastal region – "landlords, boat owners, salt furnace owners, mining and forestry labor butlers, and fish sauce workshop owners" – only "the powerful and evil landlords" were to be hit hard. Small salt furnace owners, most of whom were involved in the labor-intensive salt processing themselves, were categorized as poor or middle peasants depending on the number of workers they hired and whether they were employed simultaneously by larger salt kilns. Their salt lands would be declared public yet left untouched. As many successful salt furnace owners also possessed junks to trade salt and profited from giving loans, local cadres were instructed to "distinguish the nature of the feudal and bourgeois exploitations." As long as the salt field owners engaged in a form of

---

[91] This paragraph is based on "CHỈ THỊ CỦA BAN BÍ THƯ Số 34/CT-TW Về việc tăng cường công tác công an biên phòng (gồm biên giới, bờ bể và giới tuyến) [INSTRUCTION OF THE SECRETARIAT No. 34 / CT-TW on the strengthening of the work of border police (including land border and the coast)]," July 7, 1956, VKDTT 17 (1956), 282.

[92] "CHỈ THỊ CỦA BAN BÍ THƯ Số 41/CT-TW Về chính sách tiến hành cải cách ở miền biển Hồng Quảng," 312. For the difference between vạn, formed by salt-making and fishing communities, and làng, populated by rice cultivators, see Roszko, Fishers, Monks, and Cadres, 86–88.

[93] "CHỈ THỊ CỦA BAN BÍ THƯ Số 41/CT-TW Về chính sách tiến hành cải cách ở miền biển Hồng Quảng," 312.

[94] Ibid., 322.

trade, they were deemed industrialists and only a portion of their salt fields would be redistributed. Only those who had occupied large salt fields by collaborating with the French colonial state, collected salt as the sole source of income, and were completely removed from any participation in the production process were labeled as landlords subject to seizure of their property.[95] Following a rigid definition of landlords, the Vietnamese state constrained the class struggle in the salt making industry to extremely limited groups. To minimize disruption of a weather-sensitive industry and pillar of the local economy, the WPV asked the local government to avoid "lashing out at" the salt makers by frequently summoning them to the village center or requisitioning their salt-making equipment. For the same reason, fish sauce makers who also owned land were generally considered part of the commercial class. Their lands would be subject to redistribution, yet their business would be left intact.[96]

The WPV implemented similar moderate policies toward other private properties to protect the freshwater and inshore fishery. The reform along the coastal society would abolish the evil bullies' rights over "rivers, sea surface, and estuaries," which were often obtained by serving as "minions of imperialists and feudalists," yet avoid seizing their boats or nets. Similarly, the cadres would expropriate the land registered under the name of vessel owners who did not participate in fishing labor and then treat this economically privileged group as industrialists and protect their fishing boats and equipment. In addition, the local authorities would confiscate most land slots owned by sorcerers and soothsayers but at the same time leave enough land in their hands "to let their family make a living." As the leaders of folk religion commanded high levels of respect in the coastal communities where the livelihoods were generally precarious, cadres would refrain from labeling the liturgical offerings they received as feudal exploitation or snatching them. While seafood brokers who monopolized the local market would be "educated" to "have a more correct business attitude," they and other money lenders would not be pressed into debt forgiveness. Gangsters and sea robbers, as long as they no longer engaged in acts of sabotage, were to be absolved from guilt and granted opportunities to rehabilitate.[97] At this critical juncture of postwar economic recovery, sustaining the fishery industry topped the agenda of the Vietnamese state, instead of radically reshuffling the social hierarchy of the coast.

For the Chinese and Vietnamese communists, the social mosaic of the sea-oriented community defied the revolutionary paradigm of essentializing

---

[95] The above section is based on ibid., 313–15; first quotes on page 313; second quote on page 314.
[96] The above section is based on ibid., 316–17; quote from page 316.
[97] This paragraph is based on ibid., 317–21; first quotes are from page 317; the second and third quotes are from 319.

citizens into the ostensibly underpriviledged and the seemingly dominant elites. In comparison with the rural society of the interior, the coastal population had developed more diverse and fluid sources of livelihood and therefore stratified without clear lines between the exploiter and exploited. A fisher was often simultaneously a farmer, a "sea thief," a smuggler, and a trader, all of which were seen as "relational" categories instead of stable professions.[98] In coastal Guangxi, without the powerful lever of the poor peasantry, the initially aggressive fishery reform that imitated the land reform provoked backlash. The party cadres had to shift their policies from instigating and taking advantage of class confrontation to mending it after the hostility against junk owners paralyzed the local economy. In light of its limited coercive capacity and the exigency of economic recovery, the WPV proactively designed a more collaborative reform program to strike a tacit agreement with the seafaring people that allowed the state to assert unquestionable authority by abolishing private land ownership, while leaving marine dependent livelihoods mostly untouched.

Claiming Resources: The Fishery Agreement and the Joint Maritime Survey

Asserting authority along their respective coastlines through registering vessels, securitizing ports, and intervening in traditional fishery practices, the Chinese and Vietnamese states looked to the sea to stake claims on coastal waters and fish stocks. Fishing grounds in the Gulf of Tonkin assumed particular significance for the two countries in the mid-1950s. The division of Vietnam forced the DRV fishing industry to rely more heavily on the northern part of the Gulf. Meanwhile, for decades, fisherfolk in South China had withdrawn from several offshore fishing grounds due to Japanese fishery expansion, which had caused a decline of fish stocks in several Asian waters.[99] Upon assuming power, the Chinese revolutionary state sought to restore high catch levels. In a period when the maritime territorial disputes remained dormant, the Sino-Vietnamese Agreement on Sailboat Fishing in the Gulf of Tonkin signed in April 1957 (hereafter referred as the "1957 fishery agreement") in Hanoi marked a decisive step by the two states to enclose and divide waters, especially the near offshore fishing grounds between northern Vietnam, the Leizhou Peninsula, and Hainan that had brought the littoral

---

[98] Roszko, *Fishers, Monks, and Cadres*, 90–91.
[99] Muscolino, *Fishing Wars and Environmental Changes in Late Imperial and Modern China*, 96–97. According to John Kleinen ("Stealing from the Gods," 249), Japanese trawlers had expanded to the Gulf of Tonkin by 1928 and grew steadily in the 1930s. Also see Granados, "Japanese Expansion into the South China Sea."

society together for centuries.[100] The Sino-Vietnamese joint maritime survey conducted from September 1959 to December 1960 turned materials in the Gulf into resources that could generate wealth and geographic knowledge into military intelligence that would serve national defense needs. Mirroring the joint state invasion taking place in the mid-1950s at the borderlands, the congruence of their state-building agendas on the water frontier drove Chinese and Vietnamese authorities to collaborate in controlling the mobility, and inadvertently threatening the livelihood, of their fishing populations.

As Chinese fisherfolk who sailed on more advanced, long-distance junks had utilized the Gulf more heavily, overlapping habitual fishing grounds could easily provoke conflicts between the two revolutionary states that strived to establish authority over their respective coastal societies and derive revenues from their common-pool resources. The two countries began to look for a solution in late 1956, when fishery reforms were declared complete in both countries. At the meeting between five border provinces held in Nanning in November, the two sides acknowledged the existence of vessels from South China fishing in Vietnamese coastal waters following age-old practices and introduced several temporary measures to regulate the activities of Chinese fishing junks before the two central governments concluded a formal agreement. For the time being, Chinese fisherfolk who encountered hurricanes or other natural disasters could continue seeking shelter at Vietnamese ports as long as they reported to Vietnamese local authorities and refrained from stepping on the Vietnamese mainland. The Chinese authorities along the Gulf would meanwhile invest in deep-sea fishing in a bid to divert their junks from the Vietnamese coast, and the Vietnamese government would establish conspicuous physical markers in the littoral zone thus claiming proprietary right to fishing territories. In addition, Guangdong and Hải Ninh would collaboratively enforce boat registration, demanding that junks register with the government and carry their registration paperwork for inspection while sailing to the waters of the other side.[101] These interim arrangements heralded the two states' decisive interference into the habitual fishery practices as well as the economic network formed by the fisherfolk who berthed and traded

---

[100] For transnational connections within the region, see Li, "Epidemics, Trade, and Local Worship in Vietnam, Leizhou Peninsula, and Hainan Island," 194–213.

[101] The above section is based on UBHC KTTVB, "Trích Biên Bản Ghi Những Vấn Đề Biên Giới Được Trao Đổi Trong Cuộc Toạ Đàm Giữa Đại Biểu Các Tỉnh Cao Bằng, Lạng Sơn, Hải Ninh-Việt Nam Và Quảng Tây, Quảng Đông-Trung Quốc Họp Từ Ngày 6 Đến 9 Tháng 11 Năm 1956," 3–4. To ensure centralized control over the negotiations, the Chinese State Council instructed Guangdong Province in March 1957 that because the two central governments were holding negotiations over fishery in the Gulf, any coastal counties should refrain from conducting talks directly with the Vietnamese authorities. "Guowuyuan jiu Guangdongsheng yu Yuenan guojing tudi wenti pishi Guangdongsheng renmin weiyuanhui," March 28, 1957, in *GSBN 1957*, 199.

along the Gulf during the fishing seasons. This interventionist approach set the tone for intergovernmental negotiations over fishery regulations planned for the succeeding year.

In December 1956, while most junks were preparing for the next peak fishing season in the Gulf, growing uncertainty over the future of the fishing industry enveloped the local officials of the Chinese coastal counties. Looking toward upcoming negotiations between Beijing and Hanoi, Guangdong imposed a ban upon all Chinese vessels fishing in Vietnamese coastal waters or entering any Vietnamese ports.[102] Although a gesture of goodwill to the Vietnamese government, the measure would pose undue hardship to those who fished with engineless junks, sampans, or rafts. Although better funded fisheries along China's eastern coast had introduced net-dragging trawlers (near Shanghai) and steamboats (in Qingdao and Yantai) before the Second World War, wind-powered vessels constituted the technical reality of the fishery in the Gulf of Tonkin.[103]

Even the local authorities of the coastal counties found the ban impractical and counterproductive. The Party Committee of Hepu looked askance at the ban and cautioned that, for centuries, wind-powered fishing vessels that followed the migration of fish species and surface currents down to the Vietnamese shore had to fish there and resupply freshwater at the Vietnamese ports and that this practice had to continue unless large motorized boats were available. While wealthier counties in eastern Guangdong already acquired some modern ships, places such as Hepu had long relied on sailboat fishing and could not afford to replace wind-powered junks with engine-powered ones to ride against the currents. The political ramification of the fishing ban was even more alarming. As many fishery households in the Gulf had "one part of their families in Vietnam and the other in our country" and switched between fishing grounds seasonally, "enforcing the ban to fish in Vietnamese waters would drive them to flee to Vietnam or Hong Kong," especially those entirely living on boats. More importantly, should the ban last over the long run, the fish catches for the county would plummet by 40 percent and thus fall short of generating the dividends needed to persuade the fisherfolk to stay in fledging cooperatives.[104] Thus, the internationalist

---

[102] CCP Hepu Regional Committee, "Wo quwei dui 'yumin yilv buzhun jinru Yuenan linghai shengchan' de zhishi suo caiqu de juti banfa he dui gai zhishi de yijian [Measures taken by our region to implement the instruction of 'Chinese fisherfolk not entering Vietnamese waters' and our opinion]," January 24, 1957, no. 217-1-390-51~54, 1/GDPA.

[103] Li and Qu, *Zhongguo yuye shi*, 12.

[104] This paragraph is based on CCP Hepu Regional Committee, "Wo quwei dui 'yumin yilv buzhun jinru Yuenan linghai shengchan' de zhishi suo caiqu de juti banfa he dui gai zhishi de yijian," 3–4.

agenda pursued by Beijing was detrimental to the life and livelihood of the fisherfolk as well as the local Chinese state.

The coastal Chinese counties' preference in the negotiations, therefore, was not for interventionist changes but to maintain the status quo. Hepu County suggested to the provincial authorities that the two countries should open emergency ports of call to the other side. To redress the imbalance between Chinese junks fishing in Vietnamese waters and vice versa, the county proposed letting the Chinese fisherfolk pay a "tax" or "rent" for catches from Vietnamese waters.[105] Zhanjiang County expressed similar concerns over a possible agreement with Vietnam that denied access to Vietnamese ports for all Chinese junks. It added that the only alternative to resupplying from Vietnam was to construct larger vessels with engines that had higher load capacities and could engage in deep water fishery, which demanded sizeable investment in not only upgrading fishing gear but also increasing food supply at the port of departure for longer voyages.[106] The 1957 fishery agreement eventually reflected an uneasy compromise between the nationalist pursuit of exclusive rights over the near offshore fishing grounds, which buttressed the internationalist agenda of the two neighboring socialist countries to support each other's sovereign claims, and the transnational local demand for keeping an open marine resource pool.

Echoing the two communist countries' efforts to transform their shared land boundary from a line on paper to a physical reality, the 1957 fishery agreement utilized lines to reserve the coastal fishing grounds to adjacent countries, respectively, creating national spaces. Meanwhile, it accommodated some of the inseverable ties yet subjected them to enhanced state scrutiny. The agreement, which was set to be valid for three years and open to extension for another three years, included a main document that regulated the near offshore fishing grounds and emergency ports of call and two appendixes, one on the use of ports by foreign junks and the other on collision prevention and sea rescue.[107] The line to delimit territorial fishing grounds in the agreement was not created by the standard practice of calculating the distance from the coast but rather by connecting several islands designated by the respective sides. Chinese junks would withdraw from their historical fishing grounds in Vietnam's near offshore waters, except for those close to China around Qinglanshan (Thanh Lân Island), Litoushan, and Shuilangzhou (Xuy Long Châu). The number of Chinese vessels allowed to fish in these areas was

---

[105] Ibid., 3.
[106] CPC Zhanjiang Region Committee, "Dui Zhong-Yue yuye tanpan fang'an de yijian [Opinions on Sino-Vietnamese fishery negotiations]," January 22, 1957, no. 217-1-390-1~2, 2/GDPA.
[107] The two appendixes of the 1957 fishery agreement are titled "Regulation on Fishing Vessels Entering the Other Side's Ports and Fisherfolk' Disembarkation" and "Regulation on Preventing Collision and Sea Rescue for Fishing Sailboats."

capped at 940 in 1957 and decreased to 740 by 1959, which would be enforced by licenses. As it was less common for junks from the Vietnamese coast to sail northward and eastward during the fishing season due to surface currents of the opposite direction, the agreement generally allowed Vietnamese vessels to fish in Chinese waters so long as they also carried licenses and their number did not exceed that of the Chinese junks fishing on the Vietnamese side. Fisherfolk would pay a 5 percent tax on the catch obtained from the other side's fishing grounds. To simplify administrative procedures, this tax was to be collected by the state with which the vessel was registered, calculated by the price of fishery products on the local market of that country, and credited to the other government's account annually.[108]

While negotiations over common-pool resources were a widespread practice among countries that shared access to the same water body, a distinctively communist feature of the 1957 fishery agreement was its restriction on private trade associated with cross-border fishing. The appendix on port entry and disembarkation demanded that the fisherfolk prepare adequate reserves of food and materials for repairing fishing gear before setting sail so as to avoid purchasing them at foreign ports, barring an emergency. Banned from taking commodities for trade across the border, the fisherfolk who ran out of supplies were required to buy any necessities from the state-owned store at the other side's ports after procuring local currency at national bank branches.[109] These stringent regulations effectively criminalized the daily practices of the fisherfolk by turning private trade that had historically taken place in the contact zone of the coast into smuggling.

The local state of the Chinese coastal counties spent the summer of 1957 pressing for implementation of the fishery agreement during the forthcoming autumn fishing season. In need of effective channels to communicate with the fisherfolk, government officials first called meetings with cooperative heads, pro-party senior fisherfolk, and fishing workers association leaders – the seemingly trustworthy power delegates of the state – to ask them to lead cooperative members in formulating local conventions that would detail measures lest the fisherfolk contravened the agreement. Meanwhile, each county distributed fishing licenses received from the provincial government to the

---

[108] "Zhonghua renmin gongheguo zhengfu he Yuenan minzhu gongheguo zhengfu guanyu Beibuwan fanchuan yuye de xieding [PRC-DRV Agreement on Sailboat Fishing in the Gulf of Tonkin]," April 1957, no. 217-1-188-150~158, 1–3/GDPA; British Consulate-General in Hanoi, "Vietnam-China Agreements on Fishery," May 9, 1957, no. FO371/127381/UKNA; "Zhong-Yue liangguo zhengfu yuye daibiaotuan fabu 'guanyu Beibuwan fanchuan yuye huitan de gongbao' [The Chinese and Vietnamese fishery delegations announce 'the communique on the talks about sailboat fishery in the Gulf of Tonkin']," April 25, 1957, in *GSBN 1957*, 266.
[109] "Zhonghua renmin gongheguo zhengfu he Yuenan minzhu gongheguo zhengfu guanyu Beibuwan fanchuan yuye de xieding," 5–6.

coastal cooperatives and conducted additional background checks of the crew members of the licensed junks that would fish in Vietnamese waters. Family members of counterrevolutionaries or captains deemed lacking "political awareness" were replaced by commune cadres, party or youth league members, and those considered "loyal, credible, and with a clear background."[110]

Unsurprisingly, the internationally coordinated project to nationalize the habitual fishing grounds met with determined resistance from the seafaring community in South China. A fisherman in Lianjiang employed the state's anti-imperialist and developmentalist discourse to legitimize their bitter discontent: "Given that the government is eager to boost production, why does it impose restrictions on fishing in Vietnam and even collect a tax, which is little different than the fishing levy put up by the French imperialists?" With little knowledge of the traditional fishing grounds of each village, the county authorities mistakenly issued permits to junks that had no plan to fish in Vietnamese waters while neglecting those with a pressing need for them. Taking a less confrontational tone, a fisherman in Xuwen working on an unlicensed junk asked: "Without any physical markers of the agreement line on the sea, how are we supposed to know where to go and not to go?"[111] Grumbling about the impracticality of the agreement was the fisherfolk's most commonly used strategy to push back against the state's demands. Pointing out that the fishing zones set by lines on a map were non-enforceable, they demanded that the two countries use the depth of water to demarcate them. Citing the power of winds and currents, they told the officials that while it was possible not to fish in Vietnamese coastal waters, entering Vietnamese waters en route to the offshore sea was unavoidable. While agreeing not to buy manufactured goods from Vietnamese ports, they contended that the purchase of rice and firewood from Vietnam were essential to complete a long fishing journey for small vessels. Foreseeing formidable obstacles to honoring the agreement, several heads of the coastal cooperatives dodged appointments as the captains of junks that received cross-border fishing permits, citing difficulties in keeping the crew members disciplined while in Vietnamese ports.[112]

The incompatibility between the central authorities' pursuit of internationalist and nationalist goals and discursive local realities thwarted top-down joint state building. To enforce the fishery agreement, the state apparatus sought to subordinate the "international relationship" across the maritime frontier in the

---

[110] Office of Marine Products of Zhanjiang, "Guanyu guanche Zhong-Yue liangguo yuye xieding ji banfa buyu xukezheng gongzuo baogao [Report on implementing the Chinese-Vietnamese Fishing Agreement and issuing fishing licenses]," September 23, 1957, no. 217-1-386-77~81, 2, 7/GDPA.
[111] Ibid, 2, 8. [112] Ibid., 2–3, 5.

Gulf – defined by Brantly Womack as "the relatively spontaneous emergence of particular connections that are either indifferent to nationality or aim at mutual opportunities created by all manner of national differences"[113] – to centrally dominated international relations. Deploring the "big-nation chauvinism" of fisherfolk and grassroots cadres, the county authority of Zhanjiang defended the legitimacy of the agreement with its promised economic and political benefits of "more efficient exploitation of the marine resources," "fulfillment of the Five Principles of Peaceful Coexistence," and stronger solidarity between the Chinese and Vietnamese people. To convince the fisherfolk of the differences between socialist policies and colonial practices, the cadres insisted that the license program and the tax rate were formulated based on "equality and reciprocity" and thus contrasted with the French imperialist oppression. Emphasizing the significance of "consolidating the two countries' border defenses" and "obstructing the imperialists' scheme to drive a wedge between the two countries," they explained that vessels that entered the other country's waters would hang national flags of the PRC and the DRV and therefore "leave no opportunities for Chiang Kai-Shek's spies and counterrevolutionaries of Ngô Đình Diệm's regime to infiltrate."[114]

At this critical moment of postcolonial state building, the two central governments adopted modern maritime practices of territorializing coastal waters and nationalizing fishing grounds, as well as the Western cartographic practices of using "linear boundary" on maps to create standardized knowledge of the "homogenous" maritime national space over which the respective states claimed to rule.[115] At the same time, this territorialization was used to restrict private commerce across the maritime border that was at odds with the two communist states' autarkic economic programs. The two governments' "modern" endeavor to draw, mark, and enforce lines was nevertheless detached from the preindustrial realities of fishing societies. By connecting the implementation of the fishery agreement to the consolidation of the ideological partnership between Beijing and Hanoi and national defense against adversarial regimes, the two neighboring communist countries politicized and securitized the daily lives of the fisherfolk that up to this point had been largely constrained by customary practices and geographic conditions. Registering junks to distinguish domestic from foreign, turning foreign vessels away from coastal fishing grounds, and restricting nonemergency ports of entry imposed regulations developed upon modern, engine-powered fishing

---

[113] Womack, "International Relationships at the Border of China and Vietnam," 982.
[114] The quote and paraphrases are from Office of Aquatic Products of Zhanjiang, "Guanyu guanche Zhong-Yue liangguo yuye xieding ji banfa buyu xukezheng gongzuo baogao," 3–4.
[115] Biggs, "Putting the State on the Map," 374. For maps and modern state making, see Branch, *The Cartographic State*.

industry to a population relying on preindustrial, wind-driven fishing practices. While diplomacy centered on defining and delineating lines, an atom-width, standardized yet abstract line at ocean surface was far less meaningful to the fisherfolk than the practical navigational and hydrographic information on the depth of water, which was part of a body of indigenous knowledge incomprehensible to either state. The state and the coastal society operated on vastly different conceptual understandings and spatial knowledge of the sea.

In addition, compared to the "small, similar, connected," and "inward-regarding" honeycomb structure of interior rural society,[116] coastal societies were inherently outward-looking, and their population was engaged in more diverse professional pursuits. For the coastal community, it was the organic interdependence of fishery and commerce, instead of shared revolutionary goals, that bound China and Vietnam together. For Chinese fisherfolk to the west of Hainan, Haiphong instead of Guangzhou or Hong Kong provided the easiest access to manufactured goods. One of the most popular commodities they bought at the Vietnamese ports was the so-called French watch – a European-designed watch manufactured in Vietnam that had gained popularity for being waterproof. The Chinese communists labeled these watches as symbols of "the economic control of French imperialism" and capitalist consumerism thus had sought to ban the "smuggling" of them into China.[117] The two states' project to block the flow of commodities between private hands along the coast of the Gulf was nothing less than a major interruption of the centuries-long economic interdependence of the region.

The county-level cadres and officials thus found themselves in a difficult position in the negotiations between fisherfolk and the state. Beijing and Hanoi, both of which were even further removed from dealing with the local population, formulated foreign policies and entered into agreements, yet it was the local state that carried out central directives. During the years of the ideationally charged political consolidation, the priority of the local state was to strengthen the fishery cooperatives and to boost the catch. Promising prosperity to coastal dwellers was key to sustaining the cooperatives and the ideologies they espoused; the fishery agreement was nevertheless not conducive toward fishing capacity of the Chinese coastal communities. The officials responsible for overseeing marine products in Zhanjiang defended the nationalist and internationalist agenda of the central government publicly in front of the fisherfolk; yet in their reports to higher-ups, they asked the two

---

[116] Shue, *The Reach of the State*, 3.
[117] "Faguo shoubiao' de zui'e [The evil 'French watches']," *Guangxi ribao*, February 25, 1952, 1; Office of Aquatic Products of Zhanjiang, "Guanyu guanche Zhong-Yue liangguo yuye xieding ji banfa buyu xukezheng gongzuo baogao," 3; Yin, "The Mountain Is High, and the Emperor Is Far Away," 558.

governments to consider making an allowance for unlicensed junks to pass through coastal waters and to use emergency ports of call of the other side and for fisherfolk to exchange goods on a small scale when visiting families there.[118] When the joint state invasion of the two central governments turned predatory, the local state apparatus appeared to seek ways to "blunt the impact of demands detrimental to local interests and values."[119]

Concurrent with the fishery agreement that reenvisioned the Gulf as a common pool resource, and with both Beijing and Hanoi perceiving imminent maritime security threats posed by competitors for political legitimacy, the two states decided to acquire more firsthand knowledge of the Gulf. The 1957 fishery agreement stipulated that to conserve the marine resources and promote fisheries in the Gulf, the two countries would conduct collaborative research, exchange related knowledge, and communicate techniques and knowhow of fishery and shallow water aquaculture.[120] In June 1959, delegates of the Vietnamese National Committee of Science and Chinese National Committee for Science and Technology met in Hanoi to plan a joint maritime survey of the Gulf.[121] This project was not simply a part of "resource-creating investments" driven by the ideas of growth and technological advancement but a military operation "to examine the conditions of the sea and to collect necessary data and materials to put up an effective naval defense plan for the two countries."[122] Acquiring statistics on hydrography, meteorology, and chemistry and exploring the seabed to better exploit marine resources and support the construction of oceanography were only secondary purposes. Thus, the survey crew consisted of personnel from the two navies as well as an experimental fishery team that conducted test fishing to assess the fish

---

[118] Office of Aquatic Products of Zhanjiang, "Guanyu guanche Zhong-Yue liangguo yuye xieding ji banfa buyu xukezheng gongzuo baogao," 5–6.

[119] Friedman, Pickowicz, and Selden, *Chinese Village, Socialist State*, xv.

[120] "Zhong-Yue liangguo zhengfu yuye daibiaotuan guanyu Beibuwan fanchuan yuye huitan de gongbao (cao'an) [Draft communique between Chinese and Vietnamese governments' fishery delegations on the talk of sailboat fishery in the Gulf of Tonkin]," April 1957, 217-1-188-148~149, 5/GDPA. According to Article Ten of the 1957 fishery agreement, the South China Sea Fisheries Research Institute of Chinese Academy of Fishery Sciences and the Research Branch of Fisheries Department of the Vietnamese Ministry of Agriculture and Forestry were to establish direct contact to facilitate the scientific exchange. "Zhonghua renmin gongheguo zhengfu he Yuenan minzhu gongheguo zhengfu guanyu Beibuwan fanchuan yuye de xieding," 3.

[121] National Commission of Science, "Báo cáo của Đảng đoàn Uỷ ban Khoa học Nhà nước về đàm phán với Trung Quốc trong việc hợp tác điều tra vùng biển vịnh Bắc Bộ năm 1959 [Report of the National Commission of Science about the negotiation with China on joint survey of Gulf of Tonkin in 1959]," July 2, 1959, no. 7726, 1/PTTg/NAVC III.

[122] The first quote is from De Gregori, "Resources Are Not; They Become," 1242; second quote from National Commission of Science, "Báo cáo của Đảng đoàn Uỷ ban Khoa học Nhà nước về đàm phán với Trung Quốc trong việc hợp tác điều tra vùng biển vịnh Bắc Bộ năm 1959," 1–2.

stocks and enhance fishery technology. The Chinese National Marine Survey Office, founded in Tianjian in 1958, was responsible for providing vessels and research equipment, whereas the Vietnamese Navy would supply food and water at Vietnamese ports of call. At the insistence of the Chinese delegation, the two sides agreed to keep the data and samples obtained in "absolute confidentiality" – not to be shared with or used by a third country. Domestic civilian use of these materials, which would be preserved by the military, would only be granted when doing so was not detrimental to national defense.[123] Beijing's anxiety over secrecy might indicate its growing national security concern against the backdrop of the Sino-Soviet split.

The state projects of creating knowledge, extracting resources, and performing the socialist partnership converged in the Chinese-Vietnamese joint maritime survey, which lasted for sixteen months from September 1959 to December 1960. According to an interim report submitted by the Maritime Branch of the Chinese National Commission of Science and Technology in August 1960, the joint survey team completed eight voyages, made 27,000 graphs, collected 3,901 specimens of plankton, took 22,650 seabed floor samples, captured 1,323 underwater creatures, and obtained 2,898 bottles of geological samples. The fishery team conducted ten experimental fishing voyages, during which it caught around 200 fish specimens, created 392 maps of the distribution of marine species, and researched the ecology and reproductive patterns of 6 main commercial fish species.[124] Behind these charts and statistics was the powerful project by the two modernizing states to learn about the space to which they claimed shared access, replacing scattered, ancestral knowledge about habitual fishing grounds with systemic and standardized "scientific" knowledge on the Gulf in service to both defense and development requirements. In addition, despite the asymmetric financial investment in this resource augmenting project, the Chinese government sought to perform symbolic or ritual equality during the survey. Upon completion of the field work, the Chinese National Maritime Survey Office suggested that all biological samples collected during the survey be divided into two parts to be preserved by the two countries respectively.[125] The joint maritime survey underlined the two countries' shared ambition of discovering resources, "rendering resources legible,"[126] and deriving security and economic benefits from their Cold War partnership.

---

[123] National Commission of Science, "Báo cáo của Đảng đoàn Uỷ ban Khoa học Nhà nước về đàm phán với Trung Quốc trong việc hợp tác điều tra vùng biển vịnh Bắc Bộ năm 1959," 2–3.
[124] Maritime Branch of the National Commission of Science and Technology, "Guanyu Beibuwan haiyang diaocha Zhong-Yue lianhe jiancha xiaozu gongzuo qingkuang de baogao [Report of the work of the Sino-Vietnamese joint inspection team of the maritime investigation in the Gulf of Tonkin]," August 15, 1960, no. 306-1-35-7-8, 1–3/GDPA.
[125] Ibid., 4   [126] Lentz, *Contested Territory*, 134.

By the end of the 1950s, Beijing and Hanoi had first stamped out respective domestic power competitors at the maritime border via fishery reforms and then staked claims on marine resources through a joint maritime survey. The two processes mutually reinforced one another, as turning the natural world into known resources and recording them systematically following the modern geographic discourse gave the states greater control over the frontier population whose livelihood relied on these materials. Sino-Vietnamese interactions on their maritime frontier during the initial years after the First Indochina War were conditioned by geographic perculiarities, the limits of the reach of the communist state in a non-agrarian society, and the resilience of local fishing communities that sought to dodge and deflect the boundary-making attempts of the penetrative authorities. Abstract lines on the sea that aimed to enclose coastal waters for the adjacent nations and the maintenance of mid-Gulf common fishing grounds thus questioned the state's capacity to impose its preference in a more pressing manner in comparison with land boundaries. The two parties that ascended to power through peasant revolutions also had great difficulties in organizing and mobilizing coastal fishing societies. Tension between land-oriented policies and realities on the sea, between inward-oriented economic programs and outward-regarding means of livelihood, and between the internationalist or nationalist discourses and transnational local interests, persisted well into the 1960s as collectivization gathered pace after 1958.

The State, the Wandering People, and the Sino-Vietnamese Partnership

For the maritime border, just as with the borderlands, collectivization and the increasingly aggressive extraction of resources by the two governments tested the strength and coherence of, and generated tension in, the socialist partnership. The fishing quotas enforced by permits, whose number decreased year by year, drew a line between legal and illegal fishing activities and granted the states the power to bestow legitimate cross-boundary fishing opportunities to groups they trusted and preferred by license distribution. Unsurprisingly, fisherfolk in coastal China who failed to obtain permits and were later impoverished by the Great Leap Forward defied the agreement by continuing the practice of fishing in Vietnamese fishing grounds and thus took the risk of being arrested and detained as the DRV organized militias and picked up the pace of its cooperativization movement in the coastal area. In addition to undermining the carefully engineered socialist partnership, the hastily unleashed collectivization shook the fragile trust between the two communist states and their respective coastal societies.

The traditional livelihoods on the three Kinh populated islands, for instance, were imcompatible with the pursuit of intensity and magnitude of grain prodution during the Great Leap Forward. In comparison with other farming and fishing communities in South China that came under population pressure, the Kinh people on the three outlying islands lacked incentives to commit to large scale communization.[127] With a small population, abundant fishing resources, and a successful fish sauce business, the Kinh islanders saw no pressing need to enhance their catches by moving away from shore or shallow water fishing. By the end of 1960, 3,272 people from 714 households on these islands, together with around 250 boats, were brought into the Jiangping Commune. The ban on private holdings and the diversion of critical resources such as timber, oil, and ironware away from fishery to steel production after 1958 had left more than half of the vessels in disrepair. Building larger junks with government loans and sailing further out to the sea would also require a skill set different from that of inshore and nearshore fishing. As a result, the catch plunged in 1959 to only half of that of 1957. The most detrimental move during the Leap was against the fish sauce industry. The provincial and county-level fishery authorities demanded that the villagers dismantle all fishing ponds, insisting that this traditional fishing technique only caught small fish that should be allowed to grow up to yield a greater catch in the future. Consequently, fish sauce production shrank from 1,500 jars per year to merely 100 jars by the end of 1960.[128] Under the slogan of "taking grain production as the core task" (*yiliang weigang*), Kinh fishers had to change into farmers and traveled hours to work in the commune's fields on a daily basis.[129]

In November 1960, Beijing issued an emergency directive to restore small private plots, sideline occupation, and local markets in rural areas in a bid to rescue the national economy from Mao's utopia, following an internal report to Mao about the mass starvation in Xinyang, Henan Province.[130] Against the backdrop of a nationwide investigation into the catastrophe, the Ethnic Affairs Commission of Guangdong Province dispatched teams to ethnic

---

[127] Benedict Kerkvliet outlined four political conditions for durable collective farming: peasants' perception of a "shared serious problem" that "requires a collective solution"; their willingness to collaborate, which "may involve trade-offs between their own interests and general interests"; trust among people; and people's familiarity "with organizations and leadership" (*The Power of Everyday Politics*, 14–15).

[128] Ethnic Affairs Commission of Guangdong Province, "Pizhuan sheng minwei guanyu Dongxing gezu zizhixian Jiangping gongshe Jingzu diqu yaoqiu fazhan yuye de baogao," 2–3; also see Editorial Board, *Jiangzu jianshi*, 45–48.

[129] Du, "Renkou jiaoshao minzu shengchan fangshi zhuanxing de moshi yanjiu," 74. According to Bo Yibo, Mao first came up with the term "taking grain production as the core task" at a meeting with senior party and state leaders in June 1958. See Bo, *Ruogan zhongda juece yu shijian de huigu*, 723.

[130] Dikötter, *Mao's Great Famine*, xxii.

minority–populated areas to assess the losses incurred during the Great Famine. Alarmed by plummeting living standards, the Kinh population stood up against the commune's tight control of individual villagers over three primary "sites of negotiation" – in the words of Benedict Kerkvliet – fishing vessels, fishing ponds, and fishing loans.[131] Rather than taking a confrontational approach by advocating the restoration of family ownership, the islanders asked for materials and loans to repair the brigades' fishing vessels. To display their commitment to boosting catches, they required funding for engines and promised that motorized boats could haul more fish by traveling to the deep sea. Determined to reinstate their fish ponds and fish sauce workshops, the Kinh explained the international reputation of local fish sauce and sought to convince the authorities that what was regarded as against the spirit of "running to enter the phase of communism" could in fact bring in significant revenues for the state. In addition, the islanders probed the possibility of debt forgiveness. Repaying state loans, which had been invested in making new junks and fishing gear in the mid-1950s, had been a crippling burden because fishery equipment was collectivized during the Leap and the harvests had dropped.[132] By conveying widespread discontent against the collectivization campaign to the investigative team, the Kinh community was determined to defend their traditional occupations as shore fishers and fish sauce producers.

At the marginal spaces of state influence and state amenities, the fisherfolk were simultaneously vulnerable and powerful. The Guangdong provincial government endorsed the investigative team's suggestion to open the fisherfolk's access to funds, raw materials, and machines to repair junks and to rebuild fishing ponds. The islanders received reductions or exemptions for individual loans whereas the Jiangping Commune could amortize loans made collectively.[133] The moderate success of the Kinh community's negotiation to regain a limited autonomy from the commune underscored the overriding need of the political authorities to pull the country out of its debilitating recession. In 1961, acknowledging the Great Leap Forward as a man-made disaster, without acknowledging Mao's responsibility, the CPC Central Committee formulated guidelines of "readjustment, consolidation, expansion and raising standards for the national economy" to restore agricultural output and reduce investment in heavy industry.[134] Mirroring the Chinese state's decision to curb the exodus of Chinese to Vietnam using financial measures, the provincial government relaxed the commune's control over the Kinh people lest the latter

---

[131] Kerkvliet, *The Power of Everyday Politics*, 116.
[132] Ethnic Affairs Commission of Guangdong Province, "Pizhuan sheng minwei guanyu Dongxing gezu zizhixian Jiangping gongshe Jingzu diqu yaoqiu fazhan yuye de baogao," 2–3.
[133] Ibid., 4.   [134] Chow, *The Chinese Economy*, 50–51.

voted with their feet again by fleeing to Vietnam. The sensitivity of the transnational ethnic ties once again worked to enhance the bargaining power of the borderlanders.

Not far away from the Kinh-populated islands, the Cô Tô Islands also felt the ramifications of the Leap. After the campaign reached coastal Guangdong in May 1958, the number of unlicensed Chinese fishing vessels near the Cô Tô Islands increased dramatically. According to Hải Ninh provincial authorities, when the fishing season began in August, unlicensed junks appeared in the islands area almost every day, and some Chinese fisherfolk were either detained by the Vietnamese militias or forfeited the Vietnamese currency they carried. The fisherfolk resorted to various nonconfrontational strategies to resist state power, such as feigning ignorance of the fishery agreement, claiming to not know about the existence of government along the Vietnamese coast, pretending to have an inability to understand Cantonese, and citing the pressure to speed up production during the Great Leap Forward.[135] Not carrying any identification documents itself was a tactful way to dodge state surveillance as it could protract the time for the Vietnamese authorities to figure out who they should contact on the Chinese side and for the two sides to verify the fisherfolk's identity.[136]

The Vietnamese government was determined to exact compliance with the fishery agreement. The Great Leap Forward widened the technological gap of fisheries between the two countries. Historically, the fisherfolk of the Gulf had used gas lamps to attract fish to boost their catches, yet the Chinese coastal communes began to equip their junks with much brighter electric light bulbs in the late 1950s and thus could land larger catches than their peers across the border, putting the latter in a disadvantageous position.[137] In addition, Vietnamese authorities were alarmed by the subversive coordination among Cantonese-speaking fishing communities along the Gulf against the collectivization of maritime economy. After the DRV embarked on cooperativization in August 1958, the Cô Tô Islands were a priority for Hải Ninh province in pressing the people to join mutual aid groups or rudimentary cooperative units, as the area was close to international waters and thus had to be built into a stronghold against reconnaissance from Western warships and planes.[138] Via

[135] Department of Rural Area of CPC Guangdong Provincial Committee, "Zhuanfa Dongxing xianwei renwei guanyu Yuenan Hainingsheng fangmian tichu de jige wenti de baogao," 2–3.
[136] "Wei wosheng yuchuan feifa tingbo Yuenan Gusudao qingkuang baogao [Report on fishing boats from our province anchoring in Cô Tô Islands against regulations]," January 13, 1959.
[137] "Beibuwan yumin wenti [Fishing issue in the Gulf of Tonkin]," December 1, 1958.
[138] "Hải Ninh củng cố và xây dựng cơ sở Đảng kết hợp với phát triển hợp tác xã nông nghiệp [Hải Ninh consolidates and builds the Party base in association with agricultural cooperative development]," 1958, in *SLDQ*, 87; Department of Rural Area of CPC Guangdong Provincial Committee, "Zhuanfa Dongxing xianwei renwei guanyu Yuenan Hainingsheng fangmian tichu de jige wenti de baogao," 4.

incessant contacts with their fellow Cantonese-speaking fisherfolk from South China, the islanders nevertheless learned about the dire consequences of radical collectivization. As large junks that could sail to the open sea were snatched from private ownership and left unserviceable due to diversion of labor, funds, and material to grain and backyard iron production, some Chinese fisherfolk drifted to the Cô Tô Islands on sampans, fishing, foraging for food, or even probing the possibility of bringing children to the islands for "adoption."[139] Vương Đình Trinh, Vice Chairman of the Administrative Committee of Hải Ninh thus complained to his Chinese counterparts that it had been extremely difficult for the Vietnamese state to convince the people on its outlying territories of the benefits of collectivization and motivate the Cô Tô Islanders to join cooperatives.[140]

The Great Leap Forward and Vietnamese cooperativization renewed the tension between the alliance of state building formed by the two revolutionary states and the alliance of livelihoods sustained by the fisherfolk along the Gulf who shared ethnic, linguistic, and family connections across the Sino-Vietnamese boundary. By the late 1950s, the two socialist states' endeavor to collectivize the coastal economy became concomitant with the nationalist project of drawing lines between the seafaring peoples of Vietnam and China and assigning them into monolithic ethnic categories of being either Vietnamese or Chinese. Both the Chinese and Vietnamese local states issued fishing permits to large junks belonging to the communes or cooperatives, which interwove the fishery agreement with the reconfiguration of the social and economic order that criminalized private ownership. The transnational livelihoods alliance reponded to the state intrusion with the "hidden transcript," which, according to James Scott, "comprises a critique of power spoken behind the back of the dominant."[141] While paying lip service to the Sino-Vietnamese socialist comradeship by promising compliance with the agreement to the Chinese authorities, the fisherfolk pretended ignorance in front of the Vietnamese militia or made it difficult for the Vietnamese authorities to track them down on paper. When among their fellow "powerless" Cantonese-speaking Cô Tô Islanders, meanwhile, they tarnished the image of the socialist program by unreservedly sharing their bitter experiences during the Leap and further alienated the islands' population from the Vietnamese state's project of coaxing them into cooperative units.

State weakness blighted a foreign policy that was supposed to strengthen the two socialist economies through the enclosure of marine resources and to

---

[139] "Beibuwan yumin wenti"; Shiwanshan Autonomous County, "Yuenan minzhu gongheguo Haining shengwei bangongting fuzhuren Wang Tingzhen tongzhi dao woxian jiaohuan woguo hezuohua qingkuang."
[140] Shiwanshan Autonomous County, "Yuenan minzhu gongheguo Haining shengwei bangongting fuzhuren Wang Tingzhen tongzhi dao woxian jiaohuan woguo hezuohua qingkuang."
[141] Scott, *Domination and the Arts of Resistance*, xii.

cement their Cold War partnership by reducing room for disputes. The preponderant task of uplifting agricultural and industrial output beyond the levels previously considered feasible further marginalized fishery, including the reduction of cross-border fishing, on the local Chinese state's agenda. Lacking in control of the wandering fisherfolk's mobility on the sea, the provincial authorities' requirement of "strengthening education" fell short of pressing the fishing community into compliance with the fishery agreement.[142] On the Vietnamese side, as the DRV state's control over the society of the Cô Tô Islands remained insubstantial until 1968, the plan outlined at the border provinces meeting in November 1956 to install timber piles near the islands to separate the Vietnamese coastal waters from shared fishing grounds was shelved until late 1958.[143]

Despite resistance from below, during the first half of the 1960s, the Chinese and Vietnamese governments carried on with the closure and enclosure of maritime territory and the nationalization of marine resources by signing increasingly restrictive fishery agreements. In March 1961, the two sides signed the Protocol of Supplementing and Modifying the Agreement over Sailboat Fishery in the Gulf of Tonkin, which moved the "agreement line" of territorial waters six nautical miles away from the coast, thereby increasing the area of enclosed water, and reduced the number of vessels that could legally fish in the other side's coastal waters. In August 1963, the PRC and the DRV reached a new agreement, which expired in 1969, to extend the line to twelve nautical miles from the coastline;[144] 120 licensed boats from each country could fish in the other side's territorial water, and 700 vessels from each side were granted permits to obtain fresh water from ports on the other side.[145] This continued joint state building was interrupted and rolled backed, however, by the escalation of the Second Indochina War.

---

[142] Department of Rural Area of CPC Guangdong Provincial Committee, "Zhuanfa Dongxing xianwei renwei guanyu Yuenan Hainingsheng fangmian tichu de jige wenti de baogao," 4.

[143] Luong, "A Handbook on the Background of Ethnic Chinese from North Vietnam," 16; UBHC KTTVB, "Trích Biên Bản Ghi Những Vấn Đề Biên Giới Được Trao Đổi Trong Cuộc Toạ Đàm Giữa Đại Biểu Các Tỉnh Cao Bằng, Lạng Sơn, Hải Ninh-Việt Nam Và Quảng Tây, Quảng Đông-Trung Quốc Họp Từ Ngày 6 Đến 9 Tháng 11 Năm 1956," 4; Department of Rural Area of CPC Guangdong Provincial Committee, "Zhuanfa Dongxing xianwei renwei guanyu Yuenan Hainingsheng fangmian tichu de jige wenti de baogao," 4.

[144] "Dui Yue yuye guanxi [Fishing relations with Vietnam]," in *Guangxi tongzhi: nongye zhi*, from GZAR Gazetteers Office, *Guangxi diqing ziliaoku*, www.gxdqw.com/bin/mse.exe?seach word=&K=a&A=59&rec=383&run=13; Huang, *The Law of the Sea and Fishery Regulations*, 124–25; Nguyễn Bá Diến, "Về việc ký kết hiệp định hợp tác nghề cá ở vịnh Bắc Bộ giữa Việt Nam và Trung Quốc," 75.

[145] Revolutionary Committee on the Line of Agriculture, Forestry, and Aquaculture of Guangdong, "Guanyu Beibuwan yuye xieding wenti de qingqiu [Request regarding the fishery agreement in the Gulf of Tonkin]," March 12, 1971, no. 229-4-154-056~058, 2/GDPA.

Conclusion: State Power on the Sea

The mid-twentieth century was a critical moment for the coastal societies and fishing industry at the Sino-Vietnamese maritime frontier. Driven by technological changes and the sovereign anxieties of modernizing states, traditional fishery activities, which had been shaped by wind, currents, and preindustrial sailing techniques, became subject to the "tyranny of the national,"[146] underpinned by the geographic discourse of map, linear boundary, and natural resources. The expansion and intensification of political power in the form of joint state intrusion tied the fisherfolk more tightly to the land and to the land-based state. Socialist state building on both sides of the border unfolded following similar steps of making fishing boats and households legible through registration and census, toppling local elites and removing power intermediaries through fishery reforms, and exerting the state's control over fisherfolk livelihoods through collectivization. The simultaneity and similarities between the expansion and consolidation of the state in the two neighboring countries reduced the wiggle room for the fishing communities to exploit and manipulate the different program, pace, and intensity of state building to maintain their autonomy and mobility. In addition, fishery agreements aimed at curbing cross-border fishing aribitrarily split the integral littoral society along the Gulf of Tonkin into two – a Chinese one and a Vietnamese one – and left the daily aspects of seafaring lives, ranging from fishing to ressupplying fresh water, subject to the command of state power.

The effectiveness of an international maritime boundary largely depended on the activities of the ordinary fisherfolk. Rather than passive "weapons" used by the government to back up its territorial claim, fisherfolk were active challengers to the state-driven, internationally coordinated enclosure of the sea. The implementation of the Chinese-Vietnamese fishing agreements was thus not a notable success due to the tension between the livelihoods needs in a preindustrial society and the agenda of central governments centering on socialist internationalism, national defense, and the pursuit of a pace of growth that outperformed previous regimes. The increasing importance that the modernizing state attached to outlying territories did not always translate into enormous potency for its local apparatus to impose government priorities. Two factors led to this disparity between objectives and capability. First, a perception gap existed between the discourses of sovereignty and territoriality, which derived from a series of "horizontal" concepts, such as lines and nautical miles, and the indigenous knowledge about the sea, which was built upon a "vertical" perception reflected in notions such as marine depth, layered

---

[146] Gupta and Sharma, *Contested Coastlines*, 8.

currents, and winds, and had dictated the actual practice of navigation and fishing for centuries. The second factor was a technological gap. The fishery agreements that stipulated "agreement lines," and the delineation of national maritime space more broadly, would require engine-powered vessels, which granted the fisherfolk greater control over the navigational routes, to implement. This demand was divorced or even in conflict with the wind-powered fishery realities in the region of the time. Moreover, because establishing physical amenities on the sea was costly and sometimes technologically impossible, the states often lacked a coercive aptitude commensurate to that on land.

On July 28, 1963, twenty-six ROC commandos sneaked into the coastal town of Hà Cối in Hải Ninh via three motor boats. Detected by the local police, the squad managed to escape to the densely forested mountain region in the northern part of the province. After a fourteen-day manhunt, all members were arrested.[147] This incident harbingered the shifting priority of the state at the Sino-Vietnamese border in the next decade, when handling security threats superceded building a socialist economy as the most heavily invested task.

---

[147] "Bắt gọn toán biệt kích Mỹ-Tưởng xâm nhập địa phận Hà Cối, tỉnh Hải Ninh [Capturing the American-Chiang Kai-shek commando team infiltrating the territory of Hà Cối, Hải Ninh Province]," July 23–August 10, 1963, in *SLDQ*, 181–82. For US-ROC joint covert incursion into North Vietnam, see Conboy and Morrison, "Plausible Deniability."

5   Reversed State Building (1965–1975)*

On November 3, 1966, Zhao Jianjun, Wu Liehe, Sun Zhizhong, and Qu Shaodong – four Red Guards from Beijing – eluded the Chinese and Vietnamese border guards and snuck into Lạng Sơn under the cover of darkness. A Vietnamese truck driver offered these exhausted yet excited young men a lift to Hanoi, dropping them off at the Chinese Embassy. Meeting with the Chinese Ambassador Zhu Qiwen, they insisted on joining the guerrilla war in South Vietnam. On November 9, the Chinese State Council, in a telegram drafted by Zhou Enlai, told Zhu that the four Red Guards' crossing of the border without the endorsement from either Chinese or Vietnamese authorities had created an "awkward situation." Praising their valor, though, the telegram instructed Zhu to send them to join PLA troops stationed in northern Vietnam in assistance of the DRV's defense. Lin Biao added that this solution "shall not be taken as a precedent." In January 1967, Zhao, serving in the anti-air artillery unit, was killed during an American bombing campaign and buried at the Chinese martyrs cemetery in Lạng Sơn.[1]

In February 1967, more than two hundred Red Guards from China's interior provinces such as Anhui, Jiangxi, and Hunan gathered in Pingxiang, the border town where the Chinese and Vietnamese railway systems connected. They vehemently demanded that the local Chinese government issue them passports so that they could carry out the revolution of "Assisting Vietnam and Resisting America" (*yuanyue kangmei*). Some other Red Guards, in lieu of traveling to the border, mailed, telegrammed, or called the Vietnamese Embassy in Beijing, asking for permission to join the war effort in Vietnam. Worried that this unsolicited zeal would do a disservice to Sino-Vietnamese relations, the Central Committee of the CPC instructed local authorities to dissuade the Red Guards from going to Vietnam, emphasizing that while the "revolutionary and

---

* A few paragraphs on smuggling in this chapter have been developed from my earlier publication "The Mountain Is High, and the Emperor Is Far Away: States and Smuggling Networks at the Sino-Vietnamese Border." Copyright © 2018 Institute for Far Eastern Studies, Kyungnam University. This article first appeared in *Asian Perspective* 42, no. 4 (October–December 2018). Published with permission by Johns Hopkins University Press.

[1] Ji, "Yuanyue kangmei zhong de Zhongguo 'hongweibing zhiyuanzhe.'"

internationalist spirit" of the Red Guards was legitimate, "illegal border crossing was not only criminal but also disrespectful toward the brotherly country."[2]

Yet, amid the most chaotic factional conflicts that plunged China into virtual anarchy, the Cultural Revolution spilled over to the Vietnamese border region, which exacerbated the spiralling tension between the ethnic Chinese in the border region and the Vietnamese state. In early May of 1968, several ethnic Chinese in Móng Cái painted slogans such as "Chairman Mao is the Sun in Our Heart" outside the pottery workshops where they worked. Meanwhile, imbued with the determination to forge Chinese identity among the diaspora, the teachers at the Chinese school in the town protested the teaching of Vietnamese, labeling it as a "foreign language." Another group of ethnic Chinese organized study sessions of Maoist thought and decided to rise in rebellion against the Vietnamese authority of Móng Cái, duplicating the Red Guard attacks on government bureaucracy in China. After the Vietnamese police arrested their leaders, the rest of the group held a sit-in protest on the banks of the Beilun/Ka Long River before eventually fleeing to Dongxing.[3]

The new dynamics on the border epitomize how the escalation of the Vietnam War (Kháng chiến chống Mỹ cứu nước, "Resistance War against the US to Save the Country" in Vietnamese) and the Cultural Revolution further compounded the already wobbly state-building campaign at the border. During the decade from 1965 to 1975, the war and the chaotic sociopolitical movement militarized the Sino-Vietnamese border and made this far-off region more relevant to the decision-making in Beijing and Hanoi about both their internal power struggles and national security policies. Yet these developments also shifted state-society relations on the political periphery in favor of a more porous boundary. Thus, the extension and contraction of state power took place simultaneously. Both Chinese and Vietnamese authorities launched ambitious infrastructure projects in the border area to facilitate the transportation of aid to Vietnam and mobilized the local society against the possible expansion of the war into the region. The Sino-Vietnamese land and maritime border region, as well as the transportation lines running through it, became spaces of frequent interactions between the Chinese and Vietnamese officials

---

[2] "Zhonggong zhongyang, Guowuyuan, Zhongyang junwei guanyu quanzu hongweibing he geming qunzhong zifa fu Yue yuanyue kangmei de tongzhi [Notice about dissuading the Red Guards and revolutionary masses from spontaneously going to Vietnam by the CPC Central Committee, State Council, and the Central Military Commission]," in Research Branch of Party History and Political Affairs of the National Defense University of PLA, *"Wenhua dageming" yanjiu ziliao*, 329. According to the records of the Chinese border check station at Friendship Pass, 1,740 and 195 undocumented Red Guards were repatriated by the Vietnamese authorities in 1967 and 1968, respectively. Zeng, *YBJZ*, 171.

[3] Office for Party Rectification of CPC Fangcheng Autonomous County for Ethnic Minorities of Guangxi, *Guangxi Fangcheng gezuzizhixian "wenge" dashijian* [Chronicle of Cultural Revolution in Fangcheng Autonomous County for Ethnic Minorities, Guangxi], 1986, in *Chinese Cultural Revolution Database*; Hoàng Thị Kim Thanh, *LDTM*, 213–14.

regarding the provision of aid and the coordination of border defenses. The efficiency of these interactions, however, was increasingly susceptible to the decline of the Sino-Vietnamese partnership following the Tết Offensive and the start of negotiations between Hanoi and Washington in 1968.

As mobilizing the border population for the war effort and political struggles unleashed revolutionary zeal that the state could not tame and depleted both governments' resources that could have been used to support the local people's livelihood and reorient the border societies inward, the political authorities eventually had to become more flexible toward the revival of the spontaneous cross-border networks. As the local officials on both sides were distracted from boundary making in the late 1960s, the Sino-Vietnamese partnership declined and conflicts among the local peoples regarding border resources on the ground increased. Rising border skirmishes in the 1970s, therefore, were not just unavoidable by-products of the changing triangular relations between Beijing, Hanoi, and Moscow but the consequence of obstructed, and even reversed, state building.

The Escalation of the Vietnam War and China's Cultural Revolution

By the early 1960s, the WPV leadership had decided to make armed struggle in the South for national unification the party's priority. The Party Central Committee's Resolution 15 passed in May 1959 expanded its toolkit to prevail against the government of Ngô Đình Diệm to include military means. Later that year, Hanoi extended its logistical supply routes – the famous Ho Chi Minh Trail – to the South. Even though the country was not yet militarily prepared, Lê Duẩn and other "South-firsters" in the DRV leadership perceived armed struggle in the South as an antidote to the alienation of the people in the North caused by a series of failures in the socialist movement.[4]

Against the background of Hanoi's preparation for war, the United States increased its military presence in South Vietnam in the early 1960s yet employed significant caution to avoid another conflict akin to the Korean War. Besides sending military advisers, in March 1962 the United States launched the nationwide Strategic Hamlet Program that forcibly relocated South Vietnamese rural populations into fortified camps to segregate them from the DRV-backed National Liberation Front (NLF) insurgents.[5] As neither side was ready for a full-scale armed struggle, the civil war in Laos between the communist Pathet Lao, which was trained, equipped, and even led by the PAVN, and the US-backed Royal Lao Government led to the Declaration on the Neutrality of Laos among fourteen countries including the United States, the Soviet Union, and the PRC in July 1962. The agreement, however, broke

---

[4] Nguyen, *Hanoi's War*, 45–47.   [5] Osborne, *Strategic Hamlets in South Vietnam*, 25.

down quickly as it became well known that the DRV was using the Ho Chi Minh Trail through Laos to funnel military supplies to South Vietnam and the covert American assistance to the Laotian government continued.[6]

With the ousting and assassination of Ngô Đình Diệm and the death of John F. Kennedy in 1963, US President Lyndon B. Johnson inherited a quickly deteriorating situation in South Vietnam. In response to the fall of the Ngô Đình Diệm regime, the Ninth Plenary Session of the WPV Politburo in December 1963 envisioned a large-scale offensive against the South that could lead to a quick, decisive victory to forestall direct American intervention.[7] On August 2 and 4, 1964, North Vietnamese torpedo boats allegedly attacked the USS *Maddox* and the USS *Turner Joy*.[8] The attacks resulted in American retaliatory air strikes and then prompted the Congress to approve the Gulf of Tonkin Resolution on August 7, which granted the US president the power to launch military actions deemed necessary in Indochina without declaring war. Following an NLF attack on Camp Holloway in February 1965, the United States launched a sustained bombing campaign, dubbed Rolling Thunder, against the North Vietnamese military and industrial infrastructure as well as the Ho Chi Minh Trail, and dispatched 3,500 Marines to South Vietnam. This marked the start of the American ground war in Vietnam.[9]

Mao exploited the escalation of the Vietnam War and the American threat to push his domestic political agenda and to pursue international recognition of China's great power status.[10] The American military buildup in South Vietnam and the Soviet military pressure from the north drove Mao to launch the Third Line Program to put China on a war footing, which, according to Covell Meyskens, reversed the economic adjustment policy that prioritized agriculture and the development of coastal provinces after the failure of the Great Leap Forward.[11] Mao capitalized on mounting international crises and China's increasing isolation in the socialist bloc between 1963 and 1965 to tighten his own grip and marginalize the influence of moderates on foreign affairs.[12] Meanwhile, as quite a few revolutionary leaders in Asia and Africa claimed that they had looked to China for inspiration, Mao perceived a tide of

---

[6] Castle, *At War in the Shadow of Vietnam*, 48–61.
[7] Asselin, *Hanoi's Road to the Vietnam War*, 164–68.
[8] It was revealed later that there was no attack on August 4. McNamara et al., *Argument without End*, 167.
[9] Lawrence, *The Vietnam War*, 85–90.
[10] Following the American ground war in South Vietnam in March, Beijing signaled to Washington that China would not directly fight the United States as long as the latter confined the war to Indochina. Hershberg and Chen, "Reading and Warning the Likely Enemy," 64–73.
[11] Lüthi, "The Vietnam War and China's Third-Line Defense Planning before the Cultural Revolution," 26; MacFarquhar, *The Origins of the Cultural Revolution*, 369–73; Meyskens, *Mao's Third Front*, 2–3.
[12] MacFarquhar, *The Origins of the Cultural Revolution*, 376.

revolution in the Third World in favor of his status aspiration to project China as the undisputable model of wars for national liberation.[13]

One of the greatest ironies of China's involvement in Indochina was that its enormous military and economic aid to DRV not only failed to help the CPC wield overwhelming influence over the WPV but also laid the Sino-Vietnamese Cold War partnership in tatters. The year 1968, which began with the Tết Offensive, marked a downward turn in the Sino-Vietnamese relations. A series of coordinated general attacks launched by the NLF and the PAVN against the South Vietnamese forces, the Tết Offensive relied heavily on advanced weapons and targeted urban areas, which was in stark contrast with the Maoist strategy of protracted war with emphasis on the mobilization of the rural population. Beijing perceived both the Tết Offensive and the opening of peace talks between Hanoi and Washington in May as signs that the DRV was leaning toward the Soviet Union and thus gradually pulled out its aid.[14] Hanoi deemed the Sino-American rapprochement in 1971–1972 as Beijing's betrayal of the Vietnamese revolution while refraining from giving a negative appraisal of the Soviet-American détente unfolding simultaneously.[15]

As the military conflicts in Indochina expanded, Chinese politics further radicalized and eventually evolved into the "Great Proletarian Cultural Revolution." In January 1965, Mao began to target "capitalist roaders" in positions of authority within the party. At the end of the year, Mao removed Luo Ruiqing, an advocate of direct military intervention in case the Vietnam War further escalated, as Chief of Staff of the PLA. Meanwhile, Lin Biao, who proposed the notion of "People's War" in support of Mao's domestic mobilization, rose in status in the military. In May 1966, a CPC internal document, the "16 May Circular," claimed the existence of "representatives of the bourgeoisie" among the party leadership, which was countered by the formation of the "Central Group of Cultural Revolution" in the Politburo headed by Chen Boda. In August, Mao endorsed the students' paramilitary movement – Red Guards – and their attack on people with a non-proletarian class background and bureaucrats deemed revisionist or capitalist.[16]

The Cultural Revolution in Guangxi was particularly brutal. On one hand, influential figures in the central leadership backed conflicting armed factions there. The character of the governor of this remote region, Wei Guoqing, incited violence.[17] Wei, an ethnic Zhuang, had headed the Chinese Military Advisory Group to Vietnam during the First Indochina War. Known as "King

---

[13] Brazinsky, *Winning the Third World*, 231; Wang, "The Political Logic of Status Competition," 559, 570.
[14] Zhai, *China and the Vietnam Wars*, 179–80; Nguyen, "The Sino-Vietnamese Split and the Indochina War," 13–14; Khoo, *Collateral Damage*, 53.
[15] Lüthi, "Beyond Betrayal," 57.   [16] Dikötter, *The Cultural Revolution*, xx–xxii.
[17] Sutton, "Consuming Counterrevolution," 137.

Figure 5.1 Cultural Revolution in Guangxi
Note: Assembly held on September 17, 1968, in Nanning, Guangxi in celebration of the foundation of the GZAR Revolutionary Committee.
Source: Photo by API/Gamma-Rapho via Getty Images # 840861808.

of Guangxi," Wei enjoyed unchallenged power and the support of the local army of the region after 1954. The beginning of the Cultural Revolution nevertheless witnessed increasing hostility between Wei, supported by Zhou Enlai, and Wu Jinnan, the Deputy Party Secretary of Guangxi who was backed by Lin Biao.[18] The tension between Wei's faction, dubbed as the "Alliance Command," and Wu's supporters, known as the "22 April," turned into armed conflict in late 1967. Mao tipped the balance toward Wei by buttressing Wei as the candidate to lead the proposed GZAR Revolutionary Committee. Assuming the role of head of the committee in August 1968, Wei was the only provincial leader to survive the purges and stay in power during the Cultural Revolution (Figure 5.1).[19] On the other hand, the region's history and

---

[18] Shen, "The Revolutionary Committee Grows Out of the Barrel of a Gun during the Great Proletarian Cultural Revolution," 145–48; Dikötter, *The Cultural Revolution*, 174–76.

[19] It remains unknown as to whether Mao and Zhou preferred Wei to stay in power to stabilize China's relations with Vietnam, to check the influence of Lin Biao among the military staff in southwestern China, or to prevent the alienation of PLA in Guangxi. See Shen, "The

culture shaped "community-level collective behavior" that intensified violence. Historical migration generated "ethnic antagonism" between the indigenous population and the Han settlers as well as between different subgroups of the Han (such as between the Hakka, or "guest people," and earlier settlers). The armed forces of Guangxi, under firm control of Wei, stretched down to the rural regions with the local People's Armed Forces Department and militias, which gave the factional conflicts "an organizational structure" that extended from urban centers to the remote countryside. With Wei's endorsement to clamp down on opponents, at least 80,000 people were killed in the summer of 1968. To add on the 20,000 counted as missing during the investigation mandated by Beijing in the 1980s, the total death toll approached 100,000.[20] The most brutal massacre took place in Wuxuan County. A total of 524 "22 April" fighters who lost the battle were taken captive and executed, and 75 or 76 were actually cannibalized according to official statistics.[21]

Sino-Vietnamese Cooperation and Changing Landscape of the Border

The period of 1963–1964 witnessed a series of mutual confirmations of the Sino-Vietnamese partnership under the banner of national liberation. On August 15, 1963, Zhou Enlai met with Secretary of the Party Committee of Southern Vietnam Nguyễn Văn Linh in Beijing and praised the NLF struggle as "the greatest, most progressive, bravest, and most prominent one after the Korean War and the ceasefire in Indochina."[22] In July 1964, Zhou visited Hanoi and pledged Chinese support for the Vietnamese people.[23] The day after China successfully detonated its first atomic bomb on October 16, 1964, General Secretary of WPV Lê Duẩn paid a visit to the PRC Ministry of Transportation delegation to Haiphong to offer his congratulations. Lê Duẩn told the Chinese that the detonation "greatly enheartens the struggle in South Vietnam. Your victory is our victory." Extolling his Chinese comrades to gain Beijing's commitment of support, Lê Duẩn added that "the second thing

---

Revolutionary Committee Grows Out of the Barrel of a Gun during the Great Proletarian Cultural Revolution," 171.

[20] The above section is based on Walder, *Civil War in Guangxi*, 8, 14, 17–22, 25–26.
[21] Sutton, "Consuming Counterrevolution," 138.
[22] "Zhou Enlai zongli tong Yuenan laodongdang zhongyang nanfanju shuji Ruan Wenling de tanhua jilu [Minute of conversation between Premier Zhou Enlai and the Secretary of Southern Bureau of the WPV Central Nguyễn Văn Linh]," August 15, 1963, no. 106-01411-04, 4/ FMAPRC.
[23] Zhai, *China and the Vietnam Wars*, 131.

worthy of celebration is Khrushchev's resignation, for which the CPC should take credit."[24]

The increasing significance of Vietnam in the Cold War partnership led to further changes in the symbolic meaning of the border. Zhennan Guan/Nam Quan, just renamed to Munan Guan in 1953, once again received a new name at the behest of Vietnamese leaders. During his visit to the DRV in 1964, Zhou Enlai told Hồ Chí Minh that China agreed with the Vietnamese proposal of renaming Munan Guan as the Hữu Nghị Quan/Youyi Guan ("Friendship Pass").[25] Hanoi's insistence on renaming the gate forced Beijing to reflect on China's imperial legacy at the country's frontier region more broadly. On October 25, 1964, Zhou wrote to the Foreign Ministry that the name of places such as Andong ("to pacify the east"), Gaiping ("to overthrow and crush"), and Ji'an ("to investigate and stabilize") in Northeast China, mostly given by the Qing government, should be abandoned altogether because such "chauvinist terms" could arouse resentment from the Democratic People's Republic of Korea. He further recommended future reviews of place names along China's frontier region and change of "those that could provoke discontent of Mongolia, Burma, Laos, India, Pakistan, Nepal, Bhutan, Sikkim, Afghanistan, and Soviet Union or instigate nationalist sentiments of brotherly ethnic groups within our country."[26]

Given the importance the Vietnamese leaders attached to the renaming, China held a grand ceremony on May 5, 1965, to publicize the changing symbolic meaning of the mountain pass. The delegation from Lạng Sơn province praised the friendship between the Chinese and Vietnamese people and their united struggle, applauded Beijing's decision to change the name of the gate, and extolled "the strong support of the Chinese government for the cause of socialist construction and the struggle for national unity of [the Vietnamese] people."[27] The ceremony symbolized the delicate partnership

---

[24] The quotes and paraphrases are from Chinese Embassy to the DRV, "Duiwo baozha yuanzidan de fanying (6) [Reactions to our detonation of atomic bomb, 6]," December 20, 1964, no. 106-00778-02, 19/FMAPRC.

[25] "Guanyu jiang Munan Guan gaiwei Youyi Guan dengshi," 4.

[26] "Guanyu 'Munan Guan' gaiwei 'Youyi Guan' shi [About renaming 'South-Pacifying Gate' into 'Friendship Pass']," October 25, 1964, no. 114-00129-01, 1/FMAPRC.

[27] UBHC tỉnh Lạng Sơn, "Báo Cáo của UBHC Tỉnh Lạng Sơn v/v đoàn dại biểu của Lạng Sơn sang dự lễ đổi tên Mục Nam quan thành Hữu nghị quan [Report of the delegation of Lạng Sơn on behalf of the Provincial Administrative Committee to the ceremony of renaming South Pacifying Pass to Friendship Pass]," March 11, 1965, no. 5705, 2/UBHC KTTVB 1948–1976/NAVC III. Also see "Zhong-Yue bianjing renmin gongqing 'Munan Guan' gaiming 'Youyi Guan' [People at the Sino-Vietnamese border celebrates together the renaming of 'Munan Guan' to 'Friendship Pass']," *Jiefangjun bao*, March 6, 1965. In the same year, Mubian ("to establish rapport with the frontier") County was renamed Napo County, taking on the indigenous term of the region.

between Beijing and Hanoi at the early stage of the escalation of the Vietnam War, where the Vietnamese leadership employed pro-CPC and anti-peaceful coexistence rhetoric to secure political and military assistance from China. Meanwhile, fighting on the frontline of anti-imperialist struggle enhanced the strategic importance of the DRV to Beijing. The Chinese leadership had to formally treat the Vietnamese as an equal partner to win Hanoi to their side in the polemics with the Soviet Union.

Following the Americanization of the Vietnam War, the DRV paid lip service to the Maoist model of protracted struggle through guerrilla warfare while planning for an eventual showdown in a conventional conflict. In May 1965, the DRV Consul General to Guangzhou Đỗ Văn Mẫn returned from Hanoi and met Wang Jinchuan, Deputy Director of the Foreign Office of Guangdong, and told the latter that "the Vietnamese people will fight a long-term war yet strive for a decisive victory in the short term by concentrating the main forces. The enemy might launch sustained bombings and attack from air and sea against the North. But we need to primarily strengthen the struggle in the South so that the North could minimize losses." Emphasizing the importance of China to Vietnam's victory, Đỗ Văn Mẫn expressed his confidence that "the enemy has no choice but to take into consideration the possibility of Chinese dispatching troops. China is different from fifteen years ago and Indochina is not Korea." The mission of the WPV was "to keep fighting in the South and to produce while fighting in the North," where the Second Five-Year had to be postponed, infrastructure standards needed to be modified according to wartime requirement, and some coastal industrial sites were scheduled to be relocated to the mountainous region.[28]

The fragmented terrain in the Sino-Vietnamese border, which in the past had helped Vietnam to maintain its independence against the powerful Chinese empire, now became a geographic hurdle for Hanoi's efforts to enlist China's material assistance in the war against America. Even though the recession in the early 1960s induced a nationwide retrenchment in infrastructure construction, extension of the road network to China's southwestern border "continued unabated" to facilitate political consolidation and economic development. As a result, whereas many roads in Southeast Asia were built on natural earth and thus degenerated into trails after the rainy season, eight surfaced motor routes connected China with Burma, Laos, and Vietnam.[29] Soon after the Gulf of Tonkin Incident in August 1964, China and Vietnam embarked on sustained

---

[28] This paragraph is based on "Yuenan laodongdang zhongyang dui nanfang douzheng xingshi de kanfa ji duice [The WPV Central Committee's opinion on the situation of struggle in the South and their countermeasure]," December 28, 1964–November 20, 1965, no. 106-01302-02, 12–14/FMAPRC.

[29] "Construction of Roads in the China-Southeast Asia Border Area through 1964," April 1965, no. CIA-RDP79T01049A003100030004–0, 1/CREST/NARA College Park.

efforts to expand the roads and railways across the border and improve transloading facilities between the two countries' transport systems. Under American aerial interdiction, the construction aimed primarily at opening or restoring rails, roads, and bridges rapidly instead of building projects of high quality for long-term use. Besides land transportation, the two sides also developed additional maritime routes in the Gulf of Tonkin to increase carrying capacities and provide alternative shipping methods as a defense against bombing.

In August and September 1964, representatives of the Ministry of Transportation of the two countries met in Hanoi and laid out a plan to upgrade the cross-border railway system. Before eventually adding a standard gauge line between Hanoi and Pingxiang, the two sides decided to construct a new trans-loading station at Đồng Đăng as a transitional measure because the transloading infrastructure in Pingxiang had reached its maximum capacity and the mountainous terrain prohibited the expansion of the existing railway station. In particular, Pingxiang station was only able to trans-load 50,000 tons of oil per year, which fell far short of meeting the wartime needs. Thus, the new station in Đồng Đăng would mainly serve as an oil trans-loading point.[30] Meanwhile, in March and April 1965, the Guangxi railway authority upgraded the Nanning-Pingxiang Railway, which improved its cargo capacity in preparation for a surging volume in transports to the Sino-Vietnamese border.[31]

In April 1965, Lê Duẩn and Minister of Defense Võ Nguyên Giáp visited Beijing to negotiate the details for China's military aid. Among the requested assistance were "volunteer pilots, volunteers soldiers ... and other volunteers, including road and bridge engineering units." Hanoi hoped the pilots would help to "restrict American bombing to areas south of the 20th or 19th parallels," "defend the safety of Hanoi," "defend several main transportation lines," and "raise the morale of the Vietnamese people."[32] To avoid another head-on confrontation with the United States, however, China only decided to dispatch

---

[30] "Zhonghua renmin gongheguo tielu daibiaotuan yu Yuenan minzhu gongheguo jiaotong yunshu daibiaotuan huitan jiyao [Meeting minute between the railway representatives of the PRC and the transportation representatives of the DRV]," August 26–September 26, 1964, no. 1086/BGV 1/NAVC III. This folder contains the Chinese version of the Memorandum of Understanding from 1964–1965 between the Ministry of Transportation of the DRV and the PRC transportation delegations on the upgrade of railway and roads between Vietnam and Pingxiang.

[31] CPC Nanning Special District Committee, "Guanyu zhanbei qiangxiu Nanning zhi Pingxiang tielu huangui ji daxiu gongcheng choudiao mingong de jinji tongzhi [Urgent notice of dispatching laborers to the war preparation repair of Nanning-Pingxiang Railway and change of track]," April 22, 1965, no. 1-37-42-4/CZMA; CPC Nanning Special District Committee, "Guanyu xiujian 0521 zhanbei gongcheng choudiao mingong de jinji tongzhi [Urgent notice of sending civilian laborers to the 0521 war preparation project]," March 24, 1965, no. 1-37-42-6/CZMA.

[32] "Liu Shaoqi and Le Duan," April 8, 1965, in *77 Conversations between Chinese and Foreign Leaders on the Wars in Indochina, 1964–1977*, ed. Westad et al., 83.

railway corps, engineer corps, and anti-air artillery troops to Vietnam. In May 1965, the CPC Central Committee established the Assist Vietnam Leadership Team headed by Chief of the Joint Staff Luo Ruiqing. The leadership team then commissioned the CPC Party Central and State Council Work Team for Supporting Vietnam, which was composed of the heads of twenty-one government institutions and military services such as the Foreign Ministry, the Ministry of Railways, the Navy, and the Air Force.[33] The Vietnamese Ministry of Transportation, at the same time, set up a "24 Construction Committee" to coordinate with the Chinese "volunteer troops" in constructing railways and roads.[34]

In July 1965, the PLA Railway Corps entered Vietnam under the name of "Chinese volunteer construction teams."[35] The Corps assumed three tasks: to add a standard rail track on the line between Pingxiang and Kép (about two-thirds of the total length of the Pingxiang-Hanoi line), a transportation hub in Bắc Giang Province, build a new rail line between Kép and the Thái Nguyên industrial complex, and restore lines and bridges destroyed by bombing.[36] Despite continuous American air raids against main Vietnamese traffic routes, the Pingxiang-Kép standard gauge line was completed in December 1965. The operation of the dual-gauge railway in the DRV substantially offset the impact of aerial attacks. It eliminated the necessity for trans-loading between the Chinese standard gauge and Vietnamese narrow gauge at Pingxiang, thus enabling the Vietnamese to turn to the Chinese inventory of cars to supplement their own domestic narrow-gauge cars.[37] The dual gauges boosted the line's speed and loading capacity, and the presence of Chinese engineering troops freed the DRV construction units "for work in the Southern portions of the country."[38] The PLA Railway Corps suffered under at least nine American bombing campaigns, but for the ordinary Chinese soldiers, America was not their biggest enemy. The rainy weather, fatal malaria, deadly snakes, and declining food supply were more formidable hardships than bombardment. Li Qingde, Political Commissar of the Railway Corps, later recalled that many

---

[33] Deng, "Yuanyue kangmei shulue," 85–86.
[34] "Ke-You duan gaigui gongcheng jungong yanshou jiaojie jilu [Records of acceptance check and reception of the gauge modification project between Kép and Friendship Pass]," December 1965, no. 1093, 13/BGV 1/NAVC III. This folder contains the Chinese version of the agreements, meeting minutes, and records of acceptance and reception on the transportation projects completed by the Chinese in Vietnam from 1965 to 1970.
[35] For a review of the projects completed by the Railway Corps, see Li, *The Dragon in the Jungle*, 165–96.
[36] "Ke-You duan gaigui gongcheng jungong yanshou jiaojie jilu," 1–12.
[37] "The Situation in Vietnam: information as of 1600 29 August 1966," August 29, 1966, no. CIA-RDP79T00826A001200010005–7, VI-1/CREST/NARA College Park.
[38] "Military Storage Area Dong Dang, North Vietnam, 2158N 10641E," November 23, 1966, no. CIA-RDP78T05929A002200070001–9, 2/CREST/NARA College Park.

of the senior Chinese officers had served in the Chinese Civil War and the Korean War yet still found that the living conditions in Vietnam weighed heavily on their morale.[39]

During the reconstruction of the railway, the Chinese and Vietnamese managed to build bypass bridges at vulnerable points and flatten the terrain to improve the safety and speed of the line. The dual-gauge line was then extended to Yên Viên Railway Station, which served Hanoi and significantly increased the efficiency of shipping. According to Chinese statistics, the Pingxiang-Hanoi line – Vietnam's principal rail connection with China – was opened to traffic for 813 days (86.3 percent of all calendar days) from September 1965 to the halt of American bombing in March 1968.[40] In the summer of 1967, the two governments also planned to build a rail line connecting Thái Nguyên and Pingxiang to serve as an alternative route to transport aid to Vietnam as well as to facilitate wartime relocation. The project, however, was delayed due to the absence of detailed maps of northwestern Vietnam and was never realized after the Sino-Vietnamese relations soured in 1968.[41]

In August 1965, in exigent need of more flexible, truck-based logistic support, Hanoi secured an aid package from China to restore and build twelve new roads in Vietnam and then to connect them with Chinese roads. The two sides also agreed that the PLA engineer troops, under the name "road construction team of Chinese Ministry of Transportation," would only build temporary bridges or lay stone pavement underwater so that the construction would be less vulnerable to bombing.[42] A US appraisal of the effectiveness of intensified bombing against the Hanoi-Đồng Đăng line in July 1967 acknowledged that although the campaign had delayed rail service, it did not lead to a meaningful degradation of the DRV's ability to support the war in the South. The extensive construction projects connected the road systems of Southern China and Northern Vietnam at several points, which allowed the Vietnamese to use vehicles to overcome railway delays.[43] Even during the heyday of the Sino-Vietnamese partnership, however, border settlement remained a sensitive

---

[39] Li, "Yuanyue kangmei zhong de tiedao baozhang," 284.   [40] Ibid., 293.

[41] "Zhonghua renmin gongheguo Tiedaobu daibiao xiaozu he Yuenan minzhu gongheguo jiaotong yunshubu daibiao xiaozu huitan jiyao [Meeting minute between delegate team of the Ministry of Railways of the PRC and the delegate team of the Ministry of Transportation of the DRV]," July 9–August 4, 1967, no. 1093, 26–30/BGV 1/NAVC III.

[42] "Zhonghua renmin gongheguo zhengfu jiaotong daibiaotuan he Yuenan minzhu gongheguo zhengfu jiaotong yunshu daibiaotuan guanyu Zhongguo yuanzhu Yuenan xiujian qitiao gonglu de shishi jihua [Plan of China helping Vietnam building seven new roads between delegates of transportation of the PRC and the DRV]," August 27–September 19, 1965, no. 1089/BGV 1/NAVC III.

[43] "An Appraisal of the Bombing of North Vietnam (through 18 July 1967)," July 18, 1967, no. RDP79T00826A002400430001-2, 1–9/CREST/NARA College Park.

issue. In late 1967, the Chinese construction team transferred the management of a completed road linking Bản Chắt (in Lạng Sơn Province) and the Chinese border to the Vietnamese transportation authority. The handover certificate states that "the joint point of the road shall not be used as a basis of demarcation [in the future]."[44]

The interlinked Vietnamese and Chinese transport systems had a complicated impact on Hanoi's war efforts. In theory, the Chinese railway system provided the fastest method, except for expensive airlifts, to transport Soviet and East European weapons to Vietnam. In practice, Moscow and Beijing competed in exerting influence on Hanoi and for leadership in the world socialist movement. In particular, Hanoi's reluctant acceptance of the Maoist People's War doctrine and its requests for missiles from Moscow led Beijing to suspect that the Vietnamese leaders would eventually embrace the Soviet model of winning a conventional war with advanced and heavy weaponry.[45] In short, the Chinese leaders wanted to see their Vietnamese comrades win, but the latter had to do so in a Maoist way. Meanwhile, a desire to avoid a direct conflict with the United States constrained both Moscow and Beijing's commitment to Hanoi. When the Soviet and Chinese differed in their assessment of the level of tolerable risk, the Vietnamese were restricted over the military aid and the channels through which they could receive it.

The ongoing Sino-Soviet split led to China's opposition to a Soviet proposal of directly transporting military aid to Vietnam through China. On February 25, 1965, following Premier Alexei Kosygin's visit to Hanoi earlier in the month, the Soviets notified China of its aid plan to "send 4,000 Soviet armed forces (including a missile brigade) to Vietnam via Chinese railways," to station 500 Soviet soldiers at "one or two airports on the Sino-Vietnamese border," to assemble MiG-21s for the protection of Vietnamese airspace, and to use the air corridor over China "to transmit these MiG-21s, other weapons, and supplies for Soviet military staff during their stay in Vietnam." On March 10, Liu Xiao, Vice Foreign Minister of the PRC, rejected the proposal in an oral response to Soviet Chargé d'Affaires F. V. Mochulskii, stating that the above constituted "an extraordinary military operation, instead of conventional military aid. Comrade Kosygin did not mention this significant matter when he passed by Beijing. We were therefore surprised when you suddenly raised the issue." Liu noted critically that if implemented, the program would "put China, the Soviet Union, and Vietnam into a position of open

---

[44] "Zhonghua renmin gongheguo houqin budui xiulu zhihuibu he Yuenan minzhu gongheguo jiaotong yunshubu guanliju guanyu Banzhi zhi Zhong-Yue bianjie gonglu jiancheng de jiaojie zhengmingshu [Handover of Bản Chắt-Chinese border road from the headquater of road construction logistics corps of the PRC to Bureau of Management of Ministry of Transportation of the DRV]," n.d., no. 1089/BGV 1/NAVC III.

[45] Khoo, "Breaking the Ring of Encirclement," 20–21.

confrontation with the United States." Blaming the Soviets for trying to control Vietnam and China through its military presence, Liu told Mochulskii that China would only assist in transporting Soviet aid through rail.[46]

As a result of the Sino-Soviet squabbles, several significant delays took place during the transshipment of Soviet aid through China. According to American intelligence, throughout March 1965, the DRV "was deprived of all Soviet military aid." The operation of a Soviet-supplied surface-to-air missile system was delayed from March until July 1965, "at least in part because of Chinese pressure on North Vietnam." The first two months of 1967 also witnessed a "serious deliberate" holdup in rail shipments of Soviet military aid to the DRV.[47] After the Cultural Revolution entered the bloody "power seizing" stage in the summer of 1967, social disorder in China was to blame for the delay of Soviet transshipment, rather than Beijing's deliberate intention to use it as a way to wield coercion on Hanoi. Some trains were held at the Sino-Soviet border because the paralyzed Chinese bureaucracy was unable to protect sensitive weapons shipments from looting. At the southwest border, the rebels not only raided an ordnance depot of the PLA and militia but also targeted aid to Vietnam. On the night of August 18, 1967, about three hundred "22 April" supporters in Guangxi plundered a military freight train that was loaded with armaments in transit to Vietnam and seized more than 4,000 anti-aircraft gun cartridges. They did not return the weapons until the Central Group of Cultural Revolution in Beijing interfered. May 21, 1968 witnessed another, larger-scale raid at the Liuzhou Railway Station, a land transport hub for the region. Several thousand "22 April" fighters seized 17,000,000 cartridges from an aid package to Vietnam that had been temporarily stored at the location.[48] The "Alliance Command" members, on the other hand, were accused of detaining freight, kidnapping train drivers, and illegally searching the passengers of international trains.[49]

The paralyzed railway system and the interrupted transportation to Vietnam compelled the Chinese central government to weigh in. The CPC Central

---

[46] This paragraph is based on "Liuxiao fuwaizhang huijian Sulian zhuhua shiguan daiban Mochuli [Vice Prime Minister Liu Xiao met with Charge d'affaires of Soviet Embassy to China F.V. Mochulskii]," March 10, 1965, no. 109-03961-03, 82–84/FMAPRC.

[47] The quotes and paraphrases are from "The Sino-Soviet Dispute on Aid to North Vietnam (1965–1968)," September 30, 1968, no. 0000415086, iii/CIA Electronic Reading room, www.cia.gov/library/readingroom/docs/DOC_0000415086.pdf.

[48] Editorial group of the Chronicle of Cultural Revolution in Guangxi, *Guangxi wenge dashi nianbiao*, 48, 91.

[49] Office of the British Charge d'Affaires, Peking, "Report on the restoration of railway transport by the Liuchow Worker and Technician Alliance," July 1968, no. FCO 21/22 (FC 1/6), 27–29/ UKNA; Lucien Paye (French Ambassador in Beijing) to Michel Debre (French Foreign Minister), "Politique interieure," July 25, 1968, no. FR1480022, 2–3/ AMFEAF, obtained and re-catalogued by ECNURC.

Committee telegraphed the GZAR Revolutionary Committee Preparatory Group, the Guangxi Military District, and the regional railway authorities on June 13, 1968, urging them to forestall attacks on the railway system because Guangxi had been "on the very front line of our country's struggle to aid Vietnam and to oppose America," and it was the railway and communication technicians and workers who "[had] taken on the enormous and glorious duty to help the Vietnamese people." The telegram reprimanded the factional fighters who ransacked the storage of aid to Vietnam and PLA equipment, seized trains, and sabotaged railway equipment and the violent clashes that had "brought railway transport in the [Liuzhou] area to a complete halt" and thus "hindered the supply of goods to Vietnam and the transport of goods for foreign trade." Beijing ordered the two factions to stop armed clashes, banned external people from carrying out the Cultural Revolution in the railway system, and required all railway workers and technicians to immediately return to their posts without discriminating against each other based on factional background. It further pressed for the return of all material destined for Vietnam and all army weapons and equipment.[50] Such cases show how the Cultural Revolution jeopardized the strength and consistency of state apparatus on the ground, which inevitably strained even further the already delicate Sino-Vietnamese relations.

Besides land-based transportation, sea routes between Southern China and Vietnamese ports also assumed military importance. Before the escalation of the Vietnam War, the busiest sea lanes between China and Vietnam connected Chinese seaports such as Guangzhou and Zhanjiang with the Vietnamese harbors of Haiphong and Cẩm Phả. Chinese freighters carried manufactured goods to Vietnam and then returned with coal loaded from Hòn Gai. In the second half of 1965, these lanes took on the mission of shipping Chinese aid and transshipping Soviet and Eastern European assistance to Vietnam, but this quickly became troublesome to the local Chinese bureaucrats. In August, the GBMT reported to the provincial government that it had to undercut domestic shipping to fulfill the Guangdong Military Zone's request to freight 200,000 tons of materials to Vietnam before the end of the year. Unloading on Vietnamese coastal islands instead of well equipped harbors to dodge air strikes, the voyage of shipping aid to Vietnam also took a longer time than commercial ones, which reduced general shipping capacity.[51] The treatment of Chinese vessels by Vietnamese authorities also perturbed the Chinese officials.

---

[50] This paragraph is based on Office of the British Charge d'Affaires, Peking, "Central Committee Telegram of 13 June/ Telegram No. 68/44 Urgent," June 13, 1968, no. FCO 21/22 (FC 1/6), 25–26/UKNA; Also see "A.S. situation au Kwangsi," August 3, 1968, no. FR1480026, 1–3/ AMFEAF, obtained and re-catalogued by ECNURC.
[51] GBMT, "Guanyu yuanyue kangmei de yunshu wenti [About transportation issue of Assisting Vietnam and Resisting America]," August 18, 1965, no. 290-1-205-27~33, 28–29/GDPA.

In a report to the Ministry of Transportation in September 1965, the GBMT complained that several Vietnamese ports no longer gave the Chinese ships priority because they preferred letting more Soviet vessels anchor there so that American bombers would refrain from attacking these locations.[52]

Meanwhile, navigating the Chinese-Vietnamese sea lanes was dangerous during the war. Facing American bombing of Vietnamese ports, most Chinese ships were equipped with anti-aircraft guns. The two countries also adjusted port regulations in the face of this danger. According to a previous agreement between Beijing and Hanoi, vessels were not allowed to use transmitter-receivers after entering the ports of the other country in the interest of respecting sovereignty. But during American air raids, Vietnamese port authorities started to permit the Chinese ships staying at their ports to use transmitter-receivers when other telecommunications were interrupted by equipment damage.[53]

Ultimately, Beijing decided to provide even greater support for Vietnamese coastal shipments to sustain the latter's wartime economic development. In January 1967, the Ministries of Transportation of the two countries signed an agreement to open more sea lanes between South China and northern Vietnam to enable Vietnamese vessels to evacuate during emergencies, repair damage, and transship cargo. Under wartime conditions, Guangzhou and Huangpu – the two larger and better equipped ports in Guangdong – would receive Vietnamese state-owned freighters and merchant ships, while Beihai assumed the task of hosting smaller Vietnamese fishing boats and transshipping cargoes between Hong Kong and Haiphong. The agreement was also applicable to Vietnamese warships and Coast Guard vessels.[54]

In early 1968, against the backdrop of the Tết Offensive, Beijing decided to open new sea lanes between China and Vietnam that would be able to provide logistical backup to large-unit warfare and be less susceptible to enemy surveillance and reconnaisance. On February 7, Mao and Zhou met with Hồ Chí Minh, who was staying in China for medical treatment. Easing the pressure on the Vietnamese to fight a Maoist war, Zhou suggested that the

---

[52] GBMT, "Guanyu jiaqiang xingshi Zhong-Yue hangxian chuanbo gongzuo de baogao [Report of strengthening works of vessels on the Sino-Vietnamese sea lanes]," September 3, 1965, no. 290-1-205-7~12, 9/GDPA.

[53] GBMT, "Guanyu Nanhai 143lun zai Yuenan Jinpugang yu meiji hongzha saoshe ji ziwei fanji qingkuang de baogao [Report about vessel Nanhai no. 143 encountering American bombing and shooting and engaging in self-defense]," April 29, 1966, no. 290-1-221-67, 1–10/GDPA.

[54] "Nghị định thư giữa Bộ Giao thông vận tải nước Việt Nam Dân chủ Cộng hòa và Bộ Giao thông nước Cộng hòa Nhân dân Trung hoa về việc sử dụng đường trú ẩn đường biển, giữa hai nước Việt Trung và tàu bè Việt nam sơ tán sang cảng Trung quốc trong thời chiến [Agreement between the Ministry of Transportation of the DRV and the Ministry of Transportation of the PRC on opening sea lanes and evacuation of Vietnamese vessels to Chinese ports during wartime]," 1967, no. 8273, 1–8/PTTg 3/NAVC III.

Vietnamese armed forces organize two to three field corps that could "fight far away from their hometowns" and "engage with isolated enemies."[55] On March 22, a week before the United States halted bombing above the 20th parallel to facilitate negotiation with the DRV, the Chinese State Council ordered the secret construction of a war preparation port in the coastal county of Fangcheng, bordering on Vietnam. For the sake of secrecy, the construction was dubbed the "Guangxi 322 Project."[56]

Although Sino-Vietnamese relations chilled in 1968, mainly due to the CPC's vehement opposition to Hanoi's decision to negotiate with Washington in May of that year, the building of Fangcheng Port still commenced in June 1968. By early 1970, the Guangzhou Military Zone and the GZAR also managed to jointly build four piers, a dockyard, an oil depot, an underwater oil pipeline, and other auxiliary facilities at the port.[57] Nonetheless, the completion of the project coincided with a low tide period in the Sino-Vietnamese partnership. Chinese anti-air artillery troops had withdrawn from Vietnam by March 1969 following the halt in US bombing of North Vietnam in November 1968.[58] By July 1970, the PLA Engineer Corps and Railway Corps had also returned to China.[59]

Three developments after 1970, however, led to renewed Chinese interest in providing aid to Vietnam. First, the US expansion of the war to Cambodia in the spring of 1970 following the Cambodian coup not only gave rise to a heightened American threat but also gave Beijing another opportunity to "expose the true face of the Soviet revisionists and social-imperialists," who chose to endorse the pro-US Lon Nol government.[60] Second, China started to increase its military shipments to the DRV in 1971 in an attempt to convince its Vietnamese comrades that Beijing's rapprochement with Washington would not retard the DRV's war effort and to avoid further pushing Hanoi toward Moscow.[61] The third development was the US implementation of a mining program in the Gulf of Tonkin – dubbed "Operation Pocket Money" – in May 1972. Given the importance of seaborne transport to Vietnamese receipt of Soviet aid, Washington had speculated that Beijing would probably be reluctant to recognize the importance of Soviet aid by cooperating with Hanoi to institute countermeasures to this mining, thus eventually draining

---

[55] CPC Central Literature Research Center, *Zhou Enlai nianpu*, 217.
[56] "Fangcheng gang [Fangcheng port]," in *Fangcheng xianzhi*, from GZAR Gazetteers Office, *Guangxi diqing ziliaoku*, http://lib.gxdfz.org.cn/view-c58–414.html.
[57] Ibid.   [58] Deng, "Yuanyue kangmei shulue," 90.
[59] Li, "Yuanyue kangmei zhong de tiedao baozhang," 294.
[60] Chen, "China, the Vietnam War, and the Sino-American Rapprochement," 49 (quote); Path, "Hà Nội's Response to Beijing's Enthusiasm to Aid North Vietnam," 102.
[61] Zhai, *China and the Vietnam Wars*, 195.

Vietnamese supplies.[62] Instead, this mining crisis provided a context for greater Chinese assistance to Vietnam.

Following the American aerial mining campaign, Hanoi embarked on a strenuous effort to ensure overland resupply from China, making substantial use of roads, rail, and pipelines despite resumed American bombing. On May 9, 1972, the same day the mining against Haiphong began, Hanoi sought Chinese assistance in demining. Later in the day, Zhou Enlai met leaders of the Chinese Navy to discuss this issue, which resulted in the immediate dispatch of a "mining investigation team" to Vietnam.[63] From May 1972 to August 1973, more than three hundred Chinese navy minesweeping staff entered Vietnam.[64] Against this background, Fangcheng Port opened for military use on August 1, 1972, establishing a near-coast resupply link between South China and Northern Vietnam.[65] Chinese vessels carrying aid to Vietnam, including food supplies, departed from the port and anchored at several Vietnamese outlying islands, such as Bạch Long Vĩ, where Vietnamese lighters would transfer the cargo back to the continent.[66] By August 1972, the activation of mines had trapped many ships in the Haiphong harbor, where 85 percent of Vietnamese maritime imports had previously entered the country. This blockade diverted twenty-three foreign flagged ships with more than 155,000 tons of cargoes to Chinese ports such as Zhanjiang, Guangzhou, and Shanghai. The transportation between Pingxiang and Đồng Đăng by rail and road then surged to transship cargoes diverted to these ports.[67] Because the vast majority of Soviet aid, including significant quantities of oil, arrived in Vietnam via sea before the mine warfare began, China built five new oil pipelines to connect Fangcheng Port and Pingxiang with the Vietnamese transport pivot of Kép to mitigate the effects of the US naval blockade.[68]

Wartime construction rapidly transformed Fangcheng harbor from a fishing village to a port that could service bulk carriers. In November 1972, Zhou instructed that "no matter whether there will be a ceasefire in Vietnam, Fangcheng Port should be expanded secretly and immediately." In fact, after the United States began to remove mines in Haiphong in February 1973, Hanoi

---

[62] "Possible Alternatives to the Rolling Thunder Program," May 28, 1968, no. CIA-RDP78T02095R000900070030-0, 6/CREST/NARA College Park.
[63] Qu, *Yuanyue kangmei*, 318–22; Ma, "Zhouzongli yunchou yuanyue saolei," 35–37.
[64] Chen, "Kangmei yuanyue zhanzheng zhong de Zhong-Mei shuileizhan," 19.
[65] "Fangcheng gang."
[66] "Zhandou zai Zhong-Yue hangxianshang [Fighting on the Sino-Vietnamese sea lane]," June 1973, no. 231-A1.1-1-39, 1–8/GDPA; "The Overall Impact of the US Bombing and Mining Program on North Vietnam," August 1972, no. CIA-RDP78T02095R000700080096-3, 7/CREST/NARA College Park.
[67] "The Overall Impact of the US Bombing and Mining Program on North Vietnam," 6, 7, 33.
[68] Deng, "Yuanyue kangmei shulue," 91.

and Beijing decided to close the secret alternative shipping lane between Fangcheng and Vietnamese islands in April. Nonetheless, Fangcheng Port was expanded after May 1973 and was eventually opened as a commercial port in August 1974.[69] The development of Fangcheng Port thus highlights the long-term effects of wartime infrastructure building on the increasing presence of the state at the border.

Securitization of Border Society and Contraction of State Institutions

The rising significance of the cross-border transportation networks and persistent American and South Vietnamese intelligence reconaissance prompted renewed joint efforts by the Chinese and Vietnamese authorities to rigorously monitor their shared border. Soon after the Gulf of Tonkin Incident, the MOPS of the PRC and the DRV and the Department of General Staff of the two militaries signed an "Agreement on Cooperation in Defending the Security of the Sino-Vietnamese Border Area," which entered into force in October 1964 and superseded previous regulations for security cooperation at the border. One overriding theme of the agreement was for greater central supervision of the interactions between the local state authorities along the border. Worried about the geographically fragmented border region under the administration of KTTVB and KTTTB, Hanoi called for "unified leadership" of border regulations under the Central Military Commission and demanded that its local agents report to their superiors when encountering issues beyond their capacity, instead of acting on their own.[70]

For the two governments, the historical state weakness and ethnic mosaic of the border territory left the region particularly vulnerable. While US marines were landing at Đà Nẵng on March 8, 1965, delegates of Guangxi, Cao Bằng and Lạng Sơn met in Nanning between February 22 and March 14 to orchestrate their efforts to detect subversive activities along the border, especially "parachuted spies who could access the border area by land and sea, collect intelligence, develop networks of agents, engage in sabotage, and encourage counterrevolutionary and other destructive elements among the ethnic

---

[69] The quote and paraphrases are from "Kaifa jianshe shiji [Achievement of development and construction]," in *Fangcheng xianzhi*, from GZAR Gazetteers Office, *Guangxi diqing ziliaoku*, http://lib.gxdqw.com/view-c58–413.html.

[70] This paragraph is based on "Chỉ thị của Ban bí thư Số 86-CT/TW 4 về việc thực hiện Hiệp nghị về vấn đề hiệp đồng bảo vệ an ninh khu vực biên giới Việt-Trung [Instruction of the Secretariat No. 86-CT/TW on the implementation of the Agreement on Cooperation in Defending the Security of the Sino-Vietnamese Border Area], October 7, 1964, in *VKDTT* 25 (1964), 270–72.

minorities."[71] The Vietnamese delegation proudly told their Chinese counterparts that since their last inter-provincial meeting in 1962, the Vietnamese authorities had captured and returned 120 "counterrevolutionaries" from China, many of whom had managed to change their names and surreptitiously settle in the Vietnamese interior provinces, industrial areas, and along strategic transport lines. Sharing additional intelligence, the Vietnamese representative handed their Chinese counterparts a list of forty-two "reactionary networks" engaging in subversive and seditious activities in the border area detected by the Vietnamese authorities.[72]

With the escalation of the war against the United States, Vietnamese officials found the possibility of outside influences fermenting internal challenges to state legitimacy particularly alarming. As radical collectivization had generated unresolved tension between the border population and state authorities, the Vietnamese delegation warned that US involvement in the war would embolden South Vietnam and ROC "to take advantage of the ethnic composition and the complex terrain in the border area to expand underground networks and undertake counterrevolutionary activities." Vietnamese intelligence showed that "the US imperialists and their henchmen" had plotted to gather and train spies from "the reactionary Chinese and ethnic minorities" from the border area for future deployment.[73] With the heightened political threat, the centuries-long custom of collective gaming among the highland ethnic minorities also became potentially destructive because "armed spies and agents could sabotage the local authorities by being disguised as ordinary hunters."[74] Reframing the cross-border social fabric through the lens of national security legitimized enhanced measures against perceived enemies of the state.

---

[71] Quote from "Cuộc hội đàm về công tác biên giới giữa Khu tự trị dân-tộc Choang Quảng-tây nước Cộng-hòa nhân-dân Trung-hoa với Khu tự-trị Việt-bắc nước Việt-nam dân-chủ Cộng-hòa [Meeting on cooperation at the border between GZAR of the PRC and KTTVB of the DRV]," March 1965, no. 8104, 3/PTTg 3/NAVC III. Also see GZAR and KTTVB, "Bianjing gongzuo huitan jilu [Memorandum of meeting on border works]," March 14, 1965, no. X50-3-168, 44–48/GZARA. I thank ECNURC for sharing this document with me.

[72] "Những ý kiến của đoàn đại biểu Khu tự-trị Việt-bắc về tình hình thi hành các hiệp định giữa Khu tự-trị Việt-bắc (Việt nam) với Khu tự trị Dân tộc Choang Quảng-tây (Trung-quốc) về vấn đề trị an biên giới tại cuộc hội đàm giữa đoàn đại biểu của đoàn đại biểu Khu tự-trị Việt-bắc với Khu tự trị Dân tộc Choang Quảng-tây ngày 2/1965 tại Nam-ninh (Trung-quốc) [Opinions of the delegation of the KTTVB on the implementation of the agreements between the KTTVB (Vietnam) and the GZAR (China) on border security issues at the meeting between the delegations of the KTTVB and the GZAR in February 1965 in Nanning (China)]," February 1965, no. 8104, 17, 19/PTTg 3/NAVC III; "Cuộc hội đàm về công tác biên giới giữa Khu tự trị dân-tộc Choang Quảng-tây nước Cộng-hòa nhân-dân Trung-hoa với Khu tự-trị Việt-bắc nước Việt-nam dân-chủ Cộng-hòa," 9.

[73] The quotes and paraphrases are from ibid., 18.   [74] Ibid., 23.

The two sides, therefore, decided to improve liaison between their boundary checkpoints and border authorities. Local cadres were required to exchange views on the security situation of the border area regularly and were authorized to meet at any time in case of emergency. Moreover, the two delegations planned more comprehensive probes into those labeled as "spies, bandits, criminals, counterrevolutionaries, and suspected counterrevolutionaries" in their respective border societies and to share intelligence on those groups. If one side requested the other to investigate a suspect living in its territory, the latter should respond quickly. In addition, local administrations were responsible for inhibiting enemies or criminals from running off across the boundary. When such cases happened, though, the police were not allowed to chase the person across the border but were to inform officials on the other side, who had to assist promptly with their apprehension.[75]

The hunt for "counterrevolutionaries" was especially brutal in China's Guangxi border region in 1967 and 1968 – the most radical stage of the Cultural Revolution. In an era of self-imposed isolation from the outside world, citizens who used to travel abroad or had relatives living overseas were among the most vulnerable to persecution. Border society, where daily life blurred the distinction between the foreign and the domestic, was easily stigmatized. On August 14, 1966, Lin Biao coined the term "political border defense" (*zhengzhi bianfang*). Echoing the People's War doctrine, political border defense urged revolutionizing people's minds instead of purely relying on administrative and technical controls. Condemning existing policies toward the border communities for being "too polite" and "revisionist," Lin envisioned a strategy that relied on "military-civilian joint defense" and "supported revolutionary movements in various Southeast Asian countries." Downplaying the destabilizing effects of identifying and punishing "class enemies" in the border society, Lin boldly claimed, "Do not be afraid of driving the border people to flee the country; bad people running away is no big deal."[76]

People who had engaged in illicit cross-border activities, even minor ones, could fall victim to political stigmatization and violence. In the spring of 1968, He Guoyi, a peasant in Jingxi who was previously caught stealing the work brigade's seal to buy buffalo from Vietnam, was picked by the cadres of the local border work committee as a target for upcoming struggle sessions. To legitimize their choice, they trumped up a series of charges against He: attempting to reverse a correct verdict against his father, expressing discontent with previous political movements, murdering cadres, appropriating public

---

[75] "Cuộc hội đàm về công tác biên giới giữa Khu tự trị dân-tộc Choang Quảng-tây nước Cộng-hòa nhân-dân Trung-hoa với Khu tự-trị Việt-bắc nước Việt-nam dân-chủ Cộng-hòa," 3–4.

[76] The above is based on Zhou, *Yunnan bianfang shigao*, 54; also see Office of Party History of CPC Yunnan Provincial Committee, *Wen'ge fansi huiyi shiliao zhiba*, 233.

property, and smuggling. Under torture, He confessed to the false charge that he had participated in the Anti-Communist and National Salvation Army. Although managing to escape from custody in late July, He was shot dead after being spotted by the militia. Fearing guilt by association, He's two brothers, Guomin and Guoping, fled to Vietnam only to be repatriated to China by the Vietnamese police. Two Chinese militiamen killed the He brothers while escorting them back from the border checkpoint.[77] People who fled to Vietnam in previous political movements and famines were also vulnerable to be framed. Some of them were accused of stoking resentment against the communist government and plotting defection to South Vietnam; some others were executed for "establishing anti-revolutionary bases" on the Vietnamese border.[78]

These drastic purges were part of the broader campaign of "clearing up dangerous elements in the border area" targeting both grassroots cadres and the general public. In Pingxiang, 367 people, including 120 cadres and 247 workers, were transferred away from their posts to interior provinces due to dubious class backgrounds or "backward" thoughts during the Cultural Revolution. Meanwhile, eighty-nine households classified as landlords, rich peasants, counterrevolutionaries, and criminals were forcibly relocated further inland.[79] A consequence of this "class war" was that the state apparatus, including those responsible for border management, was constantly understaffed during the Cultural Revolution. The violent political campaign meant to reinforce border security actually turned out to be counterproductive, as the state institutions that were supposed to implement it contracted.

Similar vicissitudes of the institutional presence of the state at the border also took place in Vietnam, yet for a different reason. After the beginning of the American ground war in the South, Hanoi sought to reorganize its various security forces in order to strengthen combat capacities for military campaigns. In April 1965, the DRV downsized the People's Armed Police, including the specialized border garrison stationed along the Sino-Vietnamese border as well as Vietnamese-Laotian border, and merged it into the less-equipped local police. The rest of the armed police then replenished the PAVN.[80] This redistribution of personnel reflected the declining priority of everyday

---

[77] Office for Party Rectification of CPC Jingxi County of Guangxi, *Guangxi Jingxixian "wenge" dashijian* [Chronicle of Cultural Revolution in Jingxi County, Guangxi], 1987, in *Chinese Cultural Revolution Database*.

[78] Office for Party Rectification of CPC Chongzuo County of Guangxi, *Guangxi Chongzuoxian "wenhua dageming" dashijian, 1966–1976* [Chronicle of Cultural Revolution in Chongzuo County, Guangxi, 1966–1976], 1987, in *Chinese Cultural Revolution Database*.

[79] Nong, *Zhongguo gongchandang Pingxiang lishi*, 115.

[80] "NGHỊ QUYẾT CỦA BỘ CHÍNH TRỊ Số 116-NQ/TW Về việc phân công nhiệm vụ giữa Quân đội nhân dân và lực lượng Công an nhân dân vũ trang trong việc bảo vệ trị an ở miền Bắc và điều chỉnh tổ chức lực lượng Công an nhân an vũ trang," 146–47.

regulation on the Vietnamese northern border region under the military exigency of the war.

Even so, the WPV sought to capitalize on the anticipated military crisis to expand the social reach and consolidate the organizational strength of the party in the border region. In July 1965, the Department of Politics of the Party demanded the committee of KTTTB and KTTVB – the region bordering China assuming the critical role of producing food to sustain Hanoi's war efforts – to put cadres who had expertise in "both production and national defense" into leadership positions. Under the "new situation," Hanoi ordered that if the officials in charge of local military, police, or administration were incapable of fulfilling these new tasks, they should be replaced.[81] In a speech delivered at a cadres meeting in Cao Bằng in September 1968, Lê Duẩn insinuated his concern over the low efficiency of the bureaucracy by stating that defeating the enemy and constructing socialism relied on two irreplaceable conditions: "revolutionary zeal" and "scientific knowledge."[82] While in China under the Cultural Revolution, professional skills not only paled in comparison with political rectitude but also were condemned for being prone to revisionism; in Vietnam, the immediate need for war resources led to a more pro-pragmatic, moderate organizational principle. This principle was reflected in the backgrounds of new party members in the border area during the Vietnam War. In 1970, the party branch of Lạng Sơn admitted 259 new members, including mainly professionals who "had shouldered arduous revolutionary tasks" and "climbed the career ladder step by step."[83]

Following the economic recession caused by aggressive state acquisition of grain and prolonged drought in 1969, the rectification of cadres once again gained importance. Throughout 1970, the party committee of Lạng Sơn took disciplinary action against 330 members, the majority of whom were punished for deliquency in fulfilling their obligations.[84] In April of that year, the provincial party standing committee warned at a meeting on public security the danger of "infiltrated enemies" against the backdrop of rising public discontent over repetitive crop failures and heavy procurement quotas. According to the official narrative, some South Vietnamese agents crept into Lạng Sơn and managed to rise to influential positions in local party, state,

---

[81] NGHỊ QUYẾT CỦA BỘ CHÍNH TRỊ Số 123-NQ/TW Về việc chuyển hướng công tác tổ chức trong tình hình và nhiệm vụ mới [DECISION OF THE DEPARTMENT OF POLITICS no. 123-NQ/TW regarding the redirection of organizational work in the new situation and tasks], July 7, 1965, in *VKDTT* 26 (1965), 277.

[82] Lê Duẩn, "Lược ghi bài nói của Đồng chí Lê Duẩn bí thư thứ nhất ban chấp hành trung ương Đảng với Tỉnh ủy và cán bộ các ngành xung quanh tỉnh ở Cao Bằng ngày 10-9-1968," 2–3.

[83] Đảng cộng sản Việt Nam ban chấp hành đảng bộ tỉnh Lạng Sơn, *Lịch sử đảng bộ tỉnh Lạng Sơn* (hereafter *LDTL*), 137–38.

[84] Ibid., 138.

factory, and armed forces leadership in order to gather intelligence and commit sedition.[85]

The international crisis in the mid-1960s once again complicated the goals that the state actors sought to achieve at the border while also limiting the means to these ends. Paralyzed, and even decimated, Chinese bureaucracy during the Cultural Revolution fell far short of either enforcing the international boundary or handling the delicate relations with their Vietnamese counterparts. Ironically, a politically or ideologically rectified border, with "class enemies" purged or relocated, actually became more porous. The Vietnamese border provinces underwent less disruptive political campaigns as the paramount objective of boosting production necessitated emphasis on material gains instead of ideological zeal. The boundary-making function of the Vietnamese state nevertheless contracted too as the task had to yield to more compelling military or economic needs.

Guns and Plows: Wartime Mobilization

Besides cracking down upon the perceived enemies among cadres and the general population, both the Vietnamese and Chinese authorities set their sights on creating militarily skilled and politically conscious border citizens who rallied to the anti-imperialist cause. The Vietnam War, an armed struggle against the United States taking place right next to China's southwestern border, offered an unprecedented opportunity for the Chinese political elites to mobilize the borderlanders, who had been relatively indifferent to the country's international ambitions. At the same time, a different kind of mobilization also occurred as many local militias eventually engaged in factional struggles during the Cultural Revolution on their own initiative. The Vietnamese leaders transformed the border provinces with China into a pivot of the country's wartime food production and transportation, both of which required organizing the local population for air defense. Meanwhile, both countries further extended the reach of political authorities into the ethnic minority–populated highlands.

Similar to the pattern of mobilization during the Korean War, promoting anti-American sentiment was central to the mobilization campaign in China. Following the Gulf of Tonkin Incident, Guangxi outlined a propaganda agenda for its local administrations. It warned that American involvement in the Korea War, its support of the Nationalist government in Taiwan, and its invasion of Vietnam were all targeted against China. Urging Guangxi to serve as

---

[85] Ibid., 132.

Guns and Plows 225

"a reliable rear base" for Vietnam and "a strong front" if the conflict expand to China, the guidelines demanded that the region should "overcome the tendency to drop their guard in a period of peace...turn everybody into a soldier," and dedicate itself to production to assist the national construction.[86] This general outline set the tone for the Chinese state's tactics of mass mobilization on its southwestern border.

This campaign combined three seemingly mutually supportive yet often contradictory components: military build-up, increased food production and procurement, and ideological indoctrination. In May 1965, under the slogan of "preparing for war," border communes, which were the grassroots authority responsible for organizing militias, were required to conduct thorough background checks of existing militia members and only distribute weapons to those considered politically trustworthy.[87] A renewed emphasis on military training put an end to the practice of disbanding militia and reassigning its members for farming, a widely adopted measure during the Great Leap Forward.[88] Military drill was meant to prime the border community for possible air-drops, aerial attacks, or riots initiated by political dissidents. Meanwhile, peasants were required to achieve higher production goals and to reclaim more wasteland for vegetables and cash crops.[89]

The border community also assumed partial responsibility for the food supply of an increasing number of military personnel. By the fall of 1964, the Chinese Navy and Air Force, the Kunming Military Zone, and the Guangzhou Military Zone (which was in charge of military affairs in Guangxi) entered into combat readiness under the order of the Department of General Staff. The command of the Seventh Corps of the Air Force relocated westward from Guangdong to Nanning to strengthen the defense of Guangxi. In lieu of new mass deployments of ground forces along the border, jet fighters and anti-aircraft artillery units were stationed at the airfields of Kunming, Mengzi, Nanning, and Ningming.[90] Border communes where the

---

[86] "Tigao jingti, jiaqiang zhanbei, jianjue zhichi Yuenan renmin fandui meidi wuzhuang qinlue, suishi zhunbei fensui meidi kuoda qinlue zhanzheng de yinmou – zhichi Yuenan renmin fandui Meidi wuzhuang qinlue xuanchuan jiaoyu tigang [Enhancing alertness, strengthening war preparation, resolutely supporting Vietnamese people's resistance of American armed invasion, and crushing the plot of American expansion of war – propaganda education outline for supporting Vietnamese people's resistance of American armed invasion]," August 24, 1964, no. 1-3-1-49, 1–8/NMA.
[87] CPC Yongning County Committee, "Beizhan qingkuang huibao [Report on war preparation]," June 15, 1965, no. 1-37-34-3, 2–3/CZCA; CPC Yongning County Committee, "Yongning beizhan xuanchuan jiaoyu yundong hou qingkuang de huibao [Report of situation after war preparation propaganda campaign in Yongning]," July 17, 1965, no. 1-37-34-4, 4/CZCA.
[88] Dreyer, "The Chinese Militia," 67.
[89] CPC Yongning County Committee, "Beizhan qingkuang huibao," 1–2.
[90] Department of Politics of PLA Air Force, Zhongguo renmin jiefangjun kongjun dashidian, 283.

combat units were based organized "frontline support groups" (*zhiqian xiaozu*) to ensure adequate production and the safe transport of goods.[91]

To promote affinity to the party and the anti-imperialist cause, the local cadres transplanted psychological engineering tactics that had been proved effective elsewhere and in previous political movements. At mobilization meetings, the cadres endeavored to elicit commitment to war preparation by encouraging the attendees to "speak bitterness" and to "draw contrasts between their happy life in the new society and misery in the old one." Specifically, the cadres connected the Japanese atrocities in Guangxi during the Second World War to the American invasion of Vietnam to provoke the peasants' hatred toward the United States. A decline in alertness against external threats and an unabating fear of nuclear war among the border people were especially problematic in the eyes of the local officials, who tried to convince the people that they had to "brace themselves for fighting" and that the United States was doomed to lose.[92] By combining mass mobilization and collective readings of *The Selective Works of Chairman Mao*, participation in military preparation became an act of upholding the People's War doctrine and pledging loyalty to Mao.[93] While such "emotion work" helped the CPC gain the peasants' commitment to abstract concepts such as nationalism during the Second World War,[94] the revolutionary party encountered a different social landscape in border communities fifteen years after assuming power.

The local cadres aspired to duplicate their mobilization strategy during the Korean War to instigate anti-American sentiments. The slogan "to hate, despise, and disdain" (*choushi, bishi, mieshi*) America, which the CPC had created during the Korean War, reemerged in the propaganda campaign to curb the tendency of "being pro-America, admiring America, and fearing America" (*qinmei, chongmei, kongmei*). However, in the southwestern corner of Chinese territory, most people, including cadres, were uncommitted to the internationalist cause. The commune heads, who would bear the main responsibility for wartime mobilization locally, for instance, were chary of spearheading the campaign because they highly doubted its purpose. Many commune-level cadres dismissed the possibility of large-scale conflict in Vietnam or the expansion of the war into China in private discussion and even expressed their opposition cautiously at meetings held by the local government. A commune cadre in Heng County carefully voiced his hesitancy by praising "thirty million

---

[91] CPC Yongning County Committee, "Yongning beizhan xuanchuan jiaoyu yundong hou qingkuang de huibao," 5.
[92] Ibid., 6.
[93] CPC Wuming County Committee, "Beizhan xuanchuan gongzuo huiyi zongjie baogao [Summary of meeting for war preparation propaganda]," June 9, 1965, no. 1-37-34-6, 1–2/ CZCA.
[94] Perry, "Moving the Masses."

heroic Vietnamese people on the front" and "several million modernized troops" at their back in order to brush off war preparation as "unnecessary panic." Another commune leader attending the meeting, who was rather outspoken, told his superior categorically that the government was merely using "'assisting Vietnam and resisting America' as a pretext to promote agricultural output and extract more peasant surplus in the future."[95]

A more fundamental reason behind the local cadres' passive resistance to mobilization lay in the fact that waves of political campaigns and aggressive grain procurement in the previous decade had strained the relationship between the street-level bureaucrats and the borderlanders. While the Maoist rectification campaigns of "anti-bureaucratism" and "anti-commandism," which pitched the masses against the local officials, had been born out of the well-founded concern of popular grievances against the government caused by the "bad work style" of grassroots cadres especially in remote counties,[96] the demotions, persecutions, and humiliations during these movements significantly demoralized the bureaucrats. Furthermore, economic setbacks at the turn of the 1960s slowed down the bureaucratic expansion.[97] Limited career advancement opportunities thus discouraged the local political elite from carrying out bureaucratic tasks assigned to them.

The commune heads were especially afraid that if they arbitrarily committed the border community to war preparation, the local people would give them a hard time in the ongoing Socialist Education Movement (also known as the "Four Clean Movement"), which started in late 1962 and 1963 in some provinces, that sought to rectify communes and work teams in the hope of reinstalling confidence in socialism among cadres and poor peasants while containing any spontaneous capitalist tendencies.[98] By January 1965, it had evolved into a nationwide campaign to "clean up politics, economics, organization, and ideology."[99] A commune militia leader in Heng County spoke forthrightly at a meeting in June that if he pressed his demand for military training too hard on top of fulfilling the procurement goals, commune members would not let him "pass" the Socialist Education Movement, which was about to reach the border region. He was lagging behind his task because

---

[95] The quotes and paraphrases are from CPC Heng County Committee, "Hengxian qushe liangji ganbu huiyi qingkuang [Situation of meeting of district- and commune-level cadres]," June 17, 1965, no. 1-37-34-7, 1/CZCA.
[96] "Fandui guanliao zhuyi, mingling zhuyi, he weifa luanji [To oppose bureaucratism, commandism, and lawbreaking]," January 5, 1953, in *Mao Zedong xuanji*, vol. 5, 72–74.
[97] Su, *Collective Killings in Rural China during the Cultural Revolution*, 134.
[98] MacFarquhar, *The Origins of the Cultural Revolution*, 334–36.
[99] "Nongcun shehuizhuyi jiaoyu yundong zhong muqian tichu de yixie wenti [Several problems arising in the socialist education movement in the rural area]," January 14, 1965, in *JYZWXB* 20, 20.

"he was still haunted by the experience of the 'three-antis movement,'"[100] referring to the rectification launched in 1960 that targeted rural cadres against "corruption," "waste," and "commandism" to lessen peasant anger at the state during the Great Leap Forward.[101] With many hesitant commune-level leaders preparing for war only half-heartedly, in November 1965 the Yongning County administration had to admit that the construction of anti-aircraft installations proceeded slower than expected due to declining awareness of war danger.[102]

Laggard war preparation, nevertheless, was enough to create an apocalyptic atmosphere and trigger a widespread panic in border society. In Heng County, a widow whose late husband was killed by the Japanese during the Second World War, reportedly ate up the food she had strenuously saved for possible famine after she heard the news of war preparation, believing that she would not survive another crisis.[103] Some relatives of cadres, party members, or soldiers, who were regarded as potential activists in the mobilization, nevertheless told their fellow villagers that they regretted letting their children or spouses work for the government, fearing they would risk their lives in the looming war. The local party branch sometimes encountered hesitant veterans when requiring the latter to register and prepare for being called back for service.[104] Questioning the necessity of preparing for air defense, a villager in Binyang County told the fellow peasants in the nearby commune who were digging air-raid shelters that an atomic bomb would annihilate everyone.[105] Another poor peasant, who was selected as the representative of his commune to attend the Binyang County mobilization meeting, voiced his concern that China was able to resist the United States in the Korean War thanks to Soviet assistance, but now that the Soviet Union no longer had a cordial relationship with China, the chance to win was meager.[106]

The peasants' deepest fear was that more physical devotion to farming and war-related projects would not contribute to any actual increase in food supply due to a higher procurement quota. In an outcry against state extraction under

---

[100] CPC Heng County Committee, "Hengxian beizhan dongyuan xuanchuan qingkuang huibao [Report of war preparation propaganda in Heng County]," June 26, 1965, no. 1-37-34-8, 4/CZCA.

[101] "Zhonggong zhongyang guanyu fandui guanliao zhuyi de zhishi [CPC Central Committee's instruction on anti-bureaucratism]," March 30, 1960, in *JYZWXB 13*, 127.

[102] CPC Yongning County Committee, "Dangqian beizhan fangkong jixiang gongzuo anpai [Arrangement of war preparation and antiaircraft defense]," November 20, 1965, no. 1-37-34-5, 1/CZCA.

[103] CPC Heng County Committee, "Hengxian beizhan dongyuan xuanchuan qingkuang huibao," 4.

[104] CPC Heng County Committee, "Hengxian qushe liangji ganbu huiyi qingkuang," 3.

[105] CPC Binyang County Committee, "Beizhan jiaoyu qingkuang jianbao [Brief report of war preparation education]," June 9, 1965, no. 1-37-34-10, 4/CZCA.

[106] Ibid., 3–4.

the name of war preparation over the years, a poor peasant at a mobilization meeting in Binyang criticized the government for making new requests for grain while turning a blind eye to the villagers' need in time of famine in the past. Echoing his opposition another peasant argued, "We have not been fully prepared for famine, let alone ready for the war." Invoking wartime memories of the Japanese invasion also proved to be futile in bolstering support from a hunger inflicted community. A villager questioned his commune head: "When the Japanese invaded, it was still possible for us to take rice and hide in the Dama Mountain; now there was no extra rice, how do we deal with the arrival of garrison troops?"[107] Despite concerted state attempts to install a national awareness by the mid-1960s, borderlanders perceived military presence of outsiders, "foreign" or "national" alike, as a source of dreadful hardship. Some cases of war-induced panic or stiff resistance to mobilization alarmed the local security administrations. In 1965, a rumor emerged in Heng County that American troops had approached Friendship Pass and would occupy the area so that the Chinese currency would soon be valueless, which led to the villagers snapping up goods at local shops.[108] A bank branch in the county received anonymous letters demanding immediate food loans to sooth public anger.[109] In Binyang, a self-proclaimed "Guangxi Revolutionary Masses Command" stuck up a poster outside the local tax bureau criticizing heavy taxes and the unfulfilled promises of prosperity.[110] Contrary to the central government's wishes, the promotion of war preparation deepened the distrust of the people against the revolutionary state and incurred resistance of various forms.

The wartime mobilization on China's border nevertheless wove some parts of the society that had been on the edge of state power into the nation. To enhance rice production, the local administration decided to build dikes to reclaim land from the sea at Kinh-populated Wanwei, Wutou, and Shanxin in 1964. This ambitious project, which was completed in 1972, not only increased the amount of arable, albeit sandy, land by 7,000 *mu* but also connected the three islands more closely with each other and with mainland Guangxi.[111] Not simply a program to alter the landscape, the reclamation and the emphasis on grain self-reliance transformed a fishing society into an agricultural one and reinforced the state's control over this litoral, ethnic frontier. A paved road system facilitated transportation and communication

---

[107] This paragraph is based on ibid., 4.
[108] CPC Heng County Committee, "Hengxian beizhan dongyuan xuanchuan qingkuang huibao," 3–4.
[109] CPC Heng County Committee, "Hengxian qushe liangji ganbu huiyi qingkuang," 3.
[110] CPC Binyang County Committee, "Beizhan jiaoyu qingkuang jianbao," 5.
[111] Editorial board, *Jingzu jianshi*, 47–48.

between the mainland society and the island Kinh community, which historically had much stronger ties with the coastal society in northern Vietnam.

The ethnic and cultural connections of these islands with Vietnam, which had been an obstacle to a coherent Chinese national identity, became an asset of military significance during the Vietnam War. In the winter of 1964, the PLA General Staff Department asked the Guangdong Military Zone to recruit eighteen ethnic Kinh cadets with high school diplomas – a strong educational background of the time – from the three islands in light of the contingency in Indochina. Ruan Shiying, from Wanwei, was among them. After briefly attending the foreign languages colleges in Guilin and Zhanjiang to improve his Vietnamese reading and writing, Ruan was sent to a military school to study reconnaissance and intelligence collection. This second program was crucial for the interpreters' role in Vietnam because besides translating for the PLA Anti-Artillery Corps, the Railway Corps, and the Naval branch responsible for sea transport and minesweeping, these Kinh soldiers were also responsible for detecting South Vietnamese agents near the places where the troops were stationed so that their fellow soldiers and the construction sites would be less exposed to precision bombing. A talented learner, Ruan later joined the weapon research unit that collected and studied the wrecks of American airplanes shot down by the anti-aircraft troops.[112] The Vietnam War thus offered the young men of the Kinh community a unique, fast-track opportunity for upward mobility, while providing the state with a favorable opportunity to incorporate the Kinh elite, and the entire Kinh community, into a national campaign.

Among the 400 Vietnamese language interpreters serving in Vietnam, 137 were ethnic Kinh recruited from the islands. Others were mainly returned overseas Chinese, Chinese students in Vietnamese universities, and borderlanders conversant with the Vietnamese language. Due to staff shortages, most interpreters did not get the same chance as their fellow soldiers to rotate for rest and recuperation every six to eight months.[113] Recognizing their long service and active roles at various positions, the Chinese and Vietnamese governments awarded medals to all 137 Kinh interpreters, including Luo Zhoude who was killed in a bombing campaign in Quảng Ninh. Upon returning from service, the vast majority of these men earned jobs in various levels of government service, universities, or state-owned factories, and 62 joined the party, thus being elevated to the status of provincial elites.[114] Meanwhile, the wartime

---

[112] Liu, *Yuanyue kangmei Jingzu fanyiguan jishi*, introduction, n.p.; Luo, "Dangnian, yuanyue kangmei zhong de Jingdao fanyiguan."
[113] For the rotation policy, see Li, *The Dragon in the Jungle*, 113.
[114] The above section is based on Liu, *Yuanyue kangmei Jingzu fanyiguan jishi*, introduction, n.p.; Luo, "Dangnian, yuanyue kangmei zhong de Jingdao fanyiguan."

recruitment unintentionally sustained the existing social structure of the Kinh community. In urgent need of physically and intellectually competent Vietnamese speakers, the PLA prioritized capability, especially Vietnamese reading and writing skills, over class background when enlisting interpreters from these islands.[115] This preference of physical fitness and "expertise" over "redness" favored the better educated and nourished, whereas children of families deemed capitalist or feudal elsewhere would have had a slim chance of joining the military – the vanguard of the workers and peasants. With these decorated soldiers retiring from service and assuming government positions, these families were able to maintain their traditional influence in local society.

The Vietnamese cadres along the border encountered a more daunting task in mobilizing the society for war. Under the death and destruction caused by air raids, they had to devote their limited manpower to competing priorities of production and war, conveniently summarized as "with a plow in one hand and a gun in the other."[116] The wartime draft of young males, however, drained the labor reserve. In 1964 and 1965, former servicemen (particularly noncommissioned officers) were recalled to duty. Discharges were halted in early 1965, and a partial mobilization of males between eighteen to twenty-five years old was officially proclaimed.[117] Besides growing food and cash crops, transporting food through rugged terrain, defending against air raids, repairing damaged infrastructure, and hosting the relocated population all tapped manpower extensively. By the end of 1966, for instance, people in Cao Bằng had dug 90,000 meters of traffic trenches and 23,000 shelters, and organized engineering teams to remove unexploded ordinance.[118] The Vietnamese administration, thus, had to make a considerable effort to secure alternative labor sources by replacing men with women, although female participation in agriculture had already been high before the war.

On March 22, 1965, the Central Committee of the Vietnamese Women's Union launched the "Three Responsibilities (Ba đảm nhiệm) Movement," which was renamed in July by Hồ Chí Minh to "Three In-Charge (Ba đảm đang) Movement" to appeal to more women by hailing their role in the economy and in social life.[119] Women were placed in charge of production and work, replacing men who went to fight; in charge of the family,

---

[115] Liu, *Yuanyue kangmei Jingzu fanyiguan jishi*, introduction, n.p.
[116] "Slogan on August Revolution, National Day," August 16, 1966, in CIA, *Daily Report, Foreign Radio Broadcasts*, Issue 158, JJJ1.
[117] "NIE 14.3-66 North Vietnamese Military Potential for Fighting in South Vietnam," July 7, 1966, no. 0001166476, 4–5/CIA Electronic Reading Room, www.cia.gov/library/readingroom/docs/DOC_0001166476.pdf.
[118] Hà Minh Trần, *Lịch sử Ủy Ban Mặt Trận Tổ Quốc Việt Nam Tỉnh Cao Bằng*, 114.
[119] "LỜI KÊU GỌI CỦA CHỦ TỊCH HỒ CHÍ MINH [Calling of President Hồ Chí Minh]," July 20, 1965, in *VKDTT* 26 (1965), 308.

encouraging their husbands, brothers, or children to fight with peace of mind; and in charge of combat service, being ready to fight when called for. The wartime mobilization raised female agricultural labor from 70 to 80 percent in the border region and put more women in positions of power. Among the 603 high-level agricultural cooperatives in Lạng Sơn, more than 1,000 women were in management posts. In 1965, over 1,000 women joined the militia and self-defense corps, and the number increased to 5,000 by 1972. Among the 3,300 soldiers from the province who joined PAVN in 1972, 259 were women. Medicine and education, traditionally male-dominanted professions, were also increasingly staffed by females.[120] The neighboring Quảng Ninh province organized 92 female militia platoons, among which 150 members were awarded the designation of "model soldier" by the end of the war. At various levels of the WPV local branch, 891 female party members also assumed leadership positions.[121]

Several similar "patriotic emulation movements" initiated by nationwide umbrella social organizations under the auspices of the WPV also sought to replace the draining young male labor pool with children, older people, and government employees. The "Three Ready (*Ba Sẵn sàng*) movement," launched by the Vietnamese Youth Unions in August 1964, demanded youths be ready to enter the armed forces, to overcome all difficulties to boost production and complete school, and to "go anywhere and do anything" to answer the country's call.[122] The "Three good (*Ba giỏi*) movement," advocated by the Vietnamese Senior Citizens Association in June 1966, called for good production and savings, good combat service, and good policy advocacy from the elderly, building upon their influential roles in traditional Vietnamese societies.[123]

The two years 1965 and 1966 witnessed the peak of these labor-centered, group-specific emulation movements in the border region, which was envisioned as a rear base for Hanoi's war efforts. Viewing irrigation as key to the survival of the population in Móng Cái, a historical commercial town with little agricultural population, the town authority launched a hundred-day campaign in the second

---

[120] Thúy Long, "Phụ nữ Lạng Sơn với phong trào 'Ba đảm đang'" [Lạng Sơn women and the 'Three In Charge Movement']," *Lạng Sơn*, March 8, 2010, https://baolangson.vn/xa-hoi/29051-phu-nu-lang-son-voi-phong-trao-ba-dam-dang.html.
[121] Hoài Anh, "Phụ nữ vùng mỏ: Tiếp nối xuất sắc truyền thống 'Ba đảm đang'". Photo coverage by official party newspapers reflected this notable change in the division of labor; see *Lạng Sơn*, February 21, 1966, 1; *Cao Bằng*, January 5, 1965, 1.
[122] PV, "Kỷ niệm 50 năm phong trào Ba sẵn sàng"; "LỜI KÊU GỌI CỦA CHỦ TỊCH HỒ CHÍ MINH," 320–25.
[123] Other mobilization campaigns included "Three Clings Movement" (*Ba bám*: party members clinging to people, people clinging to land, and guerilla soldiers clinging to the enemy) in South Vietnam and "Three Determinations Movement" (*Ba quyết tâm*: being determined to serve war, production, and life) among the intellectuals. Việt Hải (st), "Ba bám, Ba nhất ... Ba sẵn sàng."

half of 1965 to expand irrigated areas from 24 percent to more than 50 percent. Relying heavily on elderly women and children, the project sought to boost the town's food self-sufficiency level by intensifying agriculture.[124] In January 1966, Lạng Sơn province launched a "campaign to boost production in Winter and Spring for resisting America and saving the nation," during which plowing, sowing, harvesting, road construction, and the production of light industrial goods were carried out almost entirely by women, children, and the elderly.[125] The campaign also enlisted government employees to promote the food self-reliance of state institutions. The armed police units in charge of border management, for instance, were required to form cooperatives and to attain pre-set goals for grain production.[126] With Hanoi's endorsement of enlisting help from Chinese border provinces to promote industrial and agricultural development,[127] local Vietnamese administrations invested in mechanizing agriculture by purchasing machines from Guangxi.[128]

Demanding enormous resources from society without much material compensation, Hanoi decided to offer political benefits. In April 1966, the WPV launched a campaign to expand the party's social base and membership in places where its influence had been circumscribed, such as Catholic-populated regions, the highlands, and border provinces. In particular, the party leadership required its grassroots branches to commend model warriors and workers by admitting them to the party. To achieve this goal, local cadres were instructed that they must "resolutely oppose any expressions of feudalism," namely patriarchy and the traditions of promotion by seniority, by recruiting young people and women into the party.[129] By the mid-1960s, females remained

---

[124] Hoàng Thị Kim Thanh, *LDTM*, 204.

[125] "Tinh ta cẩy chiêm rét vười 37% mực của Trung ương giáo va phát động Chiến dịch đẩy mạnh vụ sản xuất đồng xuân chống Mỹ cứu nước [Our province has accomplished 37% of the production task required by the central government and launched a campaign to boost production in Winter and Spring for resisting American and saving the nation]," *Lạng Sơn*, March 26, 1966, 1.

[126] "Các đơn vị Công an vũ trang nhân dân trong tỉnh tích cực tham gia công tác xã hội [Provincial People's Armed Police units actively participate in the socialist cooperatives]," *Lạng Sơn*, February 9, 1966, 3.

[127] "ĐỀ CƯƠNG BÁO CÁO TẠI HỘI NGHỊ BAN CHẤP HÀNH TRUNG ƯƠNG LẦN THỨ 11 (ĐẶC BIỆT) họp từ ngày 25 đến ngày 27 tháng 3 năm 1965 Kịp thời chuyển hướng việc xây dựng và phát triển kinh tế quốc dân phục vụ nhiệm vụ đắc lực nhiệm vụ cách mạng cả nước trong tình hình mới [Outline of the Report at the 11th Central Executive Committee Conference (SPECIAL) held from March 25 to 27, 1965 on timely redirection of the construction and development of the national economy to effectively serve the task of national revolution in a new situation]," in *VKDTT* 26 (1965), 83.

[128] "Năm 1965, hợp tác xã Na Lừm sẽ dùng máy gieo lúa Nam-ninh và lúa mùa trên một điểm tích lớn [In the year 1965, cooperatives in Na Lừm will use rice cultivators from Nanning to expand farmland]," *Cao Bằng*, January 5, 1965, 4.

[129] "CHỈ THỊ CỦA BAN BÍ THƯ Số 121-CT/TW Về việc ra sức nâng cao chất lượng và tăng cường công tác phát triển đảng song song với việc củng cố đảng [INSTRUCTIONS OF THE SECRETARY COMMITTEE No. 121-CT/TW On striving to improve the quality and

Figure 5.2 Hoàng Văn Thụ (1906–1944)
Source: Duyphuong, "Chân dung Hoàng Văn Thụ trong Hỏa Lò Hà Nội." Wikimedia Commons, https://commons.wikimedia.org/wiki/File:Hoàng_Văn_Thụ.JPG. Object in Public Domain in Vietnam. Photograph under CC BY 3.0. No changes made.

underrepresented in the party membership despite their vital roles in various sectors after the escalation of the Vietnam War. In the commercial hub of Móng Cái, only a mere 14 percent of party members were women by 1966.[130] This new emphasis on female and youth party membership acted as a supplementary scheme to the "Three In Charge Movement" and "Three Ready Movement," offering additional incentive for compliance.

The wartime mobilization campaigns also renewed the Vietnamese state's efforts to extend its reach to the "ethnic minorities"–populated highlands. To rally the highlanders to dedicate to the war against the United States, a remote enemy, local officials resorted to a more explicit acknowledgment of the role of ethnic leaders in Vietnam's struggle against French colonialism. In May 1966, the party committee of Lạng Sơn commissioned a memorial of Hoàng Văn Thụ, an ethnic Tày Việt Minh leader from the province, at his birthplace (Figure 5.2).[131] Hoàng Văn Thụ was lauded as a revolutionary martyr for his role in organizing underground Vietnamese activists in the

strengthen the party development work in parallel with strengthening the party]," April 7, 1966, in *VKDTT* 27 (1966), 74–75.
[130] Hoàng Thị Kim Thanh, *LDTM*, 210.
[131] Đảng cộng sản Việt Nam ban chấp hành đảng bộ tỉnh Lạng Sơn, *LDTL*, 116.

Guangxi-northern Vietnam border and later mobilizing armed resistance in Hanoi against the French colonial government before being arrested by the French secret police and executed in 1944.[132] Citing the idiom "drinking water, remembering the source," the provincial party leadership bestowd the memorial the symbolic meaning of the WPV and Vietnamese people's "deep gratitude" to the pioneers of national liberation from the ethnic minorities.[133] Weaving the highlands people into the revolutionary narrative and lauding their historical contribution, the state appealed to the continuous devotion of the ethnic minorities to the revolutionary and anti-imperialist cause that emulated their ancestors.

The core to the state's mobilization project in the highlands of the border region, though, was to boost grain production by intensifying agriculture, which meant a fundamental change to the ways of highland life. The state apparatus' venture into the highland community in the border region to promote lowland agricultural practice, such as wet rice cultivation, artifical pollination, weeding, and fertilizing, began as early as 1956 during the Three-Year Plan to boost yield.[134] The Fifth Party Congress of Lạng Sơn held on September 30, 1966, passed a resolution to "investigate the economic and cultural development" of the highlands to renew the campaign of agricultural intensification there. It acknowledged that previous efforts of relocating highland populations to permanent settlement, changing their agricultural practice from swiddening in forests to rice cultivation in irrigated fields, and requiring schooling for children were less fruitful because the state actors had failed to take into account the fragmented geography and centuries-long customs. Lacking appreciation of these conditions, the state had attempted to integrate the highlanders into the lowland economy and society in a hasty and forceful manner, thus alienating the ethnic minorities.[135] In mountainous Cao Bằng, to secure higher, more predictable, and more legible harvest, the local state relocated 250 highland households (1,481 people) to government-sponsored permanent villages and organized them into high-level cooperatives engaged in intensive agriculture of rice and maize in 1966.[136]

With the increase and greater severity of American night air raids, Hanoi decided to strengthen the militia, composed of elite core forces and auxiliary

---

[132] Minh Châu, "Đồng chí Hoàng Văn Thụ – người Cộng sản kiên trung."
[133] Đảng cộng sản Việt Nam ban chấp hành đảng bộ tỉnh Lạng Sơn, *LDTL*, 116.
[134] "Nhân dân các xã miền núi tỉnh Hải Ninh và Khu Hồng Quảng tích cực áp dụng khoa học kỹ thuật vào sản xuất nông nghiệp [People in mountainous communes of Hải Ninh province and Hồng Quảng area actively apply science and technology to agricultural production]," 1956, in *SLDQ*, 51–52.
[135] Đảng cộng sản Việt Nam ban chấp hành đảng bộ tỉnh Lạng Sơn, *LDTL*, 110–12; quote on page 110.
[136] Hà Minh Trần, *Lịch sử Ủy Ban Mặt Trận Tổ Quốc Việt Nam Tỉnh Cao Bằng*, 116.

self-defense corps. The WPV issued a nationwide order in May 1966 to improve the combat readiness of the militia, especially in coastal, border, and mountainous regions. Of particular importance was training in the use of anti-aircraft artillery to shoot down planes engaged in reconnaisannce or dropping leaflets in order to "crush the enemy's plots to instigate riots and maintain law and order."[137] The United States had exercised restraint toward attacking the narrow belt of territory along the Chinese border lest it provoked an open conflict with China. In August 1967, the intensified Operation Rolling Thunder reduced this "self-imposed 25-mile buffer zone" to "less than 10 miles,"[138] which subjected more areas in Cao Bằng, Lạng Sơn, and Quảng Ninh to air raids. Under enhanced pressure to engage in air defense, militia were made responsible for gearing the border society toward everyday life in wartime. With the slogan "where there are people, there are militia and self-defense squads,"[139] the elite core forces of militia in Lạng Sơn assisted the military in driving away or shooting down American aircraft. The self-defense corps meanwhile were in charge of coordinating evacuation in time of bombing, organizing emergency drills, and adjusting the society's production, education, and living schedule to a wartime routine.[140]

Hanoi installed many governmental and educational institutions, along with key industries, to the sanctuary along the Chinese border beyond the operational limitations of American bombers and tactical reconnaissance aircrafts. Beginning in mid-1966, Lạng Sơn became a main destination for such relocations, receiving the evacuated population of the Central Pharmaceutical Company, the Ministry of Health, a textile and a cigarette factory, the University of Civil Engineering, the Military Arts School, the University of Southern Students, and a warehouse of the Ministry of National Defense. Besides providing a safe haven for these resettled organizations, which took up the limited sheltering space, Lạng Sơn also had to supply the members of these relocated units with food and daily necessities.[141]

Combined with the military draft, managerial inefficiencies, and prolonged drought after 1966, the loss of farmland and other dislocations under bombardment handicapped production and plunged the North Vietnamese local

---

[137] "CHỈ THỊ CỦA BAN BÍ THƯ Số 127-CT/TW Về việc tăng cường lãnh đạo công tác dân quân, tự vệ và hậu bị trong tình hình mới [INSTRUCTIONS OF THE SECRETARY COMMITTEE No. 127-CT/TW On strengthening the leadership of militia, self-defense and rearguard work in the new situation]," May 17, 1966, in *VKDTT* 27 (1966), 171–72.

[138] Rogers, "Sino-American Relations and the Vietnam War," 314; "OXCART Reconnaissance of North Vietnam (w/ attachment)," May 15, 1967, no. 0001471747, CIA Electronic Reading Room, www.cia.gov/library/readingroom/docs/DOC_0001471747.pdf.

[139] Đảng cộng sản Việt Nam ban chấp hành đảng bộ tỉnh Lạng Sơn, *LDTL*, 147.

[140] Ibid., 107; Hoàng Văn Thường and Nguyễn Thành Hoành, *Lịch sử đảng bộ khối các cơ quan tỉnh Lạng Sơn*, 35.

[141] Đảng cộng sản Việt Nam ban chấp hành đảng bộ tỉnh Lạng Sơn, *LDTL*, 107–8.

economy into disaster in 1967. Heavy procurement, the hasty development of high-level cooperatives, and an influx of relocated populations required the further extraction of meager resources from peasant households. The disruption of transportation due to air raids and shortages of labor also hampered the society's capability to respond to crop failures. A long winter from late 1967 to early 1968 greatly reduced crops of sweet potatoes, beans, and peanuts in rural Móng Cái, which had been crucial to feeding growing populations with limited access to crop land.[142] In Lạng Sơn, the people had to forage the forests to combat hunger.[143] By the spring of 1968, rice quotas for the rural residents of the province dropped to under thirteen kilograms, and in some places only seven to eight kilograms, per month. On April 29, 1968, the Lạng Sơn provincial party committee issued an order on "preventing and combating hunger during the planting season of 1968." Local party branches were required to send out investigation teams to assess the food shortages of each household, especially families with soldiers killed in action, wounded veterans, and active service members. Besides selling 600 tons of rice at a low prices to residents, the provincial authorities required party, government, and industrial workers to increase food self-sufficiency by devoting time to irrigation, promoting intensive farming, and planting fast-growing crops.[144] Only the temporary halt of American bombing of North Vietnam in 1968 offered much-needed breathing space for the border economy, which was teetering on the brink of collapse. The centuries-long regional interdependence that disregarded the international boundaries thus gained new importance under the increasing threats to the subsistence of borderlanders during the Vietnam War.

Wartime Relocation, Cross-Border Mobility, and Deteriorating Sino-Vietnamese Relations

The Vietnam War, while creating tensions between the Chinese and Vietnamese leadership, also accelerated the momentum of spontaneous cross-border connections, which the two states had to accommodate. The continuous influx of outsiders to the Vietnamese border depleted resources in the border society, which was already overwhelmed by the need to contribute food to the war effort. The border people thus had to resort to cross-border mutual assistance networks for their survival. Meanwhile, the Cultural Revolution and Vietnam's priority of waging war in the South sapped the institutional strength of the Chinese and Vietnamese states to enforce the boundary while securing the livelihoods of border citizens, and the rocky

---

[142] Hoàng Thị Kim Thanh, *LDTM*, 214–16.
[143] Đảng cộng sản Việt Nam ban chấp hành đảng bộ tỉnh Lạng Sơn, *LDTL*, 123.
[144] Ibid., 125–26.

relations between the two central governments hindered collaboration between local Chinese and Vietnamese officials. As a result, the arduous state building of the previous decade was largely reversed, contributing to greater ambiguities in the power relationships on the borderlands.

The escalation of the Vietnam War in 1964 prompted the adjustment of local officials on their expectations of the ongoing efforts to build an inward-oriented economy and society on their respective sides of the border. At the 1965 border provinces meeting, the two countries adopted a rather lenient policy toward spontaneous cross-boundary connections among the border people so far as they did not pose a direct security threat. Border check points and the patrolling police were instructed not to arrest or detain ordinary villagers who were caught crossing the border without legal documents but to record the names of these villagers and educate them to return home on the same day. In addition, the two delegations reached an oral agreement to open four additional "convenient trails" across the boundary managed locally by the communes and unpatrolled by the border police (there were already twenty-five those trails). People living in eight communes along the Quảng Ninh-Guangxi border that originally belonged to four villages that had been arbitrarily divided in two by the boundary line were again allowed to visit each other without legal procedures.[145] Admitting that border checkpoints were too far away from the many unpatrolled mountain trails that remained the easiest way for the border people to travel, the two delegations tilted toward less intervention into daily cross-border economic activities that did not directly generate revenue to the state. Acknowledging that the international boundary had always been ignored by the borderlanders in collecting firewood in the mountain, the two states decided to focus on "avoiding collisions that affected solidarity between the two peoples" and cracking down on private trade of precious woods, instead of banning cross-border tree cutting all together. The highland agriculturalists' practice of slash-and-burn was nevertheless labeled as breach of forest planning. The two sides also vowed to "educate borderlanders on preserving border markers" and to jointly investigate "destroyed or moved" markers before reporting to the higher authorities of the respective countries.[146]

Following the meeting, the Vietnamese government shifted away from its previous stance of accelerating the shutdown of historical border markets to nationalize cross-border trade and partly returned to the economic strategy

---

[145] "Cuộc hội đàm về công tác biên giới giữa Khu tự trị dân-tộc Choang Quảng-tây nước Cộng-hòa nhân-dân Trung-hoa với Khu tự-trị Việt-bắc nước Việt-nam dân-chủ Cộng-hòa," 5, 8–9.

[146] "Những ý kiến của đoàn đại biểu Khu tự-trị Việt-bắc về tình hình thi hành các hiệp định giữa Khu tự-trị Việt-bắc (Việt nam) với Khu tự trị Dân tộc Choang Quảng-tây (Trung-quốc) về vấn đề trị an biên giới tại cuộc hội đàm giữa đoàn đại biểu của đoàn đại biểu Khu tự-trị Việt-bắc với Khu tự trị Dân tộc Choang Quảng-tây ngày 2/1965 tại Nam-ninh (Trung-quốc)," 21–22; GZAR and KTTVB, "Bianjing gongzuo huitan jilu," 47–48.

used during the First Indochina War, which took advantage of the trade networks between Southern China and Vietnam, to sustain the renewed armed conflict. In June 1965, the WPV Party Central asked border provinces to carefully study the international and regional markets and to take advantage of the border trade with China and Laos more effectively.[147] In August 1965, the Vietnamese Ministry of Foreign Trade suggested to Beijing that they reopen two pairs of border markets – Đồng Đăng-Aikou and Tà Lùng-Shuikou – for small-scale border trade "to adapt to the needs for war, production, and the livelihood of the border people."[148] Hanoi's proposal indicated the DRV's changing priority on the border. Before the war, the Vietnamese government had not only tightened sovereign control over the border region against their much more powerful northern neighbor but also sought to perform a functioning, state-dominated socialist economy in front of their Chinese comrades. Eroding, or at least increasing the regulation of, the spontaneous commercial ties between Northern Vietnam and Southern China, was essential to both goals. The demand of fighting a war in the South, however, drove the Vietnamese leaders to explore all available resources, whether in private or official hands.

The border people, who had acutely perceived the changing permeability of the boundary, took every opportunity to revive the transnational trade networks and dense kinship connections. These efforts did not go unnoticed by the state authorities. From mid-July to early August 1965, more than 2,300 residents of Đồng Đăng sought shelter at Pingxiang after receiving air strike alarms from the Vietnamese authority. Staying in Pingxiang during the day when the threat of bombing was greater while returning home after dusk, these sojourners created an awkward situation for the local officials responsible for enforcing the border. Despite "repeated persuasion" from the Vietnamese police, a seventy-six-year-old woman decided not to return to Vietnam but to make a shed in a cave on the Chinese side of the border and survive on food delivered across the border by her husband or son every few days.[149] Half a year after the reopening of Tà Lùng, the Vietnamese border authority expressed dismay over a "recent degeneration of thought among the peasants

---

[147] "CHỈ THỊ CỦA BAN BÍ THƯ Số 100-CT/TW Về việc chuyển hướng công tác tài chính thương nghiệp trong tình hình mới [INSTRUCTIONS OF THE SECRETARY COMMITTEE No. 100-CT/TW On the redirection of commercial and financial work in the new situation], June 14, 1965, in *VKDTT* 26 (1965), 211.

[148] UBHC tỉnh Lạng Sơn, "xin lập lại quan hệ mậu dịch cửa khẩu biên giới Việt-Trung [We would like to re-establish trade relations at the Sino-Vietnamese border]," August 26, 1965, no. 8183, 10/PTTg 3/NAVC III.

[149] Border Work Commission of CPC Guangxi Region Committee, "Yuenan bianmin wei yufang diren kongxi lai Pingxiangshi duobi de qingkuang [Situation of Vietnamese border residents seeking shelter from air raid at Pingxiang]," August 12, 1965, no. X50–3-193, 34–35/GZARA. I thank ECNURC for sharing this document with me.

on our side," blaming the borderlanders for making excess profits by "turning themselves to traders and illegally taking small agricultural and forestry products to China in exchange for manufactured goods."[150] Given the fact that the military draft had already reduced agricultural labor, the peasants' flagging interest in farming obstructed the state project of tying as many people as possible to the land for food production. To the disappointment of the officials, returning state-run trade firms and customs fell short of helping the state assert dominance over the border trade or steering the borderlanders to full-time agriculture.[151]

This changing agenda and declining capability of the state was even more evident in the Gulf of Tonkin. The three fishing agreements in 1957, 1961, and 1963 had substantiated the two countries' claim over maritime resources by restricting the number of vessels that could fish in the other side's coastal waters, a boundary-making project that was interrupted by the Vietnam War. On March 15, 1966, as the Operation Rolling Thunder escalated, Hanoi signed a "Protocol on the Usage of Chinese Ports by Vietnamese Fishing Boats" with China to open Chinese waters and ports to Vietnamese trawlers to reduce the deficit of the Vietnamese state-owned fishery companies. Meanwhile, many Vietnamese fishermen, especially Cantonese speakers who had relatives in China, began to seek shelter in coastal China. Facing a declining fishery tax base, the DRV dispatched "work teams" to Beihai – the main destination of these fleeing fisherfolk – to persuade those who took household vessels to China to return to Vietnam. Due to the life-threatening bombing, however, few sojourning Vietnamese fishermen obeyed this appeal.[152]

The destructive air raids against Haiphong in late April 1967 triggered an even greater outflow of Vietnamese seafaring people to China. Between December 18, 1967, and January 7, 1968, representatives from Guangxi, Quảng Ninh, and Haiphong met in Nanning and signed a "Minute on Fishing Vessels (Sail Boats) from Quảng Ninh and Haiphong Evacuating to and Fishing in Ports of GZAR." The two sides agreed that the Vietnamese commune or family-owned fishing vessels could transfer to four ports in Guangxi and fish in Chinese waters. To settle these newcomers in the existing planned economy, at least temporarily, the local Chinese authorities would provide grain to the evacuated Vietnamese citizens based on the same food quota of the Chinese citizens. The local Chinese authorities would also advance funds when the Vietnamese citizens purchased additional materials for fishing or other livelihoods, who would then reimburse the Chinese with

---

[150] UBHC tỉnh Cao Bằng, "tái mở cửa khẩu [Reopening the port]," January 25, 1966, no. 8183, 4/ PTTg 3/NAVC III.
[151] Ibid, 4–5.   [152] "Yuenan dapi yuchuan shusan Beihai."

their catch. Finally, a "fishery products work team" dispatched by the DRV would liaison with the local Chinese government to regulate the sojourner community.[153]

With the Cultural Revolution plunging the Chinese border province in chaos and the Vietnamese officials preoccupied with the war efforts, evacuations and relocations out of areas vulnerable to bombing raids rarely went as planned. The local Chinese cadres murmured discontent with the lack of planning by the Vietnamese liaison staff, who often placed urgent requests for vessels or fishing gear to the Chinese authorities but changed their mind once the materials were ready. Moreover, fishing families along the Vietnamese coast carried on with their own spontaneous evacuation to China when perceiving danger, which often caught the Chinese cadres unprepared and made it impossible for the Vietnamese authorities to notify the Chinese ports in advance as agreed in the minutes. The resettled fisherfolk, whom the Chinese authorities regarded as foreigners by law despite their ethnic ties, were dissatisfied with being charged fees for fishing information such as tide tables or sea charts. By 1968, 345 fishing boats and 3,100 fisherfolk and their families had relocated from Vietnam to Beihai, the largest port in Guangxi before the completion of Fangcheng Port.[154]

As the Paris Peace Talks between Hanoi and Washington dampened the Vietnamese and Chinese leaders' enthusiasm for their comradeship, the quickly subsiding intergovernmental cooperation also reduced the orchestrated efforts between the local administrations to regulate the flows of people and goods across the border. Along the Sino-Vietnamese land border, the deteriorating Sino-Vietnamese partnership led to the revival of the "illegal" border trade, namely large, private economic transactions not under the auspices of the two states, typically outside the officially opened border markets and therefore yielding no customs revenue. As early as 1961, against the background of the rapid collectivization movement in both countries, Dongxing and Móng Cái had been closed to earlier state-endorsed small-scale cross-border trade among the residents upon the request of the Vietnamese government. After that, annual or quarterly trade deals and barter between local state-run companies of the two countries became the only two forms of legal cross-border trade in the Dongxing-Móng Cái area.[155] At the end of 1968, the "Agreement on Sino-Vietnamese Small-Scale Border Trade" (signed in 1955) and the "Agreement on Sino-Vietnamese Local Trade" (signed in

---

[153] GZAR Gazetteers Office, *Guangxi tongzhi: waishizhi*, 110–11.
[154] "Yuenan dapi yuchuan shusan Beihai."
[155] CPC Dongxing County Committee, "Bianjing kou'an shichang qingkuang ji jinhou yijian [Situation at the border markets and opinions on moving forward]," 1973, no. 1-2-254-13, 49/FDA.

1957, "local trade" referred to trade by sub-provincial state-owned companies), both of which had been renewed several times, expired amid rocky Sino-Vietnamese relations.[156] Without any extension or renewal of the agreements, the grassroots administration of border towns found themselves in a tricky situation of a reduced and narrowed channel for legal cross-border trade that was crucial for the local economy. Nonetheless, in the summer of 1969, the representatives of Cao Bằng, Lạng Sơn, Quảng Ninh, and Guangxi managed to sign an annual inter-provincial trade contract in Nanning, which, as in previous years, helped the Vietnamese border provinces strike a favorable trade deal with a 500,000 RMB export surplus.[157]

As the Sino-Vietnamese relations navigated troubled waters, and as China pulled out its volunteer corps and reduced its aid, in 1970 the annual trade negotiations between their border provinces were entirely suspended. Having foreseen the economic ramifications of the declining Sino-Vietnamese partnership, Deputy Minister of Finance Hoàng Văn Diệm made a sober comment in his notes to the Ministry of Foreign Trade that that Chinese border provinces were disinclined to reach a trade deal at this point because "China wants to impose unified regulations on relations with Vietnam under the current situation."[158] The inter-provincial trade across the border, however, remained crucial to the Vietnamese economy. Exports to Chinese border provinces accounted for more than half of the DRV's exports to China. Imports from China, the majority of which came through the trade with Chinese border provinces, "served the economy and consuming demand of various ethnic groups of people." Moreover, the absence of a state-endorsed form of commerce only encouraged people to trade across the border illegally. As a result, in July 1970, Hoàng Văn Diệm suggested that the border provinces "find a way to talk with China to persuade the latter to maintain some border trade based on the principles of equality, reciprocity, and mutual help."[159]

Beijing's strategy of wooing Hanoi to its side with economic pressure trapped the local Chinese officials on the border in a dilemma. For the sake of social stability and people's livelihood, border authorities had to acquiesce to the spontaneous, transnational commercial ties outside the state's perimeter,

---

[156] Ministry of Foreign Trade of PRC, "Guanyu yanchang Zhong-Yue bianjing difang maoyi he xiao'e maoyi yidingshu de youxiao qixian de tongzhi [Notice on the extension of Agreements on the Sino-Vietnamese Local Trade and Small-Scale Cross-Border Trade]," October 16, 1967, no. 302-1-268-54~56/GDPA.

[157] "Difang maoyi [Provincial trade]," in *Guangxi tongzhi: waijingmaozhi*, from GZAR Gazetteers Office, *Guangxi diqing ziliaoku*, http://lib.gxdqw.com/view-a43–175.html.

[158] Hoàng Văn Diệm, "V/v uy trì mậu dịch biên giới Việt- Trung [About maintaining trade at the Sino-Vietnamese border]," March 9, 1970, no. 8602, 1/PTTg 3/ NAVC III.

[159] Hoàng Văn Diệm, "V/v tiếp tục bán với Trung-quốc về vấn đề mậu dịch địa phương giữa các tỉnh biên giới [On continuing to sell to China in the local trade between border provinces]," July 29, 1970, no. 8602, 4/PTTg 3/ NAVC III.

instead of arresting hundreds of people for illegally crossing the national boundary. The absence of any formal, top-down bilateral agreement to manage the volume of cross-border exchanges created a legal loophole that was impossible for the local authority to plug. This legal vacuum contributed to a vibrant black market for currency trading, speculation and profiteering, smuggling, and other market-oriented activities that the communist states found unacceptable. This dilemma worsened after the Nixon administration resumed bombing against North Vietnam with greater intensity in 1972. In March 1973, Dongxing border authorities observed that since December 1972, when the United States launched Operation Linebacker II, producing the heaviest bombing campaign during the Vietnam War, three hundred to five hundred Vietnamese citizens, many of whom were relocated from interior provinces, appeared at the border town on a daily basis with goods to trade yet without travel documents; around the Lunar New Year the number exceeded 1,000. In December 1972, the Revolutionary Committee of Guangxi had banned state-run companies in the border towns from trading goods not listed on the expired small-scale border trade agreement. It also demanded that local authorities stop the Vietnamese citizens from selling manufactured goods in Chinese villages, outside of the historical border markets, because the lower price of the flooding Vietnamese commodities would disadvantage the Chinese state-run stores in rural markets.[160] Trading directly with each other instead of dealing with government-run shops whenever possible, the border people created a bustling market economy under the gaze yet out of the control of the state.

The officials of Dongxing County, who were largely indifferent or impervious to the geostrategic considerations that strained the bilateral relations between the two central governments, proposed to the higher authorities that the two countries should restore small-scale trade and inter-provincial trade in the border towns and promised that regulations such as trade licenses, daily import quotas, and the state monopoly on the purchase and sale of critical goods could effectively curb smuggling and profiteering. It also pleaded with the provincial government to furnish the border town with more food and daily commodities because, to heed the decades-long internationalist spirit of prioritizing the needs of the Vietnamese people, the local state-run companies had to cut back supplies to local Chinese after selling goods to the increasing number of Vietnamese citizens who attended the market in Dongxing.[161] The proposal to formally reopen Dongxing for trade, however, was not considered until the normalization of Sino-Vietnamse relations after the end of the Cold War.

Tense Sino-Vietnamese relations created equally thorny problems in the relations between the local state and the transnational fishing community. After

[160] CPC Dongxing County Committee, "Bianjing kou'an shichang qingkuang ji jinhou yijian," 50.
[161] Ibid.

the American bombing subsided in 1969, about 80 percent of the Vietnamese fishing families who had evacuated to Guangxi gradually left. By September of the year, though, 1,215 of the sojourning fisherfolk from 202 households still chose to stay. After April 1969, the Guangxi provincial government repeatedly asked the Vietnamese Consulate in Nanning to facilitate their return, noting that the Vietnamese government had long preferred these fishing populations to "reconstruct their homes in Vietnam" and that the coastal area of Quảng Ninh and Haiphong were now safe for fisheries. The Vietnamese diplomats, however, responded that Hanoi had asked the dislocated people to stay where they were until the dust settled and suggested that the Chinese government permit the elderly and those who had relatives in China to migrate to China.[162]

On August 18, the Vietnamese government unilaterally withdrew all the work teams that had been dispatched to Chinese ports to oversee the relocated fishing community and stopped issuing subsidies in support of the fisherfolk's livelihood and production, which created a fait accompli leaving the issue in the hands of the Chinese government. In June 1970, negotiations on the return of evacuated Vietnamese citizens resumed. The Vietnamese representatives recommended that the fisherfolk who remained in Chinese ports after the end of September should apply for legal residency and be allowed to stay in China as ordinary Vietnamese overseas without the favorable treatment bestowed by the wartime relocation agreement. At the insistence of the Guangxi officials, who did not have the authorization to grant Chinese residency, though, the two sides signed a memorandum on July 1 to facilitate the repatriation of the remaining fisherfolk to Vietnam. It demanded that all evacuated Vietnamese fishing families should depart for Vietnam before September 20; otherwise, they would be denied anchorage at Chinese ports. Moreover, Chinese local governments noted that it would stop their advance payments for production, livelihood, or medical expenditure after fifteen days of the signing of the memorandum. Under mounting economic pressure, the Vietnamese fisherfolk left China grudgingly by the end of August.[163]

Similar to events on the Sino-Vietnamese land border, the Sino-Vietnamese fishing agreement, which was signed in 1957 and revised in 1961 and 1963, expired in August 1972. Despite renewed Chinese interest in providing aid to Vietnam after the Sino-US rapprochement, the state of Sino-Vietnamese relations was unfavorable to any negotiations to extend the validity period of the agreement. The long-existing practices in the Gulf of Tonkin of junks from both countries fishing on each other's side of the coastal waters, which was a central issue in the fishing agreements, became an unregulated activity that further complicated the delicate intergovernmental relations. In 1973, the

---

[162] GZAR Gazetteers Office, *Guangxi tongzhi: waishizhi*, 111.   [163] Ibid., 111–12.

Chinese Foreign Ministry and the Ministry of Agriculture and Forestry instructed the Guangxi and Guangdong provincial governments and the military that, as the bilateral fishing relations "[had] entered a state of no agreement," Chinese vessels should refrain from fishing in Vietnamese waters or, saving exceptional circumstances, obtaining fresh water from Vietnamese ports "before the two countries sign a new one in order to respect the maritime sovereignty of Vietnam."[164] Meanwhile, Chinese local administrations should "persuade foreign ships to leave the coastal water of Guangxi and expel those who do not obey."[165] The two ministries cautioned the dire political consequences of not following these instructions; yet this insistence alone was not enough to enforce their will upon the Chinese junks, whose voyages were first and foremost decided by wind directions, sea currents, and migrations of fish.

The sensitivity of the maritime border became even more apparent in the "Battle of the Paracel Islands" (*Xisha haizhan* in Chinese and *Hải chiến Hoàng Sa* in Vietnamese) between the PRC and South Vietnam in January 1974. Following this, in August 1975, two Chinese fishing boats with thirty-two crew members were detained by the DRV Coast Guards when they tried to take shelter from the wind in a Vietnamese port. Blaming the Chinese fisherfolk for not cooperating with the Vietnamese authorities in the inspection of their vessels, the Vietnamese Coast Guard asked the Chinese captain to sign a document confessing to a violation of Vietnamese territorial waters, and the captain refused.[166] The incident was a harbinger of a pattern of conflict between the two countries over fishery resources and the maritime boundary in the Gulf of Tonkin in the following years.

Conclusion: War, Political Chaos, and the State on Borderlands

The decade from 1965 to 1975 witnessed contradictory trends in the interactions between the two revolutionary states and the borderlands society. The Americanization of the war in Indochina elevated the strategic importance of the Sino-Vietnamese border area. Facing American and South Vietnamese intelligence collection and infiltration in the area, the two states carried out more stringent surveillance and repression of the identified "class enemy" at the border. Furthermore, the present day Sino-Vietnamese border, despite a

---

[164] Revolutionary Committee of Guangdong Province, "Guanyu chongshen jinzhi wo yuchuan jinru Yuenan linghainei buyu de tongzhi [Notice on reemphasis of banning our fishing vessels from fishing in Vietnamese territorial water]," October 7, 1975, no. 314-A1.4-6-196, 3/GDPA.

[165] "Haishang zhi'an guanli [Maritime security management]," in *Guangxi tongzhi: gonganzhi*, from GZAR Gazetteers Office, *Guangxi diqing ziliaoku*, www.gxdqw.com/bin/mse.exe?seach word=&K=a&A=63&rec=308&run=13.

[166] Revolutionary Committee of Guangdong Province, "Guanyu chongshen jinzhi wo yuchuan jinru Yuenan linghainei buyu de tongzhi," 1–2.

hilly terrain, still enjoys a more convenient, effective transportation system than most other borderlands in the developing world largely because of the massive infrastructure building that took place during the Vietnam War. Military significance together with a high-speed transport system that linked the border to the metropolitan area facilitated the integration of the frontier with the respective two countries.

However, the concurrence of the Cultural Revolution and the Vietnam War handicapped many of the state-building measures. The border institutions thus became slack. The purge of experienced cadres and transfer of "politically unreliable" staff away from the border in China and the reassignment of some border police to the Vietnamese military undermined the cross-border cooperative institutions between local Chinese and Vietnamese state that largely depended on camaraderie and rapport. Meanwhile, the delayed transportation of aid to Vietnam, partly caused by the social disorder during the Cultural Revolution, shook the Sino-Vietnamese partnership. At the same time, though, the Vietnam War impelled the Chinese and the Vietnamese governments to pour investment and manpower to the border area in fields such as anti-aircraft infrastructure and high-speed roads while depriving the society of other vital resources such as food and a stable supply of manufactured goods. The cross-border mutual help trade networks, therefore, revived during the war to resolve these deficiencies.

More importantly, the state building and border making of the two modernizing states at their land and maritime frontier became increasingly contingent upon the volatile relations between Beijing and Hanoi, which began to deteriorate in the late 1960s as the Soviet Union replaced China as the DRV's principal supplier of weapons.[167] A notable phenomenon in this process was that instead of building a deep-binding alliance upon a formal treaty with a relatively long period of validity, which might inherit the remnants of the historical tributary relations, the postcolonial, postimperial Sino-Vietnamese partnership was laid upon a series of more scattered agreements, protocols, or meeting memoranda on trade, aid, and cultural exchanges that were only valid for a shorter time. These cooperative mechanisms, in order to offer long-term benefits, required confirmation or reaffirmation every three to five years, or even annually. When an agreement expired at a sensitive moment that coincided with a low tide period in the bilateral relations, not renewing the agreement became part of the reservoir of diplomatic methods used by the central government – but one that did not necessarily produce the best outcomes in terms of the border relations of the two countries or the livelihoods of the borderlanders.

---

[167] Gaiduk, *The Soviet Union and the Vietnam War*, 215.

The fluctuating Sino-Vietnamese relations during the Vietnam War thus reversed some of the boundary-making and state-building progress by the two countries in the borderlands, which left more conflicts between the border peoples over resources unresolved. By the late 1960s, cross-border relationships on the ground at the land and maritime borders had intensified under war and political chaos yet entered an "agreement-less" stage. The joint and collaborated state-building and boundary-making projects that had started in the mid-1950s were thus aborted. Furthermore, even during the peak of their cooperation in enforcing a socialist border and imposing a Cold War partnership at the frontier, the local Chinese and Vietnamese institutions at the border had never fully resolved the potentially divisive issues such as cross-border farming and fishing. After the late 1960s, against the backdrop of rising nationalist sentiments in both countries together with an absence of ameliorating agreements, state agents were increasingly discouraged from seeking a solution to border skirmishes between the local Chinese and Vietnamese residents. When the bilateral relations between the two governments further deteriorated a decade later, both sides could easily weaponize the skirmish created by the chronic state weakness on the borderlands and lay blame on the other side.

Conclusion
Cold War Asia: A Borderlands Perspective

> The entire party, people, and army in the province should uphold the tradition of fighting in solidarity, rising up heroically, and overcoming difficulties. In the immediate future, with the revolutionary spirit of struggle and self-reliance, [we shall] perform outstandingly in achieving the dual tasks of stepping up production and preparing to fight to firmly protect the border, airspace, and sea of the province. [We shall] build the province into a strategic unit that is politically stable, economically prosperous, and militarily strong.
>
> Report of the Sixth Congress of WPV Hải
Ninh Committee, May 1980.[1]

> We must be clear-headed that the economy of Pingxiang, due to its special geographic situation, has long invested heavily in supporting the front (*zhiqian*) in terms of the distribution of manpower, material, and fund. With little previous attention, the economic construction here has started late, been built on a weak foundation, and progressed slowly .... In the future, how to shift our work from the chaos of war preparation to economic construction is a crucial step.
>
> Report of the Sixth Congress of CPC Pingxiang City
Committee, 20 March, 1989[2]

The wax and wane of state power at the Sino-Vietnamese borderlands continued after the temporal restoration of peace in Indochina in 1975. As the Cultural Revolution and the Vietnam War crippled the border institutions, the spontaneous cross-border ties that the two states sought to contain or sever before the mid-1960s were largely left unmonitored or unchecked afterwards. At the national level, the Vietnamese Communists emerged victorious in their war for unification yet soon encountered an economic crisis due to their frustrated attempt to industrialize Vietnam following Soviet-style central planning and the plummet of nonrefundable aid from other communist countries.[3] Following the death of Mao in 1976, it was a consensus among Chinese

---

[1] Hoàng Thị Kim Thanh, *LDTM*, 296–97.
[2] Nong, *Zhongguo gongchandang Pingxiang lishi*, 193–94.
[3] Path, *Vietnam's Strategic Thinking During the Third Indochina War*, 19, 23.

leaders that the Maoist development model of "squeez[ing] resources for urban industrialization out of the countryside" was in dire need of change, although it was still unclear to them how to reform the country in the late 1970s.[4]

At the far corners of each country, the local authorities made efforts to re-institutionalize border control and mitigate disputes over resources that might destroy the intergovernmental relationship that had already been estranged by the Sino-Soviet rift, Chinese leaders' annoyance with the Vietnamese "'ungracious' attitude" toward Chinese assistance, Hanoi's employment of age-old resentment against China for nation building, and territorial disputes both on land and at the sea.[5] In 1976, the provincial delegates of Guangxi and Quảng Ninh and officials of the two border counties of Dongxing and Bình Liêu met to reaffirm their determination to reduce and eliminate transboundary farming practiced by the highland Yao people. None of the available sources on either side reveal additional details about this meeting, yet the fact that grassroots cadres met under the auspices of higher authorities indicated a genuine effort to arrive at a solution by circumventing bureaucratic hurdles.[6] Yet the persistance of cross-border farming despite strenuous efforts coordinated by the two countries to swap or transfer farmland indicated that it was state weakness, rather than its strength, that exacerbated local disputes over borderlands resources, which would later be used by both governments to condemn each other as the aggressor.

The termination of the Sino-Vietnamese Cold War partnership led to mass involuntary migration and dislocation across the boundary. In March 1978, Hanoi decided to raid against the bourgeois class in the south, with the urban ethnic Chinese being the principal target. By the summer of the year, more than 160,000 Chinese fled Vietnam, either by crossing the land border to China or by boat toward other Southeast Asian countries, and the exodus lasted into the 1980s.[7] As a result of the expulsion of ethnic Chinese, the population of Móng Cái District plunged from 64,000 to 40,000 in 1978. A unified military command to lead the district's troops, militia, and police was formed on June 30 to buttress border defense. Together with the influx of thousands of workers and peasants from Haiphong and other places to take over jobs and lands left by the dislocated Chinese, the Vietnamese government replaced 70 to 80 percent, and in some places all, of the district's cadres and officials

---

[4] Weber, *How China Escaped Shock Therapy*, 95 (quote), 104.
[5] Khoo, *Collateral Damage*, 103–36; Path, *Vietnam's Strategic Thinking During the Third Indochina War*, 19–51; Zhang, *Deng Xiaoping's Long War*, 40–66 (quoted words on page 46).
[6] CPC Committee of Dongxing Autonomous County of Multiple Ethnicities, "Guanyu buzai guojing gengzhong he shouhuo nongzuowu de tongzhi [Notice on no longer farming and harvesting across the border]," October 4, 1977.
[7] Chang, "The Sino-Vietnamese Dispute over the Ethnic Chinese," 206–8.

250   Conclusion

in an effort to "Vietnamize" the party-state's apparatus in the region.[8] On the opposite side of the border, Pingxiang and Dongxing were mobilized to host the refugees, who would later be transferred to the interior.[9] By May 1979, Qisha port received more than two thousand fisherfolk fleeing from Vietnam, many of whom were hesitant to be relocated to the Overseas Chinese State Farms (*huaqiao nongchang*) in the inland as it would mean a farewell to their seafaring life.[10] Dongxing County thus set up an "overseas Chinese fishing brigade" within the Qisha Commune and an "overseas Chinese fishers village" to facilitate stable residence. The village was equipped with an elementary school to educate the more than five hundred children, most of whom had not received formal schooling before, from the refugees families.[11]

The demographic shift at the Sino-Vietnamese borderlands harbingered more fundamental changes in the landscape of the area during the decade-long border confrontation following the Chinese invasion of Vietnam from February to March 1979. Straddling the frontline between Vietnamese and Chinese adversaries, the Sino-Vietnamese borderlands experienced renewed militarization. Having to put the border societies on a war footing hastily, both governments overperformed the predatory functions while falling short of fulfilling their protective roles. The borderlanders thus had to maintain their livelihood by carefully navigating the cracks of state power. The Sino-Vietnamese borderlands were not known for abundant arable land, and the border conflicts set back the irrigated agriculture there for decades. Many irrigation projects in the Chinese and Vietnamese border counties were built upon rivers and streams to which the two sides shared access and thus they relied on collaboration, or at least the tacit agreement, from the authority of the other side to construct and repair, which was made impossible by the political hostility. Military operations also diverted labor away from agricultural production under the similar slogan of "producing while fighting."[12] During the Chinese offensive campaign in 1979, militias and civilians of the Chinese

---

[8] Hoàng Thị Kim Thanh, *LDTM*, 290.
[9] "Bianwuzhi [border affairs]" in *Pingxiang shizhi*, www.gxdqw.com/bin/mse.exe?seachword=%u6392%u96F7&K=c&A=54&rec=160&run=13; CPC Qinzhou Prefectural Committee, "Guanyu Fangcheng xian duiYue ziwei huanjizhan zhong mofan shiji de tongbao [Information circulated about exemplary deeds in Fangcheng County during the self-defense war against Vietnam]," June 6, 1979.
[10] State-owned farms for overseas Chinese began in the 1950s to receive overseas Chinese expelled from Southeast Asian countries during anti-communist or anti-Chinese movements. Han, "The Demise of China's Overseas Chinese State Farms"; Zhou, *Migration in the Time of Revolution*, 191–210.
[11] CPC Dongxing County Committee, "Guanyu zhiliu zai Qishagang nanqiao yumin anzhi wenti the qingshi baogao [Request for instruction on the settlement of overseas Chinese fisherfolk at Qisha Port]," May 28, 1979, no. 1-2-461-19, 59–60/FDA.
[12] CPC Dongxing County Committee, "Guanyu kaizhan yongjun huodong, jinyibu zuohao zhiqian gongzuo de tongzhi [Circulation on launching campaigns to support the military and

border counties served as guides to the PLA to navigate the only locally known mountain trails, interpreters to interrogate the Vietnamese prisoners of war, laborers to construct and repair fortification, suppliers of military provisions (especially vegetables), and porters on the logistic lines (especially transporting the killed and injured soldiers).[13] As shelling and mining encroached on the arable land, Hải Ninh District mobilized local laborers to reclaim mountain lands and repair irrigation systems in the hope of not missing the planting season. Yet the rice production of the district reached 80 percent of the plan in 1979, whereas fish catches only hit 64 percent due to the exodus of ethnic Chinese fisherfolk.[14] Around the time of the withdrawal of Chinese troops from Lạng Sơn and Cao Bằng in March 1979, the two border provinces organized a sizeable amount of manpower to build underground tunnels and repair roads to facilicate the movement of Vietnamese troops in anticipation of long-term hostilities.[15]

Evacuation of manufacturing industry and handicraft business further impoverished the borderlands during the next decade. The Móng Cái Pottery Factory and Friendship Mechanical Enterprise, the two main industrial plants in the town that had received major aid packages from China, had to relocate from the border region. The small number of remaining industries struggled to survive due to a shortage of raw materials and fuel.[16] The fact that the town's irrigation pump and industrial electricity had relied on the supply from the hydropower station of Dongxing across the border paralyzed the production in wartime Móng Cái.[17] Less threatened by large-scale invasion, Chinese border towns were not immune to the heavy blow of the war. Whereas most parts of the country had benefited from the reform of shifting priority from national defense to economic development by the early 1980s, factories were relocated from places such as Pingxiang to further inland to avoid bombardment.[18] The

getting further prepared for assisting the front]," February 26, 1979, no. 1-2-463-21, 1–2/FDA; Hoàng Thị Kim Thanh, *LDTM*, 294–95.

[13] CPC Qinzhou Prefectural Committee, "Guanyu Fangcheng xian duiYue ziwei huanjizhan zhong mofan shiji de tongbao"; CPC Qinzhou Prefectural Committee, "Guanyu xuexi Dongzhong gongshe zai duiYue ziwei huanji zhandou zhong mofan shiji de jueding [Decision to study the exemplary deeds of Dongzhong Commune during the self-defense war against Vietnam]," May 22, 1979, no. 1-2-455-13, 38–44/FDA; Zhang, *Deng Xiaoping's Long War*, 170–74; Yin and Path, "Remembering and Forgetting the Last War," 6

[14] Hoàng Thị Kim Thanh, *LDTM*, 298–99. For an overview of land reclamation in the DRV, especially during the Vietnam War, see Phạm Thị Vượng, "Hoạt động khai hoang của nông trường quốc doanh ở miền Bắc Việt Nam từ năm đến năm."

[15] Ban Chỉ đạo biên soạn, *Giao thông vận tải Lạng Sơn*, 80-2; Sở Giao thông Vận tải Cao Bằng, *Lịch sử Giao thông Vận tải Cao Bằng*, 80.

[16] Hoàng Thị Kim Thanh, *LDTM*, 299.

[17] "Guanyu Dongxing shuiku dianzhan xiang Mangjie gongdian wenti de baogao [Report on supplying electricity to Móng Cái from Dongxing hydropower station]," 1964, 284-1-107-85~88/GDPA.

[18] Nong, *Zhongguo gongchandang Pingxiang lishi*, 194.

militarized borderlands lagged behind the gradually improved living standards of the country.

The ramification of the war on the border trade, ironically, was ambivalent. The widespread use of landmines by the two states to beef up the border against each other made border-crossing a harrowing journey. Continuous planting of landmines from 1975 to 1985 formed more than four hundred minefields along the border, many of which still haunt the highlanders today.[19] The political hostility nevertheless reduced the institutional capacity of the two states to inspect, manipulate, and extract revenues from the transnational economic ties. As minefields seemed formidable enough to deter cross-border connections, border garrison and other coercive institutions lapsed in their function in enforcing the border. Among the state apparatus that evacuated from the war-torn zone were the customs houses, which were not fully restored until the normalization of bilateral relations in the early 1990s.[20] Numerous bridges across border rivers were destroyed during battles.[21] The border check stations at the two bridgeheads, which had wielded coercive power against the bodies of travelers and traders by inspecting their travel documents and cargo, thus disappeared. What had been labeled by the two governments as smuggling became the norm for trade at historic border crossings such as Jingxi–Trà Lĩnh and Dongxin–Móng Cái after large scale battles ceased.[22] Border markets reappeared at less strategic positions with the state's acquiescence as early as in 1983 in light of the sheer scale of the shadow economy after the war interrupted the legal cross-border trade. The absence of border regulation enforced by the local foreign affairs office, border police, or customs reinvigorated the transnational economic network.[23] Militarization thus did not necessarily strengthen the state at the border. The tug-of-war between the smuggling rings and the two states at the Sino-Vietnamese borderlands that persists until today is a by-product of the frustrated and interrupted joint state invasion into the organic economic interdependence there.

Focusing on the Sino-Vietnamese land-maritime border in the second half of the twentieth century, this book tells a story of the consequences of the synchronocity between geopolitical conflicts and state building. The global conflict between communism and capitalism and the regional armed conflicts

---

[19] Ibid., 157. Since the 1990s, de-mining efforts by the Chinese and Vietnamese militaries last until today. Yin, "The Mountain Is High, and Emperor Is Far Away," 568; Yin and Path, "Remembering and Forgetting the Last War," 6.

[20] GZAR Gazetteers Office, *Guangxi tongzhi: haiguan zhi*, 112, 125–26.

[21] "Lulu jiaotong [land transport]," in *Fangcheng xianzhi*, http://lib.gxdfz.org.cn/view-c58-2.html; Sở Giao thông Vận tải Cao Bằng, *Lịch sử Giao thông Vận tải Cao Bằng*, 80.

[22] GZAR Gazetteers Office, *Guangxi tongzhi: haiguan zhi*, 207–8, 210.

[23] Fan and Liu, *Zhong-Yue bianjing maoyi yanjiu*, 119–20; Brantly, "Sino-Vietnamese Border Trade," 499.

Conclusion 253

had complicated ramifications on the borderlands. The non-state space beyond the reach of centralized governments or "contact zones" where "no single group rules supreme" gradually faded at the Sino-Vietnamese borderlands and the Gulf of Tonkin beginning in the 1950s, not only because the states gained access to communicative and transportational technologies that could overcome the "friction of terrain" but also due to the institutional and procedural joint state invasion examined in this book.[24] The similar pace and method of state building as well as the simultaneous collaboration and competition between the two political powers in claiming frontier resources made less effective some long-existent strategies of state evasion, such as exploiting unequal state power or voting with feet via migration. The joint state invasion took place in two directions: a vertical one characterized by the downward extension of administration from the two centralized communist governments and a horizontal one as a result of the interactions between the corresponding levels of Chinese and Vietnamese state institutions.

This joint invasion did not constitute a total rupture from the historical state building and state rebuilding. The making of the modern Chinese state, as Huaiyin Li argues, was an "accumulative result" of the emergence of "an early modern territorial state" by the high Qing, its transformation into "a modern sovereign state" in reponse to foreign pressure during the late Qing, and its evolution into "a unified and centralized state" during the Republican and People's Republican eras.[25] From the 1800s onward, the appellation, shape, and form of the polity (and sometimes polities) existing in the geographic area known as "Vietnam" today have changed drastically.[26] The territorialization, sovereignization, and centralization of the Vietnamese nation-state, as a result, unfolded simultaneously and intensely in the second half of the twentieth century. By the mid-1950s, the state building by successive governments in China and Indochina had created a relatively stable yet "soft boundary" between China and Vietnam, where the perception of border was not buttressed by consistent enforcement on the ground. Trade, arms and drug dealing, migration, and marriage across the border constituted the basis of an organic interdependence among the borderlanders without much intimidating gaze from either state. The two communist governments coordinated and competed to confine the soft boundary into a clearly defined "hard boundary," where the states could arbitrarily, and selectively, curb the flow of people, goods, and ideas. The imposition and enforcement of boundary, for instance, turned intraethnic families into "international" ones that came under more stringent state regulation. Yet the two governments retreated from the position

---

[24] Hämäläinen and Johnson eds., *Major Problems in the History of North American Borderlands*, 1 (first two quotes); Scott, *The Art of Not Being Governed*, 43 (the third quote).
[25] Li, *The Making of Modern Chinese State*, 17. [26] Goscha, *Vietnam: A New History*, xi–xii.

of trying to register every transnational marrige or mediating cross-border matrimonial disputes lest the dense webs of kinship networks overstretch the bureaucratic capacity.

The joint state invasion did not bifurcate the borderlands societies, as the soft boundary restored itself during times of chaos, crisis, and war. Whereas the consolidation of the two communist governments maintained overall tranquility at the Sino-Vietnamese border region until the 1970s, radical collectivization programs incurred famine and mass mobilization depleted local resources. Cross-border networks bounced back whenever the political power fell short of sustaining coercive and extractive institutions. Given the resilient private trade under political pressure and the persistent border trade pattern that connected Southern China and Vietnam, it was clear that the Chinese and Vietnamese societies were neither communist nor capitalist but mercantile by characteristic. It was the adoption of the Cold War ideological discourse that created the labels of "capitalist economy" and "communist trade" that legitimized various economic statecraft to serve statist goals while delegitimizing other commercial activities. In dealing with the state, the borderlanders employed both "the art of not being governed" examined by James Scott and what Michael Szonyi characterizes as "the art of being governed" – the strategies of leveraging advantage from the "regulatory overlap and loopholes" and the discrepancies between rules and realities as well as between different systems.[27] Moreover, the ways Beijing and Hanoi enforced the international boundary also reflected their history as empire-states, in which the central authority ruled by difference, not uniformity, in service to the political unity. Neither the state-building projects nor border policies were applied equally among citizens, which was characteristic of these two countries' agenda of policing ethnic differences. Calculating the cost of enforcing a "hard" international boundary among the highland ethnic minorities vis-à-vis the gains of doing so, the two states policed the lowland border more stringently than the highland portion.

Unpacking the Sino-Vietnamese partnership, this book reveals the layered relations between the two countries – between the two parties, two central governments, different levels of local authorities, and various social fabrics. It has been argued that socialist countries did not have a clear idea of sovereignty in their relations with each other. When the concerns of inter-party relations and inter-state relations were in conflict, national sovereignty was subordinate to the agenda of revolution.[28] This book demonstrates instead that defining, displaying, and defending sovereignty was a crucial driving force of Sino-Vietnamese relations even when their Cold War partnership

[27] Szonyi, *The Art of Being Governed*, 59, 156.
[28] Shen and Lovell, "Undesired Outcomes," 89; Shen and Li, "Jiegou shiheng," 7–9.

was exuberated with ideological commitment. The seemingly anti-nationalist "socialist internationalism" contributed to the eventual formation of Vietnam as a sovereign state and China's recognition of this fundamental transformation. It was exactly because the Chinese communists sought to draw Vietnam to its orbit in the ideological and strategic competition with great powers that they accommodated the nationalist sentiments of their Vietnamese comrades and performed ritual, symbolic sovereign equality at the border as a veneer to the substantive power asymmetry. This phenomenon reflects what Maria Adele Carrai describes as a striking turn from a "total rejection" to "the adoption of sovereignty as a core principle to be asserted for the democratization of international society and as a shield against Western imperialism" in Chinese communists' perceptions of sovereignty as they came to power.[29]

What compromised the coherency of the Cold War partnership on the ground was often the divergent priorities and sometimes conflicting interests between the central government and its grassroots apparatus. The Chinese and Vietnamese communists outcompeted other nationalist movements that vied for power in their respective countries with a "highly unified" party that successfully combined a "centralized fiscal-military system with a decentralized mode of resource mobilization."[30] The tension created by state building at the borderlands was characterstic of the search for optimal relations between the political center, the regional agency, and the grassroots apparatus when the two revolutionary parties ascended to ruling elites yet ventured into a polarized world that was hostile to them. As Brantly Womack demonstrates, except for sporadic military expeditions during the Ming and Qing periods, the Chinese seepage through the Vietnamese border had historically been "driven by local opportunities rather than masterminded by Beijing."[31] An unprecendentedly high-level of centralization of power during the communist era allowed the two governments to better align the local agency with the "national" interest through the disciplined organization of the party so as to regulate such "local opportunities" in ways that were unimaginable before. Some of them were illegalized, such as cross-border farming and fishing, and others were brought within the state perimeter, such as transnational trade and transportation. With limited resources trickling down from the center, however, neither of the two political centers managed to contain the attractiveness of local opportunities at the borderlands, which often developed out of traditional livelihood practices, to various actors on the Sino-Vietnamese border. The Chinese pressure on the Vietnamese border was not effectively alleviated, notwithstanding Beijing's wish to the contrary during the period under discussion in this book.

---

[29] Carrai, *Sovereignty in China*, 153.   [30] Li, *The Making of Modern Chinese State*, 280.
[31] Womack, *China and Vietnam*, 134.

Consequently, despite the disciplinary strength of the two Leninist parties – and the two communist states they controlled – over the cadres, the local state was not simply a passive, static agent of the central government that championed a coherent national interest or abstract ideological mission. While the internationalist goal of fostering socialist brotherhood was prominent on the central governments' agenda, down at the bottom of the bureaucratic ladder, the street level cadres had more pragmatic concerns that centered on how to finance the state: hitting production targets, keeping the state-run commerce profitable, and levying taxes from land and trade – to name a few. The task of addressing the problem of historical state weakness drove these local Chinese and Vietnamese governing institutions to compete for resources at the border. Struggling to balance between internationalist and nationalist agendas, the two states made heavy institutional investment in turning frontier societies inward, which conveyed the message to the borderlanders that proletarian internationalism was for the states, yet the people were supposed to be nationalist.

Beyond the locality of Sino-Vietnamese borderlands and the particular bilateral relations, this book interrogates from a borderlands perspective what the Cold War really meant for Asia and how the Cold War became a constituent part of the broader experience of Asian societies in the second half of the twentieth century. The Cold War coincided with and accelerated the last wave of the globalization of territoriality, which made the European derived "definition of a boundary as an atom-wide line separating countries with absolutely equal claims and capabilities on both sides of that line" an international norm.[32] The postcolonial Asian leaders employed the discourse of a reciprocal "socialist brotherhood" to construct and perform these equal claims, which allowed communist China to redress some of the imperial, Sinocentric legacies, at least symbolically, and catered to the Vietnamese communists' aspiration to distinguish themselves from previous dynastical rulers who governed a tributary state of China and later French protectorates. In this regard, the revolutionary regimes were conformative, accepting and implementing the pan-global understanding of border.

Moreover, the Cold War triggered a departure in Asian powers' perception of frontier from "a terrible space of social exile and cultural desolation"[33] and made border regions a focal point of state building, ideological competition, and alliance making. For the superpowers and industrialized countries, the reach of the state, especially its ability to mobilize resources, was largely facilitated by the great wars of the twentieth century. The unprecedented outreach of the state in the Western world was one of the prerequisites and causes of the Cold War.[34] For Asian countries, though, growth in the sinews

---

[32] Tagliacozzo, "Jagged Landscapes," 8.   [33] Ibid., 9
[34] Westad, "The Cold War and the International History of the Twentieth Century," 9.

of state power, especially on its periphery, was largely a *result* of the Cold War. As a "social mechanism" and "imagined reality,"[35] the Cold War provided a cognitive shortcut for political elites to make sense out of the complicated situations of the borderlands (and elsewhere), identify threats that invoked state intervention, and respond to these challenges with the arsenals of solutions prescribed by their ideological commitment and inherited from historical experience. Although the efforts to align state-building projects on the frontier with a centrally designed agenda often proved futile, the Cold War highlighted that what happened locally at the borderlands could be international and strategic and thus lent momentum to the political center's pursuit of the uniformity of social order in its orbit of power. By understanding, adapting to, and reconstructing social reality, the modernizing states sought to generate revenues, legitimacy, and geo-strategic gains at the borderlands.

Bringing together the transnational, national, and local histories, this book demonstrates the importance of examining the mundane, everyday aspects of the territorialization of states and the development of international relations. Borderlands, as well as the shared maritime frontier, were spaces where international relations were simultaneously local relations, where the everyday function of the state could easily generate spillovers abroad, and where reactions to state building were often transnational. Investigating topics ranging from taxation, fishery regulations, binational marriage, to the evolving appellation of border gates depicts a more comprehensive and complicated picture of statecraft on the margins of political power that includes its institutional, ideational, and ritual aspects. Doing so challenges the campaign-centered history of the PRC and the war-focused narrative of the DRV. Exclusive focus on "the campaign-style governance" of communist states, as Arunabh Ghosh points out, often buries important aspects of "institutional-building and knowledge-generation" by the formal state structure and its functionaries.[36] Echoing the expanding scope of international history beyond the study of the causes of war and conditions of peace, this book reveals the most stable aspect of the ties between the two neighbors despite fluctuating intergovernmental relations: the spontaneous interdependence between their societies and the day-to-day mutual adaptation on the ground.

The cumulative effects of historical state building and post-normalization state rebuilding since the 1990s still dominate the political and social landscape of the Sino-Vietnamese borderlands today. When the new fishery agreement in the Gulf of Tonkin entered into force in 2004, the two countries both had a more industrialized economy than in the mid-twentieth century to afford

---

[35] Masuda, "The Cold War as Social Mechanism," 8.   [36] Ghosh, *Making It Count*, 9–10.

diverting the fishing population to other coastal industries.[37] Meanwhile, local iterations of global forces are more pronounced than before. Driven by the global anti-trafficking campaign, the status of long-existing undocumented marriage among highland ethnic minorities across the border has gradually changed from common marriage to illegal ones.[38] Mirroring the decision of the Chinese master potters who opened workshops in Móng Cái in 1910 to dodge the Indochinese import duties, Chinese firms race to set up projects in Vietnam mostly along the Chinese border to flee the ramifications of the Sino-US trade war after China ended the zero-COVID policy.[39] At the Sino-Vietnamese border, and in the Sino-Vietnamese relations more broadly, what is new is often old.

---

[37] Chen, "Woguo yuye ziyuan guanli zhengce yanjiu," 68–69; Trường Giang/VOV-Đông Bắc, "Đánh giá 15 năm thực thi Hiệp định Hợp tác Nghề cá vịnh Bắc Bộ VN-TQ."

[38] Barabantseva, "When Borders Lie Within," 352; Qiu, "Bei guailai de 'Yuenan xinniang,'" 7.

[39] Guarascio, "Analysis: Chinese Suppliers Race to Vietnam as COVID Let-up Opens Escape Route from Sino-U.S. Trade War."

Bibliography

Archives

China

Archives of Ministry of Foreign Affairs of the PRC, Beijing
Chongzuo County Archives, Nanning
East China Normal University Resources Center of Contemporary Chinese History, Shanghai
Fangcheng District Archives, Fangchenggang
Guangdong Provincial Archives, Guangzhou
Guangxi Zhuang Autonomous Region Archives, Nanning
Nanning Municipal Archives, Nanning
Pingxiang County Archives, Pingxiang

Vietnam

National Archives of Vietnam Center III, Hanoi
    Bộ Giao thông vận tải [Ministry of Transport]
    Phủ Thủ tướng [Prime Minister's Secretariat]
    Phủ Thủ tướng (1945–54)
    Uỷ ban Hành chính Khu tự trị Việt Bắc [Northern Vietnam Autonomous Zone Administrative Committee] (1948–76)

United States

The National Archives and Records Administration, College Park, Maryland

United Kingdom

The National Archives of the United Kingdom, Kew

Documents and Papers

Ban Nghiên cứu lịch sử Đảng tỉnh ủy Quảng Ninh. *Những sự kiện lịch sử Đảng tỉnh Quảng Ninh, 1955–1965* [Historical events of the Party in Quảng Ninh Province, 1955–1965]. Quảng Ninh: Ban nghiên cứu lịch sử Đảng tỉnh uỷ Quảng Ninh, 1984.

CIA Research Reports: China (1946–1976). Microfilm Collections. Washington, DC: Global Resources Center Gelman Library, George Washington Library.

CIA, *Daily Report, Foreign Radio Broadcasts*, nos. 135 and 158.

CPC Central Literature Research Center. *Jianguo yilai zhongyao wenxian xuanbian* [Important documents since the foundation of the PRC], vols. 6, 13, 20. Beijing: Zhongyang wenxian chubanshe, 1992, 1996, 1998.

Zhou Enlai nianpu [A Chronology of Zhou Enlai], vol. 3. Beijing: Zhongyang wenxian chubanshe, 1997.

Đảng cộng sản Việt Nam. *Văn kiện Đảng toàn tập* [Complete documents of the Party], Tập 10 (1949), Tập 11 (1950), Tập 13 (1952), Tập 16 (1955), Tập 17 (1956), Tập 19 (1958), Tập 25 (1964), Tập 26 (1965), Tập 27 (1966), Tập 28 (1967). Hanoi: NXB Chính trị quốc gia, 2001–3.

Editorial Committee of Gazetteer of Pingxiang city. *Pingxiang shizhi* [Gazetteer of Pingxiang City]. Guangzhou: Zhongshan daxue chubanshe, 1993.

Editorial Group of Biography of Xiaohua. *Xiaohua wenji* [Collection of the writings of Xiaohua], vol. 2. Beijing: Jiefangjun chubanshe, 1994.

Editorial Group of the Chronicle of Cultural Revolution in Guangxi. *Guangxi wenge dashi nianbiao* [Chronicle of Cultural Revolution in Guangxi]. Nanning: Guangxi renmin chubanshe, 1990, internal circulation.

Guangxi Zhuang Autonomous Region Gazetteers Office. *Guangxi tongzhi: gong'an zhi* [Gazetteer of Guangxi: public security]. Nanning: Guangxi renmin chubanshe, 2002.

Guangxi tongzhi: haiguan zhi [Gazetteer of Guangxi: customs]. Nanning: Guangxi renmin chubanshe, 2010.

Guangxi tongzhi: minzuzhi [Gazetteers of Guangxi: ethnic minorities]. Nanning: Guangxi renmin chubanshe, 2009.

Guangxi tongzhi: tieluzhi [Gazetteers of Guangxi: railways]. Nanning: Guangxi renmin chubanshe, 1992.

Guangxi tongzhi: waishizhi [Gazetteers of Guangxi: foreign affairs]. Nanning: Guangxi renmin chubanshe, 1992.

Hertslet, Edward. *Hertslet's China Treaties: Treaties, &c. Between Great Britain and China; and Between China and Foreign Powers; and Orders in Council, Rules, Regulations, Acts of Parliament, Decrees, &c. Affecting British Interests in China. In Force on the 1st January 1908, Volume 1, Parts II*. London: H. M. Stationary Office, 1908.

Hồ Chí Minh. *Hồ Chí Minh Toàn Tập* [Complete works of Hồ Chí Minh], Tập 9 1954–1955. Hanoi: NXB Chính trị quốc gia - Sự thật, 2021.

Institute of Contemporary China of Chinese Academy of Social Sciences. *Zhonghua renmin gonghe guoshi biannian* [Chronological history of the PRC], vols. 1949, 1950, 1951, 1954, 1955, 1957. Beijing: Dangdai Zhongguo chubanshe, 2004–11.

Lê Duẩn. "Lược ghi bài nói của Đồng chí Lê Duẩn bí thư thứ nhất ban chấp hành trung ương Đảng với Tỉnh ủy và cán bộ các ngành xung quanh tỉnh ở Cao Bằng ngày 10-

9-1968 [Summary of the speech of Comrade Lê Duẩn, First Secretary of the Central Committee of the Party, with the Provincial Party Committee and officials of branches around the province of Cao Bằng on 10 September 1968]." VN69.01864. Vietnamese National Library, Hanoi.

Mao Zedong. *Mao Zedong xuanji* [Selected Works of Mao Zedong], vol. 5. Beijing: Renmin chubanshe, 1977.

Ministry of Railway of the PRC. *Zhong-Yue guojing tielu xieding* [The PRC-DRV Border Railway Agreement]. Beijing: Renmin tiedao chubanshe, 1956.

Research Branch of Party History and Political Affairs of the National Defense University of PLA. *"Wenhua dageming" yanjiu ziliao* [Research materials of the "Cultural Revolution"], vol. 1. Beijing, 1988, internal publication.

Second Historical Archives of China. *Minguo shiqi xi'nan bianjiang dang'an ziliao huibian: Yunnan Guangxi zonghejuan* [Compilation of archival documents of southwestern frontier during the Republic era: Yunnan and Guangxi], vols. 88, 91. Beijing: Shehui kexue chubanshe, 2014.

State Council of the PRC. "Guowuyuan guanyu jiang Guangxisheng de Qinxian, Hepu, Lingshan, Fangcheng sixian he Beihaishi huagui Guangdongsheng lingdao de jueding [State Council's decision to put the four counties of Qin, Hepu, Pingshan, and Fangcheng, and the city of Beihai under the administration of Guangdong]." 31 May 1955, *Zhonghua renmin gongheguo guowuyuan gongbao* 10 (1955), 370.

"Liu Shaoqi Zhuxi he Hu Zhiming Zhuxi lianhe shengming [Joint Communique between President Liu Shaoqi and President Hồ Chí Minh]." May 16, 1963, *Zhonghua renmin gongheguo guowuyuan gongbao* 9 (1963), 166–72.

US Senate, Committee on Foreign Relations, 90th Congress, 1st Session. *Background Information Relating to Southeast Asia and Vietnam*. Washington, DC: U.S. Government Printing Office, 1967, 3rd rev. ed.

Westad, Odd Arne, Chen Jian, Stein Tonnesson, Nguyen Vu Tung, and James G. Hershberg, eds. *77 Conversations between Chinese and Foreign Leaders on the War in Indochina, 1964–1977*. CWIHP Working Paper, no. 22. Washington, DC: Woodrow Wilson International Center for Scholars, 1998.

Zeng Fusheng. *Youyiguan bianfang jianchazhan zhanzhi* [Gazetteer of the border check station of the Friendship Pass]. Nanning: Youyiguan bianfang jianchazhan zhanzhi bianweihui, 1993.

Zhang Zhidong. *Zhang Wenxianggong quanji: dianzou 2* [Complete works of Zhang Zhidong: Telegrams 2], vol. 74. Taipei: Wenhai, 1963.

"Zhong-Fa guiding Yuenan ji Zhongguo biansheng guanxi zhuantiao [Pact on the relations between Vietnam and border provinces of China signed between the ROC and France, 16 May 1930]." *Waijiao gongbao* 3, no. 4 (1930), 109–10.

Databases, Websites, and Media Sources

An Kiên-Trung Dũng/VOV-Tây Bắc. "Lực lượng biên phòng Việt Nam và Trung Quốc tuần tra phòng chống dịch [Vietnamese and Chinese border guards patrol to prevent epidemics]." *Voice of Vietnam*, June 25, 2021. https://vov.vn/quan-su-quoc-phong/viet-nam/luc-luong-bien-phong-viet-nam-va-trung-quoc-tuan-tra-phong-chong-dich-868862.vov.

"Bộ đội Biên phòng 50 năm xây dựng, chiến đấu và trưởng thành [Border guards' 50 years of development, fighting and expansion]." *Báo Biên phòng*, August 11, 2011. http://bienphongvietnam.vn/bd-bien-phong-viet-nam/truyen-thong-bo-doi-bien-phong/114-b-i-bien-phong-50-nm-xay-dng-chin-u-va-trng-thanh-.html.

Bộ Ngoại thương [Ministry of Foreign Trade]. "Nghị định 257-BNT/TCCB năm 1959 về việc thành lập Sở Ngoại thương Khu tự trị Việt Bắc [Decree No. 257-BNT / TCCB of 1959 on the establishment of the Foreign Trade Department of the Việt Bắc Autonomous Region]." September 21, 1959. https://lawnet.vn/vb/Nghi-dinh-257-BNT-TCCB-thanh-lap-So-Ngoai-thuong-Khu-tu-tri-Viet-Bac-4F78.html.

Bộ Tài chính [Ministry of Finance]. "Thông tư 140-TC-TQD-T năm 1964 bổ sung Thông tư 802-TC-TQD năm 1962 về việc trả thù lao cho những người tham gia bắt lậu [Circular 140-TC-TQD-T of 1964 supplementing Circular 802-TC-TQD of 1962 on the payment of remuneration to participants of anti-smuggling]," June 17, 1964. https://lawnet.vn/vb/Thong-tu-140-TC-TQD-T-bo-sung-Thong-tu-802-TC-TQD-tra-thu-lao-nguoi-tham-gia-bat-lau-4CC9.html.

Bộ trưởng Bộ Nội Vụ [Minister of Internal Affairs]. "Chiếu theo Sắc lệnh số 23 ngày 21 tháng 02 năm 1946 thành lập Việt Nam Công an vụ Sau khi thỏa hiệp với Bộ trưởng Bộ Tư pháp [Further instruction of order no. 23 on 21 February 1946 regarding establishing Vietnamese Public Security Forces after consultation with the Minister of Justice]." April 18, 1946. https://lawnet.vn/vb/Nghi-dinh-121-NV-ND-cong-an-vu-554F.html.

Burstein, Daniel. "Days of Danger at Friendship Pass." *Macleans*, September 6, 1982. https://archive.macleans.ca/article/1982/9/6/days-of-danger-at-friendship-pass.

CIA Freedom of Information Act Electronic Reading Room.

Chen Derong. "Kangzhanzhong de Zhong-Yue jiaotong yunshuxian [Sino-Vietnamese transportation line during the Anti-Japanese War]." *Dongfang zaobao*, July 19, 2014. www.cssn.cn/zgs/zgs_zgxds/201507/t20150720_2086103.shtml.

Chủ tịch Nước [President]. "Sắc lệnh số 268/SL về việc ban hành bản quy định việc thành lập Khu Tự trị Việc Bắc [Decree No. 268/SL on promulgating regulations on the establishment of Northern Autonomous Region]." July 1, 1956. https://lawnet.vn/vb/Sac-lenh-268-SL-ban-hanh-ban-quy-dinh-thanh-lap-khu-tu-tri-Viet-bac-8FA6.html.

COSCO Shipping (Guangzhou) Co., Ltd. "Mianhuai chuanyuan geming xianlie, hongyang guoji zhuyi jiangshen [Remember revolutionary martyr sailors and carry forward internationalist spirit]." June 12, 2017. https://gz.coscoshipping.com/art/2017/6/12/art_10096_317283.html.

Cui Heyu. "Zousi dongrou, weihe changqi lüjin buzhi? [Why does smuggled frozen meat still exist despite strict ban?]" *Liaowang Institution*, December 24, 2020. www.huxiu.com/article/401844.html.

Dacheng laojiu qikan quanwen shujuku [Dacheng Pre-1949 Periodical Full-Text Database]. Online Database. Beijing: Shangpin Dacheng Data Technology Co., Ltd.

Dan County of Hainan Province Gazetteers Office. "Juan yi: dilizhi [Section one: Geography]." *In Danxian zhi* [Gazetteers of Dan County]. 2001. www.hnszw.org.cn/data/news/2011/01/48286/.

Đảng Cộng sản Việt Nam. "Tượng đài Bác Hồ trên đảo Cô Tô [Monument of Uncle Hồ on Cô Tô Island]." *Báo điện tử - Đảng Cộng sản Việt Nam*, July 10, 2012. https://dangcongsan.vn/tu-tuong-van-hoa/tuong-dai-bac-ho-tren-dao-co-to-135099.html.

Foreign Broadcast Information Service Daily Reports (1941–1974, 1974–1996). Online Database. Naples, FL: Readex.

Guangxi Zhuang Autonomous Region Gazetteers Office. *Guangxi diqing ziliaoku* [Database of Guangxi Provincial Information]. www.gxdfz.org.cn/gdtz/.

Guarascio, Francesco. "Analysis: Chinese Suppliers Race to Vietnam as COVID Let-up Opens Escape Route from Sino-U.S. Trade War." *Reuters*, March 16, 2023. www.reuters.com/markets/asia/chinese-suppliers-race-vietnam-covid-let-up-opens-escape-route-sino-us-trade-war-2023-03-16/.

Han Shuainan. "Yunnan bianjing diqu mubiao renqun xinguan bingdu yimiao diyiji jiezhonglü yu 97% [More than 97% eligible people in the border region of Yunnan have received the first dose of COVID vaccine]." *China News Service*, May 17, 2021. www.chinanews.com/gn/2021/05-17/9478907.shtml.

Hoài Anh. "Phụ nữ vùng mỏ: Tiếp nối xuất sắc truyền thống 'Ba đảm đang' [Women of the mining region: carry on the great tradition of 'Three In Charge']." *Quảng Ninh*, August 7, 2013. https://baoquangninh.com.vn/phu-nu-vung-mo-tiep-noi-xuat-sac-truyen-thong-quot-ba-dam-dang-quot-2203808.html.

Hội đồng Chính phủ [Government Council]. "Nghị quyết về việc tiến hành hợp tác hóa nông nghiệp kết hợp hoàn thành cải cách dân chủ miền núi [Resolution on the implementation of agricultural cooperation in combination with the completion of democratic reform in the mountainous area]." November 4, 1959. https://lawnet.vn/vb/Nghi-quyet-tien-hanh-hop-tac-hoa-nong-nghiep-ket-hop-hoan-thanh-cai-cach-dan-chu-mien-nui-5ADC.html.

Hoskin, Mark. "Communication through Cartography – China 1946–1947." International Map Collectors' Society Show & Tell, February 28, 2023. www.youtube.com/watch?v=QAPP-tjqDYU.

Huang, Kristin. "Chinese Authorities Take a Leaf from the Trump Playbook and 'Build the Wall' as Part of Covid-19 Curbs." *South China Morning Post*, July 15, 2021. www.scmp.com/news/china/science/article/3141126/chinese-authorities-take-leaf-trump-playbook-and-build-wall-part.

Ji, Zhen-Gang. "The South China Sea Island China Gave Away: Bach Long Vi Island and its secret transfer from China to Vietnam." *The Diplomat*, August 14, 2019. https://thediplomat.com/2019/08/the-south-china-sea-island-china-gave-away/.

Kardon, Issac B. "The Other Gulf of Tonkin Incident: China's Forgotten Maritime Compromise." *Asia Maritime Transparency Initiative*, October 21, 2015. https://amti.csis.org/the-other-gulf-of-tonkin-incident-chinas-forgotten-maritime-compromise/.

Lã Nghĩa Hiếu. "Quảng Ninh duy trì 74 chốt kiểm soát dọc biên giới Việt – Trung để phòng Covid-19 [Quảng Ninh maintains 74 checkpoints along the Vietnam-China border to prevent COVID-19]." *Báo Thanh Niên*, July 27, 2020. https://thanhnien.vn/thoi-su/quang-ninh-duy-tri-74-chot-kiem-soat-doc-bien-gioi-viet-trung-de-phong-covid-19-1256901.html.

Liang Ying. "Guangxi xinguan bingdu yimiao jiezhong wancheng 2000wan jici [Guangxi completes 20 million doses of COVID vaccines]." People's Government of Guangxi Zhuang Autonomous Region, June 7, 2021. www.gxzf.gov.cn/gxyw/t9113597.shtml.

Lilian Goldman Law Library. The Avalon Project Documents in Law, History and Diplomacy. https://avalon.law.yale.edu/.

Li Ya'nan. "Guangxi guanbi qige lulu kou'an, yu Yuenan sisheng dingqi hutong yiqing [Guangxi closes four land border ports and communicates situation of the pandemic with four border provinces of Vietnam]." *China News Service-Guangxi*, May 18, 2020. www.gx.chinanews.com/top/2020-05-19/detail-ifzwkahv4164896.shtml.

Luo Congsheng. "Dangnian, yuanyue kangmei zhong de Jingdao fanyiguan [Interpreters from the Kinh islands during the movement of assisting Vietnam and resisting America]." *Fangchenggang Ribao*, July 31, 2016. www.fcgsnews.com/news/hot/2016-7-31/85144.shtml.

Luo Ruiqing. "Luo Ruiqing zai diliuci quanguo gongan huiyishang de zongjie [Summary by Luo Ruiqing at the sixth national meeting on public security]." June 17, 1954. Yongyi Song, *Laogai Research Foundation Database*. https://laogairesearch.org/wp-content/uploads/2019/06/B540617Luo-RQ.pdf.

Mei Zixiang. "Tiedaobing lishi: Gui-Kun tielu [History of the Railway corps: Guiyang-Kunming Railway]," December 13, 2019. www.tdbjy.com/cms/show-64300.html.

Meyskens, Covell. "There Never Was a Cold War China." History and Public Policy Program Blog. Woodrow Wilson Center for International Scholars. www.wilsoncenter.org/blog-post/there-never-was-cold-war-china.

Minh Chiến. "Trung Quốc siết nhập cảnh tại biên giới Việt-Trung do dịch Covid-19 diễn biến phức tạp [China tightens entry at the Vietnam-China border due to complicated developments of the COVID-19 epidemic]." *Báo Người Lao Động,* April 5, 2020. https://nld.com.vn/kinh-te/trung-quoc-siet-nhap-canh-tai-bien-gioi-viet-trung-do-dich-covid-19-dien-bien-phuc-tap-20200405172140356.htm.

Minh Châu. "Đồng chí Hoàng Văn Thụ – người Cộng sản kiên trung [Comrade Hoàng Văn Thụ – A Staunch Communist]." *Báo điện tử – Đảng Cộng sản Việt Nam*, September 27, 2019. https://dangcongsan.vn/tu-tuong-van-hoa/dong-chi-hoang-van-thu–nguoi-cong-san-kien-trung-537039.html.

National Palace Museum. *The Green Borderlands: Treaty and Maps That Defined the Qing's Southwest Boundaries*. Online Exhibition. Taipei. https://theme.npm.edu.tw/exh105/GreenBorderlands/ch/index.html#main.

Ngân hàng Quốc gia Việt Nam [National Bank of Vietnam]. "Thông tư 195-VP/PC năm 1958 về biện pháp cho vay Mậu dịch xuất nhập khẩu biên giới Việt-Trung [Circular 195-VP / PC of 1958 on loans to import and export companies of Vietnam-China border trade]." December 2, 1958. https://lawnet.vn/vb/Thong-tu-195-VP-PC-bien-phap-cho-vay-Mau-dich-xuat-nhap-khau-bien-gioi-Viet-Trung-D176.html.

Nguyễn Hà. "Yuenan renmin jundui canjia shiwandashan zhanyi 60 zhounian [60 anniversary of PAVN's participation of the Hundred Thousand Mountains Campaign]." *Quân đội nhân dân* (Chinese Version), May 12, 2012. https://cn.qdnd.vn/cid-7232/7298.

Pham, Bac and Bennett Murray. "Behind Vietnam's COVID-19 Response, Deep Distrust of China." *The Diplomat,* May 14, 2020. https://thediplomat.com/2020/05/behind-vietnams-covid-19-response-deep-distrust-of-china/.

Prados, John. "The Numbers Game: How Many Vietnamese Fled South In 1954?" Veteran, January/February 2005. www.vva.org/TheVeteran/2005_01/feature_numbersGame.htm.

PV. "Kỷ niệm 50 năm phong trào Ba sẵn sàng [In memory of the 50 anniversaries of the 'Three Ready Movement']." *Nhân Dân*, August 7, 2014. https://nhandan.vn/tin-tuc-su-kien/ky-niem-50-nam-phong-trao-ba-san-sang-210196.

Qiao Xiaoguang. "Guangxisheng tudi gaige jiben zongjie [A basic summary of land reform in Guangxi Province]." December 17, 1952. https://zh.wikisource.org/wiki/广西省土地改革基本总结.

Song, Yongyi, ed. *Chinese Cultural Revolution Database*. Online Database. Hong Kong: Chinese University of Hong Kong.

Thanh Nga (Trung tâm TT&VH). "Vàng không mua nổi lòng người Dao theo Đảng [Gold cannot buy the hearts of the Dao people who follow the Party]." Cổng thông tin điện tử Huyện Đầm Hà, Quảng Ninh, June 5, 2020. www.quangninh.gov.vn/donvi/huyendamha/Trang/ChiTietTinTuc.aspx?nid=9694.

Trường Giang/VOV-Đông Bắc. "Đánh giá 15 năm thực thi Hiệp định Hợp tác Nghề cá vịnh Bắc Bộ VN-TQ [An evaluation of fifteen years of implementation of the Gulf of Tonkin Fishery Agreement]." *Đài Tiếng nói Việt Nam*, September 25, 2019. https://vov.gov.vn/danh-gia-15-nam-thuc-thi-hiep-dinh-hop-tac-nghe-ca-vinh-bac-bo-vn-tq-dtnew-96476.

Thu Hằng. "Trung Quốc tính gì khi tăng tốc xây tường biên giới với Việt Nam, Miến Điện? [What does China think when speeding up the construction of border fences with Vietnam and Myanmar]." *Tạp chí Việt Nam*, February 8, 2021. www.rfi.fr/vi/tạp-ch%C3%AD/tạp-ch%C3%AD-việt-nam/20210208-trung-quoc-xay-hang-rao-o-bien-gioi-viet-nam-mien-dien.

Thủ tướng Chính phủ [Prime Minister]. "Nghị định 486-TTg năm 1958 về bản điều lệ quản lý mậu dịch tiểu ngạch nhân dân trong khu vực biên giới Việt-Trung [Decree No. 486-TTg of 1958 on the regulation on management of small-scale trade in the border area between Vietnam and China]." November 4, 1958. https://lawnet.vn/vb/Nghi-dinh-486-TTg-ban-dieu-le-quan-ly-mau-dich-tieu-ngach-nhan-dan-trong-khu-vuc-bien-gioi-Viet-Trung-5665.html.

Thủ tướng Chính phủ [Prime Minister]. "Nghị định 100-TTg năm 1959 về việc thống nhất các đơn vị bộ đội quốc phòng, công an biên phòng, cảnh sát vũ trang thành Công an nhân dân vũ trang [Decree No. 100-TTg of 1959 on the unification of the units of military defense, border police guard, and armed police into the People's Armed Forces]." March 3, 1959. https://lawnet.vn/vb/Nghi-dinh-100-TTg-thong-nhat-cac-don-vi-bo-doi-quoc-phong-cong-an-bien-phong-canh-sat-vu-trang-thanh-Cong-an-nhan-dan-vu-trang-AAFA.html.

Trương Minh Đức. "Giải quyết mối quan hệ dân tộc xuyên biên giới, góp phần bảo đảm chủ quyền, an ninh quốc gia [Resolving cross-border ethnic relations contributes to ensuring national sovereignty and security]." *Lý luận Chính trị*, July 15, 2022. http://lyluanchinhtri.vn/home/index.php/thuc-tien/item/4403-giai-quyet-moi-quan-he-dan-toc-xuyen-bien-gioi-gop-phan-bao-dam-chu-quyen-an-ninh-quoc-gia.html.

United States Provost Marshal General's Bureau. "Civil Affairs Handbook, French Indo-China, section 8: industry and commerce." Army Service Forces Manual M 359-8, January 22, 1944. Ike Skelton Combined Arms Research Library Digital Library. https://cgsc.contentdm.oclc.org/digital/collection/p4013coll8/id/2632/.

Ủy Ban Nhân Dân Thành Phố Hải Phòng [Haiphong City People's Committee]. "Đề nghị xây dựng Nghị quyết của Hội đồng nhân dân thành phố về cơ chế, chính sách đối với cán bộ, công chức, viên chức công tác tại huyện đảo Bạch Long Vỹ [Proposal of resolution of the City People's Council on institutions and policies for cadres, civil servants and public employees working in Bạch Long Vỹ island district]." 2017. https://haiphong.gov.vn/Upload/hpgov/old/2020/05/du%20thao%20to%20trinh%20danh%20gia%20tac%20dong%20thuc%20hien%20QD%20409-44821.pdf.

Việt Hải [pseud.]. "Ba bám, Ba nhất . . . Ba sẵn sàng [Three clings, Three mosts . . . Three Readies]." *Phú Yên*, January 20, 2017. www.baophuyen.com.vn/349/168299/ba-bam-ba-nhat...-ba-san-sang.html.

Vietnam News Agency. "Border Gates with China Start to Reopen." *Vietnam News*, February 7, 2020. https://vietnamnews.vn/economy/591987/border-gates-with-china-start-to-reopen.html.

Wilson Center Digital Archive. https://digitalarchive.wilsoncenter.org/.

Wyrtki, Klaus. "Physical Oceanography of the Southeast Asian Waters." La Jolla, CA. The University of California, Scripps Institution of Oceanography, 1961. NAGA report, volume 2, Scientific Results of Marine Investigations of the South China Sea and the Gulf of Thailand 1959–1961. https://escholarship.org/uc/item/49n9x3t4.

"Yuenan dapi yuchuan shusan Beihai [Large number of Vietnamese fishing vessels relocating to Beihai]." *Beihai Wenshi* 14, Foreign Relations. http://m.liuzhou520.cn/e/action/ShowInfo.php?classid=14&id=8365.

Zhou, Laura. "Why Fishing Boats Are on the Territorial Front Lines of the South China Sea." *South China Morning Post*, January 12, 2020. www.scmp.com/news/china/diplomacy/article/3045662/why-fishing-boats-are-territorial-front-lines-south-china-sea.

Zhuang, Beining, and Yan Wang. "Zhiji Yunnan bianjian diyixian: jiyao kangji yiqing, yeyao huhang tongguan [At the frontline of border control of Yunnan: fighting pandemic while facilitating custom clearance]." *Xinhua News*, June 4, 2021. www.yn.xinhuanet.com/reporter/2021-06/04/c_139988364.htm.

Newspapers and Periodicals

Cao Bằng
Guangxi ribao [Guangxi Daily]
Jiefangjun bao [PLA Daily]
Lạng Sơn
Quảng Ninh
Renmin ribao [People's Daily]

Books and Articles

Adelman, Jeremy, and Stephen Aron. "From Borderlands to Borders: Empires, Nation-States, and the Peoples in between in North American History." *The American Historical Review* 104, no. 3 (1999), 814–41.

Ahn, Byung-Joon. "The Political Economy of the People's Commune in China: Changes and Continuities." *Journal of Asian Studies* 34, no. 3 (May 1975), 631–58.

Bibliography

Amer, Ramses. "The Sino-Vietnamese Approach to Managing Boundary Disputes." *Maritime Briefing* 3, no. 5 (2002), 1–80.

——. "French Policies towards the Chinese in Vietnam: A Study of Migration and Colonial Responses." *Moussons* [En ligne] 16 (2010), 57–80. http://journals.openedition.org/moussons/192.

Amirell, Stefan Eklöf. *Pirates of Empire: Colonisation and Maritime Violence in Southeast Asia*. Cambridge: Cambridge University Press, 2019.

Anderson, James A. *The Rebel Den of Nùng Trí Cao: Loyalty and Identity Along the Sino-Vietnamese Frontier*. Singapore: National University of Singapore Press, 2007.

——. "Distinguishing between China and Vietnam: Three Relational Equilibriums in Sino-Vietnamese Relations." *Journal of East Asian Studies* 13, no. 2 (2013), 259–80.

Ang, Cheng Guan. *Vietnamese Communists' Relations with China and the Second Indochina Conflicts, 1956–1962*. Jefferson, NC: McFarland, 1998.

Anthony, Robert J. "'Righteous Yang': Pirate, Rebel, and Hero on the Sino-Vietnamese Water Frontier, 1644–1684." *Cross-Currents: East Asian History and Culture Review E-Journal*, no. 11 (2014), 1–30.

Asselin, Pierre. *Hanoi's Road to the Vietnam War*. Berkeley: University of California Press, 2013.

Aumoitte, M. A. *Tong-King: de Hanoi à la frontière du Kouang-Si, provinces de Bac-ninh et Lang-Son*. Paris: Bureaux de la Revue, 1885.

Bachman, David M. *Bureaucracy, Economy, and Leadership in China: The Institutional Origins of the Great Leap Forward*. Cambridge: Cambridge University Press, 1991.

Baldanza, Kathlene. *Ming China and Vietnam: Negotiating Borders in Early Modern Asia*. New York: Cambridge University Press, 2016.

Ban Chỉ đạo biên soạn. *Giao thông vận tải Lạng Sơn: 70 năm xây dựng và trưởng thành* [Transport in Lạng Sơn: 70 years of construction and growth]. Hanoi: NXB Giao thông vận tải, 2015.

Barabantseva, Elena. "When Borders Lie Within: Ethnic Marriages and Illegality on the Sino-Vietnamese Border." *International Political Sociology* 9, no. 4 (December 2015), 352–68.

Baud, Michiel, and Willem van Schendel. "Toward a Comparative History of Borderlands." *Journal of World History* 8, no. 2 (Fall 1997), 211–42.

Bernstein, Thomas P. "Mao Zedong and the Famine of 1959–1960: A Study in Willfulness." *The China Quarterly* 186 (June 2006), 421–45.

Bhabha, Homi K. "DesemiNation: Time, Narrative and the Margins of the Modern Nation." In *Nation and Narration*, ed. Homi K. Bhabha, 292–321. New York: Routledge, 1990.

Biggs, Michael. "Putting the State on the Map: Cartography, Territory, and European State Formation." *Comparative Studies in Society and History* 41, no. 2 (1999), 374–405.

Bo Yibo. *Ruogan zhongda juece yu shijian de huigu* [A review of several key decisions and events]. Beijing: Remin chubanshe, 1997. Rev. ed.

Bos, C. *Notes on the Lung Chow T'ing, Lang Son, and Cao Bang*. Paris: Imprimerie levé, 1909.

Bradley, Mark Philip. *Vietnam at War*. Oxford: Oxford University Press, 2009.

Branch, Jordan. *The Cartographic State: Maps, Territory, and the Origins of Sovereignty*. Cambridge: Cambridge University Press, 2014.

Brocheux, Pierre, and Daniel Hémery. *Indochina: An Ambiguous Colonization, 1858–1954*. Berkeley: University of California Press, 2011.

Brook, Timothy. "What Happens When Wang Yangming Crosses the Border?" In *The Chinese State at the Borders*, ed. Diana Lary, 74–90. Vancouver: University of British Columbia Press, 2007.

Brunet-Jailly, Emmanuel. *Border Disputes: A Global Encyclopedia*, vol. 1. Santa Barbara, CA: ABC-CLIO, 2015.

Buzan, Barry, Ole Wæver, and Jaap de Wilde. *Security: A New Framework for Analysis*. Boulder, CO: Lynne Rienner, 1998.

Bureau of Foreign Trade. *China Industrial Handbooks: Chekiang*. Shanghai: Ministry of Industry, 1935.

Calkins, Laura M. *China and the First Vietnam War, 1947–54*. Abingdon; Oxon: Routledge, 2013.

Campagne, Armel. "French Energy Imperialism in Vietnam and the Conquest of Tonkin (1873–1885)." *Journal of Energy History/Revue d'Histoire de l'Énergie* [En ligne], no. 3 (2020). http://energyhistory.eu/node/218.

Carrai, Maria Adele. *Sovereignty in China: A Genealogy of a Concept since 1840*. Cambridge: Cambridge University, 2019.

Castle, Timothy. *At War in the Shadow of Vietnam: United States Military Aid to the Royal Lao Government, 1955–1975*. New York: Columbia University Press, 1993.

Chan, Alfred L. *Mao's Crusade: Politics and Policy Implementation in China's Great Leap Forward*. Oxford: Oxford University Press, 2001.

Chandler, Andrea. *Institutions of Isolation: Border Controls in the Soviet Union and Its Successor States, 1917–1993*. Montreal: McGill-Queen's University Press, 1998.

Chang, Pao-min. "The Sino-Vietnamese Dispute over the Ethnic Chinese." *The China Quarterly*, no. 90 (June 1982), 195–230.

Chappell, Jonathan. "Maritime Raiding, International Law and the Suppression of Piracy on the South China Coast, 1842–1869." *The International History Review* 40, no. 3 (2018), 473–92.

Chen Bo. "Zhong-Su fenlie yu Yuenan Laodongdang dui guoji gongyun de renzhi he biaoda, 1961–1964 [Sino-Soviet Split and WPV's perception and expression on international communist movement]." *Dangdai shijie yu shehui zhuyi* no. 8 (2018), 77–83.

Chen Jian. "China and the First Indo-China War, 1950–1954." *The China Quarterly* 133 (March 1993), 85–110.

Mao's China and the Cold War. Chapel Hill: University of North Carolina Press, 2001.

"China, the Vietnam War, and the Sino-American Rapprochement, 1968–1973." In *The Third Indochina War: Conflict between China, Vietnam and Cambodia, 1972–79*, ed. Odd Arne Westad and Sophie Quinn-Judge, 33–64. London: Routledge, 2006.

"China and the Bandung Conference: Changing Perceptions and Representations." In *Bandung Revisited: The Legacy of the 1955 Asian-African Conference for International Order*, ed. See Seng Tan and Amitav Acharya, 132–59. Singapore: National University of Singapore Press, 2008.

Chen, King C. *Vietnam and China, 1938–1954*. Princeton, NJ: Princeton University Press, 1969.

Chen Qing. "Woguo yuye ziyuan guanli zhengce yanjiu [Policy Research on Fishery Resource Managementin China]." *Haiyang kaifa yu guanli*, no. 9 (2022), 65–72.

Chen Weixin. "Deng Chengxiu yu Zhong-Fa Gui-Yue duan bianjie jiaoshe: yi Taibei Gonggong bowuyuan diancang Gui-Yue duan bianjie tiaoyue dang'an wei zhongxin [Deng Chengxiu and Sino-French negotiation over the demarcation of the Guangxi-Vietnam border: centering on archived treaties on Guangxi-Vietnam border in Taipei National Palace Museum]." *Lishi dili yanjiu*, no. 4 (2020), 15–28.

Chen Yufei. "Kangmei yuanyue zhanzheng zhongde Zhong-Mei shuileizhan [Sino-American naval mine warfare during the war of resisting America and assisting Vietnam]." *Yanhuang chunqiu*, no. 3 (2022), 17–22.

Chen Zhengqing. "Socialist Transformation and the Demise of Private Entrepreneurs: Wu Yunchu's Tragedy." *European Journal of East Asian Studies* 13, no. 2 (2014), 240–61.

Chere, Lewis M. *The Diplomacy of the Sino-French War (1883–1885): Global Complications of an Undeclared War*. Notre Dame, IN: Cross Roads Books, 1988.

Cheung Sie-woo. "Regional Development and Cross-Cultural Linkage: The Case of a Vietnamese Community in Guangxi, China." In *Where China Meets Southeast Asia: Social and Cultural Change in the Border Region*, ed. Chris Hutton, Khun Eng Kuah, and Grant Evans, 277–311. Richmond; Surrey: Curzon Press, 2001.

Chinese Academy of Social Sciences. *Zhongguo geming genjudi jingji dashiji, 1937–1949* [Chronicles of the economy of Chinese revolutionary bases]. Beijing: China Social Sciences Press, 1986.

Chinn, Dennis L. "Cooperative Farming in North China." *The Quarterly Journal of Economics* 94, no. 2 (March 1980), 279–97.

Chow, Gregory C. *The Chinese Economy*. Singapore: World Scientific, 1987.

Chu Văn Tấn. *Một năm trên biên giới Việt-Trung* [A year on the Vietnamese-Chinese border]. Hanoi: NXB Quân đội nhân dân, 1964.

Chung, Chris P. C. "Drawing the U-Shaped Line: China's Claim in the South China Sea, 1946–1974." *Modern China* 42, no. 1 (January 2016), 38–72.

Conboy, Ken, and James Morrison. "Plausible Deniability: US-Taiwanese Covert Insertions into North Vietnam." *Air Enthusiast* 18 (November–December 1999), 28–34.

CPC Guangxi Zhuang Autonomous Region Committee. *Zhongguo gongchandang Guangxi lishi* [History of the CPC in Guangxi], vol. 1. Beijing: Zhonggong dangshi chubanshe, 2004.

Culas, Christian, and Jean Michaud. "A Contribution to the Study of Hmong (Miao) Migrations and History." *Bijdragen Tot de Taal-, Land- En Volkenkunde* 153, no. 2 (1997), 211–43.

Đảng cộng sản Việt Nam ban chấp hành đảng bộ tỉnh Lạng Sơn. *Lịch sử đảng bộ tỉnh Lạng Sơn, 1955–1985* [History of the Party Committee of Lạng Sơn province, 1955–1985]. Hanoi: NXB Chính trị quốc gia, 1996.

David, Holm. "The Language Corridor Revisited: Vernacular Scripts and Migration Pathways." *Journal of Chinese Writing Systems* 4, no. 2 (2020), 71–86.

Davis, Bradley Camp. "Black Flag Rumors and the Black River Basin: Powerbrokers and the State in the Tonkin-China Borderlands." *Journal of Vietnamese Studies* 6, no. 2 (Summer 2011), 16–41.
  Imperial Bandits: Outlaws and Rebels in the China-Vietnam Borderlands. Seattle: University of Washington Press, 2017.
Decoux, Jean. *A la barre de l'Indochine: histoire de mon Gouvernement Général, 1940–1945*. Paris: Plon, 1949.
De Gregori, Thomas R. "Resources Are Not; They Become: An Institutional Theory." *Journal of Economic Issues* 21, no. 3 (September 1987), 1241–263.
De Rugy, Marie. *Imperial Borderlands: Maps and Territory-Building in the Northern Indochinese Peninsula (1885–1914)*. Translated by Saskia Brown. London: Brill, 2021.
De Tréglodé, Benoît. "Maritime Boundary Delimitation and Sino-Vietnamese Cooperation in the Gulf of Tonkin (1994–2016)." *China Perspectives*. no. 3 (2016), 33–41.
Del Testa, David W. "Workers, Culture, and the Railroads in French Colonial Indochina, 1905–1936." *French Colonial History* 2, no. 1 (2002), 181–98.
Dell, Melissa, Nathan Lane, and Pablo Querubin. "The Historical State, Local Collective Action, and Economic Development in Vietnam." *Econometrica* 86, no. 6 (2018), 2083–121.
Deng, Kent G. "Unveiling China's True Population Statistics for the Pre-Modern Era with Official Census Data." *Population Review* 43, no. 2 (2004), 32–69.
Deng Lifeng. "Yuanyue kangmei shulue [A brief summary of China's assistance of Vietnam and resistance of the United States]." *Dangdai Zhongguoshi yanjiu* 9, no. 1 (January 2002), 84–92.
Department of Politics of PLA Air Force. *Zhongguo renmin jiefangjun kongjun dashidian* [Chronicles of the Air Force of the PLA]. Los Angeles: Service Center for Chinese Publication, 2011, originally published internally in Chinese in 1993.
Deutscher, Isaac. *Ironies of History*. London: Oxford University Press, 1966.
Dikötter, Frank. *The Tragedy of Liberation: A History of the Chinese Revolution, 1945–1957*. London: Bloomsbury, 2013.
  Mao's Great Famine: The History of China's Most Devastating Catastrophe, 1958–1962. London: Bloomsbury, 2017.
  The Cultural Revolution: A People's History, 1962–1976. New York: Bloomsbury Press, 2017. Reprint ed.
Ding, Yang, Changsheng Chen, Robert C. Beardsley, Xianwen Bao, Maochong Shi, Yu Zhang, Zhigang Lai, Ruixiang Li, Huichan Lin, and Nguyen T Viet. "Observational and Model Studies of the Circulation in the Gulf of Tonkin, South China Sea." *Journal of Geophysical Research: Oceans* 118, no. 12 (2013), 6495–510.
Dinh Quang Hải. "Vấn đề di cư xuyên biên giới của cư dân khu vực biên giới Việt Nam-Trung Quốc giai đoạn 1954–1975 [The issue of cross-border migration of residents in the Vietnam-China border area in the period 1954–1975]." *Nghiên Cứu Lịch Sử Số* 9, no. 509 (2018), 3–14.
Domenach, Jean-Luc. *The Origins of the Great Leap Forward: The Case of One Chinese Province*. Boulder, CO: Westview Press, 1995.

Dommen, J. Arthur. *The Indochinese Experience of the French and the Americans: Nationalism and Communism in Cambodia, Laos, and Vietnam.* Bloomington: Indiana University Press, 2001.

Dreyer, June Teufel. "The Chinese Militia: Citizen-Soldiers and Civil-Military Relations in the People's Republic of China." *Armed Forces & Society* 9, no. 1 (1982), 63–82.

Du Liangliang Alice. "Embodied Borders: The Sino-British Maritime Frontier, 1950–1957." Translated by Mary Ann O'Donnell. *Made in China Journal* 5, no. 3 (2020), 102–7. https://madeinchinajournal.com/2021/04/08/embodied-borders-the-sino-british-maritime-frontier-1950-1957/.

Du Shuhai. "Renkou jiaoshao minzu shengchan fangshi zhuanxing de moshi yanjiu: yi huan Beibuwan Guangxi Jingzu weili [Pattern of transformation of production mode of small-size ethnic groups: An example of the Jing along the Gulf of Tonkin]." *Heilongjiang minzu congkan,* no. 133 (2013), 72–77.

Duan, Zhidan. "At the Edge of Mandalas: The Transformation of the China's Yunnan Borderlands in the 19th and 20th Century." PhD diss., Arizona State University, 2015.

Duiker, William J. *China and Vietnam: The Roots of Conflict.* Berkeley: Institute of East Asian Studies, University of California, 1986.

Historical Dictionary of Vietnam. Metuchen, NJ: Scarecrow Press, 1989.

Vietnam: Revolution in Transition. Boulder, CO: Westview Press, 1995, 2nd ed.

The Communist Road to Power in Vietnam. Boulder, CO: Westview Press, 1996, 2nd ed.

Editorial Board. *Jingzu jianzhi* [Brief introduction of ethnic Kinh]. Nanning: Guangxi minzu chubanshe, 1984.

Jingzu jianshi [Brief history of ethnic Kinh]. Beijing: Minzu chubanshe, 2008.

Editorial Board of the Contemporary China Series. *Dangdai Zhongguo de tiedao shiye* [Railway Industry in Contemporary China]. Beijing: Zhongguo shehui kexue chubanshe, 1990.

Elliott, David W. P. *Changing Worlds: Vietnam's Transition from Cold War to Globalization.* Oxford: Oxford University Press, 2012.

Elman, Benjamin, A. *Science in China, 1600–1900: Essays by Benjamin A. Elman.* Edited by Yi Kai Ho. Singapore: World Century, 2015.

Fairbank, John K. "The Problem of Revolutionary Asia." *Foreign Affairs* 29, no. 1 (1950), 101–13.

Fan Honggui. "Zhong-Yue liangguo de kuajing minzu gaishu [A survey of Sino-Vietnamese cross-border ethnic minorities]." *Minzu yanjiu,* no. 6 (1999), 14–20.

Fan Honggui and Liu Zhiqiang. *Zhong-Yue bianjing maoyi yanjiu* [A study of Sino-Vietnamese border trade]. Beijing: Minzu chubanshe, 2006.

Fan Liping. "Lengzhan shiqi Zhong-Yue tielu guoji lianyun guankui: zhaoyan yu difang cailiao de kaocha [On the international transportation of Sino-Vietnam Railway during the Cold War: Evidence from local records]." *Guangxi shifan daxue xuebao: renwen shehui kexue ban* 46, no. 3 (June 2010), 99–103.

Fravel, Taylor. "Securing Borders: China's Doctrine and Force Structure for Frontier Defence." *The Journal of Strategic Studies* 30, nos. 4–5 (2007), 705–37.

Strong Borders, Secure Nation: Cooperation and Conflict in China's Territorial Disputes. Princeton, NJ: Princeton University Press, 2008.

Friedman, Edward, Paul G. Pickowicz, Mark Seldon, and Kay Ann Johnson. *Chinese Village, Socialist State.* New Haven, CT: Yale University Press, 1993.
FitzGerald, Stephen. *China and the Overseas Chinese: A Study of Peking's Changing Policy, 1949–1970.* Cambridge: Cambridge University Press, 1972.
Gaiduk, Ilya V. *The Soviet Union and the Vietnam War.* Chicago: Ivan R. Dee, 1996.
Gao Jiayi. "Fighting Side by Side: Cross-Border Military Exchanges and Cooperation Between the Chinese Communist Party and the Viet Minh, 1945–1949." *China Review* 19, no. 3 (2019), 123–48.
Gao, Zhiguo, and Bing Bing Jia. "The Nine-Dash Line in the South China Sea: History, Status, and Implications." *The American Journal of International Law* 107, no. 1 (January 2013), 98–124.
Garver, John W. "The Tet Offensive and Sino-Vietnamese Relations." In *The Tet Offensive*, ed. Marc Jason Gilbert and William Head, 45–62. Westport, CT: Praeger, 1996.
China's Quest: The History of the Foreign Relations of the People's Republic of China. Oxford: Oxford University, 2016.
Gavrilis, George. *The Dynamics of Interstate Boundaries.* Cambridge: Cambridge University Press, 2008.
Gérard, Auguste. *Ma Mission en Chine.* Paris: Plon, 1918.
Giersch, C. Patterson. "'Grieving for Tibet': Conceiving the Modern State in Late-Qing Inner Asia." *China Perspective* 3 (2008), 4–18.
Goscha, Christopher E. "The Borders of Vietnam's Early Wartime Trade with Southern China: A Contemporary Perspective." *Asian Survey* 40, no. 6 (2000), 987–1018.
"Courting Diplomatic Disaster? The Difficult Integration of Vietnam into the International Communist Movement (1945–1950)." *Journal of Vietnamese Studies* 1, no. 1/2 (February 2006), 59–103.
Vietnam: Un état né de la guerre, 1945–1954. Paris: A. Colin, 2011.
Historical Dictionary of the Indochina War (1945–1954): An International and Interdisciplinary Approach. Copenhagen: NIAS Press, 2011.
Vietnam: A New History. New York: Basic Books, 2016.
The Road to Dien Bien Phu: A History of the First War for Vietnam. Princeton, NJ: Princeton University Press, 2022.
Granados, Ulises. "Japanese Expansion into the South China Sea: Colonization and Conflict, 1902–1939." *Journal of Asian History* 42, no. 2 (2008), 117–42.
Grémont, Johann. "Pirates et contrebandiers le long de la frontière sino-vietnamienne: une frontière à l'épreuve? (1895–1940)" PhD diss., University of Paris-Diderot, 2017.
Grosser, Pierre. "Chinese Borders and Indigenous Parallels: France, Vietnam, and the 'Korean Model.'" *Eurasia Border Review* 3 Special Issue (2012), 55–73.
Guo, Jie. "'Going to the Land of Barbarians': Nation, Ethnicity, and the Female Body in Late Qing and Republican Travel Writing on the Yunnan-Burma Borderlands." *Frontiers of Literary Studies in China* 8, no. 1 (2014), 5–30.
Guo Ming. *Zhong-Yue guanxi yanbian sishinian* [The 40-year evolution of Sino-Vietnamese relations]. Nanning: Guangxi renmin chubanshe, 1992.
Guo Mingjin. "Zhongguo budui zai Yuenan Heyang zhengxun de rizi [Days of Chinese troops training in Hà Giang, Vietnam]." *Wenshi chunqiu* 7 (2009), 31–33.

Gupta, Charu, and Mukul Sharma. *Contested Coastlines: Fisherfolk, Nations and Borders in South Asia*. New Delhi: Routledge, 2007.
Hà Minh Trần. *Lịch sử Ủy Ban Mặt Trận Tổ Quốc Việt Nam Tỉnh Cao Bằng, 1930–2003* [History of Vietnam Fatherland Front Cao Bằng Provincial Committee, 1930–2003]. Hanoi: NXB Thanh Niên, 2000.
Hämäläinen, Pekka, and Benjamin Heber Johnson, eds. *Major Problems in the History of North American Borderlands: Documents and Essays*. Boston: Cengage Learning, 2012.
Han, Xiaorong. *Chinese Discourses on the Peasant, 1900–1949*. New York: SUNY Press, 2005.
  "Spoiled Guests or Dedicated Patriots: The Chinese in North Vietnam, 1954–1978." *International Journal of Asian Studies* 6, no. 1 (2009), 1–36.
  "The Demise of China's Overseas Chinese State Farms." *Journal of Chinese Overseas* 9, no. 1 (2013), 33–58.
  Red God: Wei Baqun and His Peasant Revolution in Southern China, 1894–1932. New York: SUNY Press, 2014.
Han, Enze. "Neighborhood Effect of Borderland State Consolidation: Evidence from Myanmar and Its Neighbors." *The Pacific Review* 22, no. 2 (2020), 305–30.
  Asymmetrical Neighbors: Borderland State-building between China and Southeast Asia. New York: Oxford University Press, 2019.
Harrell, Stevan, and Yongxiang Li. "The History of the History of the Yi, Part II." *Modern China* 29, no. 3 (July 2003), 362–96.
He, Xi, and David Faure. "Introduction: Boat-and-shed Living in Land-based Society." In *The Fisher Folk of Late Imperial and Modern China: An Historical Anthropology of Boat-and-Shed Living*, ed. Xi He and David Faure, 1–29. London: Routledge, 2016.
He Zhiming. "Qianli da 'shuxue': xin Zhongguo nanxia ganbu ['Blood fusion' across thousands of miles: cadres transferred to the south during early PRC]." *Yanhuang Chunqiu*, no. 5 (2019), 34–38.
Hershberg, James G., and Chen Jian. "Reading and Warning the Likely Enemy: China's Signals to the United States about Vietnam in 1965." *International History Review* 27, no. 1 (February 2005), 47–84.
Ho, David Yau-Fai. "On the Concept of Face." *American Journal of Sociology* 81, no. 4 (1976), 867–84.
Hoàng Phương. *Hậu phương chiến tranh nhân dân Việt Nam (1945–1975)* [Behind the Vietnamese People's War, 1945–1975]. Hanoi: NXB Quân đội nhân dân, 1997. www.quansuvn.net/index.php?topic=30184.0.
Hoàng Thị Kim Thanh. *Lịch sử đảng bộ thị xã Móng Cái, 1946–2006* [History of party committee of Móng Cái town, 1946–2006]. Hanoi: NXB Chính trị quốc gia, 2008.
Hoàng Văn Thường and Nguyễn Thành Hoành. *Lịch sử đảng bộ khối các cơ quan tỉnh Lạng Sơn* [History of party committees and agencies in Lạng Sơn province]. Hanoi: NXB Văn Hóa Thông Tin, 2013.
Hou Bo. "Xin Zhongguo chuqi Guangdong yanhai yuye minzhu gaige yu jiaqiang haifang de douzheng [The fishery reform and struggle to strengthen coastal defense in Guangdong during the early years of PRC]." *Fazhi yu shehui* 5 (2019), 247–50.
Howell, David. *Capitalism from Within: Economy, Society and the State in a Japanese Fishery*. Berkeley: University of California Press, 1995.

Huang Shuolin. *Haiyangfa yu yuye fagui* [The law of the sea and fisheries legislation]. Beijing: Zhongguo nongye chubanshe, 1999.

Huang, Shuolin, and Yuru He. "Management of China's Capture Fisheries: Review and Prospect." *Aquaculture and Fisheries* 4 (2019), 173–82.

Hui, Victoria Tin-bor. "How Tilly's State Formation Paradigm Is Revolutionizing the Study of Chinese State-Making." In *Does War Make States? Investigations of Charles Tilly's Historical Sociology*, ed. Lar Bo Kaspersen and Jeppe Strandsbjerg, 268–95. Cambridge: Cambridge University Press, 2017.

Hung, Chang-tai. *War and Popular Culture: Resistance in Modern China, 1937–1945*. Berkeley: University of California Press, 1994.

Hutchings, Graham. "A Province at War: Guangxi during the Sino-Japanese Conflict, 1937–1945." *The China Quarterly*, no. 108 (December 1986), 652–79.

Huỳnh Kim Khánh. *Vietnamese Communism, 1925–1945*. Ithaca, NY: Cornell University Press, 1986.

Hyun, Sinae. *Indigenizing the Cold War: The Border Patrol Police and Nation-Building in Thailand*. Honolulu: University of Hawai'i Press, 2023.

Ike, Kyōkichi. *Zhongguo geming shidi jianwen lu* [Firsthand account of the Chinese revolution]. Shanghai: Sanmin gongsi, 1927.

Ishikawa, Noboru. *Between Frontiers: Nation and Identity in a Southeast Asian Borderland*. Athens: Ohio University Press, 2010.

——— "Genesis of State Space: Frontier Commodification in Malaysian Borneo." In *Routledge Handbook of Asian Borderlands*, ed. Alexander Horstmann, Martin Saxer, and Alessandro Rippa, 168–79. London: Routledge, 2018.

Ito Masako. *Politics of Ethnic Classification in Vietnam*. Translated by Minako Sato. Kyoto: Kyoto University Press, 2013.

——— "Foreword." Special Issue: The Ngái in Vietnam: The History, Religion, and Ethnicity of the Minority People of Hakka Origin. *Asian and African Area Studies* 17, no. 2 (2018), 175–79.

Jerez, Montserrat López. "Colonial and Indigenous Institutions in the Fiscal Development of French Indochina." In *Fiscal Capacity and the Colonial State in Asia and Africa, c. 1850–1960*, ed. Ewout Frankema and Anne Booth, 110–36. Cambridge: Cambridge University Press, 2019.

Ji Xiaosong. "Yuanyue kangmei zhong de Zhongguo 'hongweibing zhiyuanzhe' ['Chinese Red Guards volunteers' during the assisting Vietnam and resisting America campaign]." *Wenshi bolan*, no. 8 (2008), 50–53.

Johnson, Chalmers A. *Peasant Nationalism and Communist Power: The Emergence of Revolutionary China, 1937–1945*. Stanford, CA: Stanford University Press, 1963.

Johnson, Jason B. *Divided Village: The Cold War in the German Borderlands*. New York: Routledge, 2018.

Kang, Xiaofei, ed. *Women, Family and the Chinese Socialist State, 1950–2010*. Boston: Brill, 2019.

Kaup, Katherine Palmer. *Creating the Zhuang: Ethnic Politics in China*. Boulder CO: Lynne Rienner, 2000.

Keck-Szajbel, Mark, and Dariusz Stola. "Crossing the Borders of Friendship: Mobility across Communist Borders." *East European Politics and Societies and Cultures* 29, no. 1 (2015), 92–95.

Kerkvliet, Benedict J. T. *The Power of Everyday Politics: How Vietnamese Peasants Transformed National Policy*. Ithaca, NY: Cornell University Press, 2005.

Khan, Sulmaan Wasif. *Muslim, Trader, Nomad, Spy: China's Cold War and the People of the Tibetan Borderlands*. Chapel Hill: University of North Carolina Press, 2015.

Khoo, Nicholas. "Breaking the Ring of Encirclement: The Sino-Soviet Rift and Chinese Policy toward Vietnam, 1964–1968." *Journal of Cold War Studies* 12, no. 1 (2010), 3–42.

Collateral Damage: Sino-Soviet Rivalry and the Termination of the Sino-Vietnamese Alliance. New York: Columbia University Press, 2011.

Kim, Chin. "The Marriage and Family Law of North Vietnam." *The International Lawyer* 7, no. 2 (April 1973), 440–50.

Kinzley, Judd C. *Natural Resources and the New Frontier: Constructing Modern Borderlands*. Chicago: University of Chicago Press, 2018.

Kirby, William. "The Internationalization of China: Foreign Relations at Home and Abroad in the Republican Era." *China Quarterly* 150, Special Issue on Reappraising Republic of China (June 1997), 433–58.

Kleinen, John. "'Stealing from the Gods': Fisheries and Local Use of Natural Resources in Vietnam 1800–2000." In *A History of Natural Resources in Asia: The Wealth of Nation*, ed. Greg Bankoff and Peter Boomgaard, 245–63. London: Palgrave MacMillan, 2007.

Ku, Agnes S. "Immigration Policies, Discourses, and the Politics of Local Belonging in Hong Kong (1950–1980)." *Modern China* 30, no. 3 (July 2004), 326–60.

Kraus, Charles. "A Border Region 'Exuded with Militant Friendship': Provincial Narratives of China's Participation in the First Indochina War, 1949–1954." *Cold War History* 12, no. 3 (2012), 495–514.

Lai, Chi-kong. "Li Hung-chang and Modern Enterprise: The China Merchants' Company, 1872–1885." *Chinese Studies in History* 25, no. 1 (1991), 19–51.

Laffey, Ella S. "In the Wake of the Taipings: Some Patterns of Local Revolt in Kwangsi Province, 1850–1875." *Modern Asian Studies* 10, no. 1 (1976), 65–81.

Lary, Diana. "A Zone of Nebulous Menace: The Guangxi/Indochina Border in the Republican Period." In *The Chinese State at the Borders*, ed. Diana Lary, 181–97. Vancouver: University of British Columbia, 2014.

Lawrence, Mark Atwood. *The Vietnam War: A Concise International History*. Oxford: Oxford University Press, 2008.

Le Failler, Philippe. *La rivière Noire: L'intégration d'une marche frontière au Vietnam*. Paris: CNRS, 2014.

Lê Văn Yên. *Đảng Cộng sản Việt Nam: 80 năm xây dựng và phát triển* [Vietnamese Communist Party: 80 Years of Construction and Development]. Hanoi: NXB Chính trị quốc gia, 2010.

Leake, Elisabeth, and Daniel Haines. "Lines of (In)Convenience: Sovereignty and Border-Making in Postcolonial South Asia, 1947–1965." *The Journal of Asian Studies* 76, no. 4 (2017), 963–85.

Legerton, Colin, and Jacob Rawson. *Invisible China: A Journey through Ethnic Borderlands*. Chicago: Chicago Review Press, 2009.

Lentz, Christian C. "Making the Northwest Vietnamese." *Journal of Vietnamese Studies* 6, no. 2 (June 2011), 68–105.

"Mobilization and State Formation on a Frontier of Vietnam." *Journal of Peasant Studies* 38, no. 3 (2011), 559–86.

"Cultivating Subjects: Opium and Rule in Post-colonial Vietnam." *Modern Asian Studies* 51, no. 4 (2017), 879–918.

Contested Territory: Điện Biên Phủ and the Making of Northwest Vietnam. New Haven, CT: Yale University Press, 2019.
Lessard, Micheline. *Human Trafficking in Colonial Vietnam*. New York: Routledge, 2015.
Levich, Eugene William. *The Kwangsi Way in Kuomintang China, 1931–1939*. London: M. E. Sharpe, 1993.
Li, Huaiyin. *The Making of the Modern Chinese State, 1600–1950*. London: Routledge, 2020.
Li, Ke, and Sara L. Friedman. "Wedding Marriage to the Nation-State in Modern China: Legal Consequences for Divorce, Property, and Women's Rights." In *Domestic Tensions National Anxieties: Global Perspectives on Marriage, Crisis, and Nation*, ed. Kristen Celello and Hanan Kholoussy, 148–51. Oxford: Oxford University Press, 2016.
Li Qingde. "Yuanyue kangmei zhong de tiedao baozhang [Railway support during the assisting Vietnam and resisting America campaign]." In *Tiedaobing: huiyi shiliao* [Railway corps: memoirs and materials], ed. Editorial Committee of the PLA History Series, 282–304. Beijing: Jiefangjun chubanshe, 1998.
Li Shihao and Qu Ruoqian. *Zhongguo yuye shi* [History of fishery in China]. Shanghai: Shangwu yinshuguan, 1937.
Li, Tana. "A View from the Sea: Perspectives on the Northern and Central Vietnamese Coast." *Journal of Southeast Asian Studies* 37 (2006), 83–102.
"Between Mountains and the Sea: Trades in Early Nineteenth-Century Northern Vietnam." *Journal of Vietnamese Studies* 7, no. 2 (Summer 2012), 67–86.
"Epidemics, Trade, and Local Worship in Vietnam, Leizhou Peninsula, and Hainan Island." In *Imperial China and Its Southern Neighbours*, ed. Victor Mair and Liam Kelley, 194–213. Singapore: ISEAS-Yusof Ishak Institute, 2015.
Li, Xiaobing. *The Cold War in East Asia*. New York: Routledge, 2018.
Building Ho's Army: Chinese Military Assistance to North Vietnam. Lexington: University of Kentucky Press, 2019.
The Dragon in the Jungle: The Chinese Army in the Vietnam War. Oxford: Oxford University Press, 2020.
Liang Jinrong. *Guangxi jingji nianjian 1985* [Guangxi Economic Yearbook 1985]. Nanning: Guangxi jingji nianjian bianjibu, 1985.
Litzinger, Ralph A. *Other Chinas: The Yao and the Politics of National Belonging*. Durham, NC: Duke University Press, 2000.
Liu Weidong. "Kangzhan qianqi guomin zhengfu dui Yinzhi tongdao de jingying [Management of transportation routes with Indochina by the government of Republic of China during the early years of Anti-Japanese War]." *Jindaishi yanjiu*, no. 5 (1998), 124–28.
Liu Xiaoming. *Yuanyue kangmei Jingzu fanyiguan jishi* [Memoirs of Kinh interpreters]. Self-published, 2017.
Luong, Hy Van. *Revolution in the Village: Tradition and Transformation in North Vietnam, 1925–1988*. Honolulu: University of Hawai'i Press, 1992.
Luong, Nhi Quynh. "A Handbook on the Background of Ethnic Chinese from North Vietnam." MA Thesis, California State University, Sacramento, 1988.
Lüthi, Lorenz M. *The Sino-Soviet Split: Cold War in the Communist World*. Princeton, NJ: Princeton University Press, 2008.

"The Vietnam War and China's Third-Line Defense Planning before the Cultural Revolution, 1964–1966." *Journal of Cold War Studies* 10, no. 1 (2008), 26–51.

"Beyond Betrayal: Beijing, Moscow and the Paris Negotiations, 1971–1973." *Journal of Cold War Studies* 11, no. 1 (2009), 57–107.

Ma Faxiang. "Zhouzongli yunchou yuanYue saolei: fang haijun yuan fucanmouzhang Lai Guangzu jiangjun [Premier Zhou's facilitation of helping Vietnam with minesweeping: an interview with former Deputy Chief of Staff of PLA Navy General Lai Guangzu]," *Junshi lishi*, no. 5 (1989), 35–37, 49.

MacFarquhar, Roderick. *The Origins of the Cultural Revolution, Volume 3: The Coming of the Cataclysm, 1961–1966*. New York: Columbia University Press, 1999.

MacLean, Ken. "In Search of Kilometer Zero: Digital Archives, Technological Revisionism, and the Sino-Vietnamese Border." *Comparative Studies in Society and History* 50 (October 2008), 862–94.

Maier, Charles S. "Consigning the Twentieth Century to History: Alternative Narratives for the Modern Era." *The American Historical Review* 105, no. 3 (2000), 807–31.

Marks, Robert B. *Tigers, Rice, Silk, and Silt: Environment and Economy in Late Imperial South China*. Cambridge; New York: Cambridge University Press, 1998.

Marr, David. *Vietnam, 1945: The Quest for Power*. Berkeley: University of California Press, 1995.

Masuda, Hajimu. "The Cold War as Social Mechanism: Toward an Analysis of Cold War Asia, Not of the Cold War in Asia." International Institute of Asian Studies. *The Newsletter* 72 (Autumn 2015), 8–9.

Matthews, Mervyn. *The Passport Society: Controlling Movement in Russia and the USSR*. Boulder, CO: Westview Press, 1993.

McHale, Shawn F. *The First Vietnam War: Violence, Sovereignty, and the Fracture of the South, 1945–56*. Cambridge: Cambridge University Press, 2021.

McNamara, Robert S., James G. Blight, Robert K. Brigham, Thomas J. Biersteker, and Herbert Schandler. *Argument Without End: In Search of Answers to the Vietnam Tragedy*. New York: Public Affairs, 1999.

Meisner, Maurice. "Leninism and Maoism: Some Populist Perspectives in Marxism-Leninism in China." *The China Quarterly*, no. 45 (January–March 1971), 2–36.

Mao's China: A History of the People's Republic. New York: Simon & Schuster, 1999, 3rd ed.

Meyskens, Covell F. *Mao's Third Front: The Militarization of Cold War China*. Cambridge: Cambridge University Press, 2020.

Michaud, Jean. "Economic Transformation in a Hmong Village of Thailand." *Human Organization* 56, no. 2 (Summer 1997), 222–32.

"Incidental" Ethnographers: French Catholic Missions on the Tonkin-Yunnan Frontier, 1880–1930. Boston: Brill, 2007.

Michaud, Jean, Sarah Turner, and Yann Roche. "Mapping Ethnic Diversity in Highland Northern Vietnam." *GeoJournal* 57 (2002), 291–99.

Miller, E. Willard. "Mineral Resources of Indo-China." *Economic Geography* 22, no. 4 (October 1946), 268–79.

Mo Wenhua. *Mo Wenhua huiyilu* [Memoir of Mo Wenhua]. Beijing: Jiefangjun chubanshe, 1996.

Moïse, Edwin E. *Land Reform in China and North Vietnam: Consolidating the Revolution at the Village Level*. Chapel Hill: University of North Carolina Press, 1983.

Morieux, Renaud. *The Channel: England, France and the Construction of a Maritime Border in the Eighteenth Century*. Cambridge: Cambridge University Press, 2017.

Mullaney, Thomas S. *Coming to Terms with the Nation: Ethnic Classification in Modern China*. Berkeley: University of California Press, 2012.

Muscolino, Micah S. *Fishing Wars and Environmental Change in Late Imperial and Modern China*. Cambridge, MA: Harvard University Asia Center; Distributed by Harvard University Press, 2009.

Namba, Chizuru. "Colonization and Forestry in French Indochina: The Control, Use, and Exploitation of Forests." *Asian Review of World Histories* 9, no. 1 (2020), 24–58.

Nelsen, Harvey. "Military Forces in the Cultural Revolution." *The China Quarterly*, no. 51 (1972), 444–74.

Newman, David. "On Borders and Power: A Theoretical Framework." *Journal of Borderlands Studies*, 18, no. 1 (2003), 13–25.

Ng Chin-Keong. *Boundaries and Beyond: China's Maritime Southeast in Late Imperial*. Singapore: National University of Singapore Press, 2017.

Nguyễn Bá Diến. "Về việc ký kết hiệp định hợp tác nghề cá ở vịnh Bắc Bộ giữa Việt Nam và Trung Quốc [On the signing of a fishery cooperation agreement in the Gulf of Tonkin between Vietnam and China]." *Tạp chí Khoa học – ĐẠI HỌC QUỐC GIA HÀ NỘI* 25 (2009), 74–86.

Nguyen Hong Thao and Ramses Amer. "Managing Vietnam's Maritime Boundary Disputes." *Ocean Development & International Law* 38, no. 3 (2007), 305–24.

Nguyen, Lien-Hang T. "The War Politburo: North Vietnam's Diplomatic and Political Road to the Tết Offensive." *Journal of Vietnamese Studies* 1, nos. 1–2 (February/August 2006), 4–58.

"The Sino-Vietnamese Split and the Indochina War, 1968–1975." In *The Third Indochina War: Conflict Between China, Vietnam and Cambodia, 1972–79*, ed. Odd Arne Westad and Sophie Quinn-Judge, 12–32. London: Routledge, 2006.

Hanoi's War: An International History of the War for Peace in Vietnam. Chapel Hill: University of North Carolina Press, 2012.

Nguyễn Phúc Luân and Học viện Quan hệ quốc tế. *Ngoại giao Việt Nam hiện đại: vì sự nghiệp giành độc lập, tự do: 1945–1975* [Contemporary Vietnamese diplomacy: for independence and freedom]. Hanoi: NXB Chính trị quốc gia, 2001.

Nguyễn Thị Mai Hoa. *Các nước xã hội chủ nghĩa ủng hộ Việt Nam kháng chiến chống Mỹ cứu nước* [Socialist countries' assistance to Vietnam's resistance against America to save the country]. Hanoi: NXB Chính trị Quốc gia, 2013.

Nguyễn Thị Phương Hóa, ed. *Một số vấn đề an ninh phi truyền thống ở khu vực biên giới Việt – Trung* [Some non-traditional security issues in the Vietnamese-Chinese border area]. Hà Nội: NXB Khoa học xã hội, 2018.

Nguyen, Thuy Linh. "Dynamite, Opium, and a Transnational Shadow Economy at Tonkinese Coal Mines." *Modern Asian Studies* 54, no. 6 (2020), 1876–904.

Nguyễn Văn Chính. "Memories, Migration and the Ambiguity of Ethnic Identity: The Cases of Ngái, Nùng and Khách in Vietnam." Special Issue: The Ngái in Vietnam:

The History, Religion, and Ethnicity of the Minority People of Hakka Origin. *Asian and African Area Studies* 17, no. 2 (2018), 207–26.

"Ethnic Chinese in the Sino-Vietnamese Borderlands: Debates over Loyalty and Identity." *Journal of Vietnamese Studies* 16, no. 4 (2021), 1–35.

Niu Jun. "1962: The Eve of the Left Turn in China's Foreign Policy." Cold War International History Project Working Paper No. 48. Woodrow Wilson International Center for Scholars, Washington DC, October 2005.

Notice sur le Kouang-Si rédigée à l'Etat-major des troupes de l'Indo-Chine (mars 1900). Hanoi: F.-H. Schneider, 1900.

Nong Wenke. *Zhongguo gongchandang Pingxiang lishi* [History of the CPC in Pingxiang], vol. 2, 1949–1991. Nanning: Guangxi renmin chubanshe, 2015.

Office of Party History of CPC Yunnan Provincial Committee. *Wen'ge fansi huiyi shiliao zhiba: Yunnan wenhua dageming yundong dashi jishi* [Reflection and memoirs of the Cultural Revolution, no. 8: Chronicles of the Cultural Revolution in Yunnan]. Los Angeles: Service Center for Chinese Publications, 2007 (republished).

Oi, Jean C. "The Role of the Local State in China's Transitional Economy." *The China Quarterly*, no. 144 (1995), 1132–49.

O'Leary, Greg and Andrew Watson. "The Role of People's Commune in Rural Development in China." *Pacific Affairs* 55, no. 4 (December 1982), 593–612.

Osborne, Milton E. "Strategic Hamlets in South Vietnam: A Survey and a Comparison." Data Paper no. 55. Department of Asian Studies, Cornell University. Ithaca, NY, 1965.

Pang Zi. "Zai Yuenan gongzuo he zhandou de suiyue [Years of working and fighting in Vietnam]." *Bainianchao* 12 (1999), 33–38.

Path, Kosal. "Hanoi's Response to Beijing's Enthusiasm to Aid North Vietnam, 1970–72." *Journal of Vietnamese Studies* 6, no. 3 (Fall 2011), 101–39.

"The Sino-Vietnamese Dispute over Territorial Claims, 1974–1978: Vietnamese Nationalism and Its Consequences." *International Journal of Asian Studies* 8, no. 2 (2011), 189–220.

"The Politics of China's Aid to North Vietnam during the Anti-American Resistance, 1965–1969." *Diplomacy & Statecraft* 27, no. 4 (2016), 682–700.

Vietnam's Strategic Thinking during the Third Indochina War. Madison: University of Wisconsin Press 2020.

Perry, Elizabeth. "Moving the Masses: Emotion Work in the Chinese Revolution." *Mobilization: An International Journal* 7, no. 2 (2002), 111–28.

Peterson, Glen. *The Power of Words: Literacy and Revolution in South China, 1949–95*. Vancouver: University of British Columbia Press, 1997.

Phạm Thị Vượng. "Hoạt động khai hoang của nông trường quốc doanh ở miền Bắc Việt Nam từ năm 1955 đến năm 1975 [Reclamation activities of state-owned farms in the North of Vietnam, 1955–1975]." *Nghiên Cứu Lịch Sử, Số* 8 (2019), 60–68.

Prusin, Alexander V. *The Lands Between: Conflict in the East European Borderlands, 1870–1992*. Oxford: Oxford University Press, 2010.

Qiu Geping. "Bei guailai de 'Yuenan xinniang': fanzuixue de fenxi [The Abducted 'Vietnamese Brides': Criminological Analysis]." *Jingyue Journal*, no. 3 (2020), 7–19.

Qu Aiguo. *Yuanyue kangmei: Zhongguo zhiyuan budui zai Yuenan* [Assisting Vietnam and Resisting America: Chinese assistance corps in Vietnam]. Beijing: Junshi kexue chubanshe, 1995.

Quinn-Judge, Sophie. *Ho Chi Minh: The Missing Years, 1919–1941*. Berkeley: University of California Press, 2002.

Race, Jeffrey. *War Comes to Long An: Revolutionary Conflict in a Vietnamese Province*. Berkeley: University of California Press, 2010, updated and expanded ed.

Radcheko, Sergey. *Two Suns in the Heavens: The Sino-Soviet Struggle for Supremacy, 1962–1967*. Washington, DC: Woodrow Wilson Center Press, 2009.

Readman, Paul, Cynthia Radding, and Chad Bryant, eds. *Borderlands in World History, 1700–1914*. London: Palgrave MacMillan, 2014.

Remick, Elizabeth J. *Building Local States: China during the Republican and Post-Mao Eras*. Cambridge, MA: Harvard University Press, 2004.

Roberts, Priscilla, ed. *Behind the Bamboo Curtain: China, Vietnam, and the World beyond Asia*. Stanford, CA: Stanford University Press, 2007.

Rogers, Frank E. "Sino-American Relations and the Vietnam War, 1964–66." *The China Quarterly*, no. 66 (June 1976), 293–314.

Roper, Christopher T. "Sino-Vietnamese Relations and the Economy of Vietnam's Border Region." *Asian Survey* 40, no. 6 (2000), 1019–41.

Roszko, Edyta. "Fishers and Territorial Anxieties in China and Vietnam: Narratives of the South China Sea Beyond the Frame of the Nation." *Cross-Currents: East Asian History and Culture Review*. E-Journal 21 (December 2016), 19–46.

Fishers, Monks and Cadres: Navigating State, Religion and the South China Sea in Central Vietnam. Copenhagen: Nordic Institute of Asian Studies, 2020.

Rousseau, Jean-François. "An Imperial Railway Failure: Indochina-Yunnan Railway, 1898–1941." *The Journal of Transport History* 35, no. 1 (June 2014), 1–17.

Seldon, Mark. *The Yenan Way in Revolutionary China*. Cambridge, MA: Harvard University Press, 1971.

Schoenberger, Laura, and Sarah Turner. "Negotiating Remote Borderland Access: Small-Scale Trade on the Vietnam-China Border." *Development and Change* 39, no. 4 (2008), 667–96.

Scott, James C. *The Moral Economy of the Peasant: Rebellion and Subsistence in Southeast Asia*. New Haven, CT: Yale University Press, 1976.

Domination and the Arts of Resistance: Hidden Transcripts. New Haven, CT: Yale University Press, 1990.

Seeing Like a State: How Certain Schemes to Improve the Human Condition Have Failed. New Haven, CT: Yale University Press, 1998.

The Art of Not Being Governed: An Anarchist History of Upland Southeast Asia. New Haven, CT: Yale University Press, 2009.

Shen, Zhihua, and Julia Lovell. "Undesired Outcomes: China's Approach to Border Disputes during the Early Cold War." *Cold War History* 15, no. 1 (2015), 89–111.

Shen, Zhihua, and Li Danhui. "Jiegou shiheng: Zhong-Su tongmeng polie de shencengyuan yin [Structural imbalance: the roots of the collapse of the Sino-Soviet alliance]." *Tansuo yu zhengming* 10 (2012), 7–9.

Shen, Zhihua, and Yafeng Xia. "The Great Leap Forward, the People's Commune and the Sino-Soviet Split." *Journal of Contemporary China* 20, no. 72 (2011), 861–80.

A Misunderstood Friendship: Mao Zedong, Kim Il-sung, and Sino-North Korean Relations, 1949–1976. New York: Columbia University Press, 2020, rev. ed.

Bibliography

Shen, Xiaoyun. "The Revolutionary Committee Grows Out of the Barrel of a Gun during the Great Proletarian Cultural Revolution: The Unknown Truth of 'Armed Conflict' in Guangxi." *Modern China Studies* 20, no. 1 (2013), 141–82.

Shih, Chih-yu. *Autonomy, Ethnicity, and Poverty in Southwestern China: The State Turned Upside Down.* New York: Palgrave Macmillan, 2007.

Shin, Leo K. "Ming China and Its Border with Annam." In *The Chinese State at the Borders*, ed. Diana Lary, 91–104. Vancouver: University of British Columbia Press, 2007.

Shue, Vivienne. *The Reach of the State: Sketches of the Chinese Body Politic.* Stanford: Stanford University Press, 1988.

Shum, Kui-Kwong. *The Chinese Communists' Road to Power: The Anti-Japanese National United Front, 1935–1945.* New York: Oxford University Press, 1988.

Siu, Helen F. *Agents and Victims in South China: Accomplices in Rural Revolution.* New Haven, CT: Yale University Press, 1989.

Skocpol, Theda. *States and Social Revolutions: A Comparative Analysis of France, Russia, and China.* Cambridge: Cambridge University Press, 1979.

Spence, Jonathan D. *The Search for Modern China.* New York: W. W. Norton & Company, 1999, 2nd ed.

Sở Giao thông Vận tải Cao Bằng [Department of Transport of Cao Bằng]. *Lịch sử Giao thông Vận tải Cao Bằng* [History of transport of Cao Bằng]. Hanoi: NXB Giao thông Vận tải, 1999.

Strauss, Julia C. "Paternalist Terror: The Campaign to Suppress Counterrevolutionaries and Regime Consolidation in the People's Republic of China, 1950–1953." *Comparative Studies in Society and History* 44 (January 2002), 80–105.

St. John, Rachel. *Line in the Sand: A History of the Western U.S.-Mexico Border.* Princeton, NJ: Princeton University Press, 2011.

St. John, Ronald Bruce. "The Land Boundaries of Indochina: Cambodia, Laos and Vietnam." *Boundary and Territory Briefing* 2, no. 6 (1998), 1–51.

Su, Yang. *Collective Killings in Rural China during the Cultural Revolution.* Cambridge: Cambridge University Press, 2011.

Sunderland, Willard. *Taming the Wild Field: Colonization and Empire on the Russian Steppe.* Ithaca, NY: Cornell University press, 2004.

Sutton, Donald S. "Consuming Counterrevolution: The Ritual and Culture of Cannibalism in Wuxuan, Guangxi, China, May to July 1968." *Comparative Studies in Society and History* 37, no. 1 (1995), 136–72.

Szalontai, Balazs. "Political and Economic Crisis in North Vietnam, 1955–56." *Cold War History* 5, no. 4 (2005), 395–426.

Szonyi, Michael. *Cold War Island: Quemoy on the Front Line.* Cambridge: Cambridge University Press, 2008.

The Art of Being Governed: Everyday Politics in Later Imperial China. Princeton, NJ: Princeton University Press, 2019.

Tagliacozzo, Eric. "Jagged Landscapes: Conceptualizing Borders and Boundaries in the History of Human Societies." *Journal of Borderlands Studies* 31, no. 1 (2016), 1–21,

Taylor, Keith. *A History of Vietnamese.* Cambridge: Cambridge University Press, 2013.

Thai, Philip. *China's War on Smuggling: Law, Economic Life, and the Making of the Modern State, 1842–1965.* New York: Columbia University Press, 2018.

Thaxton, Ralph A. Jr. *Force and Contention in Contemporary China: Memory and Resistance in the Long Shadow of the Catastrophic Past*. Cambridge: Cambridge University Press, 2016.

Tilly, Charles. "Reflections on the History of European State Making." In *Formation of National States in Western Europe*, ed. Charles Tilly, 3–83. Princeton, NJ: Princeton University Press, 1975.

Tønnesson, Stein. "The Tonkin Gulf Agreements: A Model of Conflict Resolution?" In *The South China Sea: A Crucible of Regional Cooperation or Conflict-making Sovereignty Claims?*, ed. C. J. Jenner and Tran Truong Thuy, 151–70. Cambridge: Cambridge University Press, 2016.

Trần Đức Lai. *The Nung Ethnic and Autonomous Territory of Hai Ninh-Vietnam*. Translated by Ngô Thanh Tùng. s.l.: The Hai Ninh Veterans & Public Administration Alumni Association Vietnam, 2013.

Trần Đức Thạnh. *Thiên nhiên và môi trường vùng biển đảo Bạch Long Vĩ* [Nature and the environment on the Island of Bạch Long Vĩ]. Hanoi: NXB Khoa học Tự nhiên và Công nghệ, 2013.

Trần Khánh. *The Ethnic Chinese and Economic Development in Vietnam*. Singapore: Institute of Southeast Asian Studies, 1993.

Trần Minh Thái, Nguyễn Văn Kỳ, and Phạm Hồng Thụy. *Quảng Ninh–Lịch sử kháng chiến chống thực dân Pháp xâm lược* [Quảng Ninh: History of resistance war against the French colonialists]. Hanoi: NXB Quân đội nhân dân, 1991.

Trần Phương. *Cách mạng ruộng đất ở Việt Nam* [Land revolution in Vietnam]. Hanoi: NXB Khoa học xã hội, 1968.

Turner, Sarah. "Borderlands and Border Narratives: A Longitudinal Study of Challenges and Opportunities for Local Traders Shaped by the Sino-Vietnamese Border." *Journal of Global History* 5, no. 2 (2010), 265–87.

Ungar, E. S. "The Struggle over the Chinese Community in Vietnam, 1946–1986." *Pacific Affairs* 60, no. 4 (Winter, 1987–88), 596–614.

Unger, Jonathan. "The Class System in Rural China: A Case Study." In *Class and Social Stratification in Post-Revolution China*, ed. James Watson, 121–41. Cambridge: Cambridge University Press, 1984.

——— "State and Peasant in Post-Revolution China." *The Journal of Peasant Studies* 17, no. 1 (October 1989), 114–36

——— "Not Quite Han: The Ethnic Minorities of China's Southwest." *Bulletin of Concerned Asian Scholars* 29, no. 3 (2000), 67–78.

Van Schendel, Willem. "Geographies of Knowing, Geographies of Ignorance: Jumping Scale in Southeast Asia." *Environment and Planning D: Society and Space* 20, no. 6 (2002), 647–68.

Van Schendel, Willem, and Erik de Maaker. "Asian Borderlands: Introducing Their Permeability, Strategic Uses and Meanings." *Journal of Borderlands Studies* 29, no. 1 (2014), 3–9.

Võ Nguyên Giáp. *Chiến đấu trong vòng vây: Trích từ Võ Nguyên Giáp - Tổng tập hồi ký* [Fighting under siege: collections from the memoirs of General Võ Nguyên Giáp]. Hanoi: NXB Quân đội Nhân dân, 2006.

Vũ Đường Luân. "Contested Sovereignty: Local Politics and State Power in Territorial Conflicts on the Vietnam-China Border, 1650s–1880s." *Cross-Currents: East Asian History and Culture Review* 20 (2016), 40–74.

Vu, Tuong. "The Revolutionary Path to State Formation in Vietnam: Opportunities, Conundrums, and Legacies." *Journal of Vietnamese Studies* 11, no. 3/4 (Summer-Fall 2016), 267–97.

Wade, Geoff. "The Southern Chinese Borders in History." In *Where China Meets Southeast Asia: Social & Cultural Change in the Border Regions*, ed. Grant Evans, Christopher Hutton, and Kuah Khun Eng, 28–50. New York: St. Martin's Press, 2000.

Walder, Andrew G. *Civil War in Guangxi: The Cultural Revolution on China's Southern Periphery*. Stanford, CA: Stanford University Press, 2023.

Wallerstein, Immanuel. "What Cold War in Asia? An Interpretive Essay." In *The Cold War in Asia: The Battle for Hearts and Minds*, ed. Zheng Yangwen, Hong Liu, and Michael Szonyi, 15–24. Boston, MA: Brill, 2010.

Wang Defa. *Zhonghua minguo tongjishi, 1912–1949* [History of the statistics of the Republic of China, 1912–1949]. Shanghai: Shanghai caijing daxue chubanshe, 2017.

Wang, Haiguang. "Radical Agricultural Collectivization and Ethnic Rebellion: The Communist Encounter with a 'New Emperor' in Guizhou's Mashan Region, 1956." In *Maoism at the Grassroots: Everyday Life in China's Era of High Socialism*, ed., Jeremy Brown and Matthew D. Johnson, 281–305. Cambridge, MA: Harvard University Press, 2015.

Wang, Tao. "Neutralizing Indochina: The 1954 Geneva Conference and China's Efforts to Isolate the United States." *Journal of Cold War Studies* 19, no. 2 (2017), 3–42.

Wang Xunzhi, and Liao Jingcun. *Guangxi bianfang jiyao* [Summary of border defense of Guangxi]. Guangxi: Guangxi qiye yinshuchang, 1941.

Wang, Ziyuan. "The Political Logic of Status Competition: Leaders, Status Tradeoffs, and Beijing's Vietnam Policy, 1949–1965." *The Chinese Journal of International Politics* 14, no. 4 (2021), 554–86.

Waters, Tony and Dagmar Waters, eds and trans. *Weber's Rationalism and Modern Society: New Translations on Politics, Bureaucracy, and Social Stratification*. Hampshire: Palgrave Macmillan, 2015.

Weber, Isabella M. *How China Escaped Shock Therapy: The Market Reform Debate*. London: Routledge, 2021.

Westad, Odd Arne. "The Cold War and the International History of the Twentieth Century." In *The Cambridge History of the Cold War: Volume 1 Origins*, ed. Melvyn P. Leffler and Odd Arne Westad, 1–19. Cambridge: Cambridge University Press, 2012.

Wheeler, Charles. "Re-Thinking the Sea in Vietnamese History: Littoral Society in the Integration of Thuận-Quảng, Seventeenth-Eighteenth Centuries." *Journal of Southeast Asian Studies* 37, no. 1 (2006), 123–53.

Whitson, William W., with Chen-hsia Huang. *The Chinese High Command: A History of Communist Military Politics, 1927–71*. London: Palgrave Macmillan, 1973.

Williams, Dee Mack. *Beyond Great Walls: Environment, Identity, and Development on the Chinese Grasslands of Inner Mongolia*. Stanford, CA: Stanford University Press, 2002.

Wilson, Thomas M., and Hastings Donnan. "Nation, State and Identity at International Borders." In *Border Identities: Nation and State at International Frontiers*, ed. Thomas M. Wilson and Hastings Donnan, 1–30. Cambridge: Cambridge University Press, 1998.

Winichakul, Tongchai. *Siam Mapped: A History of the Geo-Body of a Nation.* Honolulu: University Hawai'i Press, 1994.

Womack, Brantly. "International Relationships at the Border of China and Vietnam: An Introduction." *Asian Survey* 40, no. 6 (November–December 2000), 981–86.

——— *China and Vietnam: The Politics of Asymmetry.* Cambridge: Cambridge University Press, 2006.

Wong, Linda. "Family Reform through Divorce Law in the PRC." *Pacific Basin Law Journal* 1, no. 2 (1982), 265–84.

Woodside, Alexander B. *Community and Revolution in Modern Vietnam.* Boston: Houghton Mifflin, 1976.

Worthing, Peter. *Occupation and Revolution: China and the Vietnamese August Revolution of 1945.* Berkeley: Institute of East Asian Studies, University of California, 2001.

Yang, Kuisong. "Changes in Mao Zedong's Attitude toward the Indochina War, 1949–1973." Cold War International History Project Working Paper No. 34. Woodrow Wilson International Center for Scholars, Washington, DC, February 2002.

——— *Eight Outcasts: Social and Political Marginalization in China under Mao.* Translated by Gregor Benton and Ye Zhen. Oakland: University of California Press, 2020.

Yang, Peina. "Government Registration in the Fishing Industry in South China during the Ming and the Qing." In *The Fisher Folk of Late Imperial and Modern China: An Historical Anthropology of Boat-and-Shed Living*, ed. Xi He and David Faure, 33–44. New York: Routledge, 2016.

Yin, Qingfei. "The Mountain Is High, and the Emperor Is Far Away: States and Smuggling Networks at the Sino-Vietnamese Border." *Asian Perspective* 42, no. 4 (October–December 2018), 551–73.

——— "From a Line on Paper to a Line in Physical Reality: Joint State-Building at the Chinese-Vietnamese Border, 1954–1957." *Modern Asian Studies* 54, no. 6 (2020), 1905–48.

Yin, Qingfei, and Kosal Path. "Remembering and Forgetting the Last War: Discursive Memory of the Sino-Vietnamese War in China and Vietnam." *TRaNS: Trans-Regional and -National Studies of Southeast Asia* 9, no. 1 (2021), 11–29.

You Lan. "Zhanhou Zhong-Yue ludi bianjie wenti de lishi kaocha ji zaisikao [A historical survey and reconsideration of Sino-Vietnamese land border issues after the Second World War]." *Twenty-First Century*, no. 190 (April 2022), 64–81.

Yvon, Florence. "The Construction of Socialism in North Vietnam: Reconsidering the Domestic Grain Economy, 1954–1960." *South East Asia Research* 16, no. 1 (March 2008), 43–84.

Zhai, Qiang. *China and the Vietnam Wars, 1950–1975.* Chapel Hill: University of North Carolina Press, 2000.

Zhang, Xiaoming. *Deng Xiaoping's Long War: The Military Conflict between China and Vietnam.* Chapel Hill: University of North Carolina Press, 2015.

Zhang Zhaohe. "Zhong-Yue bianjie kuajing jiaowang yu Guangxi Jingzu kuaguo shenfen rentong [Trans-border interactions along the Sino-Vietnamese border and transnational identity of the Kinh in Guangxi]." *Lishi renleixue xuekan* 2, no. 1 (2004), 89–133.

Zhang, Zhihong. "Rural Industrialization in China: From Backyard Furnaces to Township and Village Enterprises." *East Asia* 17, no. 3 (September 1999), 61–87.

Zheng Yixing and Wang Guoping. *Xinan diqu haiwai yiminshi yanjiu: yi Guangxi, Yunnan weili* [Study of overseas migration from the Southwestern Area: the case of Guangxi and Yunnan]. Beijing: Shehui kexue wenxian chubanshen, 2013.

Zhou, Taomo. *Migration in the Time of Revolution: China, Indonesia, and the Cold War*. Ithaca, NY: Cornell University Press, 2019.

Zhou, Ziren. *Yunnan wenge shigao* [The Cultural Revolution in Yunnan Province], vol. 2. Austin, TX: Remembering, 2020.

Zhu Xie. *Yuenan shouxiang riji* [Diary of accepting surrender in Vietnam]. Shanghai: Shangwu yinshuguan, 1946.

Zou, Keyuan. "Maritime Boundary Delimitation in the Gulf of Tonkin." *Ocean Development & International Law* 30, no. 3 (1999), 235–54.

Index

aid, PRC to DRV
  assistance to Việt Minh, 51, 53
  border terrain hindering, 61, 209
  delays, 130, 214–15
  direct aid, 59–61
  DRV's financial problems, 60
  DRV's reliance on, 115
  DRV's self-reliance encouraged by PRC, 60–61
  failures of, for PRC, 205
  food supply, 60–61, 95
  indirect aid, 61
  military aid, 210, 217–18
Anti-Communist and National Salvation Army, 64, 222
Anti-French Resistance War. *See* First Indochina War
Anti-Japanese War, 53, 66, 170
Anti-Rightist Movement (CPC), 114, 120, 142
Aumoitte, M. A., 23
Autonomous Region of Thái-Mèo, 145. *See also* Khu tự trị Tây Bắc (KTTTB)

Bạch Long Vĩ (Fushuizhou) Island, 161
bandits. *See* subversives and counterrevolutionaries
"boat people," 21, 49, 172, 178. *See also* Đản people; Danjia (Tanka) people; ethnic minorities
Bandung Conference, 78
Beihai, China, 81
Beilun (Ka Long) River, 3, 18, 126, 202
Bhabha, Homi, 159
border. *See* Sino-Vietnamese border
border administration. *See* local state administration
Border Campaign (Battle of Route Coloniale 4), 39, 52, 59, 67–68, 74
border police. *See also* border securitization; subversives and counterrevolutionaries
  formalization of border police, 85–89
  Laotian border, 89

  Ministry of Public Security (MOPS), 43, 45, 67, 143
  mobilizing local support for border police, 86
  People's Armed Police (DRV), 67, 143, 222
  People's Armed Police Corps (PRC), 142
  police tasks, 87–88
  policing difficulties, 40, 64–66
border priorities
  countering subversive forces, 43
  decreasing permeability, 39, 78
  joint enforcement of boundary, 39
  limited resources for, 45
  local and linguistic knowledge, 64, 66–67
  proletarian internationalism, 44
  removal of French forces, 39
  revenue extraction, 39
  state authority's expansion, 39, 64–67, 79
  uniting national minorities with the interior, 149
border securitization. *See also* border police; subversives and counterrevolutionaries
  Agreement on Cooperation in Defending the Security of the Sino-Vietnamese Border Area, 219
  benefits of, 38
  border defense liaisons, 67
  broadly conceived, 86
  Chinese doctrine of defense, 88
  coordination between cadres, 220–21
  DRV relaxing defensive measures along Sino-Vietnamese border, 88
  ethnic minorities as threat, 219–20
  impact on fisherfolk and coastal societies, 178, 189
  implementation and enforcement, 142, 222, 237, 252
  intelligence collection, 131–33, 221
  leniency toward cross-border connections, 238
  Lin Biao's "political border defense," 221
  maritime borders, 167, 170

Index

Stalinist model, 85
state-perceived vulnerabilities, 219
territorialization coupled with, 5
border societies. *See also* coastal societies; collectivization campaigns; ethnic minorities; food supply and shortages; highlanders; Kinh people; local state administration; lowlanders; migration; trade; Yao people
  attempt to align with revolutionary objectives, 74, 77
  bargaining power of, 150
  control over, 67
  COVID-19, 3
  cross-border social ties, 105–8, 113, 220
  difficulties mobilizing, 91, 231
  evading state, 78, 102, 254
  hostility to communists, 64
  impoverishment of, 250–52
  integrating into national state, 101, 104–5, 109, 115–16
  joint state invasion and, 126, 254
  local state agents protective of, 104
  marriage and family ties, 105–8, 111, 239–40
  mercantile nature, 254
  mutual aid networks, 118–19, 140, 150, 237
  New Marriage Law (PRC), 105–6, 118
  overview, 15–22
  propaganda targeted at, 152
  resisting state incursion, 119, 141–42
  shadow economy and smuggling, 71–72, 87, 146–48, 154
  shaping state priorities and strategies, 77
  socialist brotherhood language used, 6
  stigmatized during Cultural Revolution, 221–22
  trade and, 70–72, 94, 100, 239–40
  Vietnamization of, 250
  village mentality to national identity, 84
borderlands history, 7–10, 15–22. *See also* border societies; Sino-Vietnamese border
borders, generally
  boundary making and its limits, 63–73
  contested sovereignty and border discrepancies, 103
  elements of, 79
  epitomizing the communist party-state, 85
  Geneva Accords, 84
  pan-global understanding of, 256
  ramifications of geopolitics, 12–13
  sovereignty and, 40
  Stalinist model of border control, 85
buffalo, 138, 144
Bureau of Commerce of Hainan Island, 148

cadres. *See* collectivization campaigns; cooperative movement (WPV); Cultural Revolution; Great Leap Forward; local state administration
Cẩm Phả, Vietnam, 81–82, 131, 133, 215
Cambodia, 217
Campaign of the Hundred Thousand Mountains, 36–38
Cao Bằng, Vietnam, 52, 71, 74, 147, 154
Carrai, Maria Adele, 255
Catroux, Georges, 29
Central Military Commission (CPC), 43, 45, 142, 219
Chandler, Andrea, 11
Chappell, Jonathan, 20
Chen Boda, 205
Chen Geng, 52
China (PRC). *See also* aid, PRC to DRV; border priorities; collectivization campaigns; Communist Party of China (CPC); Cultural Revolution; Great Leap Forward; Mao Zedong; Sino-Soviet split; Sino-Vietnamese border; state building; Zhou Enlai; *individual provinces, cities, and islands*
  approach to overseas Chinese problem, 110
  Civil Code of the Republic of China, 105
  COVID-19, 2
  DRV as key to national security, 115
  foreign policy reorientation, 121
  inward orientation, 77–78
  maintenance of territoriality, 32
  Ministry of Foreign Affairs, 2, 82–83, 130
  naval blockade, 170
  New Marriage Law, 105–6, 118
  partnership with DRV, 50, 77, 209
  political radicalization, 128–35
  promoting intra-socialist bloc solidarity, 128
  reunification of Vietnam, 122
  trade agenda, 129
Chinese Civil War, 30
citizenship, 20, 58, 110–11, 159
Civil Code of the Republic of China, 105
Cô Tô Islands, 158–59, 164, 196–98. *See also* coastal societies; maritime border
coastal mobility. *See* cross-border mobility; fisherfolk
coastal societies. *See also* border securitization; Cô Tô Islands; cross-border mobility; ethnic minorities; fisherfolk; fishery reforms; maritime border; migration; trade
  about, 18–20
  citizenship, 159

288 Index

coastal societies. (cont.)
  class struggle's impact, 175–76, 181–83
  collectivization campaigns and cooperative movements, 169, 177–79, 181, 190, 193–96, 199
  cross-border ties, 163–65, 197
  draft dodging, 159
  economic ties, 165, 169, 184–87
  enhanced securitization and surveillance, 178, 180
  fishing and commerce, 165, 190
  folk religion, 182
  Great Leap Forward, 194–96
  Hán rài, 159
  integration into PRC state project, 170, 178–79, 184–87
  joint state interference, 184–87
  land reform's impact, 172–73
  loyalty of islanders, 158
  nationalist project of ethnic categorization, 197
  outward-looking nature, 190
  party-state's struggle to generate legitimacy, 174
  policy reforms, 168–69, 181
  private ownership criminalized, 197
  revolutionary agenda incompatible with, 160, 179, 194–96
  state building and local customs, 167, 171
  state policies lacking consistency, 169
  sustaining fishery industry, 181–82
  tensions with and thwarting state, 159, 167, 172
  transnational arrangements, 161
collectivization campaigns. *See also* cooperative movement (WVP); Cultural Revolution; fishery reforms; food supply and shortages; Great Leap Forward; land reform; mobilization campaigns
  advanced cooperatives, 136
  among Yao people, 137–39
  border societies' resistance, 120, 136–38
  buffalo, 138
  coastal societies and, 169, 193–96, 199
  coercive tactics, 138
  ethnic minorities recruited, 136
  foreign policy reorientations and, 121
  Great Leap Forward, 119–21
  inter-state divisions, 148–49, 193
  migration and, 138–40, 150
  reunification of Vietnam and, 121
  state building hindered, 119–20

Communist Party of China (CPC). *See also* collectivization campaigns; Cultural Revolution; Great Famine; Great Leap Forward; Mao Zedong; mobilization campaigns; People's Liberation Army (PLA); socialist brotherhood
  Anti-Rightist Movement, 114, 120, 142
  Assist Vietnam Leadership Team, 211
  Central Military Commission, 43, 45, 142, 219
  cross-border transportation system, 53–55
  Five-Anti Campaign, 72, 87
  Five-Year Plan, 78
  foreign policy moderated, 78
  GZAR Revolutionary Committee, 206, 215
  influence at border and DRV, 47–48
  International Supervisory Commission operations, 84
  local elites distrusted, 64
  Maoism's agrarian focus, 51
  Socialist Education Movement (Four Clean Movement), 227
  State Council Work Team for Supporting Vietnam, 211
Convention between China and France respecting the Delimitation of the Frontier (1887 Convention), 159, 163
cooperative movement (CPC), 136, 177–78, 190
cooperative movement (WPV). *See also* collectivization campaigns; Cultural Revolution; fishery reforms; food supply and shortages; Great Leap Forward; land reform; mobilization campaigns
  agricultural cooperatives, 147–48
  along coast, 190, 197
  buffalo, 144
  Cô Tô Islands prioritized, 196
  cross-border traffic surveilled, 145–46
  expansion, 136, 143–45
  illicit trade and black market, 146–47, 154
  inter-state divisions, 148–49
  learning from CPC collectivization campaigns, 144–45
  migration and, 148, 150
  resistance to, 151, 197
  Three-Year Plan for Socialist Transformation and Development of Economy and Culture, 121
COVID-19, 3–4
cross-border connections. *See* border societies; coastal societies; local state administration

Index

cross-border mobility. *See also* migration
  escape from bombing campaigns, 239–41, 243–44
  for survival, 114
  maritime mobility, 184–87, 198, 240–41, 243–44
  state building and control over, 76–77, 126, 184–87, 198
  travel permits, 68, 112
Cultural Revolution. *See also* collectivization campaigns; cooperative movement (WPV); Great Leap Forward; mobilization campaigns
  22 April supporters, 214
  Alliance Command members, 214
  border enforcement deteriorating, 222, 237
  border societies stigmatized, 221–22
  delaying aid to Vietnam, 214–15
  disrupting railways, 214
  in Guangxi particularly brutal, 205–7
  intergovernmental relations in wake of, 248–50
  party purges, 205–6
  Red Guards, 201–2, 205
  spilling over Vietnamese border, 202
  state building and, 202–3, 215, 246
Đản (or Tàn Cá) people, 21. *See also* Danjia (or Tanka) people

Danjia (or Tanka) people, 21, 172. *See also* Đản (or Tàn Cá) people
Dao people, 16, 148. *See also* Yao people
Daxin County, China, 140
Declaration on the Neutrality of Laos, 203
Deng Xiaoping, 28, 130, 134
Đỗ Văn Mẫn, 209
Đồng Đăng, Vietnam, 53–55, 89, 210
Dongxing Autonomous County of Multiple Ethnicities, 167
Dongxing, China
  about, 17–19
  collectivization campaigns, 136
  Dongzhong Commune, 148
  hostility to communists, 65
  new bridge, 126
  People's Communes Committee, 136
  resettlement, 81, 250
  trade in, 241, 243

ethnic Chinese in Vietnam
  about, 15–17, 20–21, 38
  changing terms to refer to, 49
  citizenship and nationality, 58, 110–11

Cultural Revolution exacerbating tensions, 202
  emigration, 81–83
  enlisted into resistance movement, 58–59
  equality for, 57–59
  expulsion of, 249
  food shortages feared, 143
  Hắc-Cá (Khách) people, 21, 38
  Hán people, 21
  Hoa Kiều ("overseas Chinese"), 21, 58, 163
  Independent Regiment, 47
  land reform, 172
  Ngái people, 21, 38
  người Hoa, 21
  Nùng people, 17, 38, 163
  rights and equality for, 57–59
  as source of intelligence, 132
  tensions with state, 110, 143, 202
  trade, 71, 99–100, 154
ethnic minorities. *See also* ethnic Chinese in Vietnam; Yao people
  "boat people," 21, 49, 172, 178
  about, 20–21
  alienation of, 136
  on Cô Tô Islands, 158
  collectivization campaigns recruiting, 136
  Đản (or Tàn Cá) people, 21
  Danjia (or Tanka) people, 21, 172
  Dao people, 16, 148
  ethnic antagonism, 207
  ethnic categorization, 15–16, 197
  Hắc-Cá (Khách) people, 21, 38
  Hán people, 21
  Hmong (former Mèo) people, 16
  Kinh people in China, 166–67, 193–96, 229–31
  La Chí people, 17
  land reform, 172
  Lô Lô people, 16
  Miao people, 16, 139
  Ngái people, 21, 38, 163
  Nùng people, 17, 38
  Pà Thẻn people, 16
  Phù Lá people, 16
  Pu Péo people, 17
  Sán Chay people, 17
  Sán Dìu people, 16, 38
  Tày people, 17
  as threat, 219–20
  trade and, 99–100
  woven into the nation, 149, 229–31
  Yi people, 16
  Zhuang people, 17, 167
ethnic Vietnamese in China, 83, 111

Fan Honggui, 15
Fangcheng Port, China, 217–19
farming, 101, 103–5, 109–10, 112–14, 143, 249. *See also* food supply and shortages; land reform
First Indochina War. *See also* French Indochina; Việt Minh
  about, 63, 73
  blockade interrupting sea lanes, 62
  Border Campaign, 39, 52, 59, 67–68, 74
  borders as sites of danger and opportunity, 42, 73
  boundary making and its limits during, 63–73
  Campaign of the Hundred Thousand Mountains, 36–38
  control of transport chokepoints, 59
  Hồng Quảng region, 47
  inter-state relations institutionalized, 74
  land reform, 52
  railways during, 55
  Sino-Vietnamese revolutionary comradeship, 31, 51–52
  state building communist Vietnam, 48, 51–52
  trade, 80
fisherfolk. *See also* coastal societies; Guangdong Province, China; Hải Ninh Province, Vietnam; Kinh people; maritime border; Ngái people
  class status of, 174–75
  class struggle's impact, 175–76
  Cô Tô Islands as pivot point, 164
  collectivization campaigns and cooperative movements, 194–97, 199
  cultural and ethnic ties, 164
  dangers of fishing life, 160
  economic networks, 184–87
  fishing quotas, 193
  land reform's impact, 172–73
  lives securitized and politicized, 170–71, 189
  mobility of, 198, 243–44
  morale waning, 176
  registration, 178–80, 199
  resisting state power, 188, 196, 199
  salt supply system, 172
  state building and, 161, 171
  trade restrictions, 187, 189–90
fishery reforms. *See also* collectivization campaigns; cooperative movement (WPV); land reform; Sino-Vietnamese Agreement on Sailboat Fishing in the Gulf of Tonkin
  class struggle's impact, 175–76
  collectivization and cooperative cadres, 170, 173–74
  economic consequences, 171, 174

  goals, 173–74
  inconsistency of, 173, 176–77
  labor negotiations, 175–76
  morale of fisherfolk worsening, 176
  reallocating resources, 179
  resistance to, 173, 183
  seabed redistribution, 174
  state building and, 169–71, 176–77
  state control, 160, 171, 199
  technological gaps, 161, 185–86, 189, 195–96, 200
  WPV's collaborative approach, 181–83
Five Principles of Peaceful Coexistence, 78
Five-Year Plan (1953–1957) (PRC), 78
food supply and shortages. *See also* collectivization campaigns; cooperative movement (WPV); fishery reforms; Great Famine; land reform
  aid to DRV, 60–61, 95
  black market, 155
  causing tensions with ethnic Chinese in Vietnam, 143
  challenge to DRV leadership, 83
  Chinese invasion of Vietnam, 250–51
  cross-border crossings crucial, 95
  during mobilization campaigns, 225–26, 228–29, 232–33, 235
  during Vietnam War, 225–26, 228–29, 232–33, 235–37
  farming, 101, 103–5, 109, 112–14
  First Indochina War, 59
  Great Leap Forward, 148
  in Lạng Sơn Province, 233, 235
  migration and, 153–54
Fravel, M. Taylor, 13, 86
French Indochina. *See also* First Indochina War
  ethnic Chinese lumped together, 38
  negotiations with Japan, 29
  Pact on the Relations between Vietnam and Border Provinces of China, 123
  state power at border, 24–27
Friendship Pass, 87, 92, 208–9. *See also* Zhennan Guan
Fushuizhou (Bạch Long Vĩ) Island, 161

Geneva Accords, 84
Geneva Conference (1954), 78, 80–81, 84
Ghosh, Arunabh, 257
Goscha, Christopher, 46, 48
Great Famine. *See also* Cultural Revolution; food supply and shortages
  Guangdong-Hong Kong border, 150
  investigations into, 194
  migration and, 140–42, 150, 153–54
  rural-urban divide, 150

Index 291

Sino-Korean border, 150
social uncertainty and upheaval, 140–41
Great Leap Forward. *See also* collectivization campaigns; cooperative movement (WPV); mobilization campaigns
  about, 120
  Cô Tô Islands, 196–97
  collectivization campaigns and, 119–21, 136
  currency exchange, 146
  ethnic minorities alienated, 136
  as man-made disaster, 195
  maritime livelihoods incompatible with, 194–96
  migration to Vietnam, 136
  railways, 130–31
  Sino-Soviet split and, 121
  starvation, 148
  state building hindered, 119
  technological gap widening, 196
  tensions between PRC and DRV, 119
  tensions with fisherfolk, 197
  WPV learning from, 144–45
Guangdong Province, China
  boat registration, 184
  Border Defense Bureau, 170
  cooperatives and collectivization, 136, 194–96
  cross-border farming, 109–10, 112–14, 143
  Ethnic Affairs Commission, 194–96
  excess goods from Vietnam, 129
  fisherfolk relations, 168, 170–71, 194–96
  Foreign Trade Bureau, 129
  provincial foreign office, 132, 209
  restrictions in fishing, 185
Guangdong-Hong Kong border, 150
Guangxi Province, China
  administering coast along Gulf of Tonkin, 168
  border as transport hub, 90–92
  collectivization campaigns and cooperative movements, 136
  cross-border farming, 112–14
  Cultural Revolution in, 205–7
  ethnic antagonism in, 207
  fishery reforms, 183
  liaison office in Pingxiang, 84
  mobilization in, 91, 224
  Office of Foreign Affairs, 77, 82
  PLA takeover of, 42, 91
  School of Border Affairs, 28
  search for subversives, 221
  sojourner population, 243–44
  state vs local institutions, 91–92
Guangxi Zhuang Autonomous Region (GZAR), 5, 217
Guangxi-Vietnam border
  bandit suppression campaigns, 43, 45, 64–65, 74, 87

border check system, 43–45
border police tasks, 87–88
cross-border farming, 101–5, 109–10, 112–14, 249
cross-border marriages, 106–8
foreign and internal threats, 87
migration, 112
space of danger and subversion, 40, 44
specialized border institutions, 66
trade, 62, 94, 147, 154
as transport hub, 90
Gulf of Tonkin. *See also* coastal societies; fishery reforms; maritime border; Sino-Vietnamese Agreement on Sailboat Fishing in the Gulf of Tonkin
  about, 163
  economic alliances of trade, 169
  fishing grounds' importance, 183
  mining program, 217–19
  natural resources, 168, 184
  Protocol on the Usage of Chinese Ports by Vietnamese Fishing Boats, 240
  sovereignty, 163
  state building, 162–69
Guyot-Réchard, Bérénice, 13

Hắc-Cá (Khách) people, 21, 38
Hải Ninh Province, Vietnam
  administration of coastal regions, 168, 184, 196
  competitions for legitimacy, 38
  cooperative movement, 143, 145, 196
  ethnic Chinese population, 47, 110, 143
  Independent Regiment, 47
  land reclamation, 251
  merged into Quảng Ninh Province, 169
  as a reactionary corridor, 151–52
  salt making, 19, 181
  steel manufacturing, 144
hải phỉ (haizei/haifei), 19
Hainan Island, 62, 148
Haiphong, Vietnam, 81–82, 130–31, 215
Hán people, 21
Han, Enze, 8
He Guomin, 222
He Guoping, 222
He Guoyi, 221
Hekou-Lào Cai, 125
Hepu County, China, 185–86
highlanders. *See also* ethnic minorities; Miao people; Yao people
  about, 15–17
  collectivization campaigns and cooperative movements, 136–38, 144, 148
  cross-border ties a threat, 220
  food production and procurement, 235, 249

highlanders. (cont.)
  marriage and citizenship, 111, 258
  mine fields, 252
  mobilization campaigns among, 233–35
  state institutions weaker among, 109, 111, 254
  trade and state power, 8
  traditional practices criminalized, 238
Hmong (former Mèo) people, 16
Hồ Chí Minh, 30, 36, 61, 133, 158, 231
Ho Chi Minh Trail, 203
Hoa Kiều ("overseas Chinese"), 21, 58, 163.
  See also ethnic Chinese in Vietnam
Hoàng Chính, 145
Hoàng Văn Diệm, 242
Hoàng Văn Thụ, 234
Hoành Bồ, Vietnam, 151
Hòn Gai, Vietnam, 131
Hong Kong, 15–17, 67, 150, 168, 170, 190, 216
Hồng Quảng, Vietnam, 48, 168–69, 181
Huang Deqin (pseudonym), 76–77
Hyun, Sinae, 13

Ichi-Go Campaign, 29
Independent Regiment, 38, 47–48
Indochina Communist Party (ICP), 28, 46–49, 52, 57
International Supervisory Commission (ISC), 84

Japan, 29–31, 55, 57, 178, 183
Jing people. *See* Kinh people
Johnson, Jason B., 13
Johnson, Lyndon B., 204

Ka Long (Beilun) River, 3, 18, 126, 202
Kaup, Katherine Palmer, 17
Kennedy, John F., 204
Kerkvliet, Benedict, 195
Khách (or Hắc-Cá) people, 21
Khan, Sulmaan Wasif, 13, 84
Khrushchev, Nikita, 121–22
Khu tự trị Tây Bắc (KTTTB), 145, 219, 223
Khu tự trị Việt Bắc (KTTVB), 32, 128, 146, 148, 219, 223
Kinh people in China, 166–67, 193–96, 229–31
Korean War, 59–61, 170
Kosygin, Alexei, 213
Kraus, Charles, 10

La Chí people, 17. *See also* Zhuang people
land reform. *See also* collectivization campaigns; cooperative movement (CPC); cooperative movement (WPV); fishery reforms
  control and supervision of the masses, 76
  detecting political dissidents, 93
  exported from China to Vietnam, 52
  migration and, 167
  redistribution, 83, 172, 174
  rice surplus, 62
  social inequalities in coastal communities, 172–73
  state building and, 105
Lạng Sơn Province, Vietnam
  cross-border trade, 71, 147, 154
  ethnic minorities woven into the nation, 234
  food production and procurement, 233, 235
  governmental and institutional relocations, 236
  land reform, 52
  militia, 236
  Việt Minh power base, 74
Laos, 89, 203
Lê Duẩn, 122, 203, 207, 210, 223
Lê Đức Thọ, 122
Lê Quảng Ba, 36
Lentz, Christian, 4
Li Qingde, 211
Li, Huaiyin, 51, 253
Lin Biao, 43, 201, 205–6, 221
Ling Chunsheng, 28
"lips and teeth" relationship, 100, 115
Liu Shaoqi, 53, 55, 130, 133
Liu Xiao, 213
Liu Yongfu, 24
Lô Lô people, 16. *See also* Yi people
local state administration. *See also* border securitization; border societies; coastal societies; collectivization campaigns; cooperative movement (WPV); mobilization campaigns; state building; trade; transportation systems
  about, 10–11
  asked to be everything to everyone, 114–15, 117
  bandit suppression, 150–52
  border work committees, 87, 221
  central government and state building, overview, 66, 108–15, 188, 255–56
  cooperative movement and, 190
  cross-border collaboration hindered, 148–49, 238
  inspections of foreigners, 85
  intergovernmental cooperation and, 44, 125, 221, 241–43
  liaison office, 53
  local realities vs party-state agenda, 111–15, 117, 119, 125, 129, 153, 155, 190
  migration and, 152, 240–41
  as predatory and protective, 160
  protective of border societies, 104

Index 293

reinstitutionalizing border in 1970s, 249
Sino-Soviet split and, 135
Sino-Vietnamese partnership expensive, 130
tensions with borderlanders, 94, 227
trade regulations, 241–43
understaffing of, 222
village mentality to national identity, 84
lowlanders, 17. *See also* border societies
Lu Han, 30
Luo Guibo, 52, 60
Luo Ruiqing, 86, 205, 211
Luo Zhoude, 230
Lương Mù, 151

Mao Zedong
criticism of Guangxi, 42
exploiting Vietnam War, 204
Great Leap Forward, 120
importance of Sino-Vietnamese partnership, 55
intraparty tensions, 122, 205–6
meeting with Hồ Chí Minh, 216
Sino-Soviet split, 121, 131, 134
Third Line Program, 204
maritime border. *See also* border securitization; Cô Tô Islands; coastal societies; fisherfolk; Gulf of Tonkin; local state administration; Sino-Vietnamese Agreement on Sailboat Fishing in the Gulf of Tonkin
bandit suppression campaigns, 170
Battle of Paracel Islands, 245
border securitization, 167, 170–71
boundary settlements, 161–62
cultural and ethnic ties ignored, 164–65
defined, 180
fishing, 184, 193
fluidity of, 161
intergovernmental tensions, 244–45
internationalism, nationalism, transnational localism, 159
military importance during Vietnam War, 215–19
national spaces created, 183, 186, 189, 198–99
natural resources, 161
Protocol on the Usage of Chinese Ports by Vietnamese Fishing Boats, 240
state buildings' challenges, 161
trade, 62, 169, 175, 187, 189–90
transportation routes, 125, 210, 215–17
maritime mobility, 184–87, 198. *See also* cross-border mobility
marriage. *See also* border societies; coastal societies
Marriage and Family Law of the DRV, 106

Masako, Ito, 15
Masuda Hajimu, 12
Mèo (later Hmong) people, 16
Miao people, 16, 139
Michaud, Jean, 16
migration
across demarcation line, 80–81
attempts to curb, 152–53
bandit suppression and, 150–52
causing labor shortage, 152
collectivization campaigns and, 138–40, 150
comradeship plus brotherhood vs permeability, 78
end of Cold War partnership and, 249–50
ethnic Chinese returning to Vietnam, 81–83
food supply solutions to, 153–54
Great Famine and, 140–42, 150, 153–54
Great Leap Forward, 136
land reform and, 167
narrowing cross-border activity, 143
resettlement, 81, 148, 240–41, 250
restrictions on, 78, 82–83
states' protective function, 82
as survival strategy, 142
xia Nanyang, 83
Ming Dynasty, 23, 49, 56, 178
Ministry of Foreign Affairs (PRC), 2, 82–83
Ministry of Foreign Trade (PRC), 130
Ministry of Public Security (MOPS) (PRC), 43, 45, 67, 143
Ministry of Transportation (DRV), 89, 125–26, 211
Ministry of Transportation (PRC), 216
Mo Wenhua, 57
mobilization campaigns, 91, 224–33, 235–36
Mochulskii, F.V., 213
Móng Cái, Vietnam, 18, 126, 202, 241, 249, 251
Munan Guan, 57, 208–9. *See also* Friendship Pass; Zhennan Guan
Mutual Defense Treaty, 87

Ngái people, 21, 38, 163
Ngô Đình Diệm, 121, 203–4
người Hoa, 21
Nguyễn Duy Trinh, 83
Nguyễn Hữu Thấu, 16
Nguyễn Văn Linh, 207
Nguyễn Xuân Phúc, 2
Noboru Ishikawa, 39
Nong Zhigao (Nùng Trí Cao), 17
North Korea, 150
Nùng Autonomous Territory, Vietnam, 38, 81
Nùng people, 17, 38. *See also* Zhuang people
Nùng Trí Cao (Nong Zhigao), 17

Pà Thèn people, 16. *See also* Yao people
Paracel Islands, Battle of the, 245
Peng Dehuai, 149
People's Armed Police (DRV), 67, 143, 222
People's Armed Police Corps (PRC), 142
People's Army of Vietnam (PAVN)
  Campaign of the Hundred Thousand Mountains, 36
  corruption and organizational problems, 60
  First Indochina War, 36–39, 59
  Laotian civil war, 203
  local police replenishing, 222
  Tết Offensive, 205
  transition to national army, 52
  women in, 232
People's Liberation Army (PLA)
  border policies, 40, 44
  borders as sites of danger, 42
  Guangxi takeover, 42, 91
  railway corps, 211
  restoring order after Cultural Revolution, 33
  transportation engineering, 212
  Việt Minh and, 49
Phạm Văn Đồng, 122
Phù Lá people, 16. *See also* Yi people
Pingxiang, China
  Cultural Revolution, 222
  Guangxi liaison office, 84
  mobilization methods' ineffectiveness, 91
  population increase, 91
  refugee settlement, 250
  Sino-Vietnamese Railway, 53–55, 89–91, 130–31, 210, 212
  state vs local institutions, 91–92
pirates, 19
police. *See* border police
propaganda, 47–49, 81, 132, 152–54, 226
Protocol of Supplementing and Modifying the Agreement over Sailboat Fishery. *See also* Sino-Vietnamese Agreement on Sailboat Fishing in the Gulf of Tonkin
Protocol of Supplementing and Modifying the Agreement over Sailboat Fishery in the Gulf of Tonkin, 198
Pu Péo people, 17. *See also* Zhuang people

Qin County, China, 175–76
Qing Dynasty, 24–27, 64, 178, 208
Qinzhou, China, 178
Qisha, China, 175–77, 250
Qu Shaodong, 201
Quảng Ninh Province, Vietnam, 169

railways
  aid to DRV delayed at stations, 130
  Cultural Revolution's disruptions to, 214–15
  during First Indochina War, 55
  during Vietnam War, 210–13
  expansions, 210–12
  geopoliticization of border, 53, 55, 89–93
  Great Leap Forward and, 130–31
  Guangxi-Vietnam railway, 123
  Kunming-Haiphong Railway, 27
  Liuzhou Railway Station, 214
  looting on, 214
  Nanning-Pingxiang Railway, 210
  Pingxiang Railway Station, 130–31
  Pingxiang-Đồng Đăng connections, 125
  Pingxiang-Hanoi line, 212
  PLA Railway Corps, 211
  placement of rail lines and stops, 53, 89
  Sino-Vietnamese Railway at Đồng Đăng, 53–55, 89, 125, 167, 210
  social controls tightened along, 92
Red Guards. *See* Cultural Revolution
Regional Ethnic Autonomy System (PRC), 167
resettlement. *See* cross-border mobility; migration
Ruan Shiying, 230

sailors, 132. *See also* coastal societies; fisherfolk
Sán Chay people, 17. *See also* Zhuang people
Sán Dìu people, 16, 38. *See also* Yao people
Scott, James, 7–8, 116, 197, 254
sea lanes. *See* maritime border; trade; transportation systems
seafaring communities. *See* coastal societies; fisherfolk
Second Indochina War. *See* Vietnam War
Second World War, 29–30
Shanxin Island, 164–65, 167, 194–96, 229
shipping. *See* maritime border; transportation systems
Sino-French Convention, 26
Sino-French War, 24, 31
Sino-Korean border, 150
Sino-Soviet split
  competition for leadership, 129
  deterioration of, 131
  DRV and PRC evaluating each other during, 119, 209
  DRV playing sides off each other, 122, 131–35
  Great Leap Forward and, 121
  intelligence collection, 131–33
  joint maritime survey and, 192
  peaceful transition and peaceful coexistence, 134
  Vietnam War and, 213–14, 217

Index

Sino-Vietnamese Agreement on Sailboat Fishing in the Gulf of Tonkin. *See also* fishery reforms; maritime border
- expiration and intergovernmental tensions, 244–45
- fishing and economic networks, 184–87
- Gulf as a common pool resource, 183, 193
- implementation and enforcement, 187–90, 196–97
- joint maritime survey, 191–93
- lacunae, inconsistencies, weaknesses, 188, 190, 197, 199
- maritime mobility, 184–87
- national spaces created, 186
- private ownership criminalized, 197
- Protocol of Supplementing and Modifying the Agreement, 198
- resistance to, 188, 196–97
- trade restrictions, 187, 189–90

Sino-Vietnamese border. *See also* border priorities; border securitization; border societies; coastal societies; collectivization campaigns; cooperative movement (WPV); First Indochina War; Guangxi-Vietnam border; local state administration; maritime border; state building; trade; transportation systems; Vietnam War; Zhennan Guan
- Chinese invasion of Vietnam, 250–52
- collectivizing border economy, 143
- communications centralized, 68
- COVID-19, 2–4
- cross-border connections politicized, 75
- crucial to Sino-Vietnamese partnership, 52, 116, 123–28
- currency and exchange, 145, 153
- Guangxi-Northeast Vietnam vs Northwest Vietnam-Yunnan borderlands, 21–22
- institutionalization of border administration, 44, 67
- as internationally coordinated project, 108–15
- inter-provincial border conference, 108–10
- ISC members constraining cross-border activities, 84
- joint state invasion process, overview, 6–9, 77, 252–53
- lens on Cold War Asia, 5–7, 9–12, 256–57
- limits of state central authority, 116
- local opportunities driving pressure on, 52
- overview, 5–6
- pan-global understanding of, 256
- rear base for war efforts, 232
- site of selective coercion, 40
- soft boundary to hard boundary, 253–54
- space of opportunity and danger, 40, 46–48

symbolic meanings bestowed on, 53–57, 208–9

smuggling. *See also* trade
- border societies and, 71–72, 87
- COVID-19, 3–4
- incentivizing resistance with money, 154
- mutual aid networks treated as, 140
- norm of cross-border trade, 252
- pre-Cold War, 30
- product of micro-management of border, 148
- revival during collectivization campaigns, 140, 147
- socialist monopolies increasing, 127
- war on, 98

socialist brotherhood, 5–6, 11, 103, 149, 256
sources, discussion, 32–33
Southeast Asia Treaty Organization (SEATO), 87, 115
sovereignty, 40, 103, 163, 254. *See also* state building
St. John, Rachel, 8

state building. *See also* border societies; Communist Party of China (CPC); cross-border mobility; local state administration; maritime border; Sino-Vietnamese border; trade; transportation systems; Workers Party of Vietnam (WPV)
- border crossing procedures and, 111
- border demarcation, 66, 79, 108, 115–16
- central government vs local administration, overview, 66, 108–15, 188, 255–56
- challenges along maritime border, 159, 161
- China's historical progression, 253
- Civil Code of the Republic of China, 105
- coerciveness at border, 119
- continuing effects of, 257
- distinctive characteristics at border, 8
- First Indochina War, 48, 51–52
- fisherfolk and coastal communities, 169–70, 175–79
- as internationally coordinated project, 108–16
- nationality and citizenship, 110–11
- paradox of the border, 5
- pre-Cold War, 23–32
- reality stymying ideology and policy, 110–15
- revolutionary state building, overview, 9–10, 238
- severing cross-border social ties, 101–8, 111, 113
- Sino-Vietnamese relations, overview, 9, 246–47
- state and society divide, 84
- state power in 1970s, 248–50
- tax consequences, 102–5

state building. (cont.)
  Vietnam War, 219, 238
  Vietnam's historical progression, 253
subversives and counterrevolutionaries
  bandit suppression campaigns, 43, 45, 64–65, 74, 87–88, 150–52, 170
  concern over, 87
  counterrevolutionaries returned to China, 220
  land reform and, 93
  search for, 221
  as security threat, 219–22
Sun Yat-sen, 27
Sun Zhizhong, 201
Szonyi, Michael, 12, 254

Taiping Rebellion, 26
Tàn Cá (or Đản) people, 21
taxes
  consequences of state building, 102–5
  customs duties, 124
  farming, 102–5, 113
  trade, 69–70, 97, 100, 154
  trade tariffs, 123
Tày people, 17. *See also* Zhuang people
Thanh Lân Island, 158
Tilly, Charles, 7
Trà Cổ Island, 164
trade. *See also* smuggling
  benefits for state, 70, 128, 242
  black market, 30, 154–55
  breaking sea lane blockade, 62
  Bureau of Commerce of Hainan Island, 148
  Chinese companies, 95–96, 99, 129
  Chinese invasion of Vietnam, 252
  contradictory objectives, 72
  controlling border societies, 98
  cross-border interdependence of maritime trade, 190
  customs duties, 124
  ethnic Chinese traders, 71, 99–100, 154
  evading state regulations, 140
  First Indochina War, 80
  highlanders and, 8
  illicit trade undermining cooperative movement, 146–47
  intergovernmental tensions, 241–43
  intergovernmental trade and collaboration, 61, 68–70, 97, 123–26, 169
  itinerant traders, 94–96, 98
  lack of quality control, 129
  "lips and teeth" relationship, 100, 115
  local state and border society tensions, 94
  local state-owned companies, 96
  maritime trade, 62, 169, 175, 187, 189–90
  as mutual aid for borderlanders, 140
  nationalizing, 124
  overseas Chinese traders, 99
  Pact on the Relations between Vietnam and Border Provinces of China, 123
  policies alienating border societies, 100
  price stabilization, 154
  principle of mutual benefit and reciprocity, 130
  private economy vs state-run, 72
  regulations, 69–71, 97, 100, 114, 128, 154
  relations between borderlands and inland, 94
  renewal of cross-border networks and markets, 238–40
  reopening, 154
  restrictions, 187, 189–90
  seafood brokers (*yulan*), 175
  small-scale markets, 69, 93, 96, 127, 140, 252
  socialist and state monopolies, 93–95, 126–28
  spontaneous trade marginalized, 93–100
  state control lacking and hindered, 71–72, 80, 98
  state grafting onto traders' networks, 123
  state monopolies, 98, 143
  state-run companies, 127
  tariffs, 123
  taxes, 70, 97, 100, 154
  treatment based on ethnicity, 99–100
  Vietnam War worsening, 243
  West Guangxi Trade Company, 80
trains. *See* railways
transportation systems. *See also* railways
  24 Construction Committee, 211
  border society and construction of, 90–91
  during Vietnam War, 211–15
  economic purposes after First Indochina War, 124
  economic revival, 89
  integration into modern transportation system, 123
  international cooperation, 55, 125
  maritime routes during Vietnam War, 218–19
  Ministry of Transportation (DRV), 89, 125, 211
  Ministry of Transportation (PRC), 216
  nationalizing, 124–25
  PLA engineer troops, 212
  shipping lines and maritime routes, 125, 210, 215–17
Treaty of Tianjin, 24
Trình Coóng Phí, 151
Trường Chinh, 46
Turner, Sarah, 8

Index

United States. *See also* Vietnam War
  anti-American sentiment, 224, 226
  Gulf of Tonkin Resolution, 204
  mining program in Gulf of Tonkin, 217–19
  Operation Rolling Thunder, 204, 236
  PRC concerns about American encirclement, 87
  start of ground war in Vietnam, 203–4
  Strategic Hamlet Program, 203

Van Schendel, Willem, 16
Việt Bắc (Northern Vietnam) Inter-zone, Vietnam, 46, 58–59
Việt Kiều (overseas Vietnamese), 83, 111. *See also* ethnic minorities; Tàn Cá people
Việt Minh. *See also* First Indochina War
  about, 28
  Campaign of the Hundred Thousand Mountains, 36
  economic opportunities, 59
  general counter-offensive, 46–47, 49
  Independent Regiment and, 38
  institutionalizing state, 46
  PLA's approach to border, 49
  political position, 38, 50
  power base, 74
  pragmatic approach to Nationalists, 48
  PRC training of, 51
  propaganda strategy, 47–49
  provincialism tolerated to win over ethnic Chinese, 58–59
Vietnam (DRV). *See also* aid, PRC to DRV; border priorities; First Indochina War; local state administration; People's Army of Vietnam (PAVN); Sino-Vietnamese border; state building; Vietnam War; Workers Party of Vietnam (WPV); individual provinces, *cities, and islands*
  corruption and organizational problems, 60
  curbing emigration to South Vietnam, 81
  defining itself against PRC, 51, 53
  equality for ethnic Chinese minorities, 57–59
  independence, 12, 30, 40
  legacy of Chinese expansion, 50
  maintenance of territoriality, 32
  North-first policy, 79
  partition at 17th parallel, 80
  partnership with PRC, 50, 77, 209
  pre-colonial centricity, 51
  seeking international recognition, 48

Three-Year Plan for Economic Recovery, 79
  trade legitimizing government, 70
Vietnam War. *See also* border securitization
  border's strategic importance, overview, 245
  border's symbolism changing, 208–9
  Cambodia, 217
  depleting resources, 237
  draft and depleted male labor pool, 231–33
  exploited by Mao, 204
  Fangcheng Port, 217
  food supply, 225–26, 228–29, 232–33, 235–37
  intergovernmental relations in wake of, 248–50
  Kinh people and, 230–31
  maritime transportation's importance, 210, 215–19
  mutual assistance networks during, 237
  Paris Peace Talks, 241
  PRC's importance to DRV victory, 209–10
  Protocol on the Usage of Chinese Ports by Vietnamese Fishing Boats, 240
  railways during, 210–13
  Red Guards attempting to join, 201–2
  reunification and WPV, 121
  roles for women, 231–32
  Sino-Soviet split's impact, 213–14, 217
  socialist divisions over how to fight, 209, 213
  sojourner population due to, 239–41, 243–44
  Soviet aid for DRV, 213–14
  spontaneous cross-border connections, 237
  start of ground war, 203–4
  state building and, 202–3, 246–47
  strengthening WPV in border regions, 223–24
  terrain barriers during, 209
  Tết Offensive, 205, 216
  trade during, 238–40, 243
  Vietnamese militia, 235–36
  WPV's preparation for, 203
Võ Nguyên Giáp, 122, 210
Vương Đình Trinh, 197

Wallerstein, Immanuel, 12
Wang Jinchuan, 209
Wanwei Island, 164–67, 194–96, 229
Wanzhu Island, 164, 194–96
Wei Baqun, 28
Wei Guoqing, 205
Womack, Brantly, 50, 128, 189, 255
women, 231–32, 234

Workers Party of Vietnam (WPV). *See also* collectivization campaigns; cooperative movement (WPV); fishery reforms; mobilization campaigns; socialist brotherhood; Vietnam War
  adoption of Chinese Communist model, 51–52
  border police institutionalized, 88–89
  Border Work Committee, 151
  CPC's collectivization detrimental, 120
  Department of Politics of the Party, 223
  expanding party's base and membership, 233–34
  ISC operations, 84
  learning from Great Leap Forward, 144–45
  policies toward ethnic Chinese in Vietnam, 58
  rectification of cadres, 223
  reunification and, 121
  strengthening in border regions, 223–24
  Three Good movement, 232
  Three In-Charge Movement, 231
  Three Ready movement, 232
  Three-Year Plan for Socialist Transformation and Development of Economy and Culture, 121
  Vietnamese Senior Citizens Association, 232
  Vietnamese Women's Union, 231
  Vietnamese Youth Unions, 232
Wu Jinnan, 206
Wu Liehe, 201
Wutou Island, 164–65, 167, 229

Xia Nanyang, 83
Xiao Hua, 85

Yao people. *See also* Dao people; Pà Thẻn people; Sán Dìu people
  about, 16, 137
  collectivization campaigns, 136–39

Dongxing Autonomous County of Multiple Ethnicities, 167
farming, 249
migration, 139, 152
Yi people, 16. *See also* Lô Lô people; Phù Lá people
Yugoslavia, 133
Yunnan-Guizhou Railway, 124
Yunnan-Vietnam Railway, 123–24

Zeng Fusheng, 84
Zhan Caifang, 65–67
Zhang Zhidong, 23, 27
Zhanjiang County, China, 186, 190
Zhao Jianjun, 201
Zhennan Guan. *See also* Friendship Pass
  focal point of border inspection, 44–45
  pejorative names and symbolic meanings, 55
  renaming, 57, 208–9
  Sino-Vietnamese Railway, 53–55
Zhennan Guan Uprising, 27
Zhou Enlai
  Cultural Revolution and intraparty tensions, 206
  demining program, 218
  Fangcheng Port, 218
  Geneva Conference (1954), 78
  institutionalization of border administration, 45
  Red Guards attempting to join Vietnam War, 201
  Sino-Vietnamese partnership, 207, 216
Zhou Jiguang, 65
Zhu Qiwen, 201
Zhuang people, 17, 167. *See also* La Chí people; Nùng people; Pu Péo people; Sán Chay people; Tày people